The Forgotten Radical Peter Maurin

CATHOLIC PRACTICE IN NORTH AMERICA

SERIES EDITOR:
John C. Seitz, Associate Professor, Theology Department, Fordham University; Associate Director for Lincoln Center, Curran Center for American Catholic Studies

This series aims to contribute to the growing field of Catholic studies through the publication of books devoted to the historical and cultural study of Catholic practice in North America, from the colonial period to the present. As the term "practice" suggests, the series springs from a pressing need in the study of American Catholicism for empirical investigations and creative explorations and analyses of the contours of Catholic experience. In seeking to provide more comprehensive maps of Catholic practice, this series is committed to publishing works from diverse American locales, including urban, suburban, and rural settings; ethnic, postethnic, and transnational contexts; private and public sites; and seats of power as well as the margins.

SERIES ADVISORY BOARD:
Emma Anderson, Ottawa University
Paul Contino, Pepperdine University
Kathleen Sprows Cummings, University of Notre Dame
James T. Fisher, Fordham University (Emeritus)
Paul Mariani, Boston College
Thomas A. Tweed, University of Notre Dame

The Forgotten Radical Peter Maurin

EASY ESSAYS FROM THE CATHOLIC WORKER

Peter Maurin
Edited by *Lincoln Rice*

FORDHAM UNIVERSITY PRESS
New York 2020

Copyright © 2020 Fordham University Press

All rights reserved. No part of this publication may be reproduced, stored in a retrieval system, or transmitted in any form or by any means—electronic, mechanical, photocopy, recording, or any other—except for brief quotations in printed reviews, without the prior permission of the publisher.

Fordham University Press has no responsibility for the persistence or accuracy of URLs for external or third-party Internet websites referred to in this publication and does not guarantee that any content on such websites is, or will remain, accurate or appropriate.

Fordham University Press also publishes its books in a variety of electronic formats. Some content that appears in print may not be available in electronic books.

Visit us online at www.fordhampress.com.

Library of Congress Cataloging-in-Publication Data available online at https://catalog.loc.gov.

Printed in the United States of America

22 21 20   5 4 3 2 1

First edition

Contents

Introduction	1
Easy Essays Published in *The Catholic Worker*	19
Unpublished Easy Essays	423
Appendix I: Four Interviews with Peter Maurin	491
Appendix II: Peter Maurin's Radio Interview	505
Appendix III: Peter Maurin's Book Recommendations	509
Biographical Glossary to Peter Maurin's Easy Essays	513
Acknowledgments	561
Easy Essay Index	563
Name and Topic Index	577

The Forgotten Radical Peter Maurin

Introduction

Peter Maurin cofounded the Catholic Worker movement with Dorothy Day on 1 May 1933. During the 1930s, both Maurin and Day regularly gave talks on the Catholic Worker at churches and college campuses around the country. On one occasion, Maurin was scheduled to speak to a Knights of Columbus group. Maurin arrived in his usual shabby suit, and the pastor threw him out, complaining that he had been sent a "Bowery bum." On another occasion, in 1939, he was invited for a meal at a professor's home. The professor, believing that Maurin was extremely late to their home, complained to his wife. She responded that a poorly dressed man with a strong accent had arrived earlier. Thinking he was there to read the gas meter, she had sent him to the basement, where they discovered him patiently waiting in a chair.[1] During his lifetime and since, Peter Maurin has often been relegated to the basement and ignored both by those in the Catholic Worker movement and by its admirers.

In contrast, Dorothy Day was often revered by those in the movement during her lifetime, and her reputation has only increased in prominence since her death in 1980. In his 2015 speech to a joint session of Congress, Pope Francis singled out Day's commitment to social justice as an example for Americans. Day's cause for canonization is progressing, and she is a regular fixture in high school and college theology classes. On the other hand, her Catholic Worker cofounder, Peter Maurin, is relatively unknown. Not only were Maurin's ideas foundational for Dorothy Day and the Catholic Worker movement, his writings in the *Catholic Worker* newspaper introduced to the United States Emmanuel Mounier's personalism, which emphasized the primacy of the person over the dehumanizing effects of both rugged individualism and collectivism. Maurin promoted a return to village life and an agrarian society. He believed this was the only permanent solution for the Great Depression, of which he believed industrialism to be the primary cause. Although his message to return to the land has often been scoffed at even in the Catholic Worker movement, Catholic Worker farmer Eric Anglada notes that Maurin's vision is being embraced by Catholic Workers in the twenty-first century, "with roughly two dozen farms all over the world—from New Zealand and England to Mexico and the far reaches of northern Canada, to numerous communities in the Midwest."[2] Before Day met Maurin in 1932, he had already formulated the basic ideas and tenets of the Catholic Worker program. He was simply looking for someone to believe in his vision and put it into action.

Maurin and Day met in December 1932, as the Great Depression worsened. Either at their initial meeting or on the following day, Maurin proposed to Dorothy a three-point program for creating a functional society: (1) round table discussions, (2) houses of hospitality, and (3) farming communes. He referred to his program as the Green Revolution, indicating that he was following the example of Irish missionaries to Europe in late antiquity as opposed to the Red revolutionaries of twentieth-century Russia. Communism grew in membership and influence in American society during the 1930s, and it often played the role of a foil for Maurin.[3] Maurin not only opposed Communism but also regarded the Industrial Revolution as a harmful phase in human history in need of reversal. Maurin believed that industrialization removed creativity from the laborer and was incongruent with a localized economy because of its constant searching for new markets.[4] He believed that only a return to village life on the land could promote personalism and suitably address the problems of unemployment and isolation caused by industrialization and the expansion of cities. Saint Francis of Assisi, a person who espoused voluntary poverty, performed manual labor, and offered his labor as a gift, was his paragon. A few years before meeting Day, Maurin began emulating these aspects of Francis in his daily life and continued to do so until his death.

Maurin presented his ideas in short poetic phrases that were soon referred to as Easy Essays. These essays became a regular feature in the *Catholic Worker* and represent the bulk of his writings.[5] They were the *modus operandi* for communicating his vision. Even his letters to Day took the form of Easy Essays. At first glance, Maurin's Easy Essays appear overly simplistic and preposterous. Further investigation reveals complexity and nuance. The essays are packed with demanding ideas meant to convey dense information and encourage the listener to ponder different ways to understand and interact with reality. Jesus preached parables; Peter Maurin recited Easy Essays.

Brendan O'Grady pointed out that Maurin's essays encapsulate the teaching method of Jean-Baptiste De La Salle's *Conduite Des Ecoles Chrétiennes*: "repetition of ideas, simplicity of expression, conciseness, accuracy, and phraseology adapted to the understanding of average students."[6] The Christian Brothers in France espoused this style of teaching in the late nineteenth century. As a Christian Brother during this era, Maurin employed this method to teach children in France. O'Grady noted ten characteristics of Maurin's Easy Essays: (1) phrased format, (2) simplicity, (3) use of popular diction, (4) conciseness, (5) repetition, (6) definitions, (7) orderliness, (8) use of authorities and witnesses, (9) reading recommendations, and (10) humor.[7]

Each Easy Essay contained from one to ten or more stanzas and was part of a larger arrangement of essays. The arrangement was often titled, and within it, the individual essays, which were also titled, were arranged in such a manner as to support the overall thesis. Many individual essays were later repeated in slightly altered forms in new arrangements. It also happened that previous arrangements were repeated that omitted or added an essay. In some cases, the cause for omitting an essay from a repeated arrangement was probably space considerations.[8] In almost all instances, the first few essays of an arrangement were prominently featured on the front page of the *Catholic Worker*, with the remainder of the arrangement continued inside the paper.

Annotated Edition with Unpublished Essays

The present edition of Maurin's essays contains not only the 482 Easy Essays that were published in the *Catholic Worker* but also previously unpublished essays, in-depth explanations of obscure references, and improved formatting. Before this book, *Catholic Radicalism* (1949) was the most complete collection of Maurin's essays.[9] The foreword to that collection stated, "Everything written by Peter which he considered worthy of publication appeared in the *Catholic Worker* in his lifetime."[10] While this statement may be factual, 87 essays remained unpublished at the time of his death. Most of those essays are held at the Catholic Worker

Archives at Marquette University in Milwaukee, Wisconsin. The three essays not preserved at the archives were published in Arthur Sheehan's biography of Peter Maurin, *Peter Maurin: Gay Believer* (1959).[11] They are the last three essays presented in this volume. Maurin wrote 36 of the unpublished essays for instruction at the Catholic Worker farm near Easton, Pennsylvania, in 1938. It is uncertain why the remaining essays were never published. Of the essays not published during his lifetime, a few have been published in the newspaper and by different authors wishing to further investigate Maurin's thought. The decision by others to publish some of the essays after Maurin's death confirms that the publication and availability of these "lost" essays are essential for anyone hoping to increase his or her appreciation of Maurin's vision.

This edition also includes twenty essays published in the *Catholic Worker* during Maurin's lifetime that have not appeared in any published collection. Of the twenty essays, ten were authored by Maurin and ten were quotations from other authors. Even though these quotation essays were not original creations of Maurin's, they are included here because they were part of larger arrangements meant to be read as a whole.

As an annotated edition, this book contains more than 350 footnotes. Where Maurin published multiple versions of an essay, the original essay is always presented in this book. If future versions of an essay contained any differences, a footnote accompanying the original essay explains these differences. Footnotes also explain obscure references to historical events, most of which would have been common knowledge for *Catholic Worker* readers during the 1930s. At the end of the book is a biographical glossary with a brief biography for every person mentioned by Maurin in the Easy Essays. The entries often contain the reason Maurin was including this person in his essays and provide context for the source material if Maurin was citing something a person wrote. When possible, sources to quotations are indicated in the biographical glossary or in a footnote. This is not always possible owing to obscure sources or because Maurin often placed a statement in quotations when he was actually paraphrasing or generally stating someone's thought.

Ultimately, this edition is annotated because one's comprehension of the essays increases if one possesses a familiarity with Maurin's historical references. Although Day stressed that Maurin's thought was in the realm of theory and ideas and that he shunned conversation about personalities and personal stories, his essays were usually inspired from, or in response to, historical realities and events.[12] Maurin, keenly aware of contemporary thought in history and economics, proposed solutions that he believed were realistic responses to the social ills of his day.

Maurin also copied selections from books and speeches that he favored into an Easy Essay format, many of which were published in the *Catholic Worker*. These digests are not included in this volume not only because they would expand this book tremendously, but also because of the difficulty of securing the copyright permissions for many of the works. Within the pages of the *Catholic Worker*, Maurin liked to include lists of books that he thought were important to read. These lists are preserved in the Easy Essays if they formed an integral part of an essay arrangement. Book recommendations that stood apart from Easy Essays arrangements have been omitted. A master list of the books recommended by Maurin is presented in Appendix III. Additionally, there are appendixes for two interviews with Peter Maurin. The first is a four-part interview of Maurin as he was questioned by his future biographer, Arthur Sheehan. The second is a radio interview, the context and origin of which remain vague. Both appeared in the *Catholic Worker* and are included because they detail Maurin's vision for a functional society in concise fashion. Whereas the essays provide snapshots of individual aspects of his vision, the interviews paint the landscape.

Rubrics for the Easy Essay Arrangements

In this volume, each essay is sequentially numbered and presented chronologically as it appeared in the *Catholic Worker*. If an essay appeared again in a later issue of the paper, reference is made to its essay number, but the essay is not reprinted. Where a repeated essay contains alternate wording from the original version, the first instance of the essay includes a footnote stating how it differs from other versions that Maurin published.

The title of each arrangement is in capital letters. During the first two years it was common for the title to be simply "Easy Essays." The titles of

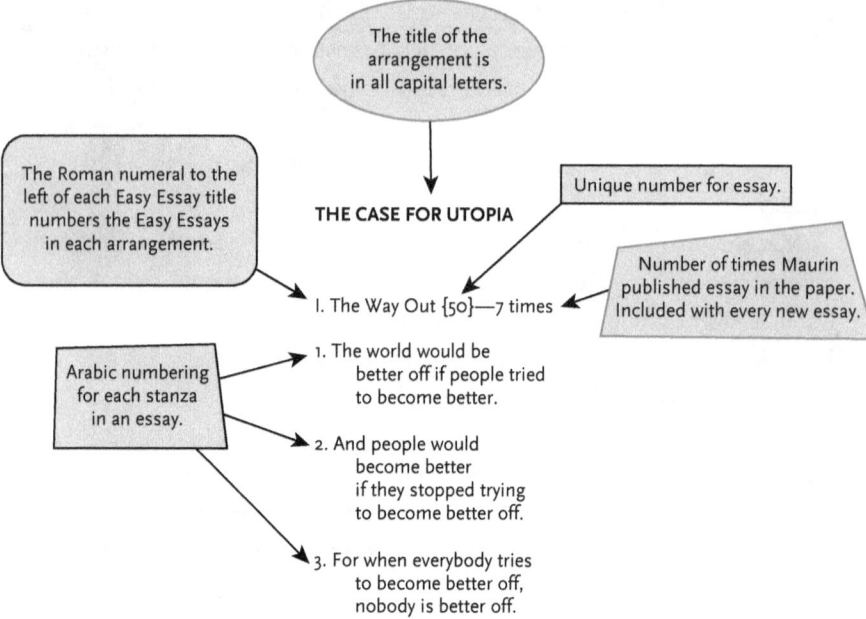

FIGURE 1. Sample Essay in Which Rubrics Are Noted

individual Easy Essays have only the first letter of each word capitalized; in the few cases where the title of the first essay of the arrangement is also the title of the arrangement, it is presented in capital letters. Each Easy Essay within an arrangement is numbered with a Roman numeral. This was a common practice for Maurin, but the newspaper did not consistently format all his essays in this manner. Each time a new essay is presented, a notation to the right of the title indicates the number of times an essay appeared in the *New York Catholic Worker*. For the sake of conformity, this volume places Roman numerals beside every essay in each arrangement. Additionally, each stanza within an essay is numbered with Arabic numerals.

Maurin never dated his essays; the dates cited in this volume refer to the date of their publication in the *Catholic Worker*. In some instances, Maurin wrote extremely long essays that included pieces of older essays. These longer essays—presented in full—include the identifying number of earlier essays within the arrangement.

The Life of Peter Maurin

Numerous biographies have been written about Maurin that are available to those wishing to further explore his life.[13] Because Maurin rarely talked about himself, his life before the Catholic Worker movement has been notoriously difficult to piece together. As Marc H. Ellis has noted, "After studying Maurin for years and laboring at writing his biography, I can say without apology that Maurin's life remains a mystery."[14]

Peter Maurin was born Pierre Joseph Aristide Maurin on 9 May 1877 in the Languedoc region of southern France. During Maurin's childhood, his village of Oultet comprised fifteen families. The village had grown to only twenty families by 2003.[15] It is likely that Maurin's vision of stable village life as a viable alternative to cities and the Industrial Revolution was based largely on his experience at Oultet. Although the Maurin family lived a life that many would equate with poverty, Maurin's half-sister asserted, "We always had what we really needed."[16] The Maurin family had a farm with fruit trees, land for growing vegetables, and space for numerous cattle, oxen, and sheep.[17] Maurin grew up in a religious household and, at the age of fourteen, left home to study at a Christian Brothers boarding school in Mende.[18] Maurin was involved with the Christian Brothers from 1891 to 1902, first as a student then, in 1893, at the age of sixteen, as a new novice for the order. From 1895 until 1899 he kept temporary vows and took a three-year vow in 1899. He taught in several elementary schools during his time as a novice.[19] As vowed religious in France were not completely exempt from military conscription, Maurin was also forced to serve in the French army from November 1898 to September 1899. At this time, Maurin became interested in social issues and, soon afterward, joined a study club that discussed the social issues of the day. Maurin left the Christian Brothers on 1 January 1903 after deciding not to renew his vows.[20]

After leaving the Christian Brothers, Maurin lived in Paris and sold the *L Éveil Démocratique* (*The Democratic Awakening*), the newspaper of *Le Sillon*, a group that promoted the reconciliation of democracy and Christianity. Though France became a republic again in 1870, tensions were still high between state and church, with the French hierarchy closely aligned with movements to reinstitute the monarchy. Maurin served two additional brief stints in the French army in 1904 and 1907. After his last stint in the military, he decided he would no longer report for duty. From 1907 to 1909, he lived in various locales in central and southern France to avoid military service. In 1909, he ended his involvement with *Le Sillon* and decided to leave France for Canada. Though the exact reason for his emigration is unclear, it is fair to speculate that he emigrated to avoid conscription.[21]

Maurin tried to homestead in Saskatchewan, Canada, for two years with a man whom he had met on the journey. In 1911, his partner in the venture died in an accident, and Maurin began working as a laborer in Alberta, digging sewers and working on the Canadian Pacific Railway. After working briefly in Ottawa, he immigrated to the United States to work as a lumberjack in New York state.[22]

After two days as a lumberjack, Maurin quit his job and traveled around New York, taking on various professions. He moved down the East Coast, even spending a couple days in a Pennsylvania jail after someone mistakenly thought he was trying to break into another person's home. Maurin also spent time laboring in the Midwest and, in 1913, settled in Chicago. With the onset of World War I, he made a good living teaching French. During this time, he visited areas that regularly featured soapbox orations and discussed the social questions of the day. Maurin taught French in Chicago until 1925, when he accepted the invitation of one of his students to teach French in New York City.[23]

After a few months teaching in New York City, Maurin moved to Woodstock, New York, where he began providing French lessons without charging a fee. He initially lived in an artist colony and later in someone's barn. Maurin then moved to Kingston, New York, where he lived for three years. He continued to teach French and lived on freewill offerings from his students. By 1927, he had started sharing his social views with others and even gave a speech to the local Rotary Club on the fallacy of saving. Up until this point, Maurin had gone by the name "Pierre," but on the advice of Fr. Joseph Scully in Kingston, he began going by "Peter."[24]

In 1929, Maurin stopped teaching French and stayed as a live-in worker at Fr. Scully's boys' camp in Phoenicia, New York. When not working there, he spent considerable time in New York City—reading at the library, arguing with soapbox orators, and striking up conversations with bystanders in various public squares. In these forums, Maurin

FIGURE 2. Formal Portrait of Peter Maurin, Chicago, ca. 1920
(Courtesy of Marquette University Archives)

would proclaim his Easy Essays and hand out printed copies when possible. Maurin recited a version the essay "Taking Back Our Name"{142}, in which he argued that authentic communism had its origin in French Catholicism, but no copies of these early essays have survived, and we cannot know how similar or different these essays were from the ones later published in the *Catholic Worker*.[25]

In December 1932, Peter Maurin appeared at Dorothy Day's apartment, which she shared with her brother and sister-in-law. Two individuals—George Shuster, the editor of *Commonweal*, and a "red-headed Irish Communist" whom Maurin had met in Union Square—had advised Maurin to introduce himself to Day. The first time Maurin stopped by, Day was away covering a hunger march in Washington, D.C. While covering the march, Day went to Immaculate Conception Basilica to make "a prayer which came with tears and with anguish, that some way would open up for me to use what talents I possessed for my fellow workers, for the poor." When she returned to New York on 8 December 1932, she found Peter Maurin waiting in her apartment.[26]

At thirty-five years old, Day was not initially impressed with the fifty-four-year-old Maurin, but he persisted in his attempt to indoctrinate her with his Catholic social vision for society. She was particularly intrigued by his idea that she should start a newspaper to convey the Catholic message to the unemployed. On 1 May 1933, Day published the first issue of the newspaper, the *Catholic Worker*. The periodical proclaimed the dignity of the poor, exposed injustice against laborers, condemned racism, promoted personal responsibility for social ills, and printed excerpts from papal social documents.

On reading proofs for the first issue of the *Catholic Worker*, Maurin was disappointed that the paper contained more than his Easy Essays. In addition, he had wanted the paper to be called the *Catholic Radical* or the *Catholic Agronomist*. To him, the *Catholic Worker* sounded too close to the Communist *Daily Worker*. Maurin apparently left New York over these disagreements and did not return for a month. The second issue of the paper included a note that only his essays spoke to his vision and that he had officially withdrawn from the editorial board to make this point even more unambiguous.[27]

Maurin contributed original Easy Essays to the newspaper from May 1933 to December 1942. These essays constitute the bulk of this volume. Maurin organized the first round table discussion at the Manhattan Lyceum on the last Sunday of June in 1933. Round table discussions were the first aspect of his three-point program, which promoted workers and scholars coming together to discuss thoughtfully the issues of the day. The Lyceum was rented because it could hold 150 people, but only about 15 people attended. The second meeting in July was attended by the same number of people but also had the good fortune of attracting Fr. John LaFarge, a Jesuit priest dedicated to racial justice. Though the discussions would never become overly popular, they did attract several significant speakers during the 1930s, including *America* editor Rev. Wilfred Parsons, liturgical reformer Virgil Michel, Catholic sociologist Paul Hanly Furfey, moral theologian Monsignor John A. Ryan, and French philosopher Jacques Maritain.[28]

Houses of hospitality to provide shelter for the homeless were the second point in Maurin's program. He had initially expected the American bishops to take a leading role in this venture, but it was Day who was compelled to open the first hospitality house on 11 December 1933. Winter temperatures had recently plummeted, and Day recognized a homeless woman who was visiting the paper's editorial offices, as she had come by with a friend the day before. Day asked about her friend, only to discover that her friend had committed suicide by throwing herself in front of a subway train because she could not bear the bitter cold. Immediately, Day begged additional money from personal contacts and combined it with previous donations for the paper to secure a large vacant apartment with five bedrooms for up to twenty homeless women; this apartment became the first house of hospitality, which was named the Teresa-Joseph Cooperative.[29] After having read the exploits of the first Catholic Worker house in the newspaper, others were inspired to take personal responsibility for the poor in their midst and began opening their own hospitality houses in various parts of the United States. The houses of hospitality have become the most prominent feature of the Catholic Worker movement.

The third point in Maurin's program was farming communes to furnish labor for the unemployed and serve as an example for a functional society. In June 1935, the Catholic Worker procured a building, garden, and an acre of land on Staten Island. This was an important development that permitted some experimentation in gardening. The first Catholic Worker farm would open near Easton, Pennsylvania, in April 1936.[30]

Maurin enacted his emulation of Franciscan poverty before he met Dorothy Day. When he met her, he owned nothing except the clothes on his back, which he would literally give away when asked. Becoming a troubadour for the Catholic Worker movement, he traveled around the country speaking about his ideas and sharing what was happening in

New York City and on the farm.[31] When in New York City, Maurin often spent his nights selling the newspaper in Union Square while arguing with Communists. After sleeping until noon the next day, he would attend Mass and eat at a cheap restaurant on the Bowery.[32]

Maurin, along with a Protestant friend, moved into a Harlem storefront that had been donated to the Worker in May 1934. Although the storefront housed a few men, it was not primarily a house of hospitality, but a base from which to evangelize and teach the Catholic program on social and racial justice to African Americans. The storefront offered literature, regular meetings, craft-making sessions, and even French classes. It seemed, at first, that the storefront might be successful, but after the first summer it never attracted more than a small crowd. By the end of 1935, the storefront was closed when the owner, a member of the National Guard, discovered the nonviolent tendencies of the Catholic Worker.[33]

By the fifth anniversary of the Catholic Worker in 1938, Catholic Worker houses of hospitality were opening all over the United States, and newspaper circulation had grown to 165,000.[34] During the first few months of 1938, Maurin organized monthly symposiums on personalist democracy. Speakers included Roger N. Baldwin of the American Civil Liberties Union, Rabbi Eugene Kohn, and Christian pacifist A. J. Muste.[35] Maurin had regularly visited the farm in Easton since its opening in 1936; during the summer of 1938 he decided to live there. That summer Maurin wrote some of the unpublished essays on cult, culture, and cultivation that are found in the latter part of this volume. He posted these essays on the bulletin board to inspire those on the farm.[36]

After that summer, Maurin traveled to the West Coast and back, giving talks and visiting friends. It appears that during spring 1939, he took a brief hiatus from the Catholic Worker. One probable reason was that Day had told Maurin the funds he had sent to her for building a farming commune had been spent on the bread line. In June, Dorothy Day wrote an open letter in the newspaper asking where he was, sharing news of her father's death, apologizing for redirecting his funds, and closing with three simple words: "We need you." Maurin must have seen the letter, because new Easy Essays appeared in the following issue of the newspaper, and he returned to lecture at the Easton farm for the remainder of the summer. He again traveled during the next fall and winter. As part of his journey, he went to Spokane, Washington, in October to attend the National Catholic Rural Life Conference, which he tried to attend each year.[37]

In December 1939, Maurin secured funds to open a Discussion Center on Catholic Doctrine that would disseminate Catholic thought to non-Catholics via clarifications of thought. The center opened at the beginning of February 1940 with a particular interest in reaching a Jewish audience. Like the storefront in Harlem, not many people visited. Before the end of the 1940, the center closed.[38]

In the early 1940s, Maurin continued to travel to and visit communities that shared a similar vision. He was involved with the creation of a folk school in Avon, Ohio, during the summer of 1941, at which he taught church history.[39] December 1942 marked the last time that the *Catholic Worker* published original Easy Essays submitted by Maurin. The reason he stopped writing essays is ambiguous but probably had its source in a recent stroke; he was becoming easily tired, and his mind was beginning to fail him.[40] By the fall of 1944, Maurin's memory was noticeably failing, and his condition worsened during 1945 and 1946. While at the New York Catholic Worker in March 1947, Maurin went missing for four days,

FIGURE 3. Peter Maurin and Dorothy Day, Maryfarm, Newburgh, New York, 1948 (Courtesy of Marquette University)

then suddenly reappeared. He had been lost. He had slept in coffee shops when possible and rode buses, hoping one might take him home. In December 1948, he was diagnosed with cardiac asthma and became increasingly lethargic. During this period, he lived at the house of hospitality in New York City, the Easton farm, a newly acquired farm near Newburgh, New York, and with friends of the Catholic Worker movement. On 15 May 1949, Maurin died at Maryfarm near Newburg and was buried in St. John's Cemetery in Queens.[41]

Concluding Remarks

As an anarchist endeavor without any central authority, the Catholic Worker movement has grown organically to more than 150 Catholic Worker houses of hospitality throughout the United States, with an additional couple dozen in other parts of the globe, including Australia, Argentina, Canada, England, Germany, Mexico, and Uganda.[42] More than a dozen farming communes continue to experiment with the third aspect of Maurin's program.[43]

The Great Recession of the early-twenty-first century was a stark reminder that we share many of the same economic problems and concerns that plagued the Western world during the Great Depression. Since the Great Depression, capitalism has become more entrenched in the Western psyche. Profit is placed before people. Technological progress is still largely viewed as an unqualified good. Businesses continue to look for new markets. So-called civilized people kill those they consider barbarians in order to civilize them. In other words, the solutions proposed by Peter Maurin more than eighty years ago continue to provide a fresh perspective for perennial problems. Peter Maurin had a gift for communicating the best of the Christian tradition, and I hope his essays will provide challenging and thoughtful ideas for readers of this book.

Notes

1. Ruth Heaney, *Voices from the Catholic Worker*, ed. Rosalie Riegle Troester (Philadelphia: Temple University Press, 1993), 105; Stanley Vishnewski, "Peter Maurin to Lead Classes at Easton Farm," *New York Catholic Worker*, June 1940, 8; Dorothy Day, "Story of Three Deaths," *New York Catholic Worker*, June 1949, 2.

2. Eric Cussen Anglada, "Our Ecological Moment," *Worcester Catholic Radical*, June/July 2018, 1–2, https://ia802704.us.archive.org/33/items/catholicradical/catholicradical-2018-06.pdf (accessed 25 June 2018).

3. Harvey Klehr and John Earl Haynes, "Revising Revisionism: A New Look at American Communism," *Academic Questions* 22 (2009): 452.

4. See Maurin's arrangement of essays from November 1935 entitled, "Back to Christ!—Back to the Land!" Because Maurin wrote supportively of the French industrialist Léon Harmel, one could argue that Maurin was not opposed to industrialism, but to industrial capitalism and industrial communism. Though he applauded Harmel's care and concern for his workers, Maurin never promoted an industrial economy. In fact, his writings indicate a belief that industrialization cannot exist outside of a capitalist or communist context.

5. It was Dorothy Day's brother John who created the name "Easy Essay" to describe the works of Maurin while helping to put together the first issue of the *Catholic Worker*; Day, *Loaves and Fishes* (1963; repr. Maryknoll, N.Y.: Orbis, 1997), 5.

6. Brendan Anthony O'Grady, "Peter Maurin, Propagandist" (Ph.D. diss., Ottawa University, 1954), 8.

7. O'Grady, "Peter Maurin," 280.

8. Luke Stocking, "When the Irish Were Irish: Peter Maurin and the Green Revolution" (M.A. thesis, St. Michael's College, 2007), 51.

9. Peter Maurin, *Catholic Radicalism: Phrased Essays for the Green Revolution*, ed. David Mason (New York: Catholic Worker, 1949).

10. David Mason, foreword to Maurin, *Catholic Radicalism*, vi.

11. Arthur T. Sheehan, *Peter Maurin: Gay Believer* (Garden City, N.Y.: Hanover House, 1959).

12. Dorothy Day, *Long Loneliness: The Autobiography of Dorothy Day* (San Francisco: Harper & Row, 1980), 169.

13. See Dorothy Day with Francis Sicius, *Peter Maurin: Apostle to the World* (Maryknoll, N.Y.: Orbis, 2004); Marc H. Ellis, *Peter Maurin: Prophet in the Twentieth Century* (New York: Paulist Press, 1981); Sheehan, *Peter Maurin*. Although not a biography of Maurin, Luke Stocking's thesis contains an excellent summary and analysis of Maurin's life before the Catholic Worker movement; Stocking, "When the Irish Were Irish."

14. Ellis, *Peter Maurin*, 75.

15. Stocking, "When the Irish Were Irish," 9; Sheehan, *Peter Maurin*, 19, 26.

16. Marguerite Maurin, quoted in Stocking, "When the Irish Were Irish,"

10. Marguerite Maurin to Arthur Sheehan, 5 June 1958, Dorothy Day–Catholic Worker Collection, Raynor Memorial Libraries, Marquette University, Series W-15, Box 3. Hereafter, this archival collection will be referred to as DD-CW.

17. Stocking, "When the Irish Were Irish," 11; Sheehan, *Peter Maurin*, 23–24.

18. Stocking, "When the Irish Were Irish," 11–13; Sheehan, *Peter Maurin*, 33–35.

19. Stocking, "When the Irish Were Irish," 13–14; Sheehan, *Peter Maurin*, 41–49.

20. Stocking, "When the Irish Were Irish," 15–18; Sheehan, *Peter Maurin*, 50–54, 58.

21. Stocking, "When the Irish Were Irish," 18–21; Sheehan, *Peter Maurin*, 61–63, 69–72.

22. Stocking, "When the Irish Were Irish," 22–24; Sheehan, *Peter Maurin*, 78.

23. Stocking, "When the Irish Were Irish," 24–27; Sheehan, *Peter Maurin*, 78–83.

24. Stocking, "When the Irish Were Irish," 28–31; Sheehan, *Peter Maurin*, 83–87. From Sheehan, we know that Maurin recited to the Rotary Club essays {38} "The Fallacy of Saving" and {567}, in which he discusses how strange he appears to others.

25. Stocking, "When the Irish Were Irish," 31–33; Day, "Peter's Program," *New York Catholic Worker*, May 1955, 2; Sheehan, *Peter Maurin*, 89, 176.

26. Day, *Long Loneliness*, 166, 169; Stocking, "When the Irish Were Irish," 34–37; Sheehan, *Peter Maurin*, 90.

27. Mel Piehl, *Breaking Bread: The Catholic Worker Movement and the Origin of Catholic Radicalism in America* (Philadelphia: Temple University Press, 1982), 57–60; Sicius, in Day and Sicius, *Peter Maurin*, 53; Ellis, *Peter Maurin*, 46; Sheehan, *Peter Maurin*, 91–93, 97.

28. Ellis, *Peter Maurin*, 51–52, 54; Day, "House of Hospitality," *Catholic Worker*, May 1939; "Day after Day—Thoughts on Breadlines and on the War," *Catholic Worker*, June 1940; Sheehan, *Peter Maurin*, 97–99, 108–9, 119.

29. Ellis, *Peter Maurin*, 53; Sheehan, *Peter Maurin*, 99; *New York Catholic Worker*, "Co-Operative Apartment for Unemployed Women Has Its Start in Parish," 15 December 1933; *New York Catholic Worker*, "The Teresa-Joseph Cooperative," 1 February 1934; Eileen Egan, interview with RTE in Dublin, 9 December 1973. The Catholic Worker archivist at Marquette University, Phil Runkel, shared this information with me via e-mail.

30. Ellis, *Peter Maurin*, 96, 98; Sheehan, *Peter Maurin*, 119–20, 131.

31. Ellis, *Peter Maurin*, 69–70; Sheehan, *Peter Maurin*, 125.

32. Ellis, *Peter Maurin*, 75.

33. Ellis, *Peter Maurin*, 82–86; Sheehan, *Peter Maurin*, 115–17.

34. Ellis, *Peter Maurin*, 122.

35. "Monthly Symposium on Personalist Democracy," DD-CW, Series W-10, Box 3, Folder "Monthly Symposium on Personalist Democracy."

36. Ellis, *Peter Maurin*, 123, 126.

37. Ellis, *Peter Maurin*, 132–40; Sheehan, *Peter Maurin*, 177–78; Day, "Open Letter to Peter Maurin from Editor," *New York Catholic Worker*, June 1939. During the time that Maurin was "missing," Day received two letters from her friend Elizabeth Burrow in Arkansas. Maurin had unexpectedly dropped in on Burrow in May, but visited for only a few hours. Maurin talked to her about possibly opening his own place in Dallas and supporting it initially by providing French lessons. Burrow was worried about Maurin and believed he was "indulging the usual little-boy complex, hiding out from home"; Burrow to Day, 7 May and 8 June 1939, DD-CW, Series D-1, Box 2, Folder 8.

38. Ellis, *Peter Maurin*, 149–53; Sheehan, *Peter Maurin*, 194.

39. Ellis, *Peter Maurin*, 154–56; Sheehan, *Peter Maurin*, 181.

40. Catholic Worker Thomas Sullivan stated that Maurin stopped writing because he disagreed with Day's pacifist stance regarding the Second World War. This line of thought contradicted Day's clear belief that Maurin was a pacifist. Nevertheless, Sullivan claimed that the Nazi invasion of Maurin's France solidified his belief that a "world police force" was needed in drastic circumstances. Nevertheless, if Sullivan was correct, it is unclear why Maurin did not stop contributing essays in 1940 when France was invaded and occupied by Nazi Germany. Although Sullivan was regularly in contact with Maurin during his last years, Sullivan was prone to exaggerate. Even Maurin's essays after the invasion of France stress the need to emulate the saints in being an example for others. Kate Hennessy, a granddaughter of Day, noted from her research that Maurin had a stroke near the end of 1941, in the wake of which "he was losing weight and tired easily." Taking everything into account, Maurin's failing health was the most likely explanation for why he stopped writing; Day, "Introduction," in *Catholic Radicalism*, iv; Hennessy, *Dorothy Day* (New York: Scribner, 2017), 139, 146; Thomas Sullivan, Interview by Francis Sicius, 24 June 1976, transcript, DD-CW. For further information on the debate of Maurin's view of nonviolence, see Stephen T. Krupa, "Dorothy Day and Spirituality of Nonviolence" (Ph.D. diss., Graduate Theological Union, Berkeley, Calif., 1998), 20–38.

41. Ellis, *Peter Maurin*, 159–62; Stocking, "When the Irish Were Irish," 151; Day, *Long Loneliness*, 273–78; Sheehan, *Peter Maurin*, 202–3; Day, "Story of Three Deaths," *New York Catholic Worker*, June 1949; Day, "On Pilgrimage," *New York Catholic Worker*, April 1947.

42. Jim Allaire, "List of States with Catholic Worker Communities," Catholic Worker Movement, http://www.catholicworker.org/communities/directory-picker.html (accessed 31 March 2020).

43. Chearcus, "Catholic Worker Farms, Catholic Community Gardens, Etc.," Catholic Worker Farms, http://farm.catholicworker.biz/listing2017.html (accessed 2 July 2017).

FIGURE 4. Peter Maurin standing in front of St. Joseph's House, 1930s (Courtesy of Marquette University)

Easy Essays Published in *The Catholic Worker*

MAY 1933
EASY ESSAYS

I. Institutions — Corporations[1] {1} — 2 times

1. Jean-Jacques Rousseau says:
    "Man is naturally good,
    but institutions make him bad,
    so let us
    overthrow institutions."
2. I say man is naturally bad,
    but corporations,
    not institutions,
    make him worse.
3. "An institution," says Emerson,
    "is the extension
    of the soul of man."
4. When institutions are no longer
    the extension of the soul of the founder
    they have become corporations.
5. Institutions are founded to foster
    the welfare of the masses.
6. Corporations are organized
    to promote the wealth of the classes.

---

1. Also known as "Institutions and Corporations." In the December 1935 version of the essay, Maurin began, "In the first issue of the *Catholic Worker* appeared this essay." He also made one of his most startling edits by changing, "I say man is naturally bad" to "I say: 'Man is partly good and partly bad.'"

7. So the question is not to organize
>   bigger corporations,
>   but to found better institutions.

II. Ethics and Economics[2] {2} — 4 times

1. Lincoln Steffens says:
   > "The social problem is not
   > a political problem;
   > it is an economic problem."
2. Kropotkin says:
   > "The economic problem is not
   > an economic problem;
   > it is an ethical problem."
3. Thorstein Veblen says:
   > "There is no ethics
   > in modern society."
4. R. H. Tawney says:
   > "There were high ethics in society
   > when the Canon Law was
   > the law of the land."
5. The high ethics of the Canon Law
   > are embodied in the encyclicals
   > of Pius XI and Leo XIII
   > on the social problem.

---

2. Also known as "Listening to the Pope" and "An Ethical Problem." The other versions of the essay omitted the sixth stanza. The November 1934 version concluded with the following lines: "So as George N. Shuster says: 'It is a case of listening to the Pope or listening to nobody.' For nobody but the Pope dares to talk ethics in terms of economics." The June 1940 version concluded with the phrase, "How society has passed from the high ethics of the Canon Law to the lack of ethics of modern society can be found in the book of R. H. Tawney: *Religion and the Rise of Capitalism*." An unpublished version of the essay entitled "No Ethics" closely followed the first three stanzas, but continued with the following: "4. Conspicuous spending is the prevailing practice in modern society. 5. A man with three bath tubs thinks he is a better man than the man with one bath tub. 6. A high standard of living has now taken the place of a high standard of loving."

6. To apply the ethics of the encyclicals
    to the problems of today,
    such is the purpose
    of Catholic Action.

III. Blowing the Dynamite[3] {3} — 4 times

1. Writing about the Catholic Church,
    a radical writer says:
    "Rome will have to do more
    than to play
    a waiting game;
    she will have to use
    some of the dynamite
    inherent in her message."
2. To blow the dynamite
    of a message,
    is the only way
    to make the message
    dynamic.
3. If the Catholic Church
    is not today
    the dominant social,
    dynamic force,
    it is because
    Catholic scholars
    have failed to blow
    the dynamite of the Church.
4. Catholic scholars
    have taken the dynamite
    of the Church,
    have wrapped it up
    in nice phraseology,
    placed it
    in an hermetic container,
    and sat on the lid.

---

3. All other versions of the essay named the radical writer as Albert J. Nock.

5. It is about time
    to blow the lid off
    so the Catholic Church
    may again become
    the dominant social dynamic force.

IV. The Money-Lenders' Dole {4} — 1 time

1. Uncle Sam does not believe
    in the unemployed dole,
    but Uncle Sam does believe
    in the money-lenders' dole.
2. Uncle Sam doles out every year
    more than a billion dollars
    to the money lenders.
3. And it is the money-lenders' dole
    that put Uncle Sam into a hole.
4. The money lenders are first citizens
    on Uncle Sam's payroll.
5. There were no money lenders
    on the payroll
    in Palestine and Ireland.
6. There were no money lenders
    on the payroll
    in Palestine and Ireland,
    because the Prophets of Israel
    and the Fathers of the Church
    forbid lending money
    at interest.
7. But Uncle Sam does not listen
    to the Prophets of Israel
    and the Fathers of the Church.

V. Mortgaged[4] {5} — 7 times

1. Because the State has legalized
    money lending at interest
    in spite of the teachings
    of the Prophets of Israel
    and the Fathers of the Church,
    home-owners have mortgaged
    their homes.
2. Because the State has legalized
    money lending at interest
    in spite of the teachings
    of the Prophets of Israel
    and the Fathers of the Church,
    farmer-owners have mortgaged
    their farms.
3. Because the State has legalized
    money lending at interest
    in spite of the teachings
    of the Prophets of Israel
    and the Fathers of the Church,
    cities, counties and states
    have mortgaged their budgets.
4. So people find themselves in all kinds
    of financial difficulties
    because the State has legalized
    money lending at interest
    in spite of the Prophets of Israel
    and the Fathers of the Church.

---

4. Also known as "Legalized Usury" and "Because the State." Some versions omit the first stanza, and one ends with the line, "So a large portion of the national income goes to the money lenders because the State has legalized money lending at interest in spite of the teachings of the Prophets of Israel and the Fathers of the Church." The December 1933 version of the essay begins, "Because John Calvin legalized money lending at interest, the State has legalized money lending at interest." It also includes the following two sentences: "Because the State has legalized money lending at interest, instutions have mortgaged their buildings. Because the State has legalized money lending at interest, congreagations have mortgaged their churches."

VI. Out of the Temple {6} — 1 time

1. Christ drove the money lenders
    out of the Temple.[5]
2. But today nobody dares
    to drive the money lenders
    out of the Temple.
3. And nobody dares
    to drive the money lenders
    out of the Temple
    because the money lenders
    have taken a mortgage
    on the Temple.
4. When church builders build churches
    with money borrowed
    from money lenders,
    they increase the prestige
    of the money lenders.
5. But increasing the prestige
    of the money lenders
    does not increase the prestige
    of the Church.
6. Which makes Archbishop McNicholas say:
    "We have been guilty
    of encouraging tyranny
    in the financial world,
    until it has become
    a veritable octopus
    strangling the life
    of our people."

---

5. This is a reference to Jesus driving the merchants and money changers out of the Jewish Temple in Jerusalem, which is documented in all four Gospels. The Gospels do not make reference to Maurin's "money lenders," but the shared message is that commercial activities should not take precedent over the spiritual life.

VII. Wealth-Producing Maniacs⁶ {7} — 4 times

1. When John Calvin
    legalized money lending at interest,
    he made the bank account
    the standard of values.
2. When the bank account
    became the standard of values,
    people ceased
    to produce for use
    and began to produce for profits.
3. When people began
    to produce for profits,
    they became
    wealth-producing maniacs.
4. When people became
    wealth-producing maniacs
    they produced
    too much wealth.
5. When people found out
    that they had produced
    too much wealth
    they went on an orgy
    of wealth-destruction
    and destroyed
    ten million lives besides.
6. And after fifteen years
    of a world-wide orgy
    of wealth and life-destruction,
    millions of people
    find themselves victims
    of a world-wide depression
    brought about

---

6. Only the December 1933 version of the essay also began stanza six with, "And after fifteen years of a world-wide orgy of wealth and life-destruction." All the other versions omitted this phrase.

by a world gone mad
on mass-production
and mass-distribution.

JUNE–JULY 1933
EASY ESSAYS

I. Round-Table Discussions[7] {8} — 5 times

  1. We need Round-Table Discussions
      to keep trained minds from being
      academic.
  2. We need Round-Table Discussions
      to keep untrained minds from
      being superficial.
  3. We need Round-Table Discussions
      to learn from scholars
      what is wrong with things as they are.
  4. We need Round-Table Discussions
      to learn from scholars
      how things would be,
      if they were as they should be.
  5. We need Round-Table Discussions
      to learn from scholars
      how a path can be made
      from things as they are
      to things as they should be.

---

[7]. Also known as "Clarification of Thought." This original essay was the longest of the essay variations. The version from June 1942 reworded each stanza to omit the opening line: "We need Round-Table Discussions." Here is how the final stanza was reworded: "Scholars must cooperate with workers in the making of a path from the things as they are to the things as they should be."

II. Houses of Hospitality[8] {9} — 7 times

1. We need Houses of Hospitality
   to give to the rich
   the opportunity to serve the poor.
2. We need Houses of Hospitality
   to bring the Bishops to the people
   and the people to the Bishops.
3. We need Houses of Hospitality
   to bring back to institutions
   the technique of institutions.
4. We need Houses of Hospitality
   to show what idealism looks like
   when it is practiced.
5. We need Houses of Hospitality
   to bring Social Justice
   through Catholic Action
   exercised in Catholic Institutions.

---

8. Later versions of this essay omitted the line, "We need Houses of Hospitality to bring the Bishops to the people and the people to the Bishops." The early essays proposed that houses of hospitality be incorporated into Catholic Action, which were cleric-led lay groups with the purpose of increasing Catholic influence in society. The September 1935 version of the essay contained the lines, "We need Houses of Hospitality to help to popularize the daily practice of the Seven Corporal and the Seven Spiritual Works of Mercy. We need Houses of Hospitality to exemplify Christian Charity and Voluntary Poverty. We need Houses of Hospitality to take the unemployed from the taxpayers' back and place them at the mercy of charitable Christians." The May 1936 version concluded with the phrase, "We need Houses of Hospitality to remind the rich 'that when man dies, he carries in his clutched hands only that which he has given away' as Jean-Jacques Rousseau used to say." The June 1942 version added the following stanzas: "We need Houses of Hospitality to give to the uneducated the opportunity to eat at the same table with the educated. We need Houses of Hospitality to give the ill-mannered the opportunity to observe the manners of the well-mannered." Unfortunately, Maurin gave the title "Houses of Hospitality" to three additional essays that were entirely different. The three other essays are {26}, {150}, and {216}.

III. Agronomic Universities[9] {10} — 7 times

1. The unemployed need
    free rent;
    they can have that
    on an Agronomic University.
2. The unemployed need
    free fuel;
    they can cut that
    on an Agronomic University.
3. The unemployed need
    free food;
    they can raise that
    on an Agronomic University.
4. The unemployed need
    to acquire skill;
    they can do that
    on an Agronomic University.
5. The unemployed need
    to improve their minds;
    they can do that
    on an Agronomic University.
6. The unemployed need
    spiritual guidance;
    they can have that
    on an Agronomic University.

---

9. Also known as "Farming Communes" and "What the Unemployed Need." The main difference with later versions of the essay was the term Maurin employed for agronomic university. Maurin originally used the term "agronomic university," then "parish subsistence camp," and then used "farming commune" and "outdoor university" interchangeably.

JULY–AUGUST 1933

EASY ESSAYS

I. Creating Problems[10] {11} — 7 times

1. Business men say
    that because everybody is selfish,
    business must therefore
    be based on selfishness.
2. But when business
    is based on selfishness,
    everybody is busy
    becoming more selfish.
3. And when everybody
    is busy becoming more selfish,
    we have classes and clashes.
4. Business cannot set its house in order
    because business men
    are moved by selfish motives.
5. Business men create problems,
    they do not solve them.

II. No Way to Turn[11] {12} — 3 times

1. Our business managers
    don't know how to manage

---

10. Also known as "Business Is Selfishness," "Business Is Business," and "Classes and Clashes." Some versions of the essay omitted the final stanza or the final two stanzas. Unlike others, the October 1938 version focused on human nature and is included here: "1. Business men believe that you cannot do anything with human nature. 2. But they do something with human nature. 3. By basing business on selfishness business men are busy making human nature more selfish. 4. Because everybody is busy becoming more selfish, we have classes, not functional classes but acquisitive classes, go-getter classes. 5. And acquisitive classes, go-getter classes give us clashes."

11. Also known as "Teaching Subjects" and "Teachers of Subjects." The other two versions omitted stanzas five and six, perhaps for space considerations.

the things they try to manage,
   because they don't understand
   the things they try to manage.
2. So they turn to college professors
   in the hope that they will understand
   the things they try to manage.
3. But college professors
   do not profess anything,
   they only teach subjects.
4. As teachers of subjects,
   college professors may enable people
   to master subjects,
   but mastering subjects
   has never enabled anyone
   to master situations.
5. So our college professors
   are as much at sea
   as our business managers.
6. And our business managers
   do not know which way to turn.

III. Liberal Fanatics[12] {13} — 7 times

1. The present would be different if
   they had made the past different.
2. The future would be different if

---

12. Also known as "Liberals Not Liberators," "Not a Liberal," "Liberals and Liberators," "Let's Be Liberators," and "Too Broadminded." This essay and some early versions used the term "tricks," where later versions used the term "habits." The October 1934 essay began with the following phrase: "They say that I am a radical. If I am a radical then I am not a liberal." The January 1936 essay was unique in that it was the only essay that began by mentioning Newman and Pius IX: "Cardinal Newman and Pius IX thought that liberalism was the greatest error of the nineteenth century." The July 1938 essay continued as follows after stanza three: "4. To give up old habits and start to contract new habits is to liberate oneself. 5. To liberate oneself is to show others how to liberate themselves. 6. Why be a liberal when you can be a liberator?" The February 1939 essay concluded with this line: "And liberals are so broadminded that they don't seem to be able to make up their minds." Last, the present essay was the only one that contained stanza eight.

we made the present different.
3. But to make the present different,
people must give up the old tricks and
start to play new tricks.
4. But it takes fanatics to give up
old tricks and play new tricks.
5. And liberals are so liberal about
everything that they cannot become
fanatics about anything.
6. And because they cannot become
fanatics about anything, they cannot be
liberators, they can only be liberals.
7. Liberals don't care to be known
as fanatics, but they are the worst kind
of fanatics.
8. They don't care to be religious,
philosophical or economic fanatics and
don't mind being liberal fanatics.

IV. The Age of Treason[13] {14} — 4 times

1. Pope Pius IX and Cardinal Newman
consider liberalism,[14] whether it be
religious, philosophical or economic,

---

13. Some versions of the essay omitted the first stanza relating the hostility of Newman and Pius IX to liberalism. Stanza two was omitted in most of the other versions. The April 1942 version of the essay also contained the following stanza: "Romanticism, positivism, pragmatism, one after another became the fashion in the nineteenth century."

14. This is the first time Maurin employed the term "liberalism," which has possessed numerous connotations over the previous two centuries. Until the late nineteenth century, it popularly referred to a more limited role for governments in economic contexts and favored the policies of laissez-faire capitalism. Liberalism in the philosophical tradition, which traces its origins to John Locke, Immanuel Kant, Thomas Hobbes, and Adam Smith, was anti-authoritarian and stressed the liberty of the individual over any authority that was not viewed as completely rational. From this viewpoint, religion was a personal matter that lacked public authority or importance. By the 1930s, many versions of philosophical liberalism advocated a larger role for the government in protecting individuals' rights and liberty. Depending on the context, Maurin utilized each aspect of liberalism noted in this footnote.

the greatest error
of the nineteenth century.
2. Modern liberalism is the logical
sequence of the so-called age
of enlightenment—the age of Voltaire,
Rousseau, Thomas Paine—
sometimes called
the age of reason in opposition
to the age of faith.
3. By sponsoring nationalism
and capitalism, modern liberals
have given up the search for truth
and have become paid propagandists.
4. Modern liberals have ceased
to appeal to reason,
and have chosen to appeal
to prejudice.
5. So the age of reason has become
the age of treason as Julien Benda
points out in his book entitled,
The Treason of the Intellectuals.

V. Commercializers of Labor[15] {15} — 6 times

1. The teachers of ethics tell us that
labor is a gift, not a commodity.
2. And "capital," says Karl Marx,
"is accumulated labor," not for
the benefit of the laborers,
but for the benefit
of the accumulators.
3. And capitalists succeed
in accumulating labor
for their own benefit,
by treating labor not as a gift,
but as a commodity,

---

15. Also known as "Capital and Labor," "Accumulators of Labor," and "Sellers of Labor."

buying it as any other commodity
at the lowest possible price.
4. And organized labor plays into the
hand of the capitalists,
or accumulators of labor,
by treating their own labor,
not as a gift, but as a commodity,
selling it as any other commodity
at the highest possible price.
5. But the buyers of labor
at the lowest possible price,
and the sellers of labor
at the highest possible price,
are nothing but
commercializers of labor.

VI. Selling Their Labor[16] {16} — 9 times

1. When the laborers place
their labor on the bargain counter,
they allow the capitalists
or accumulators of labor
to accumulate their labor.
2. And when the capitalists
or accumulators of labor
have accumulated
so much of the laborers' labor,
that they no longer find it profitable
to buy the laborers' labor,
then the laborers
can no longer sell their labor
to the capitalists
or accumulators of labor.
3. And when the laborers

---

16. Also known as "On Selling Labor" and "Getting Left." Some versions of the essay replace the term "laborer" with "worker." "Getting Left" replaces stanza four with the following: "So the laborers get left when they sell their labor to the Capitalists or accumulators of labor."

        can no longer sell their labor
        to the capitalists
        or accumulators of labor,
        they can no longer
        buy the products of their labor.
    4. And that is what the laborers get
        for selling their labor.

SEPTEMBER 1933

EASY ESSAYS

I. God and Mammon[17] {17} — 3 times

1. Christ says:
    "The dollar you have
    is the dollar you give."[18]
2. The bankers says:
    "The dollar you have
    is the dollar you keep."
3. Christ says:
    "You cannot serve two masters,
    God and Mammon."[19]
4. "You cannot?
    And all our education
    consists in trying
    to find out how we can,"
    says Robert Louis Stevenson.[20]

---

17. The June 1936 version changed the word "Christ" to "Christian" in the first stanza. The July–August 1942 version replaced stanza two with the following: "The banker says: 'The dollar you have is the dollar you lend me for your sake.'"

18. Christ never said this, but it is reminiscent of certain sayings of Jesus, such as, "It is more blessed to give than to receive" (Acts 20:35) and "For the measure you give will be the measure you get back" (Luke 6:38).

19. This quote of Jesus is from Matthew 6:24 and Luke 16:13. "Mammon" is another term for money or wealth.

20. The quote was from a posthumously published fragment of Stevenson's writing from 1879 entitled, "Lay Morals."

5. "The poor are the true children
of the Church,"
says Bossuet.[21]
6. "Modern society has made
the bank account
the standard of values,"
says Charles Péguy.

II. When Civilization Decays {18} — 1 time

1. When the bank account
is the standard of values,
the class on the top
sets the standard.
2. When the class on the top
cares only for money
it does not care for culture.
3. When the class on the top
does not care for culture,
nobody cares for culture.
4. And when nobody cares for culture,
civilization decays.
5. When class distinction
is not based on the sense
of "noblesse oblige"[22]
it becomes clothes distinction.
6. When class distinction
has become clothes distinction
everybody tries
to put up a front.

---

21. The quote is from a sermon that Jacques-Bénigne Bossuet delivered.
22. Peter Maurin employed the term "noblesse oblige," literally "nobility obligates," to indicate the social responsibility of the wealthy to provide for the necessities of the poor. He particularly utilized the term to critique business owners and managers who placed profit before the basic dignity of their workers.

III. Self-Organization[23] {19} — 4 times

1. People go to Washington,
     asking the Federal Government
     to solve their economic problems,
     while the Federal Government
     was never intended
     to solve men's economic problems.
2. Thomas Jefferson says:
     "The less government there is
     the better it is."[24]
3. If the less government there is,
     the better it is
     then the best kind of government
     is self-government.
4. If the best kind of government
     is self-government
     then the best kind of organization
     is self-organization.
5. When the organizers
     try to organize
     the unorganized
     then the organizers
     don't organize themselves.
6. And when the organizers
     don't organize themselves,
     nobody organizes himself.
7. And when nobody organizes himself,
     nothing is organized.

---

23. Also known as "Self-Government." This version of the essay was the longest version. All the other versions omit stanza seven.

24. The quote, while commonly attributed to Jefferson, originated in 1837 in the pages of the now defunct *United States Magazine and Democratic Review*.

IV. Politics Is Politics[25] {20} — 3 times

1. A politician is an artist
    in the art of keeping up
    with public opinion.
2. He who follows the mind
    of the public opinion
    is ruled by public opinion.
3. He who is ruled
    by public opinion
    does not follow
    his own judgment.
4. He who does not follow
    his own judgment
    cannot lead people
    out of the beaten path.
5. He is like the tail of the dog
    that is fastened to its body
    and tries to lead the head.
6. When the people stand back
    of their President
    and their President
    stands back to them,
    people and President
    go around in a circle,
    getting nowhere.

V. Church and State {21} — 1 time

1. Modern society
    believes in separation
    of Church and State.
2. But the Jews
    did not believe in it,
    the Greeks did not believe in it,

---

25. Also known as "Politics vs. Politics." Future versions of the essay inserted the word "politicians" for "President."

>   the Romans did not believe in it,
>   the Mediaevalists did not believe in it,
>   the Puritans did not believe in it.
> 3. Modern society
>   has separated
>   the Church from the State,
>   but it has not separated
>   the State from Business.
> 4. Modern society
>   does not believe in a Church's State;
>   it believes in a Business Men's State.
> 5. "And it is the first time
>   in the history of the world
>   that the State
>   is controlled by business men,"
>   says James Truslow Adams.[26]

VI. A Modern Plague[27] {22} — 8 times

[part 1]
> 1. Having separated the Church
>   from the State,

---

26. The quote paraphrased an 1873 speech from Wisconsin Chief Justice Edward G. Ryan in Adams, *The Epic of America* (Boston: Little, Brown, 1931), 297.

27. In June 1934, Maurin broke this essay into two essays called "A Modern Plague" and "Secularism." Afterward, he joined them back together under the names "Secularism" and "Secularism Is a Pest." The June 1934 version added the following lines to the first part: "This separation of the spiritual from the material is what we call 'Secularism.' Everything has been secularized, everything has been divorced from religion. We have divorced religion from education, we have divorced religion from politics, we have divorced religion from business." The second part of the June 1934 version replaced stanza seven with the following: "And when religion has nothing to do with either education, politics and business, you have the religion of business taking the place of the business of religion." The November 1936 version concluded with the following: "Religion is good for weekdays as well as Sunday." There is an unpublished occurrence of the essay entitled, "French Secularism." That essay, which consists of only part 2, began with the following stanza: "Official France believes in the separation of the spiritual from the material."

modern society
has separated
religion from education,
politics and business.
2. "This separation of the spiritual
from the material
is at the base
of the modern chaos,"
says Glenn Frank,
President of Wisconsin University.
3. Pope Pius XI calls this separation
of the spiritual from the material
"a modern plague."[28]
[part 2]
4. When religion has nothing
to do with education,
education is only information.
5. When religion has nothing
to do with politics,
politics is only factionalism.
6. When religion has nothing
to do with business,
business is only commercialism.
7. And when religion has nothing
to do with education,
politics or business,
people have little
to do with religion.

28. This is probably a reference to Pius XI's encyclical *Mens nostra* 7 (1929), in which Pius referred to "the deadly plague of Rationalism." In this encyclical, Pius promoted the practice of spiritual retreats as a way of infusing the spiritual in the life of the faithful.

OCTOBER 1933
TO THE BISHOPS OF THE U.S.:
A PLEA FOR HOUSES OF HOSPITALITY

By Peter Maurin

(The following is an address by Peter Maurin, one of the founders of THE CATHOLIC WORKER, *to the unemployed, at a meeting held last month at the Manhattan Lyceum, and is reprinted here at his request in order that it may be sent to all the Bishops and Archbishops meeting at the National Conference of Catholic Charities in New York these first days of October, 1933.)*

I. The Duty of Hospitality[29] {23} — 3 times

1. People who are in need
    and are not afraid to beg
    give to people not in need
    the occasion to do good
    for goodness' sake.
2. Modern society calls the beggar
    bum and panhandler
    and gives him the bum's rush.
3. But the Greeks used to say
    that people in need
    are the ambassadors of the gods.
4. Although you may be called bums
    and panhandlers
    you are in fact
    the Ambassadors of God.

---

29. Also known as "Why Not Be a Beggar?" and "Hospitality." This version of the essay was the longest and most complete version. The second instance of the essay omitted the two stanzas regarding Muslims and replaced it with the following: "We read in the Gospel: 'As long as you did it to one of the least of My brothers, you did it to Me.'" The second instance concluded with the phrase, "To be God's Ambassador is something to be proud of." The final version of the essay replaced the last two stanzas with the following: "Hospices or Houses of Hospitality have existed in Europe since the time of Constantine. An Hospice was a shelter for the sick, the poor, the orphans, the old, the traveler and the needy of every kind."

5. As God's Ambassadors
    you should be given food, clothing
    and shelter
    by those who are able to give it.
6. Mahometan[30] teachers tell us
    that God commands hospitality.
7. And hospitality is still practiced
    in Mahometan countries.
8. But the duty of hospitality
    is neither taught nor practiced
    in Christian countries.

II. The Municipal Lodgings[31] {24} — 1 time

1. That is why you who are in need
    are not invited to spend the night
    in the homes of the rich.
2. There are guest rooms today
    in the homes of the rich
    but they are not for those
    who need them.
3. And they are not for those
    who need them
    because those who need them
    are no longer considered
    as the Ambassadors of God.
4. So people no longer
    consider hospitality to the poor
    as a personal duty.

---

30. "Mahometan" is an obsolete word that formerly referred to a Muslim or follower of the Islamic faith.

31. The Municipal Lodging House, or the "Muni," was a shelter built and run by New York City from 1909 to 1949. During the Great Depression, it used additional buildings to house the homeless. Though it provided shelter for men, women, and children, it was notorious for its lack of hospitality. Catholic Worker Herman Hergenhan wrote a two-part exposé on the Municipal Lodging House for the May and June 1934 issues of the paper.

5. And it does not disturb them a bit
         to send them to the city
         where they are given
         the hospitality of the "Muni"
         at the expense of the taxpayer.
   6. But the hospitality that the "Muni"
         gives to the down and out
         is no hospitality
         because what comes
         from the taxpayer's pocketbook
         does not come from his heart.

III. Back to Hospitality {25} — 1 time

   1. The Catholic unemployed
         should not be sent to the "Muni."
   2. The Catholic unemployed
         should be given hospitality
         in Catholic houses of hospitality.
   3. Catholic houses of hospitality
         are known in Europe
         under the name Hospices.
   4. There have been Hospices in Europe
         since the time of Constantine.
   5. Hospices are free guest houses;
         hotels are paying guest houses.
   6. And paying guest houses or hotels
         are as plentiful
         as free guest houses or hospices
         are scarce.
   7. So hospitality like everything else
         has been commercialized.
   8. So hospitality like everything else
         must now be idealized.

IV. Houses of Hospitality {9}

V. Hospices[32] {26} — 2 times

1. We read in the *Catholic Encyclopedia*[33]
    that during the early ages
    of Christianity,
    the hospice (or the house of hospitality)
    was a shelter
    for the sick, the poor,
    the orphans, the old,
    the traveler
    and the needy
    of every kind.
2. Originally the hospices
    (or houses of hospitality)
    were under the supervision
    of the bishops
    who designated priests
    to administer
    the spiritual
    and temporal affairs
    of these charitable institutions.
3. The fourteenth statute
    of the so-called
    Council of Carthage
    held about 436
    enjoins upon the bishops
    to have hospices
    (or houses of hospitality)
    in connection
    with their churches.[34]

32. Also known as "Houses of Hospitality." The only differences between the two versions of the essay were grammatical.

33. This is a reference to the *Catholic Encyclopedia* that was published by the Robert Appleton Company in fifteen volumes between 1907 and 1912. It is currently available online at newadvent.org. Maurin took the information for the current Easy Essay from its entry on "hospice."

34. Carthage never held an ecumenical council that was recognized as applicable to the entire Catholic Church, but regional North African councils were convened there. It

VI. Parish Houses of Hospitality {27} — 1 time

1. Today we need houses of hospitality
    as much as they needed it then
    if not more so.
2. We have Parish Houses for the priests
    Parish Houses for education purposes
    Parish Houses for recreational purposes
    but no Parish Houses of hospitality.
3. Bossuet says that the poor
    are the first children of the Church
    so the poor should come first.
4. People with homes
    should have a room of hospitality
    so as to give shelter
    to the needy members of the parish.
5. The remaining needy members of the parish
    should be given shelter in a Parish Home.
6. Furniture, clothing and food
    should be sent
    to the needy members of the parish
    at the Parish House of Hospitality.
7. We need Parish Homes
    as well as Parish Domes.
8. In the new Cathedral of Liverpool
    there will be a Home
    as well as a Dome.[35]

---

does not appear that a North African council occurred in Carthage in 436, but the eighteenth-century collector of the canons, cited by the *Catholic Encyclopedia*, pointed out that this collection of canons was probably taken from numerous councils held in Carthage; Giovanni Domenico Mansi, ed., *Sacrorum Conciliorum: Nova et Amplissima Collectio* (Venice: Expensis Antonii Zatta Veneti, 1759), 3:945–52, https://books.google.com/books?id=7wdEFsUX_-gC&printsec=frontcover&dq=editions:kGbSiHR_PZIC&hl=en&newbks=1&newbks_redir=0&sa=X&ved=2ahUKEwifiLuAh-voAhVOB5oJHSG6BDY4FBDrATACegQIAxAB#v=onepage&q&f=false.

35. This proposed cathedral, which would have been the second-largest church in the world with the world's largest church dome, was never completed. Construction began in 1933, but was halted for financial reasons after the crypt was constructed. It was also to include a space for the poor to escape the elements at any hour of the day.

VII. Houses of "Catholic Action" {28} — 1 time

1. Catholic houses of hospitality
    should be more than free guest houses
    for the Catholic unemployed.
2. They could be vocational training schools
    including the training for the priesthood
    as Father Corbett proposes.
3. They could be Catholic reading rooms
    as Father McSorley proposes.
4. They could be Catholic Instruction Schools
    as Father Cornelius Hayes proposes.
5. They could be Round-Table Discussion Groups
    as Peter Maurin proposes.
6. In a word, they could be
    Catholic Action Houses
    where Catholic Thought
    is combined with Catholic Action.

THE SPIRIT OF THE MASS[36] {29} — 1 time

Men always ring a little bell
When the sacring time is near,
And then shalt thou do reverence
To Christ Jesus' own high presence;
That thou mayest loose all sinful bonds
Kneel and hold up both thy hands,
For this is He that Judas sold
That lifted up thou dost behold.
And He was scourged and trod the way
To shed His blood for all mankind.
He died, He rose, He went to Heaven
Whence He comes to judge mankind

---

36. This essay begins with Maurin quoting a medieval text on the Eucharistic sacrifice, followed by his own thoughts on Christ's passion, the Eucharist, and its implications for today.

For all that each of us had done.
This same is He thou lookst upon
This is the truth of Holy Church.

—From a lay-folk's Mass Book
Thirteenth Century[37]

The Spirit of the Masses

1. The central act of devotional life in the Catholic Church
    is the Holy Sacrifice of the Mass.
2. The sacrifice of the Mass is
    the unbloody repetition
    of the Sacrifice of the Cross.
3. On the Cross of Calvary Christ gave
    His life to redeem the world.
4. The life of Christ was a life of sacrifice.
5. The life of a Christian must be a life of sacrifice.
6. We cannot imitate the sacrifice
    of Christ on Calvary
    by trying to get all we can.
7. We can only imitate the sacrifice
    of Christ on Calvary
    by trying to give all we can.

—Peter Maurin

AN OPEN LETTER TO FATHER LORD, M. AG. (MASTER AGITATOR) {30} — 1 Time

Dear Father:

1. In your instructions about writing,
    you told us that the best way to learn to write,

---

37. This quote is from *The Lay Folks Mass Book; Or, The Manner of Hearing Mass, with Rubrics and Devotions for the People, in Four Texts, and Office in English According to the Use of York, from Manuscripts of the Xth to the XVth Century, with Appendix, Notes, and Glossary*, 38. The text was published in 1879 by N. Trubner. The text, which was translated into English around 1300, explained the priest's actions and provided devotional prayers to be prayed during Mass.

is to write letters
   because a letter is a message
   from someone to somebody about something.
2. So this is a message
   from an agitator to another agitator
   about a discontented world
   which begins to realize
   that things are not good enough
   to be left alone.
3. THE CATHOLIC WORKER thinks
   that you are a wonder.
4. We know what good work you are doing
   among Catholic college youth.
5. But Catholic college youth
   are a small proportion of Catholic youth
   and all Catholic youth need you
   as much as Catholic college youth.
6. Not only all Catholic youth need you
   but all youth need you.
7. And not only all those who are in their first youth
   but all those who are getting in their second youth.
8. And also all those who have reached the age of maturity
   without having reached the state of maturity.
9. That is to say
   we all need you.
10. We all need you
    because you have the knack
    of getting at the core of things
    and of presenting your findings
    in a vivid and dynamic form.
11. In one of his editorials Father Gillis says
    that this age is very much like the age of the Fall of Rome
    and that we could use another Saint Augustine.
12. Father Gillis adds
    that we need men to stir things up
    and that we have too many
    who try to smother them down.
13. You certainly can stir things up
    and you can do that with much ease.

14. It is said that Abbé Chardonnel who was a poet
     became a priest
     so he could be more of a poet.
15. You who are a born agitator
     have become a priest
     which makes you more of an agitator.
16. In St. Louis University
     you turn out Masters of Arts
     but as Diego Rivera says:
     "All art is propaganda."
17. And as all propaganda is agitation
     it behooves St. Louis University
     one of the best American Universities
     to turn out Masters of Agitation.
18. So the CATHOLIC WORKER suggests
     that you, our Master Catholic Agitator
     start in St. Louis University
     a School of Catholic Agitation
     for the popularization of Catholic Action.

—Yours for Catholic Action,
For THE CATHOLIC WORKER,
Peter Maurin

NOVEMBER 1933
EASY ESSAYS

I. To Be a Marxian {31} — 1 time

1. Before he died, Karl Marx
     told one of his friends
     "I have lived long enough
     to be able to say
     that I am not a Marxian."[38]
2. To be a Marxian,
     according to the logic of *Das Capital*,

---

38. Marx stated this jokingly, which is not readily apparent from the context.

is to maintain that the best thing to do
   is to wait patiently, till Capitalism
   has fulfilled its historic mission.
3. To be a Marxian,
   according to the logic of *Das Capital*,
   is to step back, take an academic view of things
   and watch the self-satisfied Capitalists
   dig their own graves.
4. To be a Marxian,
   according to the logic of *Das Capital*,
   is to have faith in the forces of materialism—
   forces so powerful, according to materialists,
   that they will bring the millennium
   whether man wants it or not.
5. To be a Marxian,
   according to the logic of *Das Capital*,
   is to let economic evolution do its work
   without ever attempting to give it a push.

II. Karl Marx Soon Realized {32} — 1 time

1. Karl Marx soon realized
   that his own analysis of bourgeois society
   could not be the basis
   of a dynamic revolutionary movement.
2. Karl Marx soon realized
   that a forceful Communist Manifesto
   was the necessary foundation
   of a dynamic Communist Movement.
3. Karl Marx soon realized,
      as Lenin realized,
      that there is no revolution
      without revolutionary action,
      that there is no revolutionary action
      without a revolutionary movement
      that there is no revolutionary movement
      without a vanguard of revolution,
      and that there is no vanguard of revolution
      without a theory of revolution.

III. The Communist Manifesto[39] {33} — 2 times

1. Having realized that a Communist Manifesto
    was the basis of a Communist Movement
    Karl Marx decided to write a Communist Manifesto.
2. To write the *Communist Manifesto*
    Karl Marx did not use his own analysis of Capitalism.
3. He took the criticism of the bourgeois society of his time
    by Victor Considerant, a Utopian Communist,
    and made it the first part of the
    Communist Manifesto.
4. He took the definition of Communism by Proudhon
    and made it his own.
5. He borrowed Utopian criticism and Utopian aims;
    and decided to advocate class-struggle,
    that is to say, materialist aims.
6. As some people used to think
    that we need a good honest war
    to end all wars,
    Karl Marx used to think
    that we need a gigantic class-struggle
    to bring about a classless society.

IV. For Catholic Action[40] {34} — 2 times

1. We Catholics have a better criticism
    of bourgeois society
    than Victor Considerant's criticism,
    used by Karl Marx.
2. Our criticism of bourgeois society
    is the criticism of Blessed Thomas More.
3. We Catholics have a better conception
    of Communism
    than the conception of Proudhon.

---

39. Also known as "The Communist Party." The other version is shorter, but concluded with the following sentence: "The technique of proletarian dictatorship is the technique advocated by Lenin."

40. Also known as "The Catholic Worker." The other version was highly condensed, though it concluded by explicitly stating that the Catholic Worker promotes the works of mercy and farming communes.

4. Our conception of Communism
    is the conception of Saint Thomas Aquinas
    in his doctrine of the "Common Good."
5. We Catholics have a better means
    than the means proposed by Karl Marx.
6. Our means to realize the "Common Good"
    are embodied in Catholic Action.
7. Catholic Action is action by Catholics
    for Catholics and non-Catholics.
8. We don't want to take over the control
    of political and economic life.
9. We want to reconstruct the social order
    through Catholic Action
    exercised in Catholic Institutions.

V. The Bishops' Program {35} — 1 time

1. Shortly after the War the Bishops of America
    formulated a Program of Social Reconstruction[41]
    largely based on Co-operation.
2. But the Bishops' Program failed to materialize
    for lack of co-operators.
3. Catholic laymen and women were
    more interested in a laissez-faire economy.
4. So Catholic laymen and women
    went back to Normalcy with Harding;
    they tried to Keep Cool with Coolidge,
    and now they try to See Rosy with Roosevelt.
5. Catholic laymen and women are more interested
    in political action
    than they are interested
    in Catholic Action.
6. Catholic laymen and women are more ready to follow
    the leadership of the politicians
    than they are ready to follow
    the leadership of the Bishops.

---

41. This document, called the "Program for Social Reconstruction," was published by the American bishops in 1919.

VI. Reconstructing the Social Order[42] {36} — 5 times

1. The Holy Father and the Bishops ask us
    to Reconstruct the Social Order.
2. The social order was once constructed
    through dynamic Catholic Action.
3. When the Barbarians invaded
    the decaying Roman Empire
    Irish missionaries went all over Europe
    and laid the foundations of Mediaeval Europe.
4. Through the establishment of cultural centers,
    that is to say, Round-Table Discussions,
    they brought thought to the people.
5. Through free guest houses,
    that is to say, Houses of Hospitality,
    they popularized the divine virtue of Charity.
6. Through farming colonies,
    that is to say, Agronomic Universities,
    they emphasized voluntary Poverty.
7. It was on the basis of personal Charity
    and voluntary Poverty
    that Irish missionaries
    laid the foundations of the social order.

---

42. Also known as "Reconstruction." The other versions of the essay place greater stress on the role of Irish scholars. Here is the September 1934 version: "The Holy Father asks us to reconstruct the social order. The social order was once reconstructed after the fall of the Roman Empire. The Irish scholars were the leaders in the reconstruction of the social order after the fall of the Roman Empire. Through Round-Table Discussions scattered all over Europe as far as Constantinople the Irish scholars brought thought to the people. Through Houses of Hospitality the Irish scholars exemplified Christian charity. Through Farming Communes the Irish scholars made workers out of scholars and scholars out of workers." Some of the later essays end with the phrase, "The means used by the first Christians to construct the social order and by the Irish Scholars to reconstruct the social order are the means proposed now by the CATHOLIC WORKER."

15 DECEMBER 1933
TO NATIONAL RECOVERY ACT ADMINISTRATION OFFICIALS[43] — IS INFLATION INEVITABLE?

I. Usurers Not Gentlemen[44] {37} — 3 times

1. The Prophets of Israel
and the Fathers of the Church
forbid lending money at interest;
2. Lending money at interest
is called usury[45]
by the Prophets of Israel
and the Fathers of the Church;
3. Usurers were not considered
to be gentlemen
when people used to listen
to the Prophets of Israel
and the Fathers of the Church;
4. When people used to listen
to the Prophets of Israel

---

43. This was addressed to the National Recovery Administration, which President Roosevelt established in 1933. After conferring with businesses in a specific industry, the N.R.A. was empowered to legislate prices, wages, and business practices for that industry. The administration's goal was to harmonize industry and labor under a preconceived government plan to eliminate "destructive competition" and spur growth. In 1935, the United States Supreme Court ruled these practices were unconstitutional. The N.R.A. is often viewed as a failure, but it did help solidify the forty-hour work week, end child labor, and strengthen unions with its promotion of collective bargaining.

44. The wording for the other versions is the same.

45. This is the first of many instances in which Maurin noted the Catholic Church's classical condemnation of usury. Although usury now refers to the excessive charging of interest on a loan, it had previously referred to the condemned practice of charging any interest on a loan. The Old Testament was also clear in its condemnation of charging interest on loans to fellow Jews. Around the time of the Reformation, Catholic and Protestant leaders began loosening restrictions on usury. Nevertheless, Dorothy Day and Peter Maurin held the charging of interest to be harmful for society. For Maurin, one should earn a living by the sweat of one's brow and not simply from the fact that one already has money for which they can charge others to borrow. For more on this topic, see the biographical entries for John Calvin and John Knox.

and the Fathers of the Church
they could not see anything gentle
in trying to live
on the sweat of somebody else's brow
by lending money at interest.

II. Wealth-Producing Maniacs {7}

III. Legalized Usury {5}

IV. The Fallacy of Saving[46] {38} — 7 times

1. When people save money,
    they invest that money.
2. Money invested
    increases production.
3. Increased production
    brings a surplus
    in production.
4. A surplus in production
    brings unemployment.
5. Unemployment
    brings a slump
    in business
6. A slump in business
    brings more unemployment.
7. More unemployment
    brings a depression.
8. A depression
    brings more depression.
9. More depression
    brings red agitation.
10. Red agitation
    brings red revolution.

---

46. Some versions of the essay add the following stanza at the end: "That is what people get for saving money for a rainy day."

V. Avoiding Inflation[47] {39} — 3 times

1. Some say
    that inflation
    is desirable.
2. Some say
    that inflation
    is deplorable.
3. Some say
    that inflation
    is deplorable
    but inevitable.
4. The way
    to avoid inflaction
    is to lighten the burden
    of the money borrowers
    without robbing
    the money lenders.
5. And the way
    to lighten the burden
    of the money borrowers
    without robbing
    the money lenders
    is to pass two laws,
    one law
    making immediately illegal
    all interest
    on money lent
    and another law
    obliging the money borrowers
    to pay one per cent
    of their debt
    every year
    during a period
    of a hundred years.

---

47. The other two versions of the essays omit stanza four.

ANOTHER OPEN LETTER TO FATHER LORD M. AG. (MASTER AGITATOR)[48] {40} — 1 Time

Dear Father:
1. There is a lot of talk today
    about the social value of Fascism.
2. But Fascism is only a stop-gap
    between Capitalism and Bolshevism.
3. Fascist Dictatorship is a half-way house
    between the rugged individualism of Capitalism
    and the rugged collectivism of Bolshevism.
4. There is no essential difference
    between Fascist Dictatorship
    and Bolshevik Dictatorship.
5. The trouble with the world today
    is too much dictatorship
    and too little leadership.
6. Leadership cannot be found
    among politicians, businessmen
    and college professors.
7. The appointed leaders of mankind
    are the Catholic Bishops.
8. Catholic Bishops have ceased to lead
    because Catholic laymen and women
    do not consider the Bishops as their leaders
    in political and economic matters.
9. Catholic laymen and women
    look up to the Bishops in spiritual matters
    and look up to politicians and business men
    in political and economic matters.
10. Catholic laymen and women commit the great modern error
    of separating the spiritual from the material.
11. This great modern error
    known under the name of Secularism
    is called a "modern plague"
    by Pope Pius XI.

---

48. Other collected works often refer to this essay as "A SECOND OPEN LETTER TO FATHER LORD, S.J."

12. You who are a born agitator and a theologian
    ought to make Catholic laymen and women realize
    that the Bishops are their Leaders
    in temporal as well as spiritual matters.
13. You who are a born agitator and a theologian
    should bring a thorough understanding
    between Bishops, Clergy and lay people.
14. From that understanding
    would spring a form of Catholic Action
    that would be dynamic in character.
15. We are threatened with Dynamic Bolshevik Action
    because we are sorely lacking
    in Dynamic Catholic Action.

    —Yours for Dynamic Catholic Action,

    Peter Maurin

INTERVIEW WITH MOLEY TOLD BY PETER MAURIN

The following is an address delivered by Peter Maurin at the last Round Table Discussion held by THE CATHOLIC WORKER at the Manhattan Lyceum, Sunday, December 3:

I. Legalized Usury[49] {41} — 5 times

1. Two years ago, I went to see Professor Moley,
    former head
    of President Roosevelt's Brain Trust,
    and said to him:
    "I came here to find out
    if I could make an impression

---

49. Also known as "Things Have Changed," "Business Is the Bunk," "On the Campus," and "Business Is Business." This address by Peter Maurin contains previous Easy Essays and one new one. The address is presented without change. Since other versions do not include the other essays included in this version, the next time {41} is presented in July–August 1934, it will be presented in its entirety. This second version of {41} should be used as a guide when the text of {41} is omitted.

on the depression
by starting a rumpus on the Campus.
But I found out
that agitation is not rampant
on the Campus.
Only business is rampant
on the Campus.
although business is the bunk.
May be," said I
"history cannot be made on the Campus."
2. And turning toward his secretary,
Professor Moley said:
"That's right, we don't make
history on the Campus,
we only teach it."
3. And because history is taught
but not made
on the Campus of our Universities,
THE CATHOLIC WORKER is trying
to make history on Union Square,
where people have nothing to lose.
4. A battle royal is raging
between East and West
between stock speculators
and land speculators
between money lenders
and money borrowers.
5. To go back to the gold standard
as the so-called "sound money"
people propose
is to favor the money lenders
at the expense
of the money borrowers.
6. To increase the amount of currency
as the mild inflationists propose
is to favor the money borrowers
at the expense of the money lenders.
7. To devise schemes
so as to bring about a rise in prices

is to favor both money lenders
and money borrowers
at the expense of the consuming public.
8. We made the mistake
of running business on credit,
and credit has run into debts
and debts are leading us toward bankruptcy.
9. The Jews had a way
of wiping off the slate.
10. Every fifty years,
the year of the Jewish Jubilee
all debts were liquidated.
11. But nobody, not even the Jews,
proposes this old-time solution.
12. John Maynard Keynes,
the well-known English economist, says
that we ought to ask ourselves
if the Mediaeval economists
were not sound
in condemning money lending
at interest.
13. In his book on *Religion and
the Rise of Capitalism*
R. H. Tawney, another English economist,
points out
that at the basis of our acquisitive society
we find legalized usury
or lending money at interest.
14. Because the State has legalized {5}
money lending at interest
in spite of the teachings
of the Prophets of Israel
and the Fathers of the Church
home owners have mortgaged
their homes,
farm owners have mortgaged
their farms,
institutions have mortgaged
their buildings,

governments have mortgaged
   their budgets.
15. So we are where we are
   because the State has legalized
   money lending at interest
   in spite of the teachings
   of the Prophets of Israel
   and the Fathers of the Church.
16. To go back to the teachings
   of the Prophets of Israel
   and the Fathers of the Church,
   as I propose in my Easy Essays
   in the current number
   of the *Catholic Worker*,
   would not do any injustice
   to the money lenders
   or the money borrowers
   or the consuming public.
17. Money lenders
   would get their money back,
   money borrowers
   would find their burden lightened
   and the consuming public
   would not have to pay the bill.
18. We would go back to the point
   from which we should never
   have gone.
19. We would go back to the time {37}
   when no one was called a gentleman
   who indulged in money lending
   at interest.
20. We would go back to the time
   when people could not see
   anything gentle
   in trying to live on the sweat
   of somebody else's brow
   by lending money at interest.

21. Many people say {42} — 2 times[50]
    that we cannot go back.
22. But I say
    neither can we go ahead,
    for we are parked in a blind-alley.
23. And when people are parked
    in a blind-alley
    the only thing to do is to go back.
24. For when people lend money at interest {38}
    that money is invested.
25. Money invested
    increases production.
26. Increased production
    brings a surplus in production.
27. A surplus in production
    brings unemployment.
28. Unemployment
    brings a slump in business.
29. A slump in business
    brings more unemployment.
30. More unemployment
    brings a depression.
31. A depression
    brings more depression.
32. More depression
    brings red agitation.
33. Red agitation
    brings red revolution.

---

50. This essay about being trapped in a blind alley occurs here and is expanded in the later version of the essay, which is kept in its entirety. Though it was here part of a larger essay and untitled, in the April 1935 issue it was called "Going Back."

TO OUR READERS[51]
NOTICE!
ROUND TABLE DISCUSSION

Again we meet in the Manhattan Lyceum, 66 East 4th Street,
    on Sunday, Jan. 7, at 2 p.m.
To these meetings I invite Clergymen and Communists—
    That is to say, everybody is welcome.
To a commercial industrial economy
    I am opposing a cultural agronomic economy
    —cultural implying cult plus culture
    plus cultivation; that is to say liturgy plus
    literature plus agriculture.
To systematic selfishness
    I am opposing systematic unselfishness.
To the sociology of Karl Marx, Lenin, and Stalin
    I am opposing the sociology of Saint Francis of Assisi,
    Blessed Thomas More and Léon Harmel.
To a technique of Dictatorship
    I am opposing a technique of Leadership.
To Dictatorial Pagan Communism
    I am opposing Utopian Christian Communism.
To Bolshevik Action
    I am opposing Catholic Action.
Knowing that you are deeply interested in the subject
    I am inviting you to attend the meeting.
Your presence would be a great encouragement for me
    and I hope of much profit to you.
There will not be any collection at the meeting
    but if you would care to contribute
    I will gladly accept what you can afford.
Your contribution will be used
    to help the House of Hospitality for Catholic unemployed.
Hoping to see you at the meeting,
    I am,

—Your co-worker in Christ's Kingdom,
Peter Maurin

---

51. This was a notice that Maurin placed in the paper about an upcoming round-table discussion.

1 FEBRUARY 1934
EASY ESSAYS

I. Hayes[52] of Columbia Gives Opening Night Lecture of Catholic Workers' School {43} — 1 time

1. We start next month,
    the Catholic Workers' School.
2. From 7 to 8 P.M.
    we will have a discussion
    led from the floor
    by anyone who happens to be there.
3. From 8 to 9 P.M.
    we will have a lecture,
    on a special subject
    by one who knows his subject.
4. From 9 to 10 P.M.
    we will have a discussion
    led from the platform
    by the lecturer
    or by a Catholic worker.

II. Coming to Union Square[53] {44} — 6 times

1. Two years ago,
    I went to see college professors
    and asked them to give me
    the formulation
    of those universal concepts

---

52. This is a reference to Carlton J. H. Hayes (1882–1964).
53. Also known as "Specialization," "Not My Subject," and "A College Professor." The other versions of the essay follow a variation more similar to the last instance of the essay in January 1942, which is included here: "1. I asked a college professor to give me the formulation of those universal concepts embodied in the universal message of universal universities that would enable the common man to create a universal economy. 2. And the college professor answered: 'That is not my subject.' 3. College professors enable students to master subjects but mastering subjects does not enable people to master situations. 4. College professors are specialists who know more and more about less and less and if they keep on specializing they will end by knowing everything about nothing."

embodied in the universal message
of universal universities
that will enable the common man
to create a universal economy.
2. But college professors
were too busy teaching subjects
to be interested in mastering situations.
3. College professors
were too interested in academic matters
to be interested in dynamic matters.
4. But now college professors
realize that they must be men of action
as well as men of thought—
that they must be dynamic
as well as academic,
and that Union Square
can teach something
to college professors
as well as learning
from college professors.

III. Blowing the Dynamite {3}

IV. Scholars and Bourgeois[54] {45} — 2 times

[part 1]
1. The scholar has told the bourgeois
that a worker is a man
for all of that.
2. But the bourgeois has told the scholar
that a worker is a commodity
for all of that.
3. Because the scholar has vision,
bourgeois calls him a visionary.

---

54. Also known as "Scholar and Bourgeois." There were three differences between this essay and the other version: (1) the second version divided the original into the two parts (or essays) with the second part called, "Scholar and Worker," (2) the second version omitted stanza ten, and (3), the second version changed the line "a worker is a man for all of that" to "a man is a man for all of that."

4. So the bourgeois laughs
    at the scholar's vision
    and the worker
    is left without vision.
5. And the worker left by the scholar
    without vision
    talks about liquidating
    both the bourgeois
    and the scholar.
[part 2]
6. The scholars must tell the workers
    what is wrong
    with the things as they are.
7. The scholars must tell the workers
    how the things would be,
    if they were as they should be.
8. The scholars must tell the workers
    how a path can be made
    from the things as they are
    to the things as they should be.
9. The scholars must collaborate
    with the workers
    in the making of a path
    from the things as they are
    to the things as they should be.
10. The scholars must become workers
    so the workers may be scholars.

BUILDING CHURCHES[55] {46} — 6 Times

1. Henry Adams tells us in his Autobiography
    that he could not get an education in America,

---

55. Also known as "Looking for an Education," "No Unity of Thought," "Unity of Thought," and "Henry Adams." Other versions of the essay are much shorter and consist of only the first four stanzas. In some of the other versions, Maurin explicitly mentions Adams's book on the unity of thought in the Middle Ages, *Mont Saint-Michel and Chartres* (New York: Gallery Books, 1985). Starting with the third version, he not only references the "Cathedral of Chartres," but always references both "the cathedral of Chartres and the Mont St. Michel."

      because education implies unity of thought
      and there is no unity of thought in America.
2. So he went to England
      and found that England
      was too much like America.
3. So he went to France
      and found that France
      was too much like England and America.
4. But in France he found the Cathedral of Chartres
      and from the Cathedral of Chartres he learned
      that there was unity of thought
      in thirteenth-century France.
5. People who built the Cathedral of Chartres
      knew how to combine
      cult, that is to say liturgy
      with culture, that is to say philosophy
      and cultivation, that is to say agriculture.
6. The Cathedral of Chartres is a real work of art
      because it is the real expression
      of the spirit of a united people.
7. Churches that are built today
      do not express the spirit of the people.
8. "When a church is built,"
      said to me a Catholic editor,
      "the only thing that has news value is:
      How much did it cost?"
9. The Cathedral of Chartres was not built
      to increase the value of real estate.
10. The Cathedral of Chartres was not built
      with money borrowed from money lenders.
11. The Cathedral of Chartres was not built
      by workers working for wages.
12. Maurice Barrès used to worry
      about the preservation of French Cathedrals.
13. But Charles Péguy thought
      that the faith that builds Cathedrals
      is after all the thing that matters.
14. Moscow had a thousand churches
      and people lost the faith.

15. Churches ought to be built
    with donated money,
    donated material, donated labor.
16. The motto of Saint Benedict was
    Labore et Orare, Labor and Pray.
17. Labor and prayer ought to be combined;
    labor ought to be a prayer.
18. The liturgy of the Church
    is the prayer of the Church.
19. People ought to pray with the Church
    and to work with the Church.
20. The religious life of the people
    and the economic life of the people
    ought to be one.
21. I heard that in Germany
    a group of Benedictines
    is trying to combine liturgy with sociology.
22. We don't need to wait for Germany
    to point the way.
23. Architects, artists, and artisans
    ought to exchange ideas
    on Catholic liturgy and Catholic sociology.

A QUESTION AND AN ANSWER ON CATHOLIC GUILDS

Dear Peter Maurin:

I have read many of your articles in the *Catholic Worker* and am interested in your program for Houses of Hospitality.

Why not organize Catholic Labor Guilds[56] throughout the nation such as Mr. Gunn is doing in Brooklyn?

---

56. Catholic labor guilds were common in the United States during the Great Depression. Often, they took the form of Catholic Labor Schools that taught Catholics about labor law, contract negotiations, and workers' rights. In contrast to secular unions, these guilds grounded the rights of the worker in Catholic Social Teaching. In early 1934, Michael Gunn's Labor Guild in Brooklyn consisted of a group of workers who lived in community, attended daily Mass, and shared resources as they supported each other in obtaining work. Ideally, Gunn wanted the group to consist of capital, laborers, and consumers who would collaborate to ensure that everyone's needs were met.

Then assess each member a dollar a year, using the money to build houses of hospitality such as you propose.

We have the right to organize now. Why not?

Suppose a million workers in or throughout the United States would organize in a Catholic Labor Union or Labor Guild.

A dollar a year as a special assessment would make a million dollars.

The working man has to support the unemployed anyway and Catholics may as well organize into a union by themselves (they can join other trade unions if they please). They will have to join sooner or later, why not now when the government gives the right to organize.

A reader from Bellingham, Washington.

PETER MAURIN ANSWERS[57]

Most organizations exist
> not for the benefit of the organized,
> but for the benefit of the organizers.

When the organizers try to organize the unorganized
> they do not organize themselves.

If everybody organized himself,
> everybody would be organized.

There is no better way to be
> than to be
> what we want the other fellow to be.

The money that comes from assessments
> is not worth getting.

The money that is worth getting
> is the money that is given for charity's sake.

Parish Houses of Hospitality
> must be built on Christian charity.

But Parish Houses of Hospitality
> are only half-way houses.

Parish Subsistence Camps
> are the most efficient way
> to make an impression
> on the depression.

---

57. This is not an Easy Essay, but it is included because it was typical of the way Peter Maurin responded to letters.

The basis for a Christian economy
   is genuine charity and voluntary poverty.
To give money to the poor
   is to increase the buying power of the poor.
Money is by definition a means of exchange
   and not a means to make money.
When money is used as a means of exchange,
   it helps to consume the goods
   that have been produced.
When money is used as an investment,
   it does not help to consume
   the goods that have been produced,
   it helps to produce more goods
   to bring over-production
   and therefore increase unemployment.
So much money has been put into business
   that it has put business out of business.
Money given to the poor is functional money,
   money that fulfills its function.
Money used as an investment
   is prostituted money,
   money that does not fulfill its function.
Poverty and charity are no longer looked up to,
   they are looked down upon.
The poor have ceased to accept poverty
   and the rich have ceased to practice charity.
When the poor are satisfied to be poor,
   the rich become charitable toward the poor.
Because Christianity presents poverty as an ideal
   Bolshevik Communists try to make us believe
   that religion is the opium of the people.
Karl Marx says that the worker is exploited
   at the point of production.
But the worker would not be exploited
   at the point of production
   if the worker did not sell his labor
   to the exploiter of his labor.
When the worker sells his labor
   to a capitalist or accumulator of labor

  he allows the capitalist or accumulator of labor
    to accumulate his labor.
And when the capitalist or accumulator of labor
  has accumulated so much of the worker's labor
  that he no longer finds it profitable
  to buy the worker's labor
  then the worker can no longer sell his labor
  to the capitalist or accumulator of labor.
And when the worker can no longer
  sell his labor to the capitalist or accumulator of labor
  he can no longer buy the products of his labor.
And that is what the worker gets for selling his labor
  to the capitalist or accumulator of labor.
He just gets left
  and he gets what is coming to him.
Labor is not a commodity
  to be bought and sold—
Labor is a means of self-expression
  the worker's gift to the Common Good.
There is so much depression
  because there is so little expression.
I am fostering Parish Subsistence Camps
  or Agronomic Universities
  as a means to bring about a state of society
  where scholars are workers
  and where workers are scholars.
In a Parish Subsistence Camp
  or Agronomic University
  the worker does not work for wages
  he leaves that to the University.
In a Parish Subsistence Camp
  or Agronomic University
  the worker does not look for a bank account
  he leaves that to the University.
In a Parish Subsistence Camp
  or Agronomic University
  the worker does not look for an insurance policy
  he leaves that to the University.

In a Parish Subsistence Camp
   or Agronomic University
   the worker does not look for an old age pension,
   he leaves that to the University.
In a Parish Subsistence Camp
   or Agronomic University
   the worker does not look for a rainy day
   he leaves that to the University.
Modern industry has no work for everybody
   but work can be found for everybody
   in Parish Subsistence Camps
   or Agronomic Universities.
I may later on publish a magazine entitled *The Agronomist*
   for the fostering of the idea
   of Parish Subsistence Camps
   or Agronomic Universities.
Edward Koch of Germantown, Illinois
   publishes a magazine entitled *The Guildsman*;
   you ought to get in touch with him.
              —Your co-worker in Christ's Kingdom.
                                    Peter Maurin

1 MARCH 1934
EASY ESSAYS

I. Purpose of Catholic Workers' School in Detail {47} — 1 time

1. The purpose of the Catholic Workers' School
   is to bring Catholic thought
   to Catholic workers
   so as to prepare them
   for Catholic Action.
2. Besides presenting Catholic thought
   to Catholic workers,
   the Catholic Workers' School
   presents a Program of Catholic Action
   based on Catholic thought.

3. The Program of the Catholic Workers' School
    is a three-point program
    1. Round-table Discussions
    2. Houses of Hospitality
    3. Farming Communes.

II. Round-Table Discussions {8}

III. Houses of Hospitality {9}

IV. Communes {48} — 1 time

1. We need Communes
    to help the unemployed
    to help themselves.
2. We need Communes
    to make scholars out of workers
    and workers out of scholars.
3. We need Communes
    to substitute a technique of ideals
    for our technique of deals.
4. We need Communes
    to create a new society
    within the shell of the old
    with the philosophy of the new.

V. Catholic Social Philosophy[58] {49} — 1 time

1. The Catholic social philosophy
    is the philosophy of the Common Good
    of Saint Thomas Aquinas.
2. Three books where this philosophy is expressed are:
    The Thomistic Doctrine of the Common Good
    by Suzanne Michel;[59]

---

58. This is arguably not an Easy Essay, but a book reading list. It is treated as an Easy Essay because of its first stanza on the common good.

59. The original essay in the newspaper named the author as Séraphine Michel. Perhaps Michel also went by the name Séraphine, but her actual name was Suzanne.

The Social Principles of the Gospel
by Alphonse Lugan;
Progress and Religion
by Christopher Dawson.

Below is Maurin's response to a letter by Michael Gunn about the Catholic Labor Guild in Brooklyn, which Gunn viewed as "capital's PARTNER." Gunn wrote his short article after reading Maurin's response to the reader from Bellingham, Washington, which is included earlier. Maurin's response illuminates Maurin's concerns about most unions.

MAURIN ANSWERS

Dear Mike,
In my answer to a reader
    from Bellingham, Washington,
    I said that "Most organizations exist,
    not for the benefit of the organized
    but for the benefit of the organizers."
I added that "When the organizers
    try to organize the unorganized
    they do not organize themselves."
When I wrote that
    I did not have in mind
    the Catholic Labor Guild in Brooklyn.
I had in mind
    some selfish exploiters
    of the exploitation of the exploited
    who like to be called labor leaders.
I had in mind
    some exalted rulers of secret societies
    who, while they call themselves Masons,
    have not yet learned
    to create order out of chaos.

Nevertheless, this is a reference to her French book *La Notion Thomiste du Bien Commun*, which was published in 1932 by Librairie Philosophique J. Vrin. It has never been translated into English.

I had in mind
>	some dignified regulators
>	of societies which have some secrets
>	without being called secret societies.

While I don't like some of your ideas,
>	I like you personally.

I think that you are
>	much better than some of your ideas.

I think that you are inclined
>	to lead a life of sacrifice.

During the World War you placed your life
>	at the service of the British Empire.

After the war, you placed your life
>	at the service of the Irish Republic.

And now you have placed your life
>	at the service of the Church.

You and your fellow workers
>	of the Catholic Labor Guild
>	are trying to combine
>	prayer, action and sacrifice
>	as the Holy Father suggests.

You and your fellow workers
>	want to be go-givers
>	you don't want to be go-getters.

Since you and your fellow workers
>	want to be go-givers,
>	you ought to give
>	to those who are in need of giving.

To give to people who have money to lend
>	is to give to people who are not in need.

People who have money
>	should do good with their money,
>	either give it away
>	as Our Saviour advises
>	or lend it without interest.

To pay interest on money lended
>	is to place an enterprise
>	under a too heavy burden.

Everyone must live on the sweat of his brow
    and not on the money lended.
Nobody could lend money at interest
    if nobody would borrow money at interest.
People who live on money lended at interest
    reap some of the profits of property
    without the responsibility of property.
To pay double wages to managers
    is to make the workers
    envious of the managers.
Managers should receive what they need
    and no more than they need.
Knowledge obliges
    as well as "*noblesse oblige.*"
We cannot have a Catholic democracy
    without a Catholic aristocracy.
Paying double wages to managers
    is not the way to make aristocrats
    out of efficient managers.
"The most important of all are Workmen's Associations
    and it is greatly to be desired
    that they should multiply
    and become more effective,"[60]
    says Pope Leo XIII.
To borrow money at interest
    and to pay double wages to managers
    is not absolutely necessary
    to the good functioning
    of Workmen's Associations.
You say that the Catholic Labor Guild
    does not lend money at interest.
    I hope that it will see the way
    not to borrow money at interest.

---

60. This quote of Leo XIII is from *Rerum novarum* 49. I have not found Maurin's translation of *Rerum novarum* 49. I believe he was either working with a lesser-known translation or paraphrasing the document.

You say that the Catholic Labor Guild
    stands for profit-sharing.
    I hope that your self-sacrificing example
    will lead the members of the Guild
    to stand for loss-sharing.
When the members of the Guild
    decide to allow the Guild
    to accumulate the profits
    they will not need to worry
    about their economic security.
Let the members of the Guild
    give all they can to the Guild;
    the Guild will not leave them in want.
Let the Labor Guild help
    all those that it can help
    and the Farming Communes will help
    all of those that the Guild cannot help.

            —Yours for Catholic Action.
            Peter Maurin

1 APRIL 1934
THE CASE FOR UTOPIA

I. The Way Out[61] {50} — 7 times

  1. The world would be better off,
      if people tried to become better.
  2. And people would become better,
      if they stopped trying
      to become better off.
  3. For when everybody tries
      to become better off,
      nobody is better off.
  4. But when everybody tries
      to become better,
      everybody is better off.

---

61. Also known as "A Philosophy of Labor" and "Better and Better Off." All versions contain the same exact wording.

5. Everybody would be rich,
    if nobody tried
    to become richer.
6. And nobody would be poor
    if everybody tried
    to be the poorest.
7. And everybody would be
    what he ought to be
    if everybody tried to be
    what he wants
    the other fellow to be.

II. Christianity, Capitalism, and Communism[62] {51} — 3 times

1. Christianity
    has nothing to do
    with either modern capitalism
    or modern communism
    for Christianity
    has a capitalism of its own
    and a communism of its own.
2. Modern capitalism
    is based on property
    without responsibility
    while Christian capitalism
    is based on property
    with responsibility.
3. Modern communism
    is based on poverty
    through force
    while Christian communism
    is based on poverty
    through choice.
4. For a Christian,
    voluntary poverty
    is the ideal

---

62. Also known as "Christianity, Capitalism, Communism." The other two versions of the essay used the word "trust" instead of "gift" in the final stanza.

>   as exemplified
>   by Saint Francis of Assisi
>   while private property
>   is not an absolute right,
>   but a gift
>   which as such cannot be wasted,
>   but must be administered
>   for the benefit
>   of God's children.

III. Christ's Message[63] {52} — 3 times

> 1. "No one can serve two masters,
>   God and Mammon."
> 2. "Be perfect
>   as your heavenly Father
>   is perfect."[64]
> 3. "If you want
>   to be perfect,
>   sell all you have,
>   give it to the poor,
>   take up your cross
>   and follow Me."[65]
>
>   —New Testament
>
> 4. "These are hard words,
>   but the hard words
>   of a book
>   were the only reason
>   why the book was written."[66]
>
>   —Robert Louis Stevenson

---

63. The wording is the same in all three versions, though the second instance of the essay omitted the last stanza.

64. This quote is from Jesus's Sermon on the Mount (Matthew 5:48).

65. This quote was Jesus's response to the rich young man, who asked Jesus what he must do to obtain eternal life (Matthew 19:16–22).

66. The first line of the quote was from a posthumously published fragment of Stevenson's writing entitled, "Lay Morals" (1879). The second part may be a case where Maurin put in quotes his summary of a text.

IV. What Saint Francis Desired[67] {53} — 8 times

According to Johannes Jørgensen,
    a Danish convert
    living in Assisi,
1. Saint Francis desired
    that men should give up
    superfluous possessions.
2. Saint Francis desired
    that men should work
    with their hands.
3. Saint Francis desired
    that men should offer
    their services
    as a gift.
4. Saint Francis desired
    that men should ask
    other people for help
    when work failed them.
5. Saint Francis desired
    that men should live
    as free as birds.
6. Saint Francis desired
    that men should
    go through life
    giving thanks to God
    for His gifts.

V. The Third Order[68] {54} — 1 time

1. "We are perfectly certain
    that the Third Order of Saint Francis

---

67. In one instance, it was also called "Franciscan Radicalism." Some of the later versions are abridged.

68. St. Francis of Assisi founded both the Order of Friars Minor and the Third Order of Saint Francis, which is now called the Secular Franciscan Order. The Order of Friars Minor, or Franciscans, founded in 1209, is a religious community of men who take vows of poverty, chastity, and obedience. They dedicate their lives to prayer, preaching, and penance. The Third Order, founded around 1221, is for men and women living in the

is the most powerful antidote
   against the evils that harass the present age."⁶⁹

   —Leo XIII

2. "Oh, how many benefits
   would not the Third Order of Saint Francis
   have already conferred on the Church
   if it had been everywhere organized
   in accordance with the wishes
   of Leo XIII."⁷⁰

   —Pius X

3. "We believe that the spirit of the Third Order
   thoroughly redolent of Gospel wisdom
   will do very much
   to reform public and private morals."⁷¹

   —Benedict XV

4. "The general restoration of peace and morals
   was advanced very much
   by the Third Order of Saint Francis
   which was a religious order indeed
   yet something unexampled up to that time."⁷²

   —Pius XI

---

world who want to live a life inspired by the example of Francis, but without taking vows or living in community.

69. The quote has its origins in Leo XIII's 1882 encyclical *Auspicato concessum* commemorating the 700th anniversary of the birth of St. Francis. The quote can be found in other literature of Maurin's time, but it was not an exact quote from the encyclical. The encyclical encouraged membership in the Third Order and spoke of how imitating St. Francis was an "extremely efficacious remedy . . . [against] the evils of the present time," but the document itself did not bring the two aspects together like the quote.

70. The quote brought together a couple sentences from Pius X's 1909 Apostolic Letter *Septimo iam*, which addressed issues regarding how the various Franciscan groups should be organized. Similar to the quote in the first stanza of the essay from Leo XIII, Maurin probably unknowingly employed a quote that was not, strictly speaking, a quote.

71. The quote is from Benedict's 1921 encyclical *Sacra propidium*, on the Third Order of St. Francis.

72. This quote is from Pope Pius XI's 1926 encyclical *Rite expiatis* 34, on St. Francis of Assisi. The document, in addition to heralding the Third Order of Saint Francis and Francis's imitation of Jesus, also praised Francis's sincere following of the teachings of

VI. Three Ways to Make a Living {55} — 1 time

1. Mirabeau says "There are three ways
   to make a living:
   Stealing, begging and working."
2. Stealing is against the law of God
   and against the law of men.
3. Begging is against the law of men
   but not against the law of God.
4. Working is neither against the law of God
   nor against the law of men.
5. But they say
   that there is no work to do.
6. There is plenty of work to do,
   but no wages.
7. But people do not need to work for wages;
   they can offer their services as a gift.

VII. Capital and Labor {15}

VIII. Selling Their Labor {16}

IX. Self-Organization {19}

1 MAY 1934
THE BISHOPS' MESSAGE[73]

QUOTATIONS AND COMMENTS

New York Catholic Worker Editor's Note: In presenting excerpts from the bishops' statement we hope they don't mind the *phrase formation* of these

---

the Gospels and the Catholic Church. Maurin was very familiar with this document and quoted it in two other essays.

[73]. The following is not counted among Maurin's essays, but provides his unique perspective on Catholic social teaching in the 1930s. In case the introductory paragraph from the *Catholic Worker* is not clear, the first column is a quote from the National Catholic Welfare Conference's April 1933 statement *The Present Crisis*, which argued for Christian morality on a personal, social, and economic level to be a guiding principle in healing the disastrous effects of the Great Depression. The second column is Peter Maurin's commentary on the bishops' statement.

quotations. It is the theory of Peter Maurin that sentences taken phrase by phrase strike the mind more sharply and stick there. We are not attempting to put into *poem* formation the quotations which we use so abundantly in this issue (from the bishops, from Hilaire Belloc, from Dostoievsky). Peter's contributions for the *Catholic Worker* have been called "poems" by many of the workers who have come to the school, but it is only "Big Shots and Little Shots" which he delivers in poetic style. Most of his work might be termed phrased essays.

THE BISHOPS	PETER MAURIN

In tracing the remote causes
    of the present misery of
        mankind
we must listen to him
who as a loving Father
views from an eminence
all the nations of the world.
Quoting Saint Paul our Holy Father
    says:
"The desire for money
is the root of all evil."
From greed arises mutual distrust
    that casts a blight
on all human beings.
From greed arises envy
    which makes a man
    consider the advantages of
    another
as losses to himself.
From greed arises
    narrow individualism
which orders and subordinates
    everything
to its own advantage.
In common with other nations
    we have brought about our
    present unhappy conditions
    by divorcing education,
    industry, politics, business and
        economics
	People looking
	    for a rainy day
	have put so much money
	into business
	that they have
	brought about
	an increase
	in producing power
	and a decrease
	in purchasing power.
	
	So there is a rub
	between the rich
	who like
	to get richer
	and the poor
	who don't like
	to get poorer.
	
	We have taken religion
	out of everything
	and have put
	commercialism
	into everything.

from morality and religion
    and by ignoring for long
        decades
    the innate dignity of man
    and trampling on his human
        rights.
That we are an industrial nation
    is our public boast.
Industry is considered to be of
    more importance
    than the moral welfare of man.
The lord of all is Industry.
"Save industry!" is the cry.
"Put business on its feet
    and all will be well
    as it was in the past!"
The philosophy which has ruled
    governments, groups and
    individuals
    for the past three hundred
        years
    has not taken as its guide
    the moral law
    has not considered the rights
        of men.
Money, not men
    has been the supreme
        consideration
    and the justifying end.
That philosophy permits
    individuals
    to accumulate as much wealth
    as they can,
    according to unfair methods
    of modern business
    and to use such accumulated
        wealth
    as they see fit.
This extreme of individualism
    has led to the extreme of
        Communism.

We are beginning to learn
    that to put big business
        on its feet
    does not necessarily
    put the forgotten man
        on his feet.

When people care
    for money
    they do not care
    for culture.
And when people
    do not care
    for culture
    they return
    to barbarism.

When modern society
    made the bank account
    the standard of values
    people ceased
    to produce for use
    and began
    to produce for profit.

Rugged individualism
    leads to
    rugged nationalism

We rightly fear its spread in our
    country
        and see an especial menace
        in its insidious presentation
        of fundamental troubles
        for its own destructive ends.
The brotherhood of man
    is loudly proclaimed.
Energetic protest is made
    against injustice
    done to the working class.
The abuses of the capitalist system
    are vigorously condemned.
It is insisted
    that man shall not exploit his
    fellow man
    and that all shall be dedicated
    to a life of service.
A program of social reform
    couched in such language
    and with such aims and
        purposes
    is unassailable
    because it is distinctly
    Christian in origin and purport
    but in the hands of the
        Communists
    it is merely a snare
    to allure those who are
        oppressed
    by the prevailing economic
        maladjustment
    into accepting the iniquitous
    social and religious tenets
    of Lenin and Stalin.
There is a very grave and subtle
        danger
    of infection from Communism
Special efforts are being made
    to win Negroes
    who are the victims of
        injustice.
which leads to
    rugged collectivism.

In a capitalist society
    where man
    is inhuman to man
    people cannot
    keep from dreaming
    about a society
    where man
    would be human
    to man.

According to St. Thomas
        Aquinas
    man is more
    than an individual
    with individual rights
    he is a person
    with personal duties
    toward God
    Himself
    and his fellow men.
As a person
    man cannot
    serve God
    without serving
    the common good.

The Negroes
    are beginning to find out
    that wage-slavery
    is no improvement

The Communists have as their
    objective
a world war on God
and the complete destruction
of all supernatural and even
    natural religion.

on chattel-slavery.
The Communists say
    that Christianity is a failure
    but Christianity is not a
        failure
    for the very good reason
    that Christianity has not
        been tried.[74]

EASY ESSAYS

I. Big Shots and Little Shots[75] {56} — 3 times

1. America is all shot to pieces
    since the little shots
    are no longer able
    to become big shots.
2. When the little shots
    are not satisfied
    to remain little shots
    and try to become
    big shots,
    then the big shots
    are not satisfied
    to remain big shots
    and try to become
    bigger shots.
3. And when the big shots
    become bigger shots
    then the little shots
    become littler shots.
4. And when the little shots
    become littler shots
    because the big shots

---

74. The second half of this stanza paraphrased a famous line from Chesterton's *What's Wrong with the World* (1910; repr. San Francisco: Ignatius Press, 1994).

75. The two later versions of the essay are abridged.

        become bigger shots,
        then the little shots
        get mad at the big shots
5. And when the little shots
        get mad at the big shots,
        because the big shots
        by becoming bigger shots
        make the little shots
        littler shots
        they shoot the big shots
        full of little shots
6. But by shooting the big shots
        full of little shots
        the little shots
        do not become big shots;
        they make everything all shot.
7. And I don't like
        to see the little shots
        shoot the big shots
        full of little shots,
        that is why
        I am trying to shoot
        both the big shots
        and the little shots
        full of hot shots.

1 JUNE 1934
FOR CATHOLIC ACTION

I. A Modern Plague {22} (part one)

II. Secularism {22} (part two)

III. Spiritualizing {57} — 1 time

  1. Our modern educators,
        our modern politicians,
        our modern business man,

have taken religion from everything
and have put commercialism
into everything.
2. And now we have to take commercialism
out of everything
and to put religion into everything.
3. The way to take commercialism
out of everything
and to put religion into everything
is not through political action.
4. The way to take commercialism
out of everything
and to put religion into everything
is through Catholic Action.

IV. Business-Like {58} — 1 time

1. Catholic Action is action by Catholics
for Catholics and non-Catholics.
2. Catholic Action is action by Catholic laymen
in co-operation with the Clergy.
3. Catholic laymen and women have told the Clergy
"Mind your own business
and don't butt into our business."
4. So Catholic clergymen
have ceased to mind the layman's business
and the laymen have made a mess
of their own business.
5. And Catholic clergymen
have tried to mind their business
with a business-like technique
borrowed from business-minded people.

V. Roosevelt's Experiment {59} — 1 time

1. And now business is bankrupt
and Catholic clergymen don't know
what is to be done about it.

2. Not knowing what is to be done about it,
    Catholic clergymen have made up their mind
    to let George do it,[76]
    to let the politicians do it,
    to let Roosevelt do it.
3. So President Roosevelt is trying to do it
    with the help of College Professors.
4. So with the help of College Professors
    President Roosevelt is making a stab at it
    through a hit-and-miss policy,
    through a policy of experiments,
    through a policy of muddling through.
5. And while President Roosevelt is experimenting
    Catholic clergymen are wondering.

VI. The Forgotten Man[77] {60} — 2 times

1. The forgotten man has been forgotten
    because clergymen have forgotten
    to rub shoulders with the forgotten man.
2. And clergymen have forgotten
    to rub shoulders with the forgotten man
    because clergymen have forgotten
    to use logic to find what is practical.
3. And because clergymen have forgotten
    to use logic to find what is practical,
    they have failed to give us a sociology
    that has something to do with theology.

---

76. In March 1918, almost a year after the United States had entered World War I, former President Theodore Roosevelt criticized the Woodrow Wilson administration for being too passive in the war. Roosevelt stated that Wilson's policy was to "let George do it," meaning that he was letting King George V of England fight the war against Germany on his own. For Maurin's purposes, the phrase was a way of stating that someone was passing on a responsibility that one should be taking on oneself.

77. The other version has the same first three stanzas, but ends as follows: "4. The minimum standard had been emphasized, and the maximum standard has been minimized. 5. Which makes Chesterton say that 'Christianity has not failed, for the very good reason that it has not been tried.' 6. Read *Fire on the Earth*, by Rev. Paul Hanly Furfey." The Chesterton quote is from *What's Wrong with the World* (1910).

4. If there was a sociology
    that had something to do with theology
    it was sociology of St. Francis of Assisi,
    St. Thomas Aquinas and Blessed Thomas More.
5. But the sociology of St. Francis of Assisi,
    St. Thomas Aquinas and Blessed Thomas More
    was an Utopian sociology
    and clergymen are not interested in Utopias,
    not even Christian Utopias.

VII. Rome or Moscow {61} — 1 time

1. And because clergymen are not interested
    in the sociology of St. Francis of Assisi,
    St. Thomas Aquinas and Blessed Thomas More
    the forgotten man is becoming interested
    in the sociology of Karl Marx, Lenin and Stalin.
2. And because clergymen are not interested
    in a technique of leadership
    the forgotten man is becoming interested
    in a technique of dictatorship.
3. And because clergymen are not interested
    in Dynamic Catholic Action
    the forgotten man is becoming interested
    in Dynamic Bolshevik Action.

IS POLITICAL ACTION AN ANSWER?[78]

John J. Cummings wrote Peter Maurin that he only ever heard about injustice and never a plan for action. He asked Maurin why there was not a Catholic political party. Cummings further commented that "Mussolini seems to know how to rule" and suggested the elimination of "Protestant Pagan laws and the establishment of laws in harmony with Christianity." To this letter Maurin responded:

---

78. The response from Peter Maurin is not counted as an Easy Essay. It is included to show Maurin's response to proposed Catholic political solutions.

Dr. John Cummings:
As Father Fulton Sheen says:
>"The issue is between
>Christianity and Paganism."
The Communists say
>that Christianity is a failure.
But Christianity is not a failure
>and this for the very good reason
>that it has not been tried.[79]
You would like to see the formation
>of a Catholic Political Party.
Our Holy Father does not ask us
>to reconstruct the social order
>through Catholic political action,
>but through Catholic social action.
Catholic political parties
>have been done away with
>in Italy, as well as Germany.
You would like to stop Communism,
>but a Catholic Political Party
>cannot stop Communism.
Fascism, whether Catholic or Protestant,
>cannot stop Communism.
Fascism is only a stop-gap
>between the rugged individualism
>of Bourgeois Capitalism
>and the rugged collectivism
>of Bolshevik Communism.
There is no substitute
>for Catholic Social Action.
Fascist Dictatorship makes the bed
>for Bolshevik Dictatorship to lie in.
A German Catholic in Canada writes us
>that the German Catholic Party
>which his father helped to found
>did a lot of harm to the Church.

---

79. This stanza paraphrased a famous line from Chesterton's *What's Wrong with the World* (1910).

The Catholic Workers' School
is a clearing-house of thought,
and, therefore, welcomes
the expression of any opinion.
The Catholic Workers Movement
fosters Catholic social action
and not Catholic political action.
While we disagree with you,
we offer you the opportunity
to freely express your views
and win people to your cause.
—Your co-worker in Christ's Kingdom,
Peter Maurin

JULY–AUGUST 1934
COMMUNIST ACTION IN SCHOOLS CHALLENGE
TO CATHOLICS DECLARES PETER MAURIN

CATHOLIC AGITATION FOLLOWS THAT OF BOLSHEVIKS
IN EDUCATION CENTERS

I. [No Title][80] {62} — 2 times

1. I was told
    by a young Porto Rican[81]
    that the president
    of his school's study club
    was a Communist,
    and that in the meetings
    of the school's study club
    the Communist president
    did most of the talking,
    and that the school teacher
    was an interested listener
    to the Communist president
    of the school's study club.

---

80. Also known as "I Was Told." The wording between two versions is identical.
81. "Porto Rican" is a traditional variant spelling for Puerto Rican.

2. I was told
>	by the dean of a Catholic college
>	that Catholic professors
>	of Catholic colleges
>	neither have
>	the knowledge nor the courage
>	to bring Catholic social thought
>	to the man of the street.

II. Looking for Light[82] {63} — 2 times

1. So while Catholic professors
>	of Catholic colleges
>	do not have
>	enough knowledge or courage
>	to bring Catholic social thought
>	to the man of the street,
>	Communist propagandists,
>	yet in their 'teens
>	find enough knowledge or courage
>	to bring Communist social thought
>	to the men of the school.
2. The schools used to teach:
>	"If you want peace
>	prepare for war";
>	we prepared for war
>	and are still looking for peace.
3. The schools used to teach:
>	"If you want prosperity
>	save your money";
>	people saved their money,
>	and we are still looking for
>	prosperity.
4. The modern man looks for thought
>	so he can have light,
>	and is unable to find it
>	in our modern schools.

---

82. The wording of the other version is identical.

III. Shouting with Rotarians[83] {64} — 8 times

1. According to Glenn Frank,
    president of the University of Wisconsin,
    "Schools reflect the environment,
    they do not create it."
2. According to Professor Meiklejohn,
    of the same university,
    students go to school
    not to be directed,
    but to be business men.
3. Shortly after their graduation
    school graduates can be heard
    shouting with Rotarians:[84]
    "Service for profits,
    Time is money,
    Cash and carry,

---

83. Also known as "Shouting with Anglo-Saxons," "Bourgeois Slogans," "A Commencement," and "Materialist Slogans." "Bourgeois Slogans" only includes the slogans. "A Commencement" begins by stating, "1. The act of giving a degree is called a commencement. 2. After the commencement the student commences to look for a job. 3. In order to get a job he commences. . . ." "Shouting with Rotarians" from October 1935 begins with, "1. Modern colleges give you a bit of this, and a bit of that, a bit of something else and a degree." And then adds the beginning from the just-mentioned "A Commencement" before moving on to stanza three in the presented essay. "Materialist Slogans" begins by stating, "1. The fruit of secularism is materialism. 2. The materialist philosophy growing out of secularism finds its expression in materialist slogans." Slogans that are found in other variations are the following: "So is your old man," "Survival of the fittest," "So what?" and "You're all wet." The December 1934 version of the essay contains some unique aspects and so is reproduced here: "1. Now that Irish is Greek to the Irish and Jewish is Chinese to the Jews, they shout with the Anglo-Saxons: Service for profits; Time is money; Cash and carry; Business is business; Keep smiling; Watch your step; How is the rush? How are you making out? How is the world treating you? The law of supply and demand; Competition is the life of trade. Your dollar is your best friend. So is your old man. 2. So the Jews are no longer Jews. 3. So the Irish are no longer Irish. 4. So the Jews and the Irish are no longer green. 5. And that is what makes the Reds Red." The September 1936 and December 1936 versions of the essay only list the slogans.

84. Rotarians are members of Rotary Clubs. Together, these local clubs make up a service-oriented international organization that is composed of business and professional leaders. They began in 1905 in Chicago.

Keep smiling,
Business is business,
Watch your step,
How is the rush?
How are you making out?
How is the world treating you?
The law of supply and demand,
Competition is the life of trade,
Your dollar is your best friend."

IV. Things Have Changed[85] {41}

1. A few years ago
    I went to the campus
    of New York universities
    to try to find out
    if I could make an impression
    on the depression
    by starting a rumpus
    on the campus.
2. But I found out
    that agitation
    was not rampant
    on the campus;
    only business was rampant
    on the campus,
    although business
    is the bunk.
3. But things have changed
    and Bolshevik agitation
    is now rampant
    on the campus.
4. So thanks to our Bolshevik agitators
    public schools, colleges and universities
    can now be made centers
    of Catholic agitation.

85. Further editions of this essay follow this version more closely than the first appearance of {41} in December 1933.

V. Only Twenty-Five Cents {65} — 1 time

1. But while Communist propagandists
    yet in their 'teens
    are learning the art
    of Communist agitation,
    Catholic teachers
    teaching in Catholic or public schools
    have a terrible sense
    of inferiority complex
    when it comes to Catholic agitation.
2. While Communist propagandists
    yet in their 'teens
    are enough interested
    in Communist propaganda
    to buy the daily Communist paper
    named the *Daily Worker*
    a great number of Catholic teachers
    teaching in Catholic or public schools
    have not yet found the way
    to gather twenty-five cents
    for a yearly subscription
    to the monthly *Catholic Worker*.

VI. A Protestant Agitator {66} — 1 time

1. Catholic teachers
    teaching in Catholic or public schools
    who do not know how to present
    Catholic social thought
    either to the men on the street
    or to the pupils in the schools
    will be interested to learn
    that a Protestant agitator
    well known in Union Square
    is presenting the Thomistic doctrine
    of the common good
    to the men of the street
    in the streets of Harlem.

2. H. Hergenhan, such is his name,
    does not believe
    in the rugged individualism
    of capitalism
    or in the rugged nationalism
    of Fascism
    or in rugged collectivism
    of Bolshevism.

VII. The Common Good {67} — 1 time

1. He believes in the gentle personalism
    of gentlemen who are gentle,
    gentleness that finds its roots
    in the common doctrine
    of the common good.
2. H. Hergenhan believes
    that the doctrine of the common good
    is common
    to humanists who are human
    to Jews who are orthodox
    to Protestants who are Christian
    and to Catholics who are Catholic.
3. The common good movement
    is not a movement that divides
    it is a movement that unites.
4. The common good movement
    is not a new deal,
    it is an old game.
5. The common good movement
    is not a revolution to the left,
    it is a revolution to the right.

VIII. Tawney's Book[86] {68} — 2 times

1. When in 1891 Pope Leo XIII
    wrote his encyclical

---

86. Also known as "R. H. Tawney." The other version of the essay has minor differences in wording and is condensed.

on the condition of labor
he emphasized the lack of ethics
in modern society.
2. When in 1899 Thorstein Veblen
wrote *The Theory of the Leisure Class*
he emphasized the same thing.
3. R. H. Tawney, then an Oxford student,
learned that when the canon law,
that is to say, the law of the church,
was the law of the land,
there were high ethics in society.
4. So R. H. Tawney decided to study
how society has passed down
from the high ethics of canon law
to the no ethics of today.
5. What R. H. Tawney found out
about the history of ethics
of the last five hundred years
is embodied in his book,
Religion and the Rise of Capitalism.

SEPTEMBER 1934
A MESSAGE TO THE CATHOLIC ACTION SUMMER SCHOOL

Peter Maurin's Message to the Summer School of Catholic Action, Conducted by Father Daniel Lord, S.J., at St. Francis Xavier High School

I. I Was Told {62}

II. Looking for Light {63}

III. Shouting with Rotarians {64}

IV. Things Have Changed {41}

V. Catholic Social Research[87] {69} — 2 times

1. "When a social system
    fails to feed the poor,
    it is time to look out
    for one that does,"
    says Archbishop Keating
    of Liverpool.
2. And because Archbishop Keating realized
    that our modern social order
    fails to feed the poor
    he founded in Oxford
    a Catholic Labor College.
3. And the Catholic Labor College
    conducted in Oxford
    has been going on
    for the last twenty-five years.
4. At its last general meeting
    Cardinal Bourne declared
    that we are badly in need
    of Catholic social research.
5. If there had been
    more Catholic social research
    Catholics would not now
    pass the buck
    to the politicians.

VI. School of Social Studies[88] {70} — 1 time

1. To found a School of Social Studies
    such was the aim
    of Father Patrick Sheely, S.J.

---

87. Also known as "School of Social Studies." The other version of the essay added these two stanzas to the end: "Catholic social research ought to be carried out in a School of Social Studies. A School of Social Studies—such was the dream of Father Patrick Sheely, S.J."

88. This essay is being counted as a distinct Easy Essay, even though it is very similar to both {8} and {45}, part 2.

2. In a School of Social Studies
    we would be able to learn
    why things are what they are.
3. In a School of Social Studies
    we would be able to learn
    how things would be
    if they were as they should be.
4. In a School of Social Studies
    we would be able to learn
    how a path can be made
    from things as they are
    to things as they should be.
5. A School of Social Studies
    would give us Catholic Action
    based on Catholic Thought
    realized in Catholic Institutions.

VII. Putting Patches {71} — 1 time

1. Having no School of Social Studies
    we don't know how to pass
    from things as they are
    to things as they should be.
2. Having no School of Social Studies
    we have no Catholic Social Program
    based on Catholic Social Thought.
3. Having no School of Social Studies
    we try to put patches
    to the existing social order
    and call it a New Deal.
4. Having no School of Social Studies
    we let college professors
    carry on costly experiments
    at the expense of the taxpayers.
5. Having no School of Social Studies
    we are not occupied
    in Reconstructing the Social Order
    as the Holy Father wants us to be.

VIII. I Agree[89] {72} — 4 times

1. I agree
    with seven Bishops,
    three of whom
    are Archbishops,
    that the Communist criticism
    of modern rugged individualism
    is a sound criticism.
2. I agree
    with seven Bishops,
    three of whom
    are Archbishops,
    that the main social aim
    of the Communist Party
    is a sound social aim.
3. I agree
    with seven Bishops,
    three of whom
    are Archbishops,
    that the Communists are not sound
    when they advocate class struggle
    in order to realize
    their sound social aim.
4. I agree with the Apostolic Delegate[90]
    when he advocates the practice
    of the Seven Corporal and
    Seven Spiritual Works of Mercy[91]

---

89. The last two versions of the essay inserted the following phrase after the words "Communist Party" in stanza two: "which is to create a new society where everyone works according to his ability and gets according to his needs." The final version from May 1941 replaced stanza four with, "They are not pure means; they are impure means."

90. This is a reference to Archbishop Amleto Giovanni Cicognani (1883–1973).

91. The corporal and spiritual works of mercy are part of the Catholic tradition through which Catholics bring the mercy of Christ to others. The seven corporal works of mercy are to feed the hungry, to give drink to the thirsty, to clothe the naked, to shelter the homeless, to visit the sick, to ransom the captive, to bury the dead. Except for the last, they have their origin in the biblical parable of the judgment of the nations (Matthew 25:31–46). The seven spiritual works of mercy are to instruct the ignorant, to counsel

as the best practical means
of making man human to man.

IX. Personal Sacrifice[92] {73} — 2 times

1. To be our brother's keeper
   is what God wants us to do.
2. To feed the hungry
   at a personal sacrifice
   is what God wants us to do.
3. To clothe the naked
   at a personal sacrifice
   is what God wants us to do.
4. To shelter the homeless
   at a personal sacrifice
   is what God wants us to do.
5. To instruct the ignorant
   at a personal sacrifice
   is what God wants us to do.
6. To serve man
   for God's sake
   is what God wants us to do.

X. Reconstruction {36}

---

the doubtful, to admonish sinners, to bear wrongs patiently, to forgive offenses, to comfort the afflicted, and to pray for the living and the dead. Maurin believed that a functional economy needed to be grounded in charity and voluntary poverty. The works of mercy embodied this practice, in which one became poorer by sharing their goods through charity. Maurin believed that Catholic Worker houses of hospitality would play an instrumental role in the contemporary practice of the works of mercy.

92. Also known as "At a Sacrifice." The September 1935 version of the essay omitted stanza one and replaced stanza six with the following two lines: "To practice the Seven Corporal and the Seven Spiritual Works of Mercy is what God wants us to do. The daily practice of the Seven Corporal and the Seven Spiritual Works of Mercy by the First Christians made the Pagans say 'See how they love each other.'" The quote, "See how they love each other," is from the *Apology* (197), written by the early Christian author and theologian, Tertullian (c. 155–c. 240).

A THIRD OPEN LETTER TO FATHER LORD, M. AG. (MASTER AGITATOR) {74} — 1 time

Dear Father:
1. D. C. Roper, Secretary of Commerce,
    suggested some time ago
    the establishment in Washington
    of "A Laboratory for Leadership in Public Affairs."
2. H. McCall, assistant to Secretary Roper,
    says that "youth movements
    have occupied dominant and
    aggressive positions
    in the social and governmental changes
    that have taken place throughout the world
    since the World War."
3. H. McCall proposes
    the establishment in Washington
    "of a forum
    for study and training
    in public affairs."
4. Colleges and universities
    have failed
    to give their students
    a technique of leadership
    based on scholarship.
5. And because colleges and universities
    have failed
    to make leaders out of their students
    politicians propose
    to make bureaucrats out of them.
6. College professors
    have become so academic
    that their students
    refuse to be scholarly-minded
    and consent to be politically-minded.
7. College professors
    have failed
    to train their students

in a technique of leadership,
   so their students wish to be trained
   in a technique of dictatorship.
8. In Cuba, Germany, China, Mexico, Italy, Russia,
   dictators have found their greatest support
   among college students
   eager for action.
9. Academic college professors
   are interested in thought,
   not in action.
10. So we have on one hand
    thought without action
    and on the other hand
    action without thought.
11. People go to Washington
    asking the Federal Government
    to solve their economic problems
    while the Federal Government
    was never intended
    to solve men's economic problems.
12. Catholic action
    based on Catholic thought
    is the Catholic solution
    of men's economic problems.
13. To impart Catholic thought
    and train in Catholic action,
    such is the function
    of Catholic universities.
14. Some way ought to be found
    to send Catholic workers
    to Catholic universities
    or to bring Catholic universities
    to Catholic workers.
15. When Catholic scholars
    and Catholic workers
    become acquainted with each other
    Catholic workers
    will cease to be politically-minded
    and begin to be scholarly-minded.

16. When Catholic scholars
    are dynamic
    and not academic
    and Catholic workers
    are scholars
    and not politicians
    we will have dynamic Catholic Action.

    —Yours for dynamic Catholic Action,
    Peter Maurin

OCTOBER 1934
CHRIST THE KING ALONE CAN RECONSTRUCT THE WORLD

The Practice of the Seven Corporal and Seven Spiritual Works of Mercy is Basis of Christian Society.

I. On Being Crazy[93] {75} — 2 times

1. People went crazy
    for Democracy
    majority rule,
    mob rule.
2. Then they went crazy
    for the War
    for Democracy[94]
    trying to bring Peace
    through War.
3. Then they went crazy
    for Normalcy;[95]

---

93. While both versions of the essay employ the same wording, they possess minor stylistic differences.

94. When President Woodrow Wilson went before Congress on 2 April 1917 to seek a declaration of war against Germany, he famously stated that the war would make the world "safe for democracy."

95. "A Return to Normalcy" was a campaign promise by Warren G. Harding in 1920 that indicated returning to a way of life before World War I. This theme helped put Harding in the White House with over 60 percent of the popular vote.

then they went crazy
for Technocracy;[96]
then they went crazy
for the N.R.A.
and they say that I am crazy.
4. They say that I am crazy
because I refused to be crazy
the way everybody else is crazy.
5. For, if I tried to be crazy
the way everybody else is crazy
I know that I would be crazy.
6. So I persist in being crazy
in my own crazy way
and I am trying
to make other people crazy
my way.

II. Not a Liberal {13}

III. Not a Conservative {76} — 1 time

1. If I am a radical,
then I am not a conservative.
2. Conservatives try to believe
that things are good enough
to be let alone.
3. But things are not good enough
to be let alone.
4. Conservatives try to believe
that the world is getting better
every day in every way.
5. But the world is not getting better
every day in every way.
6. The world is getting worse
every day in every way.

---

96. The technocracy movement promoted the idea of replacing politicians and business people with scientists and engineers who had expertise to adequately address the Great Depression. The idea became popular in the early 1930s, but waned by the mid-1930s with the arrival of Roosevelt's New Deal.

7. And the world is getting worse
    every day in every way
    because the world is upside down.
8. And conservatives do not know
    how to take the upside down
    and to put it right side up.
9. When conservatives and radicals
    will come to an understanding
    they will take the upside down
    and they will put it right side up.

IV. A Radical Change[97] {77} — 2 times

1. The order of the day
    is to talk about the social order.
2. Conservatives would like
    to keep it from changing
    but they don't know how.
3. Liberals try to patch it
    and call it a New Deal.
4. Socialists want a change
    but a gradual change.
5. Communists want a change
    an immediate change
    but a socialist change.
6. Communists in Russia
    do not build communism
    they build socialism.
7. Communists want to pass
    from capitalism to socialism
    and from socialism to communism.
8. I want a change
    and a radical change.
9. I want a change
    from an acquisitive society

---

97. Both versions of the essay are the same.

to a functional society,
from a society of go-getters
to a society of go-givers.

V. When Bankers Rule[98] {78} — 3 times

1. Modern society has made the bank account
   the standard of values.
2. When the bank account
   becomes the standard of values
   the banker has the power.
3. When the banker has the power
   the technician has to supervise
   the making of profits.
4. When the banker has the power
   the politician
   has to assure law and order
   in the profit making system.
5. When the banker has the power
   the educator trains students
   in the technique of profit making.
6. When the banker has the power
   the clergyman is expected
   to bless the profit making system
   or to join the unemployed.
7. When the banker has the power
   the Sermon on the Mount
   is declared unpractical.

---

98. The second instance of the essay omits stanza six. The last version of the essay (June 1936) was changed dramatically and is included here: "1. When the bank account is the standard of values, the Bankers have the power. 2. When Bankers rule, the Business men have to do the bidding of the Bankers. 3. When Bankers rule, the Politicians have to assure law and order according to the wishes of Business men. 4. When Bankers rule, the Educators have to prepare the minds of the students so that they can be good specialists knowing more and more about less and less. 5. When Bankers rule, the Clergymen have to endorse this scheme of things or starve. 6. When Bankers rule, the Christian ideal is used to camouflage a Pagan practice."

8. When the banker has the power
   we have an acquisitive
   not a functional society.

VI. When Christ Is King[99] {79} — 2 times

1. When the Sermon on the Mount
   is the standard of values
   then Christ is the Leader.
2. When Christ is the Leader
   the priest is the mediator.
3. When Christ is the Leader
   the educator
   trains the minds of the pupils
   so that they may understand
   the message of the priest.
4. When Christ is the Leader
   the politician
   assures the law and order
   according to the priest's teachings.
5. When Christ is the Leader
   the technician
   devises way and means
   for the economical production
   and distribution of goods.
6. When Christ is the Leader
   the administrator administrates
   according to the directions
   from the technicians.
7. When Christ is Leader
   we have a functional
   not an acquisitive society.

---

99. The only difference between the two versions is that the March 1935 version adds two stanzas at the end: "8. The Catholic Church stands for the reunion of our separated brothers. 9. The Catholic Church stands for the Reconstruction, not the patching up of the social order."

VII. Rebellion Is Rebellion {80} — 1 time

1. Boloney is boloney
    no matter how you slice it
    and rebellion is rebellion
    no matter when it happens
    whether it is
    the religious rebellion
    of the 16th century
    or the political rebellion
    of the 18th century
    or the economic rebellion
    of the 20th century.
2. Someone said
    that the Catholic Church
    stands for Rome, rum, and rebellion.
3. But the Catholic Church
    does not stand for Rome, rum, and rebellion.
4. The Catholic Church stands
    for Rome, Reunion, and Reconstruction.
5. The Catholic Church stands
    as Rome used to stand
    for law and order.
6. The Catholic Church stands
    for the reunion of our separated brothers.
7. The Catholic Church stands
    for the Reconstruction
    not the patching up
    of the social order.

VIII. Constructing the Social Order[100] {81} — 2 times

1. The Holy Father asks
    to reconstruct the social order.
2. The social order was constructed
    by the first Christians
    through the daily practice

---

100. The other version possessed the same wording.

of the Seven Corporal
and Seven Spiritual
Works of Mercy.
3. To feed the hungry
at a personal sacrifice,
to cloth the naked
at a personal sacrifice,
to shelter the homeless
at a personal sacrifice,
to instruct the ignorant
at a personal sacrifice
such were the works
of the first Christians
in times of persecution.
4. If you want to know more about it
read the two following books:
a) *The Great Commandment*
by the Apostolic Delegate.
b) *The Valerian Persecution*
by Father Patrick Healy
of the Catholic University.

IX. Reconstructing the Social Order {36}

EASY ESSAYS

I. Looking for an Education {46}

II. Flying from America {82} — 1 time
1. In his book entitled
Re-discovery of America
Waldo Frank says
that America is a lost continent.
2. And the way for America
to rediscover itself
is to go back to Mediterranean culture.

3. According to Waldo Frank
    Mediterranean culture
    embodied Greek philosophy
    plus the Roman system of law
    plus Christian morality.
4. There are still a few spots
    around the Mediterranean Sea
    where the rugged individualism
    of bourgeois capitalism
    has not yet penetrated.
5. In one of these rare spots
    an American artist
    has decided to make his home.

III. Carl Schmitt the Artist {83} — 1 time

1. American Catholics thought
    that no one but Al Smith
    could save America.
2. But it seems that Al Smith
    is as much at sea
    as President Roosevelt.
3. But while Roosevelt is experimenting
    and Al Smith is wondering
    Carl Schmitt is planning.
4. Carl Schmitt the artist
    plans to go to some Dalmatian island
    where people still combine
    cult, that is to say liturgy,
    with culture, that is to say literature,
    with cultivation, that is to say agriculture.

IV. What America Needs {84} — 1 time

1. Carl Schmitt the artist
    does not want his ten children
    to be super salesmen,

       he wants them to be
       cultured peasants.
2. Carl Schmitt the artist
       is far from thinking
       that all America needs
       is a good five-cent cigar
       as Vice President Marshall
       was in the habit of saying.
3. Carl Schmitt the artist
       thinks that America
       needs to be revitalized
       with healthy peasant blood
       from those parts of Europe
       where the rugged individualism
       of bourgeois commercialism
       has not yet penetrated.
4. Carl Schmitt the artist
       is not interested
       in any kind of New Deal
       he is interested
       in the old Catholic game
       of the Seven Corporal
       and Seven Spiritual
       Works of Mercy.

V. Carl Schmitt Believes {85} — 1 time

1. Carl Schmitt believes
       that Catholicism
       has the solution
       of all man's problems.
2. Carl Schmitt believes
       that the Catholic religion
       is the hope of the people,
       not the dope of the people.
3. Carl Schmitt believes
       that the mysticism of the faith
       should not be separated
       from the mysteries of the faith.

4. Carl Schmitt believes
    in ascetic theology
    as well as he believes
    in dogmatic theology
5. Carl Schmitt believes
    in a functional society
    and he does not believe
    in an acquisitive society.
6. Carl Schmitt believes
    in a democratic aristocracy
    and he does not believe
    in a plutocratic democracy.

VI. What Makes Man Human[101] {86} — 5 times

1. Charles Péguy used to say
    "There are two things in this world
    politics and mysticism."
2. Politics is just politics
    and is not worth bothering about it
    and mysticism is mysterious
    and is worth all our striving.
3. To give and not to take
    that is what makes man human.
4. To serve and not to rule
    that is what makes man human.
5. To help and not to crush
    that is what makes man human.
6. To nourish and not to devour
    that is what makes man human.
7. And if need be
    to die and not to live
    that is what makes man human.
8. Ideals and not deals
    that is what makes man human.

---

101. Also known as "Human to Man." All other versions omit the first two stanzas. The last version, with the alternate name, ends each of its stanzas by stating, "that is what makes man human to man."

9. Creed and not greed
that is what makes man human.

I. Peter Maurin Says Usurers Are Not Gentlemen![102] {37}

II. Legalized Usury {5}

Fighting Communism {87} — 1 time

1. THE CATHOLIC WORKER proposes
fighting Communism
the way the first Christians
fought Pagan Romanism
through the Works of Mercy.
2. THE CATHOLIC WORKER proposes
fighting Communism,
the way the Irish scholars
fought Pagan Feudalism,
through Round Table Discussions,
Houses of Hospitality,
Farming Communes.
3. The Communists do not build Communism
they build Socialism.
4. THE CATHOLIC WORKER
does not build Catholic Socialism
it builds Catholic Communism.
5. THE CATHOLIC WORKER
builds Catholic Communism
the way the first Christians
and the Irish scholars
built Catholic Communism.
6. THE CATHOLIC WORKER believes
that there is no better Communism
than Catholic Communism
and that there is no better way
to build Catholic Communism
than by building Catholic Communes.

---

102. The name of this short arrangement of essays and the name of the first essay are the same.

7. Catholic Communes
    are not a new thing
    they are an old thing.
8. Catholic Communes are so old
    that Catholics have forgotten them.
9. Communists have not invented anything,
    not even the name Commune.
10. The Communist ideal
    is the Common Good ideal—
    the ideal of Blessed Thomas More,
    the ideal of Saint Thomas Aquinas,
    the ideal of the Irish scholars,
    the ideal of the first Christians.
11. The doctrine of the Common Good
    of Saint Thomas Aquinas
    is still Catholic doctrine.
12. We don't need a new doctrine,
    we need an old technique.
13. We need the old technique
    of the first Christians
    and the Irish scholars.
14. What was good for the first Christians
    and the Irish scholars
    ought to be good enough for us.
15. What was practical for them
    ought to be practical for us.

NOVEMBER 1934
HUMAN REHABILITATION

I. Listening to the Pope {2}

II. Robertson's Book {88} — 1 time

1. When in 1891, the Pope Leo XIII,
    sent out his famous encyclical
    On the Condition of Labor,
    the rugged individualists

of bourgeois capitalism
paid little attention
to what he had to say.
2. When in the year after, in 1892,
a wealthy Englishman,
John M. Robertson,
published his book
on *The Fallacy of Saving*,
he received still less attention.
3. Whether they be
financial magnates
or captains of industry,
or distinguished economists,
or plain college professors,
they are perfectly willing
to let disturbing prophets
talk in the wilderness.

III. Before the Crash {89} — 1 time

1. Two years before the crash, in 1927,
I spoke to a Rotary Club
on *The Fallacy of Saving*,
the same subject
that John M. Robertson
expounded in his book
thirty-five years before.
2. Like John M. Robertson,
thirty-five years before
I told business men
that if they continued
to put money into business
they would put business
out of business.
3. But business men thought
that America
had found the secret
of mass distribution

as well as the secret
of mass production
and that the day had come
of a two-car garage,
a chicken in every pot
and a sign "To Let"
in front of every poorhouse.

IV. The Great Folly {90} — 1 time

1. While John M. Robertson and I
    were telling people:
    "If you want prosperity
    don't save your money,"
    nobody paid any attention.
2. People preferred
    to listen to President Coolidge
    who was telling them
    just the opposite.
3. On the fallacy of saving
    a great boon was promoted
    which was bound to be followed
    by a great depression
    as was pointed out
    by a Minneapolis business man
    as far back as 1926.[103]
4. On the wave of the great boom
    people got crazy for stocks
    and stock promoters
    stocked people with stocks
    till they got stuck.
5. So in October, 1929,
    stocks ceased to go up
    and went down with a bang.

---

103. This is probably a reference to Charles Reinold Noyes (1884–1954), an American economist from St. Paul, Minnesota. Maurin referenced him again in the March 1942 *Catholic Worker* to further explain Noyes's prognostication of the Great Depression.

V. We Were Told[104] {91} — 2 times

1. We were told in 1929
   that "business would go on
   as usual."[105]
2. We were told in 1930
   that "the economic system
   was fundamentally sound."
3. We were told in 1931
   that "prosperity
   was around the corner."[106]
4. We were told in 1932
   that "the depression was fought
   on one hundred fronts."[107]
5. We were told in 1933
   that "most of the unemployed
   would be employed by Labor Day."[108]
6. And now we are told
   that "it is not a question
   of bringing back prosperity,"
   that "it is not a question
   of economic recovery,"
   that "it is not a question

---

104. Also known as "1933—New Deal." The other version of the essay from June 1935 omitted stanza six and concluded with the following sixth and seventh stanzas: "6. And in 1934 people went crazy for the N.R.A. 7. And in 1935 the N.R.A. is scrapped and economic recovery is a long way off."

105. This was a common refrain from many areas of American society in 1929. Like the following quotes, it was not an exact quote, since the verb tenses were wrong.

106. As the Great Depression continued and his economic policies failed, the quotes from stanzas two and three were spoken by President Hoover.

107. This is an inexact quote from President Hoover's "Radio Address on the Hoarding of Currency," which he delivered on 6 March 1932. The exact quote states, "Fighting a great depression is a war with destructive forces in one hundred battles on one hundred fronts."

108. This is probably referencing a statement by Hugh S. Johnson, a major figure in the Roosevelt administration. During July 1933, he stated on the radio that up to 600,000 workers would be reemployed by Labor Day.

of emergency relief,"
that "it is a question
of human rehabilitation."[109]

VI. What Is Needed {92} — 1 time

1. Our experienced business men,
    our clever politicians,
    our distinguished college professors,
    had to have the experiments of
    the NRA, AAA,[110] CCC,[111] PWA,[112]
    CWA,[113] and what not
    before they were able to learn
    that "it is not a question
    of economic recovery,"
    that "it is a question
    of human rehabilitation."
2. I am saying now
    to our experienced business men,
    our clever politicians,
    our distinguished college professors,
    that the way

---

109. In November 1934, Roosevelt touted that his New Deal federal programs were putting people back to work. He believed that this was positive not only for the health of the state and economy, but also for "human rehabilitation" because the programs aided people in supporting themselves and their families. This is a fine example of Maurin using a contemporary headline as a hook for an arrangement title for an Easy Essay.

110. The Agricultural Adjustment Administration was a farm program of the Roosevelt administration during the 1930s. Part of the program gave farmers money for not growing certain crops to raise prices on those commodities.

111. The Civilian Conservation Corps was another of Roosevelt's programs that provided work for young, unmarried, unemployed men in conservation and the development of natural resources.

112. The Public Works Administration was another part of the New Deal legislation, which paid over six billion dollars to private companies to build dams, bridges, hospitals, and schools.

113. The Civil Works Administration was a $200 million program established during the winter of 1933–34 that created construction jobs for bridges and buildings.

>   to make an impression
>   on the depression
>   is self-expression.
> 3. I am saying now
>   that the best thing
>   to give to labor
>   is a philosophy of labor.

VII. A Philosophy of Labor {50}

VIII. Capital and Labor {15}

IX. Selling Their Labor {16}

X. Self-Organization {19}

XI. Farming Communes {10}

XII. Professors of a Farming Commune[114] {93} — 5 times

> 1. Professors of a Farming Commune
>   do not look
>   for endowments;
>   they leave that
>   to the Farming Commune.
> 2. Professors of a Farming Commune
>   do not tell their students
>   what to do;
>   they show them
>   how to do it.
> 3. Professors of a Farming Commune
>   do not enable their students
>   to master subjects;
>   they enable them
>   to master situations.
> 4. Professors of a Farming Commune
>   do not prepare their students

---

114. Also known as "Professors of an Outdoor University." Other variations often omitted the last stanza. In the alternately named essay, each stanza began with "Professors of an Outdoor University" instead of "Professors of a Farming Commune."

>   for a position
>   where they will have to play
>   somebody else's game;
>   they train them
>   for a profession,
>   where they will be able to play
>   their own game.
> 5. Professors of a Farming Commune
>   do not teach their students
>   how to make
>   profitable deals;
>   they teach them
>   how to realize
>   worthy ideals.

XIII. Laborers of a Farming Commune[115] {94} — 8 times

> 1. Laborers of a Farming Commune
>   do not work for wages;
>   they leave that to the Farming Commune.
> 2. Laborers of a Farming Commune
>   do not look for a bank account;
>   they leave that to the Farming Commune.
> 3. Laborers of a Farming Commune
>   do not look for an insurance policy;
>   they leave that to the Farming Commune.
> 4. Laborers of a Farming Commune
>   do not look for unemployment insurance,
>   they leave that to the Farming Commune.

---

115. Also known as "Farming Commune," "Farming Communes," and "Laborers of an Outdoor University." The version entitled "Laborers of an Outdoor University" began each stanza with that title instead of "Laborers of a Farming Commune." Some versions of the essay concluded with the following line: "Laborers do not look for economic security on a Farming Commune; they leave that to the Farming Commune." The March 1935 version began with the line, "Laborers of a Farming Commune do not teach their students how to make profitable deals they teach them how to realize worthy ideals." This version also added an additional stanza: "Laborers of a Farming Commune do not look for a rainy day they leave that to the Farming Commune."

5. Laborers of a Farming Commune
      do not look for an old age pension;
      they leave that to the Farming Commune.
6. Laborers of a Farming Commune
      do not look for economic security;
      they leave that to the Farming Commune.

XIV. The Common Good {95} — 1 time

1. Helen Keller says:
      "Dazzled by inventions
      and exploitation
      of the vast resources
      in which this country abounded,
      the people lost the vision
      of the Kingdom of God.
2. "The time came
      when every American
      was afraid to be poor,
      and despised anyone
      who elected to remain poor
      in order
      to simplify his life
      and save his conscience.
3. "They lost even the power
      of imagining
      what their forefathers' ideal
      of a nation of God-fearing men
      had been.
4. "We begin to realize
      that there is only
      one true kind of national greatness,
      and that is
      to hold fast to,
      and conscientiously work for
      the ideal
      of the Common Good
      which is mightier

than any man
and worthy
of all men."[116]

DECEMBER 1934
ESSAYS ON COMMUNISM

I. On Being Crazy {75}

II. Not Communists[117] {96} — 3 times

1. There is nothing wrong
with Communism;
but there is something wrong
with Bolshevism.
2. The wrong thing with Bolshevism is
that Bolshevists
are not Communists;
they are Socialists.
3. For if the Bolshevists
were Communists,
they would build Communism.

---

116. This essay was almost an exact quote from an article entitled, "The Common Good," which Keller published in the November 1934 issue of *Home Magazine*. The article focused on the need for Americans to live more simply and not be "dazzled" into a materialistic lifestyle.

117. Also known as "Bolshevik Socialists." The May 1936 version of the essay began with two stanzas that were very similar to the present essay, but then continued as follows: "3. There is no Communism in Soviet Russia; there is State Socialism in Soviet Russia. 4. Communism is a state of society where each one works according to his ability and gets according to his needs. 5. The State has not withered away, the wage system prevails, and you can buy 7% government bonds in Soviet Russia. 6. By selling 7% government bonds they are creating a parasitic class in Soviet Russia." The January 1937 version of the essay began with two stanzas that were very similar to the present essay, but then continued as follows: "3. 'Communism,' according to the definition of the *Communist Manifesto*, 'is a state of society where each one works according to his capacity and gets according to his needs.' 4. According to this definition there is no Communism in Soviet Russia. 5. Communists do not deserve the name 'Communists.' 6. They should be called 'Bolshevik Socialists.'"

4. And the Bolshevists
   do not build Communism;
   they build Socialism;
   they build State Socialism.
5. The Bolshevists probably hope
   that the State
   "will wither away,"[118]
   and that they will be able to pass
   from State Socialism
   to Communism without State.

III. Two Reds {97} — 1 time

1. Some time ago
   I was discussing in Harlem
   with a Russian Red
   and an Irish Red.
2. And the Russian Red
   understood me sooner
   than the Irish Red.
3. Having understood
   what I was saying,
   the Russian Red
   started to explain
   to his friend, the Irish Red,
   what I was talking about.
4. When the Russian Red
   had finished explaining,
   the Irish Red
   turned toward me
   and said that while he agreed
   with most of what I said
   he still believed

---

118. This phrase was coined by Friedrich Engels in his book *Anti-Dühring* (1878). He used the phrase to explain that the state would not need to be abolished when Communism came to fruition, but that it would simply be superfluous and "wither away."

that the Catholic Church
was not the friend
of the workingmen.
5. Many Catholics
are much disappointed
when Wall Street corporations
or political organizations
or Catholic associations
fail to provide them
with economic security.

IV. Looking for a Boss {98} — 1 time

1. A Catholic workingman
once said to me:
"There is only one thing
between me and the Reds,
and that is a good job."
2. Everybody
is looking for a boss,
and nobody wants
to be his own boss.
3. And because everybody
looks for a boss
the Reds want the State
to be the boss of everybody.
4. Because everybody
consents to play somebody else's game
for the sake of a pay-envelope
the Reds try to find the way
to assure a pay-envelope to everybody
so as to force everybody
to act like everybody.
5. But nothing will be changed
when the Reds
will force everybody
to act like everybody,

since nobody is nobody
when everybody
tries to keep up with everybody.

V. American and Russia {99} — 1 time

1. American Republicans
    want their friends
    on the public payroll,
    but only *their* friends.
2. American Democrats
    want their friends
    on the public payroll,
    but only *their* friends.
3. But the Reds want everybody
    on the public payroll;
    not only their friends.
4. The American idea
    is to keep the Government
    out of business
    and to put everybody
    into business.
5. The Russian idea
    is to put the Government
    into business
    and to keep everybody
    out of business.
6. But business
    is only business,
    whether it is
    the State business
    or private business;
    and I am trying
    to make it my business
    to put all business
    out of business.
    including State business,
    which is a big business.

VI. Red and Green {100} — 1 time

1. Our business managers
    have made such a mess of things
    that people are inclined
    to see Red.
2. And when people see Red
    it is useless
    to present to them
    the Red, White and Blue,
    because they can no longer see
    the White and the Blue
    of the Red, White and Blue;
    all they can see is Red.
3. The only way
    to keep people
    from seeing Red
    is to make them
    see Green.
4. The only way
    to prevent
    a Red Revolution
    is to promote
    a Green Revolution.
5. The only way
    to keep people
    from looking up
    to Red Russia
    of the twentieth century
    is to make them look up
    to Green Ireland
    of the seventh century.

VII. Then and Now {101} — 1 time

1. Three thousand years ago,
    when a Jew
    met a Jew

  he asked him
  "What can I
  do for you?"
2. Now, when a Jew
  meets a Jew,
  he asks him
  "What can I
  get out of you?"
3. Two thousand years ago,
  when a Greek
  met a Greek
  they started to philosophize.
4. Now when a Greek
  meets a Greek
  they start a business.
5. A thousand years ago
  when an Irishman
  met an Irishman
  they started a school.
6. Now when an Irishman
  meets an Irishman
  you know what they start—
  I don't have to tell you.

VIII. A Thousand Years Ago {102} — 1 time

1. When Irish were Irish
  a thousand years ago,
  the Irish were scholars.
2. And when the Irish were scholars
  the Irish were Greek scholars.
3. And when the Irish were Greek scholars,
  the Irish spoke Greek
  as well as Irish.
4. And when the Irish spoke Greek
  as well as Irish
  Greek was Irish
  to the Irish.

5. Greek was Irish
    to the Irish
    a thousand years ago;
    and now
    Irish is Greek
    to the Irish.
6. Irish is Greek
    to the Irish now,
    and Hebrew is Chinese
    to the Jews.

IX. Shouting with Anglo-Saxons {64}

X. Palestine, Ireland, America {103} — 1 time

1. It was forbidden to the Jews
    to hold title to land
    in Palestine.
2. But it is not forbidden to the Jews
    to hold title to land
    in America.
3. It was forbidden to the Irish
    to lend money at interest
    in Ireland.
4. But it is not forbidden to the Irish
    to lend money at interest
    in America.
5. The Prophets of Israel
    and the Fathers of the Church
    wanted the Jews and the Irish
    to try to become better;
6. But the American politicians don't mind
    if the Jews and the Irish
    are trying to become better off
    in America.
7. But America is not better off
    since the Jews and the Irish
    are trying to become better off
    in America.

XI. Reconstructing the Social Order {36}

XII. Irish Scholars at Work {104} — 1 time

Marie Schulte Kallenback says:
1. "Upon gifts of land,
    often bleak and barren,
    huts were built
    about the little church,
    all work being done
    by the missionaries themselves.
2. "Thus they exhibited
    almost at the very outset
    to their pagan observers
    that moving spectacle
    of Christians
    living in united peace
    and harmony,
    prayer and good works,
    so utterly foreign
    to their own turbulent lives.
3. "All was done
    for the love of God,
    work being suspended
    at fixed hours of the day
    for worship, prayer and song.
4. "By such tactics
    the hearts of the people
    were won;
    a most civilizing influence
    was extended,
    ending in their conversion
    and complete confidence."

JANUARY 1935
A PROGRAM FOR IMMEDIATE NEEDS

I. School of Social Studies {69}

II. Social Missionaries {105} — 1 time

1. A School of Social Studies
would be a training ground
for Social Missionaries,
priests, laymen and women.
2. As Al Smith says:
"The social problem
is not a problem
for politicians,
business men
and lawyers."[119]
3. The social problem
is a problem
for Social Missionaries.
4. The task of Social Missionaries
is not to help people
to adjust themselves
to the existing environment.
5. The task of Social Missionaries
is to teach people
the difficult art
of creating order
out of chaos.
6. To be a Social Missionary
requires social-mindedness,
historical-mindedness
and practical idealism.

---

119. The source of this quote is uncertain, but it likely expressed Smith's strong opposition to the Eighteenth Amendment, which prohibited alcoholic beverages in the United States. Smith believed that it was not the place of the state to ban the use of alcohol.

III. Study Clubs {106} — 1 time

1. Social Missionaries
    would be official leaders
    of Study Clubs.
2. The conduct of a Study Club
    does not require
    a fluent speaker.
3. As Bishop O'Hara[120] says:
    "The purpose of Study Clubs
    is to make people articulate;
    and lectures do not help
    to make people articulate."
4. Social Missionaries
    would be able
    to impart their knowledge
    through easy conversation.
5. Easy conversations
    about things that matter
    would keep people
    from going to the movies,
    from talking politics,
    from cheap wisecracking.
6. Easy conversation
    about things that matter
    would enable Catholics
    to understand Catholicism,
    to give an account of their Faith,
    and to make non-Catholics
    curious about Catholicism.

IV. Works of Mercy {107} — 1 time

1. The best kind of apologetics
    is the kind of apologetics
    people do not have
    to apologize for.

---

120. This is a reference to Edwin Vincent O'Hara (1881–1956), who promoted adult study clubs as Bishop of Great Falls, Montana, in 1931.

2. In the first centuries
   of Christianity
   pagans said about Christians:
   "See how they love each other."
3. The love for God and neighbor
   was the characteristic
   of the first Christians.
4. This love was expressed
   through the daily practice
   of the Works of Mercy.
5. To feed the hungry,
   to clothe the naked,
   to shelter the homeless,
   to instruct the ignorant
   at a personal sacrifice
   was considered
   by the first Christians
   as *the right things to do*.
6. Superfluous goods
   were considered
   to be superfluous;
   and therefore
   to be used
   to help the needy members
   of the Mystical Body.

V. Houses of Hospitality {26}

VI. Self-Employing Centers {108} — 1 time

1. The remedy for unemployment
   is employment,
   and there is no better employment
   than self-employment.
2. Self-Employing Centers
   are small shops
   where repairs can be made
   and workers can be found
   to do work outside.

3. With the Self-Employing Centers
         could be connected
         Houses of Hospitality
         where the self-employing workers
         could find shelter.
   4. This complicated world
         is too complicated
         to be dealt with
         in an efficient manner
         by specialized technicians.
   5. Specialized technicians
         knowing more and more
         about less and less
         do not know
         how to simplify
         a complicated world.
   6. We need less specialists
         and more encyclopedists,
         less masters of one trade
         and more jacks-of-all trades.

VII. Farming Communes {10}

FEBRUARY 1935
EASY ESSAYS

The following is an analysis of the Definitions given by John Strachey (Communist), Lawrence Dennis (Fascist), Norman Thomas (Socialist) and Stanley High (Democrat) as to their respective beliefs.

I. What Communists Say They Believe {109} — 1 time
   1. Communists believe
         that the capitalist system
         has reached the point
         when it does no longer work.

2. Communists believe
    that when the workers
    come to the realization
    of the downfall of capitalism
    they will no longer tolerate it.
3. Communists believe
    that the capitalist class
    will resort to all means
    that may be in their power
    to maintain its existence.
4. Communists believe
    that the Communist Party
    knows how to assure
    the production and distribution
    in an orderly manner
    according to a predesigned plan.

II. What Fascists Say They Believe {110} — 1 time

1. Fascists believe
    in a national economy
    for the protection
    of national and private interests.
2. Fascists believe
    in the regulation of industries
    so as to assure
    a wage for the worker
    and a dividend for the investor.
3. Fascists believe
    in class collaboration
    under State supervision.
4. Fascists believe
    in the co-operation
    of employers' unions
    and workers' unions.

III. What Socialists Say They Believe {111} — 1 time

1. Socialists believe
    in a gradual realization
    of a classless society.
2. Socialists believe
    in the social ownership
    of natural resources
    and the means of production
    and distribution.
3. Socialists believe
    in a transition period
    under democratic management
    between two economic systems
    the system of production for use
    and the one of production for profits.
4. Socialists believe
    in freedom of the press
    freedom of assemblage
    freedom of worship.

IV. What Democrats Say They Believe {112} — 1 time

1. Democrats believe
    in universal suffrage
    universal education
    freedom of opportunity.
2. Democrats believe
    in the right of the rich
    to become richer
    and of the poor
    to try to become rich.
3. Democrats believe
    in labor unions
    and financial corporations.
4. Democrats believe
    in the law of supply and demand.

V. What the Catholic Worker Believes {113} — 1 time

1. The Catholic Worker believes
   in the gentle personalism
   of traditional Catholicism.
2. The Catholic Worker believes
   in the personal obligation
   of looking after
   the needs of our brother.
3. The Catholic Worker believes
   in the daily practice
   of the Works of Mercy.
4. The Catholic Worker believes
   in Houses of Hospitality
   for the immediate relief
   of those who are in need.
5. The Catholic Worker believes
   in the establishment
   of Farming Communes
   where each one works
   according to his capacity
   and gets according to his need.
6. The Catholic Worker believes
   in creating a new society
   within the shell of the old
   with the philosophy of the new.

MARCH 1935
EASY ESSAYS

I. A Radical Change {77}

II. When Bankers Rule {78}

III. When Christ Is King {79}

IV. Constructing the Social Order {81}

V. Reconstructing the Social Order {36}

VI. Round-Table Discussions {8}

VII. Houses of Hospitality {9}

VIII. Farming Communes {10}

IX. Professors of a Farming Commune {93}

X. Laborers of a Farming Commune {94}

APRIL 1935

A LETTER TO JOHN STRACHEY AND HIS READERS

Peter Maurin Answers English Communist's Defense of His Beliefs after Immigration Officers Charge Author Entered United States under False Pretenses

I. [No Title] {114} — 1 time

1. You say that "no Communist
    believes in
    or favors the use
    of force and violence."[121]
2. But the Communists
    believe in class war
    in the same way
    that the Capitalists
    believe in class war.
3. The Capitalists believe
    in keeping what they have
    and in getting
    what other Capitalists have.

---

[121]. In early 1935, Strachey came to the United States on a speaking tour and was arrested by the federal government in a failed attempt to deport him. During this time, a letter was published in the *Modern Thinker* that contained the quote, though Strachey denied that he was the author of the article. In any case, the letter and the quote were the topic of numerous newspaper articles and editorials around the country during March 1935.

4. The Communists believe
     in getting
     what the Capitalists have.
5. To keep what they have
     the Capitalists
     use all the means
     that the modern State
     allows them to use.
6. To get what the Capitalists have
     the Communists
     are not afraid to use
     all the means
     that the Capitalists
     are allowed to use.

II. Taking Over {115} — 1 time

1. The aim of the Communists
     is to take over the control
     of the means of production
     and distribution.
2. The means of production
     and distribution
     are now in the hands
     of Capitalists.
3. The class war is a war
     between Communists
     and Capitalists
     over the control
     of the means of production
     and distribution.
4. Patriots believe
     that the way to peace
     is to prepare for war.
5. Communists believe
     that the way to bring about
     a classless society
     is a class war
     between the Capitalist class
     and the working class.

III. What Is Communism? {116} — 1 time

1. Communists believe
    in capturing the State
    so as to be able
    to use it as a club
    to prevent anybody
    from becoming a Capitalist.
2. The *Communist Manifesto*
    defines Communism as
    "a state of society
    where each one works
    according to his capacity
    and gets
    according to his needs."[122]
3. Using the power of the State
    will enable Communists
    to prevent anybody
    from becoming
    a successful Capitalist
    but it will not
    make anybody
    Communist at heart.
4. To be a Communist
    according to the definition
    of the *Communist Manifesto*
    is to be willing
    to give one's labor
    for the benefit
    of a Communist Community.

IV. What Labor Needs {117} — 1 time

1. A Communist Community
    is a Community
    with common unity.

---

122. For more on this quote, see the entry on Proudhon.

2. A common belief
    is what makes the unity
    of a community.
3. Norman Thomas says
    that "Ramsay MacDonald
    has failed to give to Labor
    a philosophy of labor."[123]
4. What Labor needs
    is not higher wages,
    shorter hours,
    sickness insurance,
    unemployment insurance,
    old age pensions.
5. What Labor needs
    is not economic security.
6. What Labor needs
    is a philosophy of labor.

V. Accumulators of Labor[124] {15} [part 1]

VI. Sellers of Labor {15} [part 2]

VII. Getting Left {16}

VIII. What Makes Man Human {86}

IX. Christianity, Capitalism, Communism {51}

X. What Saint Francis Desired {53}

XI. An Old Philosophy {118} — 1 time

1. Norman Thomas
    as well as Ramsay MacDonald
    have failed to give to Labor
    a philosophy of labor.

---

123. The origin of this quote is uncertain.
124. In this instance, Maurin breaks the original essay {15} into two parts. Part 2 of the essay is composed of the last two stanzas of the original essay {15}.

2. While the Communist Party
    carries on a class war,
    it is not giving to Labor
    a philosophy of labor.
3. THE CATHOLIC WORKER
    is trying to give to Labor
    a philosophy of labor
    and a technique
    in harmony
    with the philosophy.
4. For we believe
    that we can create
    a new society
    within the shell of the old
    with the philosophy of the new
    which is not a new philosophy
    but an old philosophy
    a philosophy so old
    that it looks like new.

XII. Going Back {42}[125]

1. You realize
    as Robert Briffault realizes
    that the British Empire
    is breaking down.
2. Not only the British Empire,
    but all the other empires
    are breaking down.
3. You realize
    as we realize
    that modern society
    "is parked in a blind-alley."
4. And when one is parked
    in a blind-alley
    the only thing to do
    is to turn back.

---

125. The previous version of the essay was inserted into a much larger essay in December 1933. This was the only other instance of this essay.

5. By giving to Labor
    a philosophy of labor
    we can go back to the time
    when people tried to be
    gentle personalists
    and refused to be
    rugged individualists,
    when gentlemen
    tried to be gentle
    living on the sweat
    of their own brow
    and not living on the sweat
    of somebody else's brow.

XIII. *Esprit* {119} — 1 time

1. The French magazine *Esprit*
    carried on a campaign
    for Communitarianism.
2. In the January issue
    Emmanuel Mounier
    has a 32-page article
    on the "Communitarian Revolution."
3. Other articles are entitled:
    "Russian Communitarian Tradition,"
    "German Communitarian Tradition,"
    "French Communitarian Tradition."
4. The last article is entitled:
    "Christian Communities."
5. The magazine *Esprit*
    is not a Catholic magazine.
6. It is a magazine
    where Catholics, Protestants,
    Jews and Humanists
    are trying to promote
    a kind of society
    where man
    will be human
    to man.

XIV. Communist Ideal {120} — 1 time

1. Communism is an ideal
    but the Russian brand
    of Communism
    is not the ideal
    of Communism.
2. The ideal of Communism
    is Irish Communism.
3. Through Round-Table Discussions
    the Irish scholars
    brought thought
    to the people.
4. Through Houses of Hospitality
    the Irish scholars
    emphasized Christian charity.
5. Through Farming Communes
    the Irish scholars
    made scholars
    out of workers
    and workers
    out of scholars.
6. You are trying
    to make a case
    for Russian Communism
    which is not Communism
    but Socialism.
7. I am trying to make a case
    for Irish Communism
    which is the Communism
    of Christian communities.

XV. The Hope of the People {121} — 1 time

1. We believe that religion
    is the hope of the people
    not the dope of the people.
2. We believe that the world
    would be better off
    if people tried

    to become better
    and that people would
    become better
    if they stopped trying
    to become better off.
3. We believe that the best way to be
    is to be
    what we want
    the other fellow to be.
4. We believe that to be
    what we want
    the other fellow to be
    is to be
    what St. Francis
    wants us to be.
5. We believe that to be
    what St. Francis
    wants us to be
    is to be
    real Christians.

—Your fellow worker in Christ's Kingdom,

Peter Maurin

MAY 1935
FEED THE POOR—STARVE THE BANKERS

I. Share Your Wealth[126] {122} — 2 times

1. God wants us
    to be our brother's keeper.
2. To feed the hungry,
    to cloth the naked,
    to shelter the homeless,
    to instruct the ignorant,
    at a personal sacrifice,
    is what God
    wants us to do.

126. The other instance of the essay is the same.

3. What we give to the poor
> for Christ's sake
> is what we carry with us
> when we die.
4. As Jean-Jacques Rousseau says:
> "When man dies
> he carries
> in his clutched hands
> only that which
> he has given away."[127]

II. Why Not Be a Beggar? {23}

III. What Saint Francis Desired {53}

IV. The Wisdom of Giving[128] {123} — 6 times

1. To give money to the poor
> is to enable the poor to buy.
2. To enable the poor to buy
> is to improve the market.
3. To improve the market
> is to help business.
4. To help business
> is to reduce unemployment.
5. To reduce unemployment
> is to reduce crime.
6. To reduce crime
> is to reduce taxation.

---

127. This quote is regularly attributed to Rousseau, but its exact origin is unknown.

128. In some versions, the word "God's" in the last stanza is replaced with "Christ's." The last stanza of the final four versions of the essay states, "So give your surplus to the poor for business' sake, for humanity's sake, for God's sake." At times, the last stanza is phrased as a question: "So why not give to the poor. . . ?" Some versions of the essay attach this addition at the end: "And don't forget that 'when man dies he carries in his clutched hands only that which he has given away in his lifetime,' as Jean-Jacques Rousseau used to say." The October 1936 version was unique in beginning with the following line: "Archbishop Keating says that 'when a social system fails to feed the poor it is time to look out for one that does.'"

7. So why not give to the poor
   for business' sake,
   for humanity's sake,
   for God's sake.

V. The Fallacy of Saving {38}

VI. Wealth-Producing Maniacs {7}

VII. Mortgaged {5}

VIII. Avoiding Inflation {39}

JUNE 1935
IN THE LIGHT OF HISTORY

I. I Agree {72}

II. The Communist Party {33}

III. The Catholic Worker {34}

IV. Ethics and Economics {2}

V. 1200—Guild System {124} — 1 time

1. In 1200 A.D.
   there was no Capitalist System,
   there was the Guild System.[129]
2. The doctrine of the Guilds
   was the doctrine
   of the Common Good.
3. People used to say,
   as they do now:
   "What can I do for you?"
   but they meant what they said.

---

129. The guild system of the Middle Ages was usually an association of individuals in the same trade formed with the intention of protecting common interests, maintaining standards of quality, and ensuring a just price.

4. Now they say one thing
    and they mean another.
5. They did not look for markets,
    they let the markets
    look for them.

VI. 1400—Middle Men {125} — 1 time

1. Around 1400 A.D.
    appears the middle man.
2. He offers to buy the goods
    and to find a market.
3. The guild's man
    thinks about the money
    offered for his goods
    and forgets the Common Good.
4. And the middle man
    is not interested
    in selling useful goods
    but in making money
    on any kind of goods.
5. And the consumer
    never meets the producer
    and the producer
    ceases to think
    in terms of service
    and begins to think
    in terms of profits.

VII. 1600—Banker {126} — 1 time

1. Before John Calvin
    people were not allowed
    to lend money at interest.
2. John Calvin decided
    to legalize
    money lending at interest
    in spite of the teachings

of the Prophets of Israel
and the Fathers of the Church.
3. Protestant countries
tried to keep up with John Calvin
and money lending at interest
became the general practice.
4. And money ceased to be
a means of exchange
and began to be
a means to make money.
5. So people lend money on time
and started to think of time
in terms of money
and said to each other:
"Time is money."

VIII. 1700—Manufacturer[130] {127} — 2 times

1. With the discovery of steam
the factory system
made its appearance.
2. To take drudgery out of the home
was supposed to be
the aim of the manufacturer.
3. So the guildsman
left his shop
and went to the factory.
4. But the profit making manufacturer
found it more profitable
to employ women
than to employ men.

---

130. Also known as "Factory Capitalism." The other version of the essay from March 1942 contained some unique features and is reproduced here: "1. When the use of steam was discovered the middle men started factories. 2. The craftsmen deserted their craft shops and went to work in the factories and became factory hands. 3. Factory owners turned out gadgets to take drudgery out of the home. 4. And then they took women out of the home and brought them into factories. 5. And then they took children out of the home and brought them into factories. 6. And men had to stay home to look after young children."

5. So the women left the home
    and went to the factory.
6. Soon the children
    followed the women
    into the factory.
7. So the men have to stay at home
    while women and children
    work in the factory.

IX. 1800—Economist {128} — 1 time

1. Since Adam Smith
    who published his book
    in 1776[131]
    we have been told
    that competition
    is the life of trade
    and that it is a case
    of survival of the fittest.
2. So since 1776
    looking for markets
    has engaged men's activities.
3. And since trade follows the flag
    industrial nations
    have also become
    imperialist nations.
4. The fight for markets
    between two industrial nations
    England and Germany,
    was the main cause
    of the World War.

X. 1914—World War {129} — 1 time

1. As President Wilson said,
    the World War
    was a commercial war.

---

131. This is a reference to Smith's most well-known book, *An Inquiry into the Nature and Causes of the Wealth of Nations*, often simply called *The Wealth of Nations*.

2. But a commercial war
    had to be idealized,
    so it was called
    a War for Democracy.
3. But the War for Democracy
    did not bring Democracy
    it brought
    Bolshevism in Russia,
    Fascism in Italy,
    Nazism in Germany.

XI. 1929—World Depression {130} — 1 time

1. After the World War
    people tried to believe
    that a New Era
    had dawned upon the world.
2. People thought
    that they had found a solution
    to the problem
    of mass-distribution.
3. People thought
    that the time had come
    of a two-car garage
    a chicken in every pot
    and a sign "To Let"
    in front of every poor-house.
4. And everybody
    wanted to cash in
    on the future prosperity.
5. So stock promoters got busy
    and stocked people with stocks
    till they got stuck.

XII. 1933—New Deal {91}

XIII. 1933—Catholic Worker {131} — 1 time

1. The aim of THE CATHOLIC WORKER
    is to create order
    out of chaos.

2. The aim of THE CATHOLIC WORKER
   is to help the unemployed
   to employ themselves.
3. The aim of THE CATHOLIC WORKER
   is to make an impression
   on the Depression
   through expression.
4. The aim of THE CATHOLIC WORKER
   is to create a new society
   within the shell of the old
   with the philosophy of the new
   which is not a new philosophy,
   but a very old philosophy,
   a philosophy so old
   that it looks like new.

JULY–AUGUST 1935
EASY ESSAYS

I. No Recourse[132] {132} — 6 times

1. Politicians used to say:
   "We make prosperity
   through our wise policies."
2. Business men used to say:
   "We make prosperity
   through our private enterprise."
3. The workers did not seem
   to have anything to do
   about the matter.

---

132. Also known as "Makers of Depressions." Some of the versions add the following two stanzas at the end: "1. The refusal of business men to accept the responsibility for business depressions is what makes the workers resort to sit-down strikes. 2. If prosperity is brought about by business men, then depressions are also brought about by business men." The version called "Makers of Depressions" from April 1937 ends with the stanza, "If business men understood business they would find the way to increase the demand for manufactured products, instead of increasing the supply through the speed-up system and the extensive use of improved machinery."

4. They were either
   put to work
   or thrown out
   of employment.
5. And when unemployment came
   the workers had no recourse
   against the professed
   makers of prosperity—
   politicians
   and business men.

II. Politics Is Politics {20}

III. Maker of Deals[133] {133} — 3 times

1. A business man
   is a maker of deals.
2. He wants to close
   a profitable deal
   in the shortest possible time.
3. To close a profitable deal
   in the shortest possible time
   he tells you
   what a good bargain
   you are getting.
4. And while he tells you
   what a good bargain
   you are getting
   he is always thinking
   what a good bargain
   he is getting.
5. He appeals
   to the selfishness in you
   to satisfy
   the selfishness in him.

---

133. Also known as "Business Is Business" and "Business Is the Bunk." There were only minor variations in future iterations of the essay.

IV. Business Is Selfishness {11}

V. Teaching Subjects {12}

VI. Specialization {44}

VII. Another Experiment {134} — 1 time

1. General Johnson says
    that the N.R.A.
    was like a horse
    trying to pull
    in different directions.
2. And when the Supreme Court
    examined the "whole thing"
    it came to the conclusion
    that the "whole thing"
    did not make sense.
3. The Prohibition Law[134]
    was called by Hoover
    "A noble experiment."
4. The National Recovery Act
    was considered by all
    "A noble experiment."
5. To live by experiment
    is known in philosophy
    under the name of Pragmatism.[135]

---

134. This refers to the national ban on the sale and making of alcohol in the United States from 1920 to 1933, which was enacted with the Eighteenth Amendment to the Constitution and ended with the Twenty-first Amendment.

135. Pragmatism is a philosophical tradition that began in the United States around 1870 and was very influential during the 1930s. Leading figures in this movement included Charles Sanders Peirce (1839–1914), William James (1842–1910), and John Dewey (1859–1952). This tradition stresses that the perceived practical consequences of an action are the principal factor in judging a hypothesis. Or to quote Peirce, "Consider what effects, which might conceivably have practical bearings, we conceive the object of our conception to have. Then, our conception of these effects is the whole of our conception of the object." Maurin's critique of pragmatism likely came from the insistence of many of its proponents to dismiss religious truths in the forming of moral judgments, though Maurin could also be alluding to the fact that the pragmatists generally supported state-oriented programs for social welfare.

6. The doctrine of Pragmatism
    was exploded
    by Van Wyck Brooks.
7. If the doctrine of Pragmatism
    is wrong philosophically
    it must also
    be wrong economically.

VIII. Christianity Untried[136] {135} — 5 times

1. Chesterton says
    "Christianity has not failed
    because it has not been tried."
2. Christianity has not been tried
    because people thought
    it was impractical.
3. And men have tried everything
    except Christianity.
4. And everything
    that men have tried
    has failed.
5. And to fail
    in everything
    that one tries
    is not to be practical
6. Men will be practical
    when they try to practice
    the Christianity
    they profess
    to believe in.

IX. The Wisdom of Giving {136} — 1 time

1. General Johnson used to say
    "The problem of the depression
    is to increase

---

136. Also known as "Not Practical." There were only minor variations in the different versions of the essay.

   the buying power
   and decrease
   the producing power."
2. When people invest money
   they increase
   the producing power.
3. When people spend money
   or give it to the poor
   they increase
   the buying power.
4. To feed the hungry,
   clothe the naked,
   shelter the homeless
   at a sacrifice,
   is what God
   wants us to do.
5. "When man dies,
   he carries
   in his clutched hands
   only that which
   he had given away,"
   says Jean-Jacques Rousseau.

SEPTEMBER 1935
THE COMMUNISM OF THE CATHOLIC WORKER

St. Ambrose says: "The Church presents the most perfect form of admirable communism and social life."

I. Christianity, Capitalism, Communism {51}

II. Looking at Property {137} — 1 time

  Fr. Henry Carr, Superior of the Basilians, says:
  1. Socialists and Communists
    battle against
    the unequal conditions
    of the poor.

2. Presumably they would be satisfied
    if all were on a level.
3. Do you not see
    that this does not touch
    the question that is vital,
    namely, whether or not the people,
    no matter how much
    or how little they possess,
    regard it and use it
    in the way they should?
4. The right way
    is to regard it
    as something entrusted to us
    to use for the benefit
    of ourselves and others.
5. The wrong way
    is to look on it
    as something we own
    and can use as we desire
    without any duty to others.
6. Good or bad conditions
    will follow
    good or bad use
    of property.

III. For Christ's Sake {138} — 1 time

1. "Come, ye blessed of My Father,
    possess you the Kingdom
    prepared for you
    from the foundation of the world.
2. "For I was hungry
    and you gave me to eat.
3. "I was thirsty
    and you gave me drink.
4. "I was a stranger
    and you took me in.
5. "Naked
    and you covered me.

6. "Sick
   and you visited me.
7. "I was in prison
   and you came to me.
8. "Amen, I say to you
   as long as you did it
   to one of these,
   my least brethren,
   you did it to me."

—Matthew 25:34–36, 40

IV. At a Sacrifice {73}

V. The Wisdom of Giving {123}

VI. What Saint Francis Desired {53}

VII. Better and Better Off {50}

VIII. Capital and Labor {15}

IX. Selling Their Labor {16}

X. Round-Table Discussions {8}

XI. Houses of Hospitality {9}

XII. Farming Communes {10}

XIII. Professors of a Farming Commune {93}

XIV. Laborers of a Farming Commune {94}

INVADERS AND INVADED[137] {139} — 2 times

1. When the German Barbarians
      invaded Christian Gaul
      after the Fall of the Roman Empire
      the Christian Gauls

---

137. Also known as "Germans and French." The other version of the essay was condensed.

did not waste their time
trying to exterminate
the German Barbarians.
2. They allowed the German Barbarians
to take possession
of Christian Gaul
and set themselves to the task
of Christianizing German Barbarians.
3. And the German Barbarians
gave up their pagan religion
and took up the religion
of the invaded Gauls.
4. Not only did they give up
their pagan religion
but they also gave up
their German language
and took up the language
of the invaded Gauls.
5. It was not the invaders
that civilized the invaded
it was the invaded
that civilized the invaders.

OCTOBER 1935
THE COMMUNIST PARTY VS. THE CATHOLIC WORKER[138] {140} — 3 times

Catholics Call for Personalist Leadership Rather Than for Dictatorship by One Class as in Russia.

1. The Communist Party
credits bourgeois capitalism
with an historical mission.

---

138. Also known as "The C.P. and C.M." and "The Catholic Worker." "C.P. and C.M." replaces the term "Catholic Worker" with "Communitarian Movement."

2. The Catholic Worker
    does nothing of the kind,
    it condemns it
    on general principles.
3. The Communist Party
    throws the monkey-wrench
    of class-struggle
    into the economic machinery
    and in doing so
    delays the fulfilling
    of the historical mission
    it credits capitalism.
4. The Catholic Worker
    aims to create
    a new society
    within the shell of the old
    with a philosophy of the new
    which is not a new philosophy
    but a very old philosophy,
    a philosophy so old
    that it looks like new.
5. The Communist Party
    stands for
    proletarian dictatorship.
6. The Catholic Worker
    stands for
    personalist leadership.

II. Taking Back Our Thunder {141} — 1 time

1. Announcing the coming out
    of the Catholic Worker
    the editor of *Columbia*[139] said
    that the Catholic Worker
    was stealing the thunder
    of the Communist Party.

---

139. This is a reference to John B. Donahue, who was at that time the editor of *Columbia*, the monthly magazine published by the Knights of Columbus since 1921.

2. And seven American Bishops
    said in 1933
    that the criticism
    of the Communist Party
    is a sound criticism.
3. Writing about the Catholic Church
    Albert J. Nock said,
    "Rome will have to do more
    than to play the waiting game;
    She will have to make use
    of some of the dynamite
    inherent in her message."
4. The Catholic Worker
    is making use
    of some of the dynamite
    inherent in the message
    of the Catholic Church.

III. Taking Back Our Name {142} — 1 time

1. The name Communism
    does not come from Karl Marx
    it comes from Proudhon.
2. Proudhon was a Frenchman
    and France is a country
    with a Catholic tradition.
3. And Catholic tradition
    gave to Proudhon
    the word communism.
4. The word communism
    exists in French history
    since the eleventh century.
5. The Communist Party
    has taken the word communism
    from the Catholic tradition
    and has failed to give us
    a sample of communism.
6. No member of the Communist Party
    has ever said

       that there was Communism
          in Soviet Russia.
7. What they have in Soviet Russia
          is State Socialism.
8. State Socialism is not part
          of Catholic tradition
          but Catholic Communism is.
9. When we call ourselves
          Catholic Communists
          we reclaim our own.

IV. Confused Marxists {143} — 1 time

1. The Catholic Worker is accused
          of confusing the workers.
2. We do not confuse the workers,
          they are already confused.
3. Not only are the workers confused
          but Marxists themselves
          are confused.
4. That's why we have
          a Communist Party
          a Workers' Party
          a Socialist Party
          a Socialist Labor Party.
5. And Marxists are confused
          because Karl Marx himself
          was confused.
6. So they write books
          to help to understand Karl Marx.
7. But the writers of these books
          have not thrown any light
          on Karl Marx's confusion.

V. Confused Catholics {144} — 1 time

1. That the Catholic Worker
          confuses Marxists
          is an admitted fact.

2. But many Catholics say
    that the Catholic Worker
    confuses also Catholics.
3. But modern Catholics
    were always confused.
4. Because they were confused
    modern Catholics
    listened to modern economists
    who were telling them
    that the time had come
    at least in America
    for a two-car garage
    a chicken in every pot
    and a sign "To Let"
    in front of every poorhouse.
5. And when the depression came
    they believed with everybody
    that prosperity
    was just around the corner.
6. And when it failed to appear
    they tried to bring it back
    by backing the N.R.A.

VI. From a Non-Catholic {145} — 1 time

A French non-Catholic
    Andre Siegfried says:
1. The Puritan
    is proud to be rich.
2. If he makes money,
    he likes to tell himself
    that Divine Providence
    sends it to him.
3. His wealth itself
    becomes in his eyes
    as well as the eyes of others
    a mark of God's blessing.

    4. A time comes
            when he no longer knows
            if he acts for duty's sake
            or for interest's sake.
    5. It becomes difficult
            in those conditions
            to make a demarcation
            between religious aspiration
            and the pursuit of wealth.

VII. From a Catholic {146} — 1 time

    An English Catholic
            Henry Somerville says:
    1. Those who want to find out
            the intellectual errors
            from which England is suffering
            ought to read the book
            of R. H. Tawney,
            a non-Catholic,
            entitled *Religion
            and the Rise of Capitalism.*
    2. The religion taught by Christ
            does not make wealth
            a desirable objective.
    3. Puritanism,
            the most virile form
            of Protestantism,
            made the mistake
            of indorsing the pursuit of wealth
            in the name of religion.

BOURGEOIS COLLEGES

I. Catholic Bourgeois[140] {147} — 2 times

    1. A bourgeois is a man
            who tries to be somebody,

---

140. The other version omitted the second stanza.

>   by trying to be like everybody,
>   which makes him a nobody.
> 2. Catholic bourgeois
>   try to be
>   like non-Catholic bourgeois
>   and think they are
>   just as good
>   as non-Catholic bourgeois.
> 3. Right after the War
>   Catholic Bourgeois
>   tried to believe
>   what non-Catholic bourgeois
>   tried to believe
>   that the time had come
>   in America
>   for a two-car garage
>   a chicken in very pot
>   and a sign "To Let"
>   in front of every poorhouse.
> 4. And Catholic colleges
>   as well as non-Catholic colleges
>   turned out stock promoters
>   stock brokers
>   and stock salesmen
>   who stocked people with stocks
>   till they got stuck.

II. Business Is the Bunk {41} & {133}[141]

III. Not My Subject {44}

IV. Shouting with Rotarians {64}

V. College Graduates[142] {148} — 2 times

> 1. Sociology is not a science,
>   it is an art.

---

141. Maurin combined two separate essays: {41} and {133}. After printing the first two stanzas of essay {41}, he added stanzas one, three, and four from essay {133}.

142. Also known as "In a Changing World." The other version was abridged.

2. The art of sociology
>   is the art
>   of creating order
>   out of chaos.
3. Bourgeois colleges
>   turn out college graduates
>   into a changing world
>   without ever telling them
>   how to keep it from changing
>   or how to change it
>   so as to make it fit
>   for college graduates.
4. College graduates
>   think in term of jobs,
>   not in terms of work.
5. Since the world is upside down,
>   taking the side down
>   and putting it up
>   should be the task
>   of college graduates.
6. But college graduates
>   would rather
>   play somebody else's game
>   in a position
>   than to create order
>   out of chaos.

VI. An Unhappy Lot[143] {149} — 2 times

1. But the job providers
>   are not on the job
>   and college graduates
>   are disappointed.
2. They have degrees
>   but their degrees
>   do not give them jobs.

---

143. Also known as "Looking for Jobs." The other version was abridged.

3. They have been told
    that the road to success
    is a college education.
4. They have a college education
    and they do not know
    what to do
    with themselves.
5. The over-production
    of college graduates
    is a fertile ground
    for social demagogues.
6. The unemployed college graduates
    are getting sore
    at their parents
    for sending them into colleges
    which have not prepared them
    for a changing world.
7. And they ask themselves
    if their educators
    know what it is
    to be educated.

VII. Houses of Hospitality {150} — 1 time

1. In the *New Masses*[144]
    a Communist cartoonist
    represents
    a line of college graduates
    receiving their degrees
    from the Alma Mater
    and joining a soup line
    on the other side of the square.

---

144. The *New Masses* was a prominent American Communist publication that existed from 1926 to 1948. The *New Masses* was an allusion to an earlier socialist publication called *The Masses*. Dorothy Day wrote articles for both publications before the founding of the Catholic Worker. Day had served briefly on the editorial board of *The Masses*; her close friend Mike Gold edited the *New Masses*.

2. Social reconstruction
     will be the result
     of social indoctrination.
3. But unemployed college graduates
     cannot be indoctrinated
     without first being fed,
     as well as clothed,
     as well as sheltered.
4. Houses of hospitality
     for unemployed college graduates
     are a pressing need.

VIII. Indoctrination[145] {151} — 2 times

1. In Houses of Hospitality
     unemployed college graduates
     will be fed, clothed, sheltered,
     as well as indoctrinated.
2. Unemployed college graduates
     must be told
     why the things are
     what they are,
     how the things would be
     if they were
     as they should be
     and how a path
     can be made
     from the things
     as they are
     to the things
     as they should be.
3. Unemployed college graduates
     must be told
     how to create
     a new society
     within the shell of the old
     with the philosophy of the new

---

145. The other version was abridged.

which is not a new philosophy
but a very old philosophy,
a philosophy so old
that it looks like new.

IX. On Farming Communes[146] {152} — 2 times

1. When unemployed college graduates
    will have been indoctrinated
    they will be moved
    to Farming Communes.
2. On Farming Communes
    unemployed college graduates
    will be taught
    how to build their houses,
    how to gather their fuel,
    how to raise their food,
    how to make their furniture
    that is to say
    how to employ themselves.
3. Unemployed college graduates
    must be taught
    how to use their hands.
4. Unemployed college graduates
    have time
    on their hands.
5. And while time is on the hands
    of college graduates
    their heads don't function
    as they should function.
6. On Farming Communes
    unemployed college graduates
    will learn to use
    both their hands
    and their heads.

---

146. The other version was abridged.

NOVEMBER 1935
BACK TO CHRIST!—BACK TO THE LAND!

I. On the Level {153} — 1 time

  1. Owen Young says:
      "We will never have prosperity
      as long as
      there is no balance
      between industry
      and agriculture."
  2. The farmer sells
      in an open market
      and is forced to buy
      in a restricted market.
  3. When the farmer gets
      a pair of overalls
      for a bushel of wheat
      the wheat and the overalls
      are on the level.
  4. When the farmer
      has to give
      two bushels of wheat
      for a pair of overalls
      the wheat and the overalls
      are not on the level.
  5. Wheat and overalls
      must be on the level.

II. Industrialization {154} — 1 time

  1. Lenin said:
      "The world cannot be
      half industrial
      and half agricultural."[147]

---

147. This is probably not an exact quote, but Maurin's summation of Lenin's thought on the agrarian question. Lenin, and Marx before him, assumed that peasant agriculture (small farms owned or rented by families) would eventually be subsumed into

2. England, Germany,
   Japan and America
   have become
   industrialized.
3. Soviet Russia
   is trying to keep up
   with England, Germany,
   Japan and America.
4. When all the world
   will be industrialized
   every country
   will be looking
   for foreign markets.
5. But when every country
   will be industrialized
   you will not have
   foreign markets.

III. Mechanized Labor {155} — 1 time

1. Gandhi says:
   "Industrialism is evil."
2. Industrialism is evil
   because it brings idleness
   both to the capitalist class
   and the working class.
3. Idleness does no good
   both to the capitalist class
   and the working class.
4. Creative labor
   is what keeps people
   out of mischief.
5. Creative labor
   is craft labor.

---

industrial capitalism and become industrial farming, where people who worked the land would be wage laborers. This was required for history to take its natural course toward Communism. By this logic, industrialism could not coexist with peasant farming in the long term.

6. Mechanized labor
> is not creative labor.

IV. No Pleasure in Work {156} — 1 time

1. Carlyle says
   > "He who has found his work
   > let him look
   > for no other blessedness."
2. But workmen
   > cannot find happiness
   > in mechanized work.
3. As Charles Devas says,
   > "The great majority
   > having to perform
   > some mechanized operation
   > which requires little thought
   > and allows no originality
   > and which
   > concerns an object
   > in the transformation of which
   > whether previous or subsequent
   > they have no part,
   > cannot take pleasure
   > in their work."
4. As D. Marshall says
   > "Previously the workman
   > fashioned every article
   > with his own hands,
   > bringing to bear on it
   > all the skill of the craft
   > which was his;
   > now all of this
   > is done by the machine."

V. Industrialism and Art {157} — 1 time

Eric Gill says:
1. The notion of work
    has been separated
    from the notion of art.
2. The notion of the useful
    has been separated
    from the notion of the beautiful.
3. The artist,
    that is to say,
    the responsible workman,
    has been separated
    from all other workmen.
4. The factory hand
    has no responsibility
    for what he produces.
5. He has been reduced
    to a sub-human condition
    of intellectual irresponsibility.
6. Industrialism
    has released the artist
    from the necessity
    of making anything useful.
7. Industrialism
    has also released the workman
    from making anything amusing.

VI. From a Chinese {158} — 1 time

A Chinese says:
1. I thought I had become Westernized
    but now I am becoming repatriated.
2. The material progress of America
    has dazzled me.
3. I wished while there
    to transplant what I saw
    to China.

4. But now that I am home again
    I see that our two civilizations
    have irreconcilable differences.
5. Yours is a machine civilization;
    ours is a handicraft civilization.
6. Your people
    work in factories;
    our people
    work in shops.
7. Your people
    produce quantity things
    that are alike.
8. Our people
    produce quality things
    that are different.
9. What would Western industrialism
    do to us?
10. Our people
    would become robots.
11. Our cultural traditions
    would be destroyed.

VII. Regard for the Soil {159} — 1 time

Andrew Nelson Lytle says:
1. The escape from industrialism
    is not in socialism
    or in Sovietism.
2. The answer lies
    in a return to a society
    where agriculture is practiced
    by most of the people.
3. It is in fact impossible
    for any culture
    to be sound and healthy
    without a proper respect
    and proper regard
    for the soil,

no matter
how many urban dwellers
think that their food
comes from groceries
and delicatessens
or their milk from tin cans.
4. This ignorance
does not release them
from a final dependence
upon the farm.

VIII. Up to Catholics {160} — 1 time

Ralph Adams Cram[148] says:
1. What I propose
is that Catholics
should take up
this back to the land problem
and put it into operation.
2. Why Catholics?
Because they realize
more clearly than any others
the shortcomings
of the old capitalist
industrial system.
3. They, better than others,
see the threat
that impends.
4. They alone understand
that while the family
is the primary social unit,
the community comes next.
5. And there is
no sound
and righteous
and enduring community

148. The current essay was inspired by an article Cram wrote, "Cities of Refuge," for the 16 August 1935 issue of *Commonweal*.

where all its members
are not substantially
of one mind
in matters of the spirit—
that is to say
of religion.

IX. Farming Communes {10}

X. Professors of a Farming Commune {93}

XI. Laborers of a Farming Commune {94}

DECEMBER 1935
INSTITUTIONS VS. CORPORATIONS— CATHOLIC TACTIC

C.W. Writer Defines Fascist, Communist and Personalist Communitarian

I. Institution and Corporations {1}

II. Some Institutions {161} — 1 time
   1. Round-Table Discussions
         to learn from scholars
         how the things would be
         if they were
         as they should be—
   2. Campion Propaganda Committees
         for the indoctrination
         of the man of the street—
   3. Maternity Guilds
         for the welfare
         of needy mothers
         bringing young children
         into the world.
   4. Houses of Hospitality
         to give the rich
         the opportunity
         to serve the poor—

5. Farming Communes
   where the scholars
   may become workers
   so the workers
   may be scholars.

III. American Institutions {162} — 1 time

1. The American Constitution,
   the American Congress
   the American Supreme Court
   are also considered
   as institutions.
2. The American Constitution
   was devised
   by the American Founders
   to protect the individual
   against the majority
   whether in Congress
   or Government.
3. The American Supreme Court
   was established by the Founders
   to watch over the Constitution
   so as to prevent
   its misrepresentation
   and its misapplication.
4. And when the N.R.A.
   was brought to the Supreme Court
   for examination
   the Supreme Court found out
   that it did not harmonize
   with the Constitution.

IV. The N.R.A.[149] {163} — 2 times

1. The National Recovery Act
   promised recovery
   and pursued Reformation.

---

149. The other version of this essay from December 1936 possessed minor differences and omitted the first stanza.

2. General Johnson says
     that the N.R.A.
     was like a horse
     trying to pull
     in different directions.
3. At the head of the horse
     stood Recovery,
     at the tail of the horse
     stood Reformation.
4. The tail wanted to be the head
     the head did not want
     to be the tail,
     and the Supreme Court
     could not make
     head or tail
     out of it.
5. The Supreme Court
     seems to admit
     that social reform
     cannot be brought about
     by promising Recovery
     and making the eagle scream.[150]

V. Bureaucracy {164} — 1 time

1. Bureaucracy has failed
     whether in America,
     in France or Germany.
2. The failure of the N.R.A.
     is a striking example
     in America.
3. In France we say:
     "Plus ça change,
     plus c'est la même chose."[151]

---

150. Maurin's mention of an eagle was a reference to the symbol of the National Recovery Administration, the Blue Eagle. Companies that complied with or businesses that supported the N.R.A displayed a poster with the Blue Eagle. Businesses that did not do so were often subject to boycotts.

151. Translated into English: The more things change, the more they stay the same.

4. Governments change,
> but the bureaucracy remains.
5. Political corruption
> has made the French people
> disgusted with their politicians.
6. The most efficient bureaucracy
> was the German bureaucracy.
7. And the faith in Bureaucracy
> was so great
> among German Catholics
> that they failed
> to create a public opinion
> for democratic reform.
8. So the Nazis beat them to it
> and created a public opinion
> for racial demagogy.
9. THE CATHOLIC WORKER
> is trying to create
> a public opinion
> for Communitarian Reform.

VI. Five Definitions[152] {165} — 3 times

1. A Bourgeois is a fellow
> who tries to be somebody
> by trying to be like everybody
> which makes him a nobody.
2. A Dictator is a fellow
> who does not hesitate
> to strike you over the head
> if you refuse to do
> what he wants you to do.
3. A Leader is a fellow
> who refuses to be crazy
> the way everybody else is crazy
> and tries to be crazy
> in his own crazy way.

---

152. Also known as "Three Definitions." The May 1936 essay had slight changes from the original. The last version only contained the first three stanzas.

4. A Bolshevist is a fellow
    who tries to get
    what the other fellow has
    and to regulate
    what you should have.
5. A Communitarian is a fellow
    who refuses to be
    what the other fellow is
    and tries to be
    what he wants him to be.

VII. They and We[153] {166} — 8 times

1. People say:
    "They don't do this,
    they don't do that,
    they ought to do this,
    they ought to do that."
2. Always "They"
    and never "I."
3. People should say:
    "They are crazy
    for doing this
    and not doing that
    but I don't need
    to be crazy
    the way they are crazy."
4. The Communitarian Revolution
    is basically
    a personal revolution.
5. It starts with I
    not with They.
6. One I plus one I
    makes two I
    and two I makes We.

---

153. The September 1938 and November 1939 renditions concluded, "'They' is a crowd, 'they' is a mob, 'they' is a gang, and 'they' are gangsters. Don't be a gangster, 'be yourself,' says Shakespeare."

7. We is a community
   while "they" is a crowd.

VIII. A New Movement[154] {167} — 2 times

1. The Nazis, the Fascists
   and the Bolshevists
   are Totalitarians.
2. The CATHOLIC WORKER
   is Communitarian.
3. The principles of Communitarianism
   are expounded every month
   in the French magazine
   Esprit (the *Spirit*).
4. Emmanuel Mounier,
   editor of the magazine,
   has a book entitled
   *La Revolution Personaliste
   et Communitaire.*
5. Raymond de Becker
   is the leader in Belgium
   of the Communitarian movement.
6. The Premier of Belgium
   van Zeeland,
   is a Communitarian.

---

154. Also known as "Communitarian Movement." The other version from May 1936 replaced stanzas one and two with the following: "Communitarianism is the rediscovery and the exemplification of what the Kiwanis and Rotarians used to talk about, namely, the Community Spirit." It also replaced the final stanza with the following: "Dr. Kagawa the Japanese co-operator is truly imbued with the Communitarian spirit." Kiwanis International is a service club founded in 1915 in Detroit that boasts about 275,000 members. In its earlier years, its purpose was service and business networking. It now places greater emphasis on service.

JANUARY 1936
A NEW SOCIAL ORDER

I. No Unity of Thought {46}

II. Liberalism {13}

III. Secularism {22}

IV. A Blackfriars Editorial[155] {168} — 1 time

1. "Disinterestedness,
    based on objective truth,
    is the keynote of Christianity.
2. "The Cross is the symbol
    not only of sacrifice
    but of self-sacrifice.
3. "And the Cross
    must be shouldered
    not merely by the few
    on rare and heroic occasions,
    but daily.
4. "In other words,
    Self-sacrifice
    is the primary
    and essential principle
    in the Christian's
    daily rule of life.
5. "Whether it be
    a question of personal well-being,
    of work or play,
    of social contact,
    of national life
    or international relations,
    men are not true Christians
    and therefore not true men
    who do not regard

---

155. The essay is a quote from "Editorial," *Blackfriars* 16, no. 187 (October 1935): 725–27.

first and always
the teaching and example
of the Divine Prototype
of all men."

V. Christianity Untried {135}

VI. The Hope of the People {169} — 1 time

1. The Marxists say
    that religion
    is the dope of the people.
2. Religion
    is not the dope of the people
    it is the hope of the people.
3. Modern society
    is a materialist society
    because Christians have failed
    to translate the spiritual
    into the material.
4. If Christians knew
    how to make a lasting impression
    on the materialist depression
    through spiritual expression
    Marxists would not say
    that religion
    is the dope of the people.
5. As Raymond de Becker says:
    "The social task of the laity
    is the sanctification
    of secular life
    or more exactly
    the creation
    of a Christian secular life."[156]

---

156. Since Maurin read French-language theology journals and translated passages of importance for the *New York Catholic Worker*, it is likely that he translated this quote from one of the French-speaking journals in which de Becker wrote.

VII. The Christian Front {170} — 1 time

1. The Christians
    who consider religion
    the hope of the people
    should not unite
    with the Marxists
    who consider religion
    the dope of the people.
2. As the editors of the *Christian Front*[157] say:
    "Marxism not only falsifies
    the origin and the end of man
    but it seeks to make of him
    an anonymous animal
    a servant
    of the proletarian State."
3. The editors of the *Christian Front*
    are not liberals,
    they think that men
    "must take their choice
    to stand for Christianity
    or to stand for what opposes it."
4. They ask the Christians
    "to dissociate themselves
    from an un-Christian social order
    and prepare the way
    for a social order
    compatible with their beliefs."

---

157. The *Christian Front* was a journal begun in January 1936 by two lay Catholics who had been involved with the Catholic Worker for the two years previous: Richard L. G. Deverall (1911–80) and Norman C. McKenna (1910–97). They wanted to provide a journal on Catholic social thought that was more intellectually sophisticated than the *Catholic Worker* newspaper. In 1938, they changed the name of their paper to *Christian Social Action* to avoid confusion with the name of the group that supported Rev. Charles Coughlin. Although the paper began with very radical roots, it soon adopted a more liberal stance and then ceased publication in June 1942.

VIII. The New Apologetics {171} — 1 time

1. In his lectures
    on the New Christendom
    Jacques Maritain
    emphasizes the necessity
    of trying the foundations
    of a new social order.
2. Laying the foundations
    of a new social order
    is the task of the laity.
3. The task of the laity
    is to do the pioneer work
    of creating order
    out of chaos.
4. The Clergy teach the principles;
    the task of the laity
    is to apply them
    without involving the Clergy
    in the application.
5. The application of the social problems
    by the Catholic laity
    of the Catholic principles
    taught by the Catholic clergy
    is a new kind of apologetics
    a kind of apologetics
    Catholics will not have
    to apologize for.

IX. Putting Idle Land to Use {172} — 1 time

1. The letter "Putting the Land to Use"
    is worth a thousand
    of the panaceas
    and fantastic schemes
    of Upton Sinclair
    Father Coughlin

Dr. Townsend[158]
and the whole bunch
of brainless trustees
who have been telling the President
how to abolish unemployment
and to restore prosperity
by issuing more currency
or by cutting down production.
2. It is what I have been advocating
for nearly fifty years.
3. Give to the people
access to the millions of acres
of vacant land
held out of use by speculators
and the burden
on public relief funds
would be quickly cut down
at least one-half.
4. If the principles
behind this policy
were fully applied
it would altogether
abolish unemployment.

—Bolton Hall
(*Three Acres and Liberty*)

FEBRUARY 1936
IDLE HANDS AND IDLE LANDS

I. Rendering a Great Service {173} — 1 time

1. On my last trip west
I was asked several times
what I thought
of Fr. Coughlin.

---

158. This is a reference to Dr. Francis Townsend (1867–1960).

2. My answer was
    that Fr. Coughlin
    was rendering
    a great service
    by taking from the bankers
    a prestige
    that was not due to them.
3. I was told
    by a Catholic banker
    that this prestige,
    given to the bankers
    by almost everybody,
    did no good
    to the bankers.
4. Bankers knew
    that they did not know
    what it was all about,
    but thanks to Fr. Coughlin
    now everybody knows
    that the bankers
    never did know.

II. Bolton Hall's Panacea {174} — 1 time

1. In the January issue
    reference was made
    "to that whole bunch
    of brainless trustees."
2. I was away
    when the paper was printed
    and was not able
    to correct the proofs.
3. If I had been in New York
    I would have said
    that the last part
    was a quotation
    from a letter

   to the *New York Times*
   by Bolton Hall,
   author of *Three Acres and Liberty*.
 4. Bolton Hall's panacea
   is ruralism
   and I prefer ruralism
   to industrialism.
 5. The industrial revolution
   did not improve things;
   it made them worse.
 6. The industrial revolution
   has given us
   technological unemployment.
 7. And the best way
   to do away
   with technological unemployment
   is to place idle hands
   on idle land.

III. Brainless Trustees {175} — 1 time

 1. It was not through the trust
   in the brains
   of Fr. Coughlin
   that the N.R.A.
   became a flop.
 2. It was through the trust
   in the brains
   "of that whole bunch
   of brainless trustees"
   as Bolton Hall puts it.
 3. According to General Johnson,
   the N.R.A.
   was like a horse
   trying to pull
   in different directions
   and therefore
   had to stand still.

4. That "whole bunch
    of brainless trustees"
    were Pragmatists;
    they were not
    Aristotelians.
5. They would do better to go back
    to Aristotle
    and learn something
    about Philosophy.
6. And when they know something
    about Aristotelian philosophy
    they may become interested
    in Thomistic philosophy
    and Augustinian theology.

APRIL 1936
YES! I AM A RADICAL!

I. Down to the Roots {176} — 1 time

1. I was once thrown out
    of a Knights of Columbus[159] meeting
    because as the K. of C. official said,
    I was radical.
2. I was introduced as a radical
    before the college students
    of a Franciscan college.
3. And the Franciscan Father added
    "I am as radical
    as Peter Maurin."
4. Speaking in a girls' college
    near Saint Cloud, Minnesota,[160]
    I was told by Bishop Busch,

---

159. The Knights of Columbus are a fraternal Catholic service organization. It was originally founded in Connecticut in 1882 as a mutual benefit society for Catholic immigrants. It is now the largest Catholic fraternal organization in the world and focuses on charitable work and Catholic education.

160. This was a reference to the College of Saint Benedict in Joseph, Minnesota.

"Conservatives
are up in a tree
and you are trying
to go down to the roots."

II. Poor Conservatives {177} — 1 time

1. After another meeting
    I was told by a sociologist
    "I still think
    that you are a radical."
2. And I told the sociologist
    "We have to pity
    those poor conservatives
    who don't know
    what to conserve;
    who find themselves
    living in a changing world
    while they do not know
    how to keep it from changing
    or how to change it
    to suit themselves."

III. Radically Wrong {178} — 1 time

1. Monsignor Fulton Sheen says:
    "Modern society is based on greed"
2. Father McGowan[161] says:
    "Modern society
    is based on systematic selfishness."
3. Professor John Dewey says:
    "Modern society
    is based on rugged individualism."
4. When conservatives
    try to conserve a society
    based on greed,
    systematic selfishness

---

161. This was a reference to Rev. Raymond A. McGowan.

and rugged individualism
they try to conserve something
that is radically wrong,
for it is built
on a wrong basis.
5. And when conservatives
try to conserve
what is radically wrong
they are also
radically wrong.

IV. A New Society {179} — 1 time

1. To be radically right
is to go to the roots
by fostering a society
based on creed,
systematic unselfishness
and gentle personalism.
2. To foster a society
based on creed
instead of greed;
on systematic unselfishness
instead of systematic selfishness;
on gentle personalism
instead of rugged individualism,
is to create a new society
within the shell of the old
with the philosophy of the new
which is not
a new philosophy
but a very old philosophy,
a philosophy so old
that it looks like new.

V. Creating Order {180} — 1 time

1. Modern society
is in a state of chaos.

2. And what is chaos
 if not a lack of order?
3. Sociology
 is not a science,
 it is an art,
 the art of creating order
 out of chaos.
4. All Founders of Orders
 made it their personal business
 to try to solve the problems
 of their own day.
5. If Religious Orders
 made it their business
 to try to solve the problems
 of our own day
 by creating order
 out of chaos,
 the Catholic Church
 would be the dominant
 social dynamic force
 in our day and age.

VI. Christ's Message {52}

VII. Franciscan Radicalism {53}

COLONIAL EXPANSION

I. Right or Wrong[162] {181} — 3 times

1. Some people say:
 "My country
 is always right."
2. Some people say:
 "My country
 is always wrong."

---

162. Also known as "Right and Wrong." The words were the same in each version with only minor grammatical changes.

3. Some people say:
    "My country
    is sometimes right
    and sometimes wrong,
    but my country,
    right or wrong."
4. To stick up for one's
    country when one's
    country is wrong
    does not make the
    country right.
5. To stick up for the right
    even when the world is wrong
    is the only way we know of
    to make everything right.

II. Protecting France[163] {182} — 2 times

1. To protect French citizens
    living in Algeria
    the French took Algeria
    from the natives.
2. To protect Algeria
    the French took control
    of Tunisia.
3. To protect Senegal
    the French took Dahomey
    the Gabon and the Congo.
4. To protect the isle of Reunion
    the French took Madagascar.

---

163. The other version of the essay began with, "The French believe in protection," and added the line, "To protect Indo-China they took the Tonkin," after stanza three. Maurin was recounting the history of the second wave of France's colonial empire, which began with the invasion of Algeria in 1830. France obtained the other listed colonies in the latter half of the nineteenth century as the European powers literally divided the African continent among themselves. By the early 1960s, most of the colonies gained their independence.

5. They took Madagascar
   for another reason.
6. The other reason was
   that the English
   wished to take it.
7. When the English
   take something
   the French say
   "the English do that
   because they are grabbers."
8. When the French take something,
   the French say
   "We do that
   because we are
   good patriots."

III. Protecting England[164] {183} — 2 times

1. To protect the British Isles
   the English took the sea.
2. To protect the sea
   the English took Gibraltar,
   Canada and India.
3. To protect India
   the English went to Egypt.
4. To protect Egypt
   the English took the Sudan.
5. To protect the Sudan
   the English forced the French
   to leave Fashoda.

---

164. The other version of the essay from July to August 1940 replaced the last stanza with the following World War II reference: "The English drove the Spanish from the sea and now the Germans are doing their best or their worst to drive the English from the sea." This essay was a basic review of English imperialism from its founding of colonies in North America during the latter half of the sixteenth century to the Agadir Crisis in 1911. Many of the conquests listed were still British colonies when Maurin wrote the essay.

6. To protect the Cape and Natal
    the English took the Transvaal.
7. To protect South Africa
    the English prevented the French
    from giving Agadir
    to Germany.
8. So the English
    are just as good
    or just as bad
    as the French.

IV. Civilizing Ethiopia[165] {184} — 1 time

1. The French believe
    that trade follows the flag.
2. So do the English,
    so do the Germans,
    so do the Japanese,
    so do the Italians.
3. Italy is in Ethiopia
    for the same reason
    that the French
    are in Algeria,
    the English in India,
    the Japanese in Manchuria.
4. The Italians say
    that the Ethiopians
    are not civilized.
5. The last war proves
    that Europeans
    are no more civilized
    than the Africans.

---

165. In this arrangement of essays, Maurin began noting earlier British and French conquests to compare them with the contemporary Italian conquest of Ethiopia and the Japanese conquest of Manchuria. Though there was criticism worldwide against the actions of Italy and Japan, Maurin believed that a critique of imperialism as a whole was missing.

6. So Europeans
    ought to find the way
    to become civilized
    before thinking
    about the best way
    to civilize Africans.

V. League of Nations[166] {185} — 1 time

1. The League of Nations
    did not keep Japan
    from going to Manchuria
    or Italy
    from going to Ethiopia.
2. The League of Nations
    is not a League
    based on right.
3. It is a League
    based on might.
4. It is not a protection
    for poor nations
    against rich nations.
5. It is a protection
    for rich nations
    against poor nations.

VI. Moral Disarmament {186} — 1 time

1. Theodore Roosevelt used to say:
    "If you want peace
    prepare for war."

---

166. The League of Nations formed after World War I to prevent another world war. It failed in preventing World War II, and numerous factors prevented its effectiveness from the start. These included the refusal of the United States to join, the League's initial refusal to permit the membership of the Soviet Union, and the dependency of the League's enforcement of decisions on the victorious armies of the First World War (i.e., France, Italy, Britain, and Japan). The last point played a pivotal role in the League's favoring of wealthier nations that possessed military might.

2. So everybody prepared for war
    but war preparations
    did not bring peace;
    they brought war.
3. Since war preparations
    brought war,
    why not quit
    preparing for war.
4. If nations prepared for peace
    instead of preparing for war,
    they might have peace.
5. Aristide Briand used to say:
    "The best kind of disarmament
    is the disarmament
    of the heart."
6. The disarmament of Germany
    by the Allies
    was not the product
    of a change of heart
    on the part of the Allies
    toward Germany.

VII. Room Could be Found {187} — 1 time

1. There is too much wheat
    in the United States.
2. There is too much cattle
    in Argentina.
3. There are too many sheep
    in Australia.
4. There are too many Germans
    in Germany,
    too many Italians
    in Italy,
    too many Japanese
    in Japan.
5. Room could be found
    in the United States
    for the Germans,

>   in Argentina
>   for the Italians,
>   in Australia
>   for the Japanese.
> 6. To make room
>   for the Germans, Italians, Japanese
>   is a better way
>   to establish peace
>   than to build
>   more battleships,
>   more submarines
>   and more aeroplanes.

MAY 1936
COMMUNISM OF COMMUNITARIANISM

I. Not Communists {96}

II. Five Definitions {165}

III. They and We {166}

IV. Communitarian Movement {167}

V. The C.P. and C.M. {140}

VI. Big Shots and Little Shots {56}

VII. Capital and Labor {15}

VIII. Selling Their Labor {16}

IX. Farming Communes {94}

FEEDING THE POOR

I. The Fallacy of Saving {38}

II. The Wisdom of Giving {123}

III. Hospitality {23}

IV. At a Sacrifice[167] {188} — 5 times

1. In the first centuries
    of Christianity
    the hungry were fed
    at a personal sacrifice,
    the naked were clothed
    at a personal sacrifice,
    the homeless were sheltered
    at a personal sacrifice.
2. And because the poor
    were fed, clothed and sheltered
    at a personal sacrifice,
    the pagans used to say
    about the Christians
    "See how they love each other."
3. In our own day
    the poor are no longer
    fed, clothed and sheltered
    at a personal sacrifice
    but at the expense
    of the taxpayers.
4. And because the poor
    are no longer
    fed, clothed and sheltered
    at a personal sacrifice
    the pagans say about the Christians
    "See how they pass the buck."

---

167. This essay is also known as "Then and Now," "Primitive Christianity," "Christian Charity," and "First Christians." Some versions concluded with different phrases such as, "See how they pass the buck to the taxpayers" and "See how they pass the buck to the W.P.A." Two of the essays included the following line near or at the end: "Father Arthur Ryan, born in Tipperary, used to call this period of history 'Christian Communism.' But it is a long, long way to Tipperary."

V. Four Million Catholics {189} — 1 time

   1. Four million Catholics
      are fed, clothed and sheltered
      by the politicians
      at the expense
      of the taxpayers.
   2. And those four million Catholics
      are badly fed,
      badly clothed,
      and badly sheltered,
      by the politicians
      at the expense
      of the taxpayers.
   3. And because
      those four million Catholics
      are badly fed,
      badly clothed,
      badly sheltered,
      by the politicians
      at the expense
      of the taxpayers,
      they are indoctrinated
      by the Marxists
      in the Unemployed Councils.

VI. Houses of Hospitality {9}

JUNE 1936
BANKING ON BANKERS

I. God or Mammon {17}

II. Usurers Not Gentlemen {190} — 1 time

   1. When the Canon Law
      and not the Roman Law
      was the Law of the Land,

money lending at interest
was called usury.
2. Usurers were not considered
to be gentlemen
when Canon Law
was the Law of the Land.
3. People could not see
anything gentle
in trying to live
on the sweat
of somebody else's brow
by lending money
at interest
when the Canon Law
was the Law of the Land.

III. Wealth-Producing Maniacs {7}

IV. The Fallacy of Saving {38}

V. When Bankers Rule {78}

VI. Mortgaged {5}

VII. Avoiding Inflation {39}

JULY 1936
RADICAL OF THE RIGHT

I. Shouting a Word {191} — 1 time

Fr. Parsons[168] says:
1. There is
confusion of mind
2. When there is
confusion of mind
someone has only

168. This a reference to Rev. Wilfrid Parsons (1887–1958).

      to shout a word
      and people flock.
3. When Mussolini
      shouted discipline
      people flocked.
4. When Hitler
      shouted restoration
      people flocked.

II. The Right Word {192} — 1 time

1. Mussolini's word is
      discipline.
2. Hitler's word is
      restoration.
3. My word is
      tradition.
4. I am a radical
      of the right.
5. I go right to the right
      because I know
      it is the only way
      not to get left.
6. Sound principles
      are not new;
7. They're very old;
      they are as old
      as eternity.
8. The thing to do
      is to restate
      the never new
      and never old principles
      in the vernacular
      of the man of the street.
9. Then the man on the street
      will do
      what the intellectual

has failed to do;
that is to say,
"do something about it."

III. No Unity of Thought {46}

IV. Philosophy and Sophistry {193} — 1 time

Mortimer Adler says:
1. Modern philosophers
    have not found
    anything new
    since Aristotle.
2. Modern philosophers
    are not philosophers;
    they are sophists.
3. Aristotle
    had to deal
    with sophists
    in his day and age.
4. What Aristotle said
    to the sophists
    of his own day
    could be read
    with profit
    by modern philosophers.

V. The City of God {194} — 1 time

Jacques Maritain says:
1. "There is more in man
    than man."[169]
2. Man was created
    in the image of God;

---

169. The origin of this quote is uncertain. It could be Maurin's translation from a French text or a summary Maurin made regarding an argument by Maritain. The statement is representative of Maritain's anthropology, in which humans have a transcendent orientation and end in God.

therefore
there is the image of God
in man.
3. There is more to life
than life
this side of the grave;
there is life
the other side of the grave.
4. Science leads to biology,
biology to psychology,
psychology to philosophy,
philosophy to theology.
5. Philosophy
is the handmaid
of theology.
6. To build up the city of God,
that is to say,
to express the spiritual
in the material
through the use
of pure means,
such is the task
of professing Christians
in this day and age.

VI. Integral Humanism {195} — 1 time

1. Through the influence
of Maxim Gorky
the Marxists
have come to the conclusion
that Marxists writers
should be more
than proletarian writers;
that they should be
cultural writers.
2. Waldo Frank thinks
that the cultural tradition
must be brought

to the proletarian masses,
who will appreciate it
much more
than the acquisitive classes.
3. What the Marxists
call culture
Maritain calls
Socialist Humanism.
4. But Socialist Humanism
is not all Humanism,
according to Maritain.
5. In a book entitled
L'Humanisme Intégral[170]
Jacques Maritain points out
what differentiates
Integral Humanism
from Socialist Humanism.

VII. Thought and Action {196} — 1 time

1. Integral Humanism
is the Humanism
of the Radicals of the Right.
2. The Radicals of the Left
are now talking about
Cultural Tradition.
3. The bourgeois idea is
that culture
is related to leisure.
4. Eric Gill maintains
that culture
is related to work,
not to leisure.
5. Man is saved through faith
and through works,
and what one does
has a lot to do
with what one is.

---

170. This book was later translated into English under the title *Integral Humanism*.

6. Thought and action
 must be combined.
7. When thought
 is separated from action
 it becomes academic.
8. When thought
 is related to action
 it becomes dynamic.

AUGUST 1936
GO-GETTERS VS. GO-GIVERS

I. Two Bourgeois {197} — 1 time

1. The bourgeois capitalist
 believes in rugged individualism;
2. The Bolshevist socialist
 believes in rugged collectivism.
3. There is no difference
 between the rugged individualism
 of bourgeois capitalism
 and the rugged collectivism
 of Bolshevist socialism.
4. The bourgeois capitalist
 tries to keep
 what he has,
 and tries to get
 what the other fellow has.
5. The Bolshevist socialist
 tries to get
 what the bourgeois capitalist has.
6. The Bolshevist socialist
 is the son
 of the bourgeois capitalist.
7. And the son
 is too much
 like his father.

8. All the sins of the father
   are found in the son.

II. Bourgeois Capitalist {198} — 1 time

1. The bourgeois capitalist
   calls himself conservative
   but has failed to conserve
   our cultural tradition.
2. He thinks that culture
   is related to leisure.
3. He does not think that culture
   is related to cult
   and to cultivation.
4. He believes in power,
   and that money
   is the way to power.
5. He believes that money
   can buy everything,
   whether it be labor or brains.
6. But as the poet Emerson says,
   "People have only
   the power we give them."[171]
7. When people will cease
   selling their labor power
   or their brain power
   to the bourgeois capitalist,
   the bourgeois capitalist
   will cease being
   a gentleman of leisure
   and begin being
   a cultured gentleman.

---

171. For the probable source of this quote, see the biographical glossary entry on Emerson.

III. Bolshevist Socialist {199} — 1 time

1. The Bolshevist socialist
    is the spiritual son
    of the bourgeois capitalist;
2. He credits bourgeois capitalism
    with an historic mission
    and fails to condemn it
    on general principles.
3. The bourgeois socialist
    does not believe
    in the profit system,
    but he does believe
    in the wage system.
4. The bourgeois capitalist
    and his spiritual son,
    the Bolshevist socialist,
    believe in getting
    all they can get
    and not in giving
    all they can give.
5. The bourgeois capitalist
    and his spiritual son,
    the Bolshevist socialist,
    are go-getters,
    not go-givers.

IV. Personalist Communitarian {200} — 1 time

1. A personalist
    is a go-giver,
    not a go-getter.
2. He tries to give
    what he has,
    and does not
    try to get
    what the other fellow has.

3. He tries to be good
    by doing good
    to the other fellow.
4. He is altro-centered,
    not self-centered.
5. He has a social doctrine
    of the common good
6. He spreads the social doctrine
    of the common good
    through words and deeds.
7. He speaks through deeds
    as well as words,
    for he know that deeds
    speak louder than words.
8. Through words and deeds
    he brings into existence
    a common unity,
    the common unity
    of a community.

V. Community Spirit {201} — 1 time

1. Communitarianism
    is the rediscovery
    and the exemplification
    of what the Kiwanis
    and Rotarians
    used to talk about,
    namely,
    the community Spirit.
2. The community spirit
    is no more common
    than common sense
    is common.
3. Everybody knows
    that common sense
    is not common,

but nobody believes
   that common sense
   should not be common.
4. The community spirit
   should be common
   as well as common sense
   should be common.
5. If common sense was common,
   Bolshevist socialists
   would not be
   rugged collectivists;
   they would be
   communitarian personalists.

VI. Franciscans and Jesuits {202} — 1 time

1. Franciscans and Jesuits
   believe in the community spirit
   just as much
   as Kiwanis and Rotarians.
2. While Kiwanis and Rotarians
   used to talk about the common spirit,
   Franciscans and Jesuits
   did something about it.
3. Kiwanis and Rotarians
   used to talk
   about service,
   but never forgot
   profitable service.
4. Franciscans and Jesuits
   may not say much
   about service,
   but continue to render
   unprofitable service.
5. Franciscans and Jesuits
   believe in the responsibility
   of private property

but they believe also
in the practicality
of voluntary poverty.

VII. Counsels of the Gospel[172] {203} — 1 time

1. Someone said
    that THE CATHOLIC WORKER
    is taking monasticism
    out of the monasteries.
2. The Counsels of the Gospel
    are for everybody,
    not only for monks.
3. Franciscans and Jesuits
    are not monks.
4. Franciscans are Friars,
    and the world is their monastery.
5. Jesuits are the storm troops
    of the Catholic Church,
    and ready to be sent
    where the Holy Father
    wishes to send them.
6. The Counsels of the Gospel
    are for everybody,
    and if everybody
    tried to live up to it
    we would bring order
    out of chaos,
    and Chesterton would not have said
    that Christianity
    has not been tried.

---

172. The counsels of the Gospel, or the evangelical counsels, refer to the three vows taken by those entering religious orders: chastity, poverty, and obedience. Traditionally, Catholic theology has viewed these Gospel-inspired counsels as not necessary for salvation, but as voluntary practices for those wishing to obtain Christian perfection. Maurin and Day critiqued minimalist visions of Christianity that judged the counsels as unnecessary and advocated a maximalist vision in which all strived for Christian perfection.

SEPTEMBER 1936
COMMUNITARIAN PERSONALISM

I. They and We {166}

II. Basic Power {204} — 1 time
1. Bourgeois Capitalism
    is based on the power
    of hiring and firing.
2. Fascist Corporatism
    and Bolshevist Socialism
    are based on the power
    of life and death.
3. Communitarian Personalism
    is based on the power
    of thought and example.

III. Thinking Individual {205} — 1 time
1. Thinking is individual,
    not collective.
2. Fifty million Frenchmen
    may be wrong,
    while one Frenchman
    may be right.
3. One thinks
    better than two,
    and two
    better than two hundred.
4. The national thinking
    of Benito Mussolini,
    the racial thinking
    of Adolph Hitler,
    and the mass thinking
    of Joseph Stalin
    are not what I mean
    by thinking.
5. Read *The Crowd*,
    by Gustave Le Bon.

IV. Social Power {206} — 1 time

1. Social power
    is more important
    than political power.
2. And political power
    is not the road
    to social power.
3. The road to social power
    is the right use
    of liberty.
4. Read *Our Enemy the State*
    by Albert J. Nock.

V. Give Me Liberty {207} — 1 time

1. Patrick Henry said,
    "Give me liberty,
    or give me death!"
2. What makes man
    a man
    is the right use
    of liberty.
3. The rugged individualists
    of the Liberty League,
    the strong-arm men
    of the Fascist State,
    and the rugged collectivists
    of the Communist Party
    have not yet learned
    the right use
    of liberty.
4. Read *Freedom in the Modern World*,
    by Jacques Maritain.

VI. Leadership {208} — 1 time

1. Everybody
    looks for a leader
    and nobody
    likes to be dictated to.

2. Mussolini, Hitler, and Stalin
    try to be at the same time
    leaders and dictators.
3. A leader is a fellow
    who follows a cause
    in words and deeds.
4. A follower is a fellow
    who follows the leader
    because he sponsors the cause
    that the leader follows.
5. Read *Leadership or Domination*,
    by Paul Pigors.
6. Paul Pigors
    makes a case for domination
    in times of crisis,
    and in this he is wrong.
7. Domination is not the way
    to create order
    out of chaos.
8. Leadership is always the way
    to create order
    out of chaos.

VII. Communitarian Personalism {209} — 1 time

1. "A man is a man
    for all of that,"
    says Robert Burns.
2. To bring out
    that man in man,
    such is the purpose
    of the Communitarian Movement.
3. A Communitarian is a fellow
    who refuses to be
    what the other fellow is,
    and chooses to be
    what he wants
    the other fellow
    to be.

4. Read *Easy Essays*,[173]
by Peter Maurin.

VIII. The Forgotten Man {60}

IX. Bourgeois Slogans {64}

OCTOBER 1936
SUPERFLUOUS GOODS

I. The Problem of Today {210} — 1 time

1. General Johnson says
    that the problem of today
    is not to increase
    producing power,
    but to increase
    consuming power.
2. Saving to invest
    is considered
    a bourgeois virtue,
    while spending to consume
    is considered
    a bourgeois vice.
3. While the thrifty bourgeois
    increases the producing power
    the bourgeois spendthrift
    increases the consuming power.

II. With Our Superfluous Goods {211} — 1 time

1. Bishop von Ketteler says
    that we are bound
    under the pain of mortal sin
    to relieve the extreme needs

---

173. When this essay was published, Maurin had recently published his first collection of essays in book form: Peter Maurin, *Easy Essays* (New York: Sheed & Ward, 1936).

of our needy brother
with our superfluous goods.
2. With our superfluous goods
we build white elephants
like the Empire State Building.
3. With our superfluous goods
we build power houses
which increase the producing power
and therefore
increase unemployment.
4. With our superfluous goods
we build colleges
which turn out students
into a changing world
without telling them
how to keep it from changing
or how to change it
to suit college graduates.

III. The Wisdom of Giving {123}

IV. Ambassadors of God {212} — 1 time

1. What we give to the poor
for Christ's sake
is what we carry with us
when we die.
2. We are afraid
to pauperize the poor
because we are afraid
to be poor.
3. Pagan Greeks used to say
that the poor
"are the ambassadors
of the gods."
4. To become poor
is to become
an Ambassador of God.

V. We Seem to Think {213} — 1 time}

1. St. Francis thought
    that to choose to be poor
    is just as good
    as if one should marry
    the most beautiful girl in the world.
2. We seem to think
    that poor people
    are social nuisances
    and not the Ambassadors of God.
3. We seem to think
    that Lady Poverty
    is an ugly girl
    and not the beautiful girl
    that St. Francis of Assisi
    says she is.
4. And because we think so,
    we refuse to feed the poor
    with our superfluous goods
    and let the politicians
    feed the poor
    by going around
    like pickpockets,
    robbing Peter
    to pay Paul,
    and feeding the poor
    by soaking the rich.

VI. If {214} — 1 time

1. If Spanish Catholics
    had fed the poor
    with their superfluous goods,
    the Reds would not now
    want to relieve them
    of their superfluous goods.
2. If American Catholics
    were building churches
    in rural districts

with their superfluous goods
they would increase
the consuming power
and make an impression
on the depression
through the expression
of their Catholic faith.

VII. The Stuff and the Push {215} — 1 time

1. I was in a cafeteria
    in Greenwich Village.
2. Two young fellows
    were talking.
3. One said to the other,
    "Your father has the stuff,
    but he hasn't the push."
4. And the other said:
    "And I have the push,
    but not the stuff."
5. The father had the stuff,
    but he could not push it,
    and the son had the push,
    but he had nothing to push.
6. Catholic journalists
    have the stuff,
    but do not have the push,
    and non-Catholic journalists
    have the push,
    but do not have the stuff.

VIII. Blowing the Dynamite {3}

HOUSES OF HOSPITALITY {216} — 1 time

1. The Pagan Greeks thought
    that people in need
    are the ambassadors
    of the gods.

2. A House of Hospitality
    is a house where the guests
    are considered
    as the Ambassadors of God.
3. The Ambassadors of God
    must not be
    bossed or bounced.
4. It is a privilege
    for Catholic workers
    to be of service
    to the Ambassadors of God
    in a House of Hospitality.
5. The Ambassadors of God
    are obliged
    to adjust themselves
    to our ways.
6. The Ambassadors of God
    are not saints
    but they give us
    the opportunity
    to become saints
    by serving them
    for Christ's sake.

OPEN LETTER TO FATHER LORD, S.J.[174] {217} — 1 time

Dear Father:
1. We are living
    in a period of chaos.
2. Our task must be
    to create order
    out of chaos.
3. Creating order
    out of chaos
    ought to be the task
    of religious orders.

---

174. In some collected editions, this essay is referred to as "Fourth Open Letter to Fr. Lord, S.J."

4. The Jesuit Order
   would do well
   to open up
   Houses of Hospitality
   for the benefit
   of all college graduates,
   non-Catholics,
   as well as Catholics.
5. In those Houses of Hospitality
   unemployed college graduates
   would be given
   an historical background.
6. Professor Carlton Hayes says
   that our religion
   is the only
   historical religion.
7. A Catholic historical background
   given the unemployed
   college graduates
   in Houses of Hospitality
   would be
   the best antidote
   to Marxist materialism.
8. It ought also to be
   that kind of historical background
   that would make them
   Co-operators
   or Guildists
   or Distributists
   or Communitarians.
9. It would make them
   look up to the individual,
   not to the State,
   for the solution
   of social problems.

—Yours for the Green Revolution,
Peter Maurin

NOVEMBER 1936
THE PLURALIST STATE

I. Secularism Is a Pest {22}

II. Liberals Not Liberators {13}

III. The Age of Treason {14}

IV. Utilitarian Thought {218} — 1 time

1. When English philosophers
    broke away
    from Medieval thought
    they formulated
    what is called
    a utilitarian philosophy.[175]
2. Locke, Hobbes and Hume,
    the utilitarian philosophers,
    had for disciples
    the futilitarian economists
    of the Manchester School.[176]
3. Since the advent
    of the Manchester School,
    the School of Laissez Faire,
    religion has nothing to do

---

175. Utilitarianism is a philosophy that is consequentialist. One of its modern founders, Jeremy Bentham (1748–1832), wrote, "It is the greatest happiness of the greatest number that is the measure of right and wrong." Maurin was critical of utilitarian philosophy for separating divine revelation from morality. In this essay, Maurin made a tendentious claim that Locke, Hobbes, and Hume were utilitarians even though they all died before the term was coined and held views that were distinct from utilitarianism (and from one another). It may be fair to say that all three of them, plus the real utilitarians, tried to find philosophical truth without a transcendent reference point, and this was Maurin's complaint. In the next essay, Maurin referred to futilitarian economics, which he believed carried utilitarianism's harmful separation to its futile conclusion in economics.

176. "The Manchester School" is a term for the political, economic, and social movements that emerged in the nineteenth century with a group of businessmen in Manchester, England. Building on the economic theories of Adam Smith, this group was known for advocating free trade, laissez-faire government policies in economics, and the separation of church and state.

with political economy
because political economy
has nothing to do
with social ethics.

V. Futilitarian Economics {219} — 1 time

1. The Futilitarian Economists
of the Manchester School
thought that the general interest
of human society
would be well served
if everybody
was always mindful
of his material interest.
2. The Futilitarian Economists
of the Manchester School
thought that everything
would be lovely
if everybody took in
each other's washing.
3. The Futilitarian Economists
of the Manchester School
believed in the law
of supply and demand
and could never conceive
of the possibility
of too much supply
and not enough demand.

VI. Futilitarian States {220} — 1 time

1. The Futilitarian Economists
of the Manchester School
thought that business
is just business
and that politics
should keep out of business.

2. The Futilitarian Economists
   of the Manchester School
   thought that the State
   is only useful
   when it helps business men
   to collect their debts.
3. The war of 1914
   and the peace of 1919
   are the logical result
   of the foolish notions
   of the Futilitarian Economists
   of the Manchester School.
4. England, France and America,
   our Futilitarian States,
   are now busy
   trying to solve the problems
   brought about
   by the lack of understanding
   of the Futilitarian Economists
   of the Manchester School.

VII. Totalitarian States {221} — 1 time

1. England, France and America
   think they can muddle through
   with their eighteenth-century politics.
2. Russia, Italy and Germany
   have given up the idea
   of two, three or more
   political parties
   and have adopted the idea
   of one political party.
3. In the Futilitarian States
   everybody is told
   "Mind your own business."
4. In the Totalitarian States
   everybody is told
   "Do what we tell you

or out you go
to the Concentration Camp."

VIII. Pluralist Thought {222} — 1 time

1. Humanists believe
    with Robert Burns
    that "a man is a man
    for all of that."
2. Theists believe
    that God created the world,
    that He is our Father,
    and that we are all brothers.
3. Protestants believe
    that God, our Father,
    sent His only begotten Son
    to save the world
    from sin.
4. Catholics believe
    that Jesus Christ
    established a Church,
    and that this Church
    is the Catholic Church.
5. Humanists
    are just Humanists.
6. Theists are Humanists
    plus Theists.
7. Protestants are Humanists
    plus Theists
    plus Christians.
8. Catholics are Humanists
    plus Theists
    plus Christians
    plus Catholics.

IX. Pluralist State {223} — 1 time

1. The belief in the human personality
    is the common belief

of Humanists, Theists,
Protestants, Catholics.
2. On this common belief
of human personality
Humanists, Theists,
Protestants, Catholics,
could very well build up
a Pluralist State.
3. Futilitarian States
as well as Totalitarian States
are not based
on the cultural tradition
of the Western World.
4. The Pluralist State
is a State
where Humanists
try to be human;
Orthodox Jews
try to be Jews;
Christian Protestants
try to be Christians,
and Catholics
try to be Catholics.

X. Allied Techniques {224} — 1 time

1. Social movements
based on personal responsibility
are not hindered
by the Pluralist State.
2. The Cooperative Movement,
the Guildist Movement,
the Agrarian Movement,
the Communitarian Movement,
find themselves at home
in the Pluralist State.
3. The Pluralist State
does not try
to solve the social problem

by passing laws
or creating bureaus,
but by removing
from the Statute Book
all the laws
that hinder the activities
of the social movements
based on personal responsibility.
4. The Pluralist State
stands for leadership,
not dictatorship.

DECEMBER 1936
BACK TO NEWMANISM

I. No Recourse {132}

II. Politics vs. Politics {20}

III. Business Is Business {11}

IV. Bourgeois Slogans {64}

V. Teachers of Subjects {12}

VI. Not My Subject {44}

VII. THE N.R.A. {163}

VIII. Unity of Thought {46}

IX. About Textbooks {225} — 1 time

President Hutchins of the University
of Chicago says:
1. "How can we call
a man educated
who has never read
any of the great books
of the Western World?

2. "Yet today,
    it is entirely possible
    for a student
    to graduate
    from the finest
    American colleges
    without having read
    any of them
    except perhaps Shakespeare.
3. "Of course the student
    may have heard of these books
    or at least
    of their authors.
4. "But this knowledge
    is gained in general
    through textbooks.
5. "And the textbooks have probably
    done as much
    to degrade American intelligence
    as any single force."[177]

X. It Must Be Used {226} — 1 time

Cardinal Newman says:
1. "If the intellect
    is a good thing,
    then its cultivation
    is an excellent thing.
2. "It must be cultivated
    not only as a good thing,
    but as a useful thing.
3. "It must not be useful
    in any low,
    mechanical,
    material sense.

---

177. The quote is from Robert Maynard Hutchins, *The Higher Learning in America* (New Haven: Yale University, 1936), 78.

4. "It must be useful
       in the spreading
       of goodness.
5. "It must be used
       by the owner
       for the good
       of himself
       and for the good
       of the world."[178]

JANUARY 1937
OUTDOOR UNIVERSITIES

I. Scholar and Bourgeois {45} [part 1]

II. Scholar and Worker {45} [part 2]

III. On to the Street {227} — 1 time

1. Fr. Bede Jarrett says:
       "The truths of a generation
       become the platitudes
       of the next generation."
2. Henrik Ibsen says:
       "Thought must be rewritten
       every twenty years."
3. That is to say
       eternal principles
       must at all times
       be presented
       in the vernacular
       of the man on the street.
4. Emerson says
       that the way
       to acquire the vernacular

---

178. The quote was a paraphrase from Newman's 1852 book *Discourses on the Scope and Nature of University Education*, Discourse Eight. This quote was also in Robert Maynard Hutchins, *Higher Learning in America*, 63–64.

of the man of the street
is to go to the street
and listen
to the man of the street.[179]
5. The way to become dynamic
and cease to be academic
is to rub shoulders
with the men on the street.

IV. What the Unemployed Need {10}

V. Professors of an Outdoor University {93}

VI. Laborers of an Outdoor University {94}

VII. Hands and Heads {228} — 1 time

1. Someone said
    that the Catholic Worker
    is a movement
    for down-and-outs.
2. And it is a movement
    for down-and-outs,
    including
    down-and-out business men,
    down-and-out college graduates,
    and down-and-out college professors.
3. In the Catholic Worker
    besides being fed,
    clothed and sheltered,
    people learn
    to use their hands
    as well as their heads.
4. And while they learn
    to use their heads
    to guide their hands,

---

179. For the likely source of this quote, see the biographical glossary entry on Emerson.

>   the use of their hands,
>   improves a great deal
>   the working of their heads.

VIII. Silver Springs {229} — 1 time

1. In Silver Springs
    a few miles
    from Washington, D. C.,
    the Missionaries
    of the Holy Trinity
    combine manual labor
    with intellectual pursuits.
2. They go to the Catholic University
    in the morning,
    build their own campus
    or cultivate their land
    in the afternoon
    and do their homework
    in the evening.
3. While they do manual labor
    their mind is taken off
    their studies,
    which is to the benefit
    both of their health
    and their studies.
4. In Silver Springs
    scholars
    try to be workers
    and workers
    try to be scholars.

IX. Three Books[180] {230} — 1 time

1. The machine
    is not an improvement
    on man's skill;

---

180. Normally, book lists are not counted as Easy Essays, but this book list included commentary.

it is an imitation
of man's skill.
2. Read *Post-Industrialism*
by Arthur Penty.
3. The best means
are the pure means
and the pure means
are the heroic means.
4. Read *Freedom
in the Modern World*
by Jacques Maritain.
5. The future of the Church
is on the land,
not in the city;
for a child
is an asset
on the land
and a liability
in the city.
6. Read *The Church
and the Land*
by Fr. Vincent McNabb, O.P.

SO-CALLED COMMUNISTS
(Written for Bolshevik Socialists)

I. Bolshevik Socialists {96}

II. In Bolshevik Russia {231} — 1 time

1. The State withers away
in a Communist society,
but the State
has not withered away
in Bolshevik Russia.
2. There is no wage system
in a Communist society,
but there is a wage system
in Bolshevik Russia.

3. There is no dictatorship
    in a Communist society,
    but there is a dictatorship
    in Bolshevik Russia.
4. There is no investing class
    in a Communist society,
    but they sell Government bonds
    in Bolshevik Russia.

III. Economic Determinism {232} — 1 time

1. Bolshevik Socialists
    stand for economic determinism.
2. According to the theory
    of economic determinism,
    Bourgeois Capitalism
    creates Bourgeois ideology
    and Bolshevik Socialism
    creates Bolshevik ideology.
3. According to the same theory,
    Bolshevik ideology
    can never be the product
    of Bourgeois Capitalism.
4. But Marx and Lenin
    expressed Bolshevik ideology
    while living
    under Bourgeois Capitalism.
5. Marx and Lenin
    must be a mystery
    to Bolshevik Socialists.

IV. Class Struggle[181] {233} — 2 times

1. Bolshevik Socialists
    credit Bourgeois Capitalism
    with an historical mission.

---

181. The other occurrence of the essay was abridged.

2. If Bourgeois Capitalism
    fulfills an historical mission,
    it should not be
    interfered with
    in the fulfilling
    of that historical mission.
3. When Bolshevik Socialists
    foster the class-struggle,
    they delay the fulfilling
    of the historical mission
    which they credit
    to Bourgeois Capitalism.
4. There is no sense
    in delaying the fulfilling
    of the historical mission
    of Bourgeois Capitalism
    by throwing the monkey-wrench
    of class-struggle
    into the economic machinery.

V. Proletarian Dictatorship {234} — 1 time

1. Bolshevik Socialists
    stand for proletarian dictatorship.
2. A bourgeois without money
    may be as bourgeois
    as a bourgeois with money.
3. The bourgeois-minded
    proletarian
    and the bourgeois-minded
    capitalist
    are spiritually related.
4. The bourgeois-minded
    proletarian
    is a chip off the old block—
    the bourgeois-minded
    capitalist.

5. All the sins of the father—
        the bourgeois-minded
        capitalist—
        are found in the son—
        the bourgeois-minded
        proletarian.
   6. The bourgeois-minded
        proletarian
        is no more fit to rule
        than the bourgeois-minded
        capitalist.
   7. Proletarian dictatorship
        as well as
        capitalist dictatorship,
        are no substitutes
        for personalist leadership.

VI. Personalist Leadership[182] {235} — 1 time

   1. A Leader is a fellow
        who follows a cause.
   2. A Follower is a fellow
        who follows the Leader,
        because he sponsors the cause
        that the Leader follows.
   3. Thought must be expressed
        in words and deeds,
        and deeds speak
        louder than words.
   4. To be a Leader
        requires thought
        as well as technique.
   5. The thought must appeal to reason,
        and the technique
        must be related to the thought.

VII. The Catholic Worker {140}

182. There are two stanzas in this essay that are like essay {208}, but it is otherwise quite different.

FEBRUARY 1937
EASY ESSAYS

This essay appeared in *The Record*, the student paper of St. John's University, Collegeville, Minnesota. *The Record* has just celebrated its fiftieth anniversary.

I. The Thinking Man's Journalist[183] {236} — 2 times

1. Mark Hanna used to say,
    "When a dog
    bites a man,
    it is not news;
    but when a man
    bites a dog,
    it is news."
2. To let everybody know
    that a man
    has bitten a dog
    is not good news;
    it is bad news.
3. To tell everybody
    that a man died
    leaving two million dollars,
    may be journalism,
    but it is not
    good journalism.
4. But to tell everybody
    that the man died
    leaving two million dollars
    because he did not know
    how to take them with him
    by giving them to the poor
    for Christ's sake
    during his lifetime
    is good journalism.

---

183. Also known as "Journalism: Good and Bad." The other instance of the essay contained minor changes in phrasing, but was essentially the same.

5. Good journalism
    is to give the news
    and the right comment
    on the news.
6. The value of journalism
    is the value of the comment
    given with the news.
7. To be a good journalist
    is to say something interesting
    about interesting things
    or interesting people.
8. The news is the occasion
    for the journalist
    to convey his thinking
    to unthinking people.
9. Nothing can be done
    without public opinion,
    and the opinion
    of thinking people
    who know how
    to transmit their thinking
    to unthinking people.
10. A diary is a journal
    where a thinking man
    records his thinking.
11. The *Journal Intime*,
    of Frederic Amiel
    is the record of the thinking
    of Frederic Amiel.
12. The thinking journalist
    imparts his thinking
    through a newspaper
    by relating his thinking
    to the news of the day.
13. By relating his thinking
    to the news of the day,
    the thinking journalist
    affects public opinion.

14. By affecting public opinion,
    the thinking journalist
    is a creative agent
    in the making of news
    that is fit to print.
15. The thinking journalist
    is not satisfied
    to be just a recorder
    of modern history.
16. The thinking journalist
    aims to be a maker
    of that kind of history
    that is worth recording.

MARCH 1937
CAESARISM OR PERSONALISM

I. Caesar or God {237} — 1 time

1. Christ says:
    "Render to Caesar
    the things that are Caesar's
    and to God
    the things that are God's."[184]
2. The Fascist Caesar,
    the Nazi Caesar,
    the Bolshevik Caesar

---

184. This quote, attributed to Jesus, is found in the Gospels of Matthew, Mark, and Luke. In each telling of the story, Jesus is asked if it is lawful to pay taxes to the Roman government. Jesus asks that a coin be brought forward. Noting that the coin has the likeness and inscription of Caesar, Jesus tells them, "Render to Caesar the things that are Caesar's and to God the things that are God's." This passage has traditionally been interpreted as noting the different responsibilities that a person has for God and country. Some biblical scholars have observed that people are made in the likeness of God (Genesis 1) and have God's law inscribed on their hearts (Jeremiah 31:33). Therefore, while the likeness and inscription on the coin denote it as Caesar's property, the likeness and inscription on the human person denote that we belong to God and that our duty to God supersedes our duty to the state.

are not satisfied
with the things
that are Caesar's;
they also want
the things that are God's.
3. When Caesar sets up a claim
to the things that are God's
he sets himself up
as God.
4. And when Caesar
sets himself up as a god
he sets himself up
as a faker.
5. When Caesar
sets himself up as a faker
he should be denounced
as a faker.

II. Fascist Caesar {238} — 1 time

1. The Fascist Caesar
claims that the child
belongs to the state.
2. The child does not belong
to the state;
it belongs
to the parents.
3. The child
was given by God
to the parents;
he was not
given by God
to the state
4. The parents
must teach the child
to serve God,
from whom
they received the child.

5. When the parents
    allow the state
    to grab the child
    and to act
    toward the child
    as if God
    did not matter
    they lose their claim
    to the allegiance
    of the child.

III. The Nazi Caesar {239} — 1 time

1. The Nazi Caesar
    claims that there are
    superior races
    and inferior races.
2. The superior race
    is always the one
    one happens to belong to.
3. The inferior race
    is always the one
    that refuses to recognize
    that superiority
    and claims to be
    the superior race.
4. If a race is superior
    to another race
    then the extermination
    of the inferior race
    is the moral duty
    of the superior race.
5. The superior race
    tries to believe
    that God works
    through the superior race.
6. The superior race
    conceives God
    as a racial god.

IV. The Bolshevik Caesar {240} — 1 time

1. The Bolshevik Caesar
    says that there is no God,
    but that there is
    a messianic class.
2. And that the working class
    needs to be guided
    by those who are aware
    of the messianic mission
    of the working class.
3. The Communist Party
    claims to be the guide
    of the working class
    in the fulfilling
    of its messianic mission.
4. Those who contest
    the superior wisdom
    of the master minds.
    of the Communist Party
    are considered
    as the enemies
    of the Bolshevik revolution.
5. Many old-timers
    in the Bolshevik movement
    are now considered
    the worst enemies
    of the Bolshevik revolution.

V. Three Definitions {165}

VI. They and We {166}

VII. The Use of Liberty[185] {241} — 1 time

1. Patrick Henry said:
    "Give me liberty
    or give me death."

---

185. This essay begins the same as {207}, but then diverges significantly.

2. Liberty is a great thing,
    but few people
    know how to use it.
3. Some use liberty
    to become
    rugged individualists.
4. Some would like to be
    rugged individualists,
    but don't know how,
    and choose to be
    rugged collectivists.
5. Some use liberty
    by serving their fellowmen
    for God's sake.
6. Some are moved by greed,
    some are moved by grudge,
    and some are moved by creed.

VIII. Modern Education {242} — 1 time

1. Thomas Jefferson says:
    "The less government there is
    the better it is."
2. If the less government there is
    the better it is,
    then the best kind of government
    is self-government.
3. To teach people
    to govern themselves,
    such is the purpose
    of education.
4. If we are threatened
    with Caesarism
    it is because educators
    have failed
    to educate.
5. Modern educators
    do not educate
    because they lack
    unity of thought.

6. Modern educators
    ought to read
    Maritain's book,
    Freedom in the Modern World.

IX. What Makes Man Human {86}

APRIL 1937
THE SIT-DOWN TECHNIQUE

I. On Gandhi Lines {243} — 1 time

1. Strike news
    doesn't strike me,
    but the sit-down strike
    is a different strike
    from the ordinary strike.
2. In the sit-down strike
    you don't strike anybody
    either on the jaw
    or under the belt,
    you just sit down.
3. The sit-down strike
    is essentially
    a peaceful strike.
4. If the sit-down strike
    remains a sit-down strike,
    that is to say,
    a strike in which you strike
    by just sitting down,
    it may be a means
    of bringing about
    desirable results.
5. The sit-down strike
    must be conducted
    on Gandhi lines,
    that is to say,

according to the doctrine
of pure means
as expressed by Jacques Maritain.

II. In the Middle Ages {244} — 1 time

1. The capitalist system
    is a racketeering system.
2. It is a racketeering system
    because it is
    a profiteering system.
3. It is a profiteering system
    because it is
    a profit system.
4. And nobody
    has found the way
    to keep the profit system
    from becoming
    a profiteering system.
5. Harold Laski says:
    "In the Middle Ages
    the idea of acquiring wealth
    was limited
    by a body of moral rules
    imposed under the sanction
    of religious authority."[186]
6. But modern business men
    tell the clergy:
    "Mind your own business
    and don't butt into our business."

III. Economic Economy {245} — 1 time

1. In the Middle Ages
    they had a doctrine,
    the doctrine
    of the Common Good.

186. The quote is from Harold Laski, *The Rise of European Liberalism: An Essay in Interpretation* (1936; repr. Delhi: Aakar, 2005), 22.

2. In the Middle Ages
> they had an economy
> which was economical.
3. Their economy
> was based on the idea
> that God wants us
> to be our brothers' keepers.
4. They believed
> in the right to work
> for the worker.
5. They believed
> in being fair
> to the worker
> as well as the consumer.
6. They believed
> in doing their work
> the best they knew how
> for the service
> of God and men.

IV. Proper Property {246} — 1 time

1. Léon Harmel,
> who was an employer,
> not a labor leader,
> says: "We have lost
> the right concept of authority
> since the Renaissance."[187]
2. We have not only lost
> the right concept of authority,
> we have also lost
> the right concept
> of property.
3. The use of property
> to acquire more property

---

187. The source of this quote is uncertain. Since Harmel was French, it is likely that Maurin translated it from a French source.

is not the proper use
of property.
4. The right use of property
is to enable the worker
to do his work
more effectively.
5. The right use of property
is not to compel the worker,
under threat of unemployment,
to be a cog in the wheel
of mass production.

V. Speed-Up System {247} — 1 time

1. Bourgeois capitalists
believe in the law
of supply and demand.
2. Through mass production,
bourgeois capitalists
increase the supply
and decrease the demand.
3. The speed-up system
and the extensive use
of improved machinery
has given us
technological unemployment.
4. As a Catholic worker
said to me:
"Ford speeds us up,
making us do
in one day
three times as much work
as before,
then he lays us off."
5. To speed up the workers
and then lay them off
is to deny the worker
the right to work.

VI. Makers of Depressions {132}

VII. Collective Bargaining {248} — 1 time

1. Business men
    have made
    such a mess of things
    without workers' cooperation
    that they could do no worse
    with workers' cooperation.
2. Because the workers
    want to cooperate
    with the business men
    in the running of business
    is the reason why
    they sit down.
3. The sit-down strike
    is for the worker
    the means of bringing about
    collective bargaining.
4. Collective bargaining
    should lead
    to compulsory arbitration.
5. Collective bargaining
    and compulsory arbitration
    will assure the worker
    the right to work.

VIII. In the Rumble Seat[188] {249} — 1 time

1. There is nothing wrong
    with the sit-down strike
    if it is used to bring about
    collective bargaining.

---

188. The rumble seat was the compartment on pre–World War II cars that opened out of the rear where most cars today have trunks. The seat was exposed to the elements and was often used for servants. It was also called the dicky seat or the mother-in-law seat.

2. The aim of the N.R.A.
      was to bring about
      collective bargaining
      but, as Father Parsons said:
      "The N.R.A.
      made the mistake
      of placing labor
      in the rumble seat."
3. Labor must sit
      in the driver's seat—
      not in the rumble seat.
4. Bourgeois capitalists
      are not such good drivers
      as to be able to drive
      without the cooperation
      of organized labor.

IX. The Modern Mind {250} — 1 time

1. Organized labor,
      whether it be
      the A.F. of L.
      or the C.I.O.,[189]
      is far from knowing
      what to do
      with the economic setup.
2. Organized labor,
      as well as
      organized capital,
      is the product
      of the modern mind.

---

189. The American Federation of Labor and the Congress of Industrial Organizations were both federations of labor unions that were very prominent during the 1930s. The AFL organized workers by specific trades (e.g., carpenters, bricklayers, etc.), and the CIO organized entire industries (e.g., autoworkers, mine workers, etc.). In 1955, they merged and became the AFL-CIO, which still exists today. Maurin was very critical of unions, which he viewed as prone to violence and too willing to treat their labor as a commodity, though in essay {243}, he admired a union that used Gandhian nonviolence to achieve its goal.

3. The modern mind
      is in such a fog
      that it cannot see the forest
      for the trees.
4. The modern mind
      has been led astray
      by the liberal mind.
5. The endorsement
      of liberal economics
      by the liberal mind
      has given us
      this separation
      of the spiritual
      from the material,
      which we call
      secularism.

X. Paul Chanson {251} — 1 time

1. Organized labor,
      organized capital,
      organized politics
      are essentially
      secularist minded.
2. We need leaders
      to lead us
      in the making of a path
      from the things as they are
      to the things as they should be.
3. I propose the formation
      of associations
      of Catholic employers
      as well as associations
      of Catholic union men.
4. Employers and employees
      must be indoctrinated
      with the same doctrine.

5. What is sauce for the goose
    is sauce for the gander.
6. Paul Chanson,
    President of the Employers' Association
    of the Port of Calais (France),
    has written a book
    expounding this doctrine,
    *Workers' Right
    and the Guildist Order.*

MAY 1937
CHRISTIANITY UNTRIED

I. Not Practical {135}

II. Blowing the Dynamite {3}

III. Just as Bad {252} — 1 time
   1. Non-Catholics say
       that Catholic laymen
       are led by the nose
       by the clergy;
   2. Catholic laymen
       are not led by the nose
       by the clergy.
   3. As a matter of fact
       Catholic laymen
       are led by the nose
       by non-Catholics.
   4. Catholic laymen
       are the imitators
       of non-Catholics;
   5. Catholic laymen
       consider themselves
       just as good
       as non-Catholics;

6. Catholic laymen
    should tell non-Catholics
    "We are just as bad
    as you are."

IV. Secularism {22}

V. Christ's Message {52}

VI. The Law of Holiness {253} — 1 time

In his encyclical
    on St. Francis of Sales
    the Holy Father says:
1. "We cannot accept the belief
    that this command of Christ
    concerns only
    a select and privileged group,
    and that all others
    may consider themselves
    pleasing to Him
    if they have attained
    a lesser degree
    of holiness.
2. "Quite the contrary is true,
    as appears
    from the generality
    of His words.
3. "The law of holiness
    embraces all men
    and admits
    of no exception."[190]

---

190. Maurin was quoting *Rerum omnium perturbationem*, an encyclical by Pius XI, issued on 26 January 1923, to mark the third centenary of St. Francis de Sales's (1567–1622) entrance to eternal life. Pius offered de Sales as an example of personal holiness who prized meekness over personal gain. This essay also continued Maurin's belief from essay {203} that a life of holiness as envisioned in the evangelical counsels was for all Christians, not just for vowed religious.

VII. What St. Francis Desired {53}

VIII. Rich and Poor[191] {254} — 2 times

1. There is a rub
    between the rich
    who like
    to get richer,
    and the poor
    who don't like
    to get poorer.
2. The rich, who like
    to get richer
    turn to the Church
    to save them
    from the poor
    who don't like
    to get poorer.
3. But the Church
    can only tell the rich
    who like

---

191. The other version of the essay from July–August 1941 omitted the first stanza and added the following two stanzas to the end of the original essay: "It is the rich who choose to become richer who make the poor dissatisfied to be poor. But it is the rich who choose to become poor who make the poor satisfied to be poor." There was also a version of the essay that was not published until after Maurin's death in the February 1951 issue of the newspaper. It was significantly longer than the two published during his lifetime. It is included here: "1. They say that the rich are getting richer and the poor are getting poorer. 2. And the rich like to get richer and the poor don't like to get poorer. 3. So there is a rub between the rich who like to get richer and the poor who don't like to get poorer. 4. Afraid of the poor who don't like to get poorer, the rich who like to get richer look to the State for protection. 5. But the State is not only the State of the rich who like to get richer it is also the State of the poor who don't like to get poorer. 6. So the State sometimes chooses to help the many poor who don't like to get poorer to the expense of the few rich who like to get richer. 7. Dissatisfied with the State the rich who like to get richer turn to the Church to save them from the poor who don't like to get poorer. 8. But the Church can only tell the rich who like to get richer 'Woe to you rich who like to get richer if you don't help the poor who don't like to get poorer.' 9. It is the rich who try to become richer who make the poor dissatisfied to be poor. 10. But it is the rich who try to become poor who make the poor satisfied to be poor. 11. 'The poor are the true children of the Church,' says Bossuet. 12. In the economy of the Church the poor come first and the rich come last."

to get richer,
"Woe to you rich,
who like to get richer
if you don't
help the poor
who don't like
to get poorer."

IX. Better and Better Off {50}

JUNE 1937
UTILITARIANS FUTILITARIANS TOTALITARIANS

I. Utilitarian Philosophers {255} — 1 time

  1. After a century
      of Protestantism,
      England and Scotland
      saw the coming out
      of a philosophical thought
      known in history
      as Utilitarian Philosophy.
  2. While Luther and Calvin
      discarded the authority of the Church
      the Utilitarian Philosophers
      discarded the authority
      of Divine Revelation.
  3. They tried to convince themselves
      and convince other people
      that the Church and the Bible
      were a handicap,
      rather than a help,
      in man's striving
      towards the good life.

II. Futlitarian Economists {256} — 1 time

  1. The Utilitarian Philosophers,
      Hobbes, Locke, Hume,

were followed
by the Futilitarian Economists
Adam Smith, Ricardo.
2. The Futilitarian Economists
thought that religion
had nothing to do
with business.
3. They thought that everything
would be lovely
if everybody took in
each other's washing.
4. They thought that everybody
should try to sell
what he has to sell
to the highest bidder.
5. So people started
to think of time
in terms of money,
and ended by shouting:
"Time is money!"

III. Harold Laski Says {257} — 1 time

Harold Laski,
    professor of Political Science
    in the London School of Economics,
    has this to say:
1. "In the Middle Ages
the idea of acquiring wealth
was limited
by a body of moral rules
imposed under the sanction
of religious authority.
2. "After 1500
those rules were evaded,
criticized, abandoned.
3. "New concepts were needed to legalize
the new potentialities of wealth.

4. "The liberal doctrine
      is the philosophical justification
      of the new practices."[192]

IV. Liberals and Liberators {13}

V. The Age of Treason {14}

VI. Fascism and Marxism {258} — 1 time

1. Now that economic liberalism
      is dying out,
      modern liberals
      find themselves
      on the spot.
2. They try to escape,
      from what they consider to be
      an untenable position.
3. In their attempt to escape
      the shifting sands of liberalism,
      they look for authority;
      not the authority
      of the teaching Church,
      but the authority
      of the political State
      whether it be
      the Marxist State
      or the Fascist State.
4. Fascism is a stop-gap
      between the dictatorship
      of Bourgeois Capitalism
      and the dictatorship
      of Marxian Socialism.

VII. Capitalism, Fascism, Communism {259} — 1 time

In an article
      published in the *Christian Front*,
      Charles P. Bruehl says:

---

192. Like the other Laski quote, this quote is from Laski, *Rise of European Liberalism*, 22.

1. "Those who fondly believe
    that Fascism
    will save the world
    from Communism
    are laboring
    under a fatal delusion.
2. "The Ideologies
    of these two are too closely allied.
3. "They have too much in common
    and their differences
    can be readily effaced.
4. "The three, Capitalism, Fascism, Communism
    are links in a chain.
5. "Imperceptibly
    the one passes
    into the other.
6. "All three are fundamentally
    materialistic,
    secularistic,
    totalitarian."[193]

JULY 1937
FIGHTING COMMUNISM

I. Without Comments[194] {260} — 1 time

1. "I understand Catholic apologetics
    but I don't understand
    Catholic sociology."

    —A Catholic Editor

2. "Your stuff is new to us."

    —A Catholic Layman

---

193. The quote is from Bruehl, "Communism and Capitalism," *Christian Front* 2, no. 3 (March 1937): 40–41.

194. The sources of the quotes in this essay are unknown. Based on the last quote, these could be statements made to Maurin personally.

3. "There is nothing new about it;
>   it is Catholic doctrine."

—A Catholic Priest

4. "You are an idealist
>   and I am a materialist,
>   but I like to listen to you."

—A Communist

II. Twenty and Forty {261} — 1 time

1. A Dutch convert
>   used to say:
>   "When one is not a Socialist
>   at twenty,
>   there is something wrong
>   with his heart;
>   but if one is a Socialist
>   at forty
>   there is something wrong
>   with his head."[195]
2. Dorothy Day,
>   Grace Branham,
>   and Marguerite Gage
>   were Socialists
>   at twenty.
3. And they did not
>   wait to be forty
>   to give up Socialism.
4. So there is nothing wrong
>   either with their hearts
>   or with their heads.

---

195. It is unclear to which Dutch convert Maurin is referring. The quote is often attributed to English statesmen Winston Churchill or French statesman Georges Clemenceau, but its true origin is unknown.

III. Works of Mercy {262} — 1 time

1. The order of the day
    in Catholic circles
    is to fight Communism.
2. To denounce Communism
    in Catholic halls
    is not an efficient way
    to fight Communism.
3. The daily practice
    of the Works of Mercy
    is a more efficient way
    to fight Communism.
4. The daily practice
    of the Works of Mercy
    by the first Christians
    made the Pagans
    say about the Christians
    "See how they love each other."

IV. Irish Scholars {263} — 1 time

When the Irish scholars
    decided to lay the foundations
    of Mediaeval Europe,
    they established:
1. Centers of Thought
    in all the cities of Europe
    as far as Constantinople
    where people
    could look for thought
    so they could have light.
2. Houses of Hospitality
    where Christian charity
    was exemplified.
3. Agricultural Centers
    where they combined
    a) Cult
        that is to say Liturgy

b) with Culture
      that is to say Literature
   c) with Cultivation
      that is to say Agriculture.

V. Chinese Catholics[196] {264} — 2 times

1. Chinese Catholics
     are showing us the way
     to fight Communism.
2. Non-Catholic writers
     are writing about
     the mode of living
     of the Brothers of St. John Baptist.[197]
3. Chinese Communists
     went to visit the Brothers
     and told them
     that their mode of living
     is more perfect
     than the mode of living
     of the Communist Party.
4. The Brothers of St. John Baptist
     try to exemplify
     the Sermon on the Mount.
5. The Sermon on the Mount
     is considered practical
     by the Chinese Brothers
     of St. John Baptist.

---

196. The September 1937 version has minor word changes from the original. The most significant is the use of term "Marxist Socialists" in stanza three instead of "Communist Party."

197. The Chinese Catholics were Little Brothers of St. John the Baptist. They had been recently established in China in 1928 by the Belgian priest Fr. Vincent Lebbe. To support China against the Japanese invasions of the 1930s, the Little Brothers rescued and treated thousands of Chinese soldiers from the front lines. The most recent invasion, the Second Sino-Japanese War, had begun in July 1937, the month this issue of the paper was published. The non-Catholic writer that Maurin was alluding to is uncertain. Most Western literature about the Little Brothers is in French, so it possible that Maurin was referring to something he read in a French periodical.

VI. Five Books {265} — 1 time

1. If you want to know
    what industrialism
    has done to man,
    read *Man, the Unknown*
    by Dr. Alexis Carrel.
2. If you want to know
    how we got that way,
    read *A Guildsman's
    Interpretation of History*,
    by Arthur Penty.
3. If you want to know
    what it is
    to be a bourgeois,
    read *The Bourgeois Mind*,
    by Nicholas Berdyaev.
4. If you want to know
    what religion
    has to do with culture,
    read *Enquiries Into
    Religion and Culture*,
    by Christopher Dawson.
5. If you want to know
    what to do with freedom,
    read *Freedom
    in the Modern World*,
    by Jacques Maritain.

FAITH AND REASON {266} — 1 time

1. St. Thomas Aquinas believed
    in reason with faith.
2. Martin Luther believed
    in faith without reason.
3. Thomas Paine believed
    in reason without faith.
4. Modern Liberals believe
    neither in faith nor reason.

5. Modern Fascists believe
   in blood-thinking.
6. Modern Marxists believe
   in dialectic materialism.
7. Mortimer Adler believes
   that philosophers
   have not found
   anything new
   since Aristotle.
8. And St. Thomas Aquinas believed
   what Aristotle believed
   as well as
   what St. Augustine believed.

AUGUST 1937
AGAINST CLASS WAR

I. No Recourse {132}

II. Business Is Business {11}

III. The Trouble Has Been {267} — 1 time

Hilaire Belloc says:
1. The modern proletarian
   works less hours
   and does far less
   than his father.
2. He is not even
   primarily in revolt
   against insecurity.
3. The trouble has been
   that the masses
   of our towns
   lived under
   unbearable conditions.
4. The contracts
   they were asked to fulfill
   were not contracts

that were suitable
to the dignity of man.
5. There was no personal relation
between the man
who was exploited
and the man
who exploited him.
6. Wealth had lost
its sense of responsibility.

IV. Twin Cities {268} — 1 time

1. In St. Paul,
there are few strikers
and few Reds.
2. In Minneapolis
there are plenty of strikes
and plenty of Reds.
3. In St. Paul
the employers
try to play fair
with the workers
and the workers
with the employers.
4. In Minneapolis
the employers
choose to be
rugged individualists
and the workers
consent to be
rugged collectivists.
5. Rugged individualists
and rugged collectivists
are spiritually related.

V. Class-Consciousness {269} — 1 time

1. Georges Sorel thought
that violence

is the midwife
   of existing societies.
2. When the employers
   believe in violence
   the workers also
   believe in it.
3. Class-consciousness
   among employers
   brings class-consciousness
   among the workers.
4. To do away
   with class-struggle
   we must first of all
   do away
   with class-consciousness
   among employers.
5. The workers are
   what the employers
   make them.
6. When employers
   are moved by greed
   the workers are inclined
   to carry a grudge.

VI. Paul Chanson Says {270} — 1 time

1. Whether we like it or not
   the economic system
   is necessarily related
   to the regime of appropriation
   of the tools of production.
2. If Bourgeois Capitalism
   appropriates the ownership
   the worker becomes a serf.
3. If Bolshevik Socialism
   monopolizes the ownership
   the worker's condition
   is not better.

4. He is reduced
   to a state of slavery.
5. Only a Guildist
   and Communitarian Economy
   will bring about
   the worker's emancipation.
6. Paul Chanson
   who says those things
   is not a labor leader.
7. He is the President
   of the Employers' Association
   of the Port of Calais (France).

SEPTEMBER 1937
UNPOPULAR FRONT

I. Four in One {271} — 1 time

The Unpopular Front
   is a front composed of:
1. Humanists
   who try to be human
   to man.
2. Theists
   who believe
   that God wants us
   to be our brother's keeper.
3. Christians
   who believe
   in the Sermon on the Mount
   as well as
   the Ten Commandments.
4. Catholics
   who believe
   in the Thomistic Doctrine
   of the Common Good.

II. They and We {166}

III. What Makes Man Human {86}

IV. Jewish Jubilee {272} — 1 time
   1. The Jews had a way
         to solve their financial
         problems.
   2. Every fiftieth year
         debts were remitted,
         land went back
         to the owners,
         slaves were set free.
   3. The Jews did that
         because they believed
         that God created the world.
   4. The Jews believed
         in the Fatherhood of God
         as well as
         the Brotherhood of Man,
         for God wants us
         "to be our brother's keeper."

V. Let the Jews Be Jews {273} — 1 time
   Ludwig Lewisohn says:
   1. Nowhere in the world
         have the Jews
         made the effort
         they did in Germany
         to become assimilated.
   2. They ceased to be Jews
         and were merely Germans.
   3. What did it profit them?
   4. And what does it
         profit anyone
         at any time,
         to be just

       a second rate imitation
       of the real thing?
    5. Let the Jews be Jews
       which is perfectly compatible
       with being
       as good Americans
       as the best.
    6. By so doing
       they will command respect.

VI. For Christ's Sake {274} — 1 time

    1. The First Christians
       were real Christians.
    2. They died for their faith.
    3. Before dying for Christ's sake
       the First Christians
       fed the hungry
       for Christ's sake;
       clothed the naked
       for Christ's sake;
       sheltered the homeless
       for Christ's sake;
       instructed the ignorant
       for Christ's sake.
    4. And because they did
       all those things
       for Christ's sake,
       their Pagan contemporaries
       said about them,
       "See how they love each other."
    5. The First Christians
       did everything
       for Christ's sake
       and nothing
       for business' sake.

VII. Chinese Catholics {264}

OCTOBER 1937
BOURGEOIS COLLEGES

I. Catholic Bourgeois {147}

II. On the Campus {41}

III. Business Is Business {133}

IV. Not My Subject {44}

V. A Commencement {64}

VI. In a Changing World {148}

VII. Looking for Jobs {149}

VIII. Indoctrination {151}

IX. On Farming Communes {152}

DECEMBER 1937
WAR AND PEACE

I. Right and Wrong {181}

II. Barbarians and Civilized[198] {275} — 2 times
1. We call barbarians
    people living
    on the other side of the border.
2. We call civilized
    people living
    on this side of the border.
3. We civilized,
    living on this side of the border,
    are not ashamed
    to arm ourselves to the teeth

---

198. The other version contained slightly different wording and concluded with the following stanza: "Barbarian people don't understand civilization but civilized people think they themselves do."

so as to protect ourselves
against the barbarians
living on the other side.
4. And when the barbarians
born on the other side
of the border,
invade us,
we do not hesitate
to kill them
before we have tried
to civilize them.
5. So we civilized
exterminate barbarians
without civilizing them.
6. And we persist
in calling ourselves civilized.

III. Germans and French {139}

IV. Italians and Ethiopians {276} — 1 time

1. Italian soldiers
went to Ethiopia
to civilize the Ethiopians.
2. The Italian soldiers
still think
that invaders
can civilize the invaded.
3. But the Ethiopians
do not like the way
the Italian soldiers
try to civilize them.
4. The best way
to civilize the Ethiopians
is to prepare
Ethiopian young men
for the priesthood.[199]

---

199. It should be noted that Ethiopia has practiced Christianity for about as long as Italy, though the church in Ethiopia has long been associated with the Coptic Orthodox Church.

5. As Christopher Dawson says,
      culture
      has a lot to do
      with religion.[200]

V. Spaniards and Moors[201] {277} — 1 time

   1. Moors from Morocco
      ruled part of Spain
      for eight hundred years.
   2. They imposed Mohammedism
      on the Spaniards
      through the power of the sword.
   3. After eight hundred years,
      the Spanish Christians
      decided to give the Moors
      a dose of their own medicine.
   4. So the Spanish Christians
      drove the Moors out of Spain
      through the power of the sword.
   5. Before the war,
      Spanish Christians
      failed to make use
      of the power of the word.
   6. Spanish Christians
      seem to have more faith
      in the power of the sword
      than the power of the word.
   7. So had the Moors
      when ruling part of Spain
      for eight hundred years.

---

200. This is probably a reference to Christopher Dawson's book of essays *Enquiries into Religion and Culture* (New York: Sheed & Ward, 1933).

201. This essay briefly recounts the history of the Islamic conquest of the southern Iberian Peninsula in the eighth century and Spain's "reconquest" of the peninsula in the late fifteenth century. The years following the "reconquest" entailed the forced conversions or expulsion of Jews and Muslims.

VI. Stalinites and Trotskyites {278} — 1 time

1. Eugene Lyons says
    that Lenin and Trotsky
    accepted the idea
    that the end
    justifies the means.
2. They thought
    that an idealistic end
    could be reached
    by bloody means.
3. Because they resorted
    to bloody means,
    Stalin resorts
    to bloody means.
4. The State has not yet
    withered away
    and the Communist ideal
    is still out of sight.

JANUARY 1938
BUSINESS IS THE BUNK

I. No Recourse {132}

II. Business Is Selfishness {11}

III. Money Making {279} — 1 time

1. Business men
    are not in business
    for their health.
2. They are in business
    to make money.
3. Because business men
    are in business
    to make money
    they replace men
    with machinery.

4. But as Mussolini says
   "Machines
   do not eat."
5. Because machines
   do not eat
   they decrease
   the consuming power
   and increase
   the producing power.
6. Our economic system
   is out of joint
   because
   people with money
   do not buy,
   and people without money
   cannot buy
   what they wish to buy.

IV. Providing Jobs[202] {280} — 2 times

1. In the years
   of prosperity
   the employers
   were providing jobs.
2. But the job providers
   do no longer
   provide jobs.
3. And the job hunters
   are sore
   because the job providers
   do no longer know
   how to provide jobs.
4. And the job hunters
   turn to the State
   and ask the State

---

202. Also known as "Employers of Labor." The first two stanzas of the other version replaced the term "job provider" with "employer of labor" and the phrase "provide jobs" with "employ labor."

> to do for them
> what business men
> fail to do.
> 5. Because business men
> do no longer know
> how to provide jobs,
> the State
> takes up the job
> of providing jobs.

V. W.P.A.[203] {281} — 3 times

> 1. Someone said
> that what is needed
> is a machine
> that could do the work
> of one man
> and would take ten men
> to run it.
> 2. But as somebody else said
> "We don't need it;
> we have it already,
> the W.P.A."
> 3. In England
> they have the dole.
> 4. Here, we don't have the dole;
> we have the W.P.A.
> 5. W.P.A. jobs
> cost three times as much
> as home relief.
> 6. That money comes
> from taxpayers
> or investors
> in Government bonds.

---

203. The two other versions omitted stanzas three and four. In addition, the October 1938 version concluded with the following stanza: "To take the profits out of the profit system is to replace the profit system by another system; a system of more supervision and less vision." The December 1939 version concluded with the following stanza: "By replacing men with machinery business men have brought about bigger and better taxes."

7. And because of it
    the Government
    is no longer able
    to balance the budget.

VI. Government Control {282} — 1 time

1. Because the job providers
    sat down on the job
    of providing jobs,
    the Government
    took up the job.
2. The job providers
    who talk about service
    and think about profits,
    were told by technicians
    that the profit system
    could be made
    more profitable
    if machines
    were substituted.
3. And now politicians
    are doing their best
    to take the profits
    out of the profit system.
4. But you cannot
    take profits
    out of the profit system
    and still have
    the profit system.
5. What you have
    is more and more
    Government control
    and less and less
    personal control.

VII. State Supervision {283} — 1 time

1. Someone said:
   "There is no vision
   in Washington."
2. I say: "There is a lot
   of supervision
   in Washington."
3. Glenn Frank says:
   "Where there is
   too much supervision
   people perish."[204]
4. State supervision
   leads to
   State bureaucracy.
5. State bureaucracy
   leads to
   the Totalitarian State.
6. In the Totalitarian State
   the individual exists
   for the State
   and not the State
   for the individual.

VIII. Jeffersonian Democracy {284} — 1 time

1. The Founders of America
   wrote a Declaration
   of the Independence
   of the individual.
2. They established
   a Constitution
   for the protection
   of the individual.
3. They set up
   nine watch-dogs

---

[204]. This quote appears to be play on words from the King James Bible translation of Proverb 29:18: "Where there is no vision, the people perish."

to protect the Constitution
   against misinterpretation.
4. Thomas Jefferson says:
   "The least government
   there is,
   the better it is."
5. The Totalitarian State
   is not a substitute
   for Jeffersonian Democracy.

FEBRUARY 1938
JOURNALISM: GOOD AND BAD {236}

MARCH 1938
CHARITY AND POVERTY

I. Fallacy of Saving {38}

II. Wisdom of Giving {123}

III. Then and Now {188}

IV. Better and Better Off {50}

V. Human to Man {86}

VI. What Saint Francis Desired {53}

APRIL 1938
PEACE PREPAREDNESS

I. 1638–1938 {285} — 1 time
   1. In 1638—France and Sweden
      were helping
      Protestant Germany against
      Catholic Germany
      and Catholic Austria.
   2. In 1938—Protestant Germany
      is helping Catholic Spain.

3. In 1638—Germany was divided
in 300 principalities.
4. In 1938—Germany and Austria
form a united nation.
5. After 300 years the French policy
of 1638 to keep Germany divided
has proved to be
a complete failure.

II. Ethiopia and Austria {286} — 1 time

1. France believes in colonial expansion
and denies to Germany
colonial expansion.
2. France went to Tunisia
with Bismarck's[205] approval
who did not deny to France
colonial expansion.
3. The Treaty of Versailles[206]
reduced Germany's colonial expansion
as well as continental expansion.
4. The colonial expansion of Fascist Italy
in Ethiopia
and the continental expansion of Nazi
Germany in Austria
is the result of the colonial expansion
of both France and England.

III. France and England {287} — 1 time

1. President Wilson stood for
a Peace Treaty
without annexations or indemnities.

---

205. This is a reference to Otto von Bismarck.
206. The Treaty of Versailles formally ended World War I in 1919. Maurin believed that the treaty, particularly its requirement for Germany to pay reparations to countries that it had harmed, was too strict and that the ensuing economic stress played a role in Germany's support of Nazism. The current essay notes another provision of the treaty that transferred Germany colonies to other political powers.

2. Clemenceau and Lloyd George
         wanted to have their way
         and kept President Wilson
         from having his way.
   3. In 1919—Clemenceau and Lloyd George
         had their way
         and now Mussolini and Hitler
         have their way.
   4. France and England who have failed
         to revise the Treaty of Versailles
         talk about good will
         while Italy and Germany
         talk about force.

IV. Disarmament of the Heart {288} — 1 time

   1. The Pope Benedict XV
         and Aristide Briand spoke
         about the disarmament of the heart.
   2. France and England
         who refused to follow Wilson
         refused also to follow
         the Pope Benedict XV and Aristide Briand.
   3. They are increasing armaments
         in the fallacious hope
         that they will preserve peace
         by preparing for war.
   4. Before 1914 they prepared for war
         and got it.
   5. Nations have too long
         prepared for war;
         it is about time
         they prepared for peace.

V. A Practical Question {289} — 1 time

   Archbishop McNicholas says:
   1. Governments have
         no fixed standards of morality
         and consequently no moral sense.

2. They can scarcely settle
    the question of war for Christians.
3. Christians see and know the injustice
    of practically all wars
    in our modern pagan world.
4. There is the very practical question
    for informed Christians
    who acknowledge
    the supreme dominion of God.
5. Will such Christians
    in our own country
    form a mighty league of conscientious
    non-combatants?[207]

MAY 1938
THE RACE PROBLEM

I. Not Better {290} — 1 time

1. The Jews think
    that they are better
    than the Negroes.
2. The Germans think
    that they are better
    than the Jews.
3. I don't think
    that the Jews
    are better
    than the Negroes
    or the Germans
    better than the Jews.
4. The way for the Jews
    to be better
    than the Germans

---

207. In this essay, Maurin lightly paraphrased a passage from Archbishop John T. McNicholas's pastoral letter on peace, which he released at the beginning of Lent 1938. This portion of the letter can be found in McNicholas, quoted in "Potpourri," *Catholic World*, May 1938, 186. Portions of the letter were also reprinted in "Archbishop Urges League of 'C.O.'s," *New York Catholic Worker*, April 1938.

is to behave
the way the Prophets
want the Jews
to behave.
5. The way for the Negroes
to be better
than the Jews
or the Germans
is to behave
the way Saint Augustine
wants everybody
to behave.

II. Germans and Irish {291} — 1 time

1. Hitler wants all the Germans
to join the German Reich.
2. Hitler seems to think
that only the German Reich
can make good Germans
out of the Germans.
3. According to Hitler's
way of thinking
to make good soldiers
out of the Germans
is to make good Germans
out of the Germans.
4. When the Irish
were Irish
they did not try
to make good soldiers
out of the Irish,
they tried
to make good scholars
out of the Irish.

III. Soldiers and Scholars {292} — 1 time

1. Soldiers rely
on the power
of the sword.

2. Scholars rely
   on the power
   of the word.
3. Soldiers think
   in terms of Empire.
4. Scholars think
   in terms of culture.
5. When after the fall
   of the Roman Empire
   the Irish scholars
   made up their mind
   to lay the foundations
   of medieval Europe,
   they established
   agricultural centers
   where they combined
   cult—
   that is to say liturgy,
   with culture—
   that is to say literature
   with cultivation—
   that is to say agriculture.

IV. The Negro Problem[208] {293} — 1 time

1. There is in America
   a Negro problem.
2. White people in America
   have not yet found
   the right solution
   of the Negro problem.

---

208. Maurin did not create the term "Negro problem." It was a common term at the time to refer to the discrimination faced by African Americans. There was even a book, *The Negro Problem* (1907), composed of essays from leading African American literary figures like Booker T. Washington and W. E. B. DuBois. By the 1930s, most black intellectuals used the term with irony or disapproval because of the implication that the presence of African Americans was the source of racism in America and not a culture of white prejudice. Nevertheless, it was still common during the 1930s for whites to use the term without irony or disapproval.

3. It is up to the Negroes
    to find the right solution
    of the Negro problem.
4. When the Negroes
    try to force themselves
    on white people
    or to imitate
    white people
    they do not solve
    the Negro problem.
5. The way for Negroes
    to solve
    the Negro problem
    is to behave
    not the way
    the white people behave
    but the way
    Saint Augustine
    wants the white people
    to behave.[209]

V. The Power of Example {294} — 1 time

1. The white people
    are in a mess
    and the Negro people
    will be in a mess
    as long as
    they try to keep up
    with white people.
2. When the Negro people
    will have found the way
    out of their mess
    by evolving a technique
    in harmony
    with the ideology

---

209. Although St. Augustine was a North African Roman, he did not have a concept of whiteness or racial superiority based on skin color.

　　　　of Saint Augustine
　　　　the white people
　　　　will no longer
　　　　look down
　　　　on Negro people
　　　　but will look up
　　　　to Negro people.
　　3. When the white people
　　　　will look up
　　　　to the Negro people
　　　　they will imitate
　　　　the Negro people.
　　4. The power of Negro people
　　　　over white people
　　　　will then be
　　　　the power of example.

JUNE 1938
NO PARTY LINE

I. The Outstretched Hand {295} — 1 time

　　1. The Marxists
　　　　of Western Europe
　　　　are stretching out
　　　　their hand
　　　　to Catholic Bishops.
　　2. Referring
　　　　to that outstretched hand,
　　　　the Holy Father
　　　　in an address
　　　　to eleven French Bishops
　　　　said last fall
　　　　to offer the outstretched hand
　　　　because the Marxists
　　　　do not have the truth
　　　　and that our duty
　　　　is to bring to them
　　　　the Catholic truth.

    3. With the giving of the truth
        we must give to them
        assistance
        said the Holy Father
        through the practice
        of the Works of Mercy.

EASY ESSAYS

I. Cardinal Verdier {296} — 1 time

   1. Cardinal Verdier
        has never been
        called a Fascist
        by Reds or Pinks.
   2. He was called to Rome
        by the Holy Father
        who wanted to give him
        personal instructions
        as how to deal
        both with the Reds
        and the Fascists.
   3. What Cardinal Verdier,
        Archbishop of Paris,
        has to say
        about modern problems
        deserves much consideration
        for he expresses the views
        of the Holy Father.

II. Cardinal Liénart {297} — 1 time

   1. The bishop of Lille
        was not satisfied
        with company unions
        which were fostered
        by Catholic employers.

2. Bishop Liénart
    made up his mind
    to organize unions
    of Catholic workers.
3. The existence
    of Catholic unions
    did not satisfy
    Catholic employers.
4. Catholic employers
    accused Catholic unions
    of being Red unions.
5. The Church in Rome
    gave its approval
    to the Catholic unions
    founded by Bishop Liénart
    and the Holy Father
    made him a Cardinal.

III. Cardinal Hinsley {298} — 1 time

1. Archbishop Hinsley
    of Westminster
    took cracks at Mussolini
    while he waged a war
    in Ethiopia.
2. Archbishop Hinsley
    was made a Cardinal
    last Fall.
3. The Holy Father
    does not seem to object
    to the criticism
    of Mussolini
    by Archbishop Hinsley
    during the Ethiopian War.

IV. No Party Line {299} — 1 time

1. The Catholic Worker
    is a freelance movement,
    not a partisan movement.

2. Some of the Bishops
    agree with our policies
    and some don't.
3. We are criticized
    by many Catholics
    for some of our policies
    and especially
    our Spanish policy.[210]
4. The Communist Party
    has a Party line.
5. The Catholic Worker
    has no Party line.
6. There is no Party line
    in the Catholic Church.

JULY 1938
THE CURSE OF LIBERALISM

I. Three Jews {300} — 1 time

1. Harold Laski,
    an English Jew,
    says that Liberals
    have endorsed
    bourgeois capitalism
    in the name of liberalism.
2. Julien Benda,
    a French Jew,
    says that Liberals

---

210. This is in reference to the Spanish Civil War, which broke out in 1936 after a failed military coup against the Republican government. Almost every bishop and Catholic publication supported the military fascist Nationalists led by Francisco Franco, who defended the Catholic faith and was anti-Communist. The anti-Catholic Republican government was an alliance of Communists, socialists, and anarchists. Franco finally defeated the Republicans in 1939 and took control of Spain. The *Catholic Worker*, with its pacifist stance, refused to support either side in the Spanish Civil War and lost many newspaper subscriptions. Several bishops even banned the *Catholic Worker* in the parishes and schools of their diocese.

have given up
the search for truth
and consented to become
paid propagandists
for nationalism
as well as capitalism.
3. Mortimer Adler,
an American Jew,
says that Liberals
are sophists
and not philosophers.

II. Let's Be Liberators {13}

III. Modern Education {301} — 1 time

1. Henry Adams says
that you cannot get
an education
in America
because there is
no unity of thought
in America.
2. Norman Foerster
of the University of Iowa
says that State Universities
do not know what it is
to be educated.
3. President Hutchins
of the University of Chicago
says that Universities
turn out graduates
without giving them
an appreciation
of the human values
that are embodied
in the masterpieces
of literature.

IV. Secularism {22}

V. Materialist Slogans {64}

VI. Looking for Dictators {302} — 1 time

   1. Patrick Henry said:
       "Give me liberty
       or give me death."

   2. Men have liberty
       but intellectual liberals
       have failed to tell people
       what to do with it.

   3. And because men don't know
       what to do with liberty
       they look for dictators
       to tell them what to do.

   4. And the dictators tell them
       "You do what I tell you
       or I will knock your head off."

   5. Men look for dictators
       because intellectual liberals
       through their so-called
       liberal education
       have made man
       unknown to man.

   6. Intellectual liberals
       ought to read the book
       of Dr. Alexis Carrel,
       Man, the Unknown.

SEPTEMBER 1938
BEYOND MARXISM

I. U.S.S.R.[211] {303} — 3 times

   1. The U.S.S.R. means
       the Union of Socialist
       Soviet Republics.

---

211. Also known as "A Communist Society." The other versions of the essay were abridged.

2. There is no Communism
   in Soviet Russia.
3. According to Karl Marx
   "Communism is a society
   wherein one works
   according to his ability
   and gets according to his
   needs."
4. Such a society
   is found in Catholic
   monasteries
   but not in Soviet Russia.
5. That is why Strachey
   was told by Father McNabb,
   an English Dominican,
   "I am a Communist;
   you are only an amateur."[212]

II. Primitive Christianity {188}

III. What St. Francis Desired {53}

IV. Selling Their Labor {16}

V. Self-Government {19}

VI. They and We {166}

---

212. This is not an exact quote, but a paraphrase of what McNabb told Strachey in a debate between the two held in Manchester, England, in February 1937. The debate was published as a book: Vincent McNabb and John Strachey, *Communism or Distributism* (London: Distributist League, 1937).

OCTOBER 1938
BUSINESS AND SUCH

I. No Recourse {132}

II. Business Is Selfishness {11}

III. Priests and Policemen {304} — 1 time

    1. Jean-Jacques Rousseau said:
        "Man is naturally good."
    2. Business men say:
        "Man is naturally bad;
        you can do nothing
        with human nature."
    3. If it is true
        as business men say
        that you can do nothing
        with human nature,
        then we need less priests
        and more policemen.
    4. But if God the Father
        sent His own begotten Son
        to redeem men,
        then we need more priests
        and less policemen.

IV. More Profitable[213] {305} — 2 times

    1. Business men believe
        in the profit system.
    2. Because they believe
        in the profit system,
        they try to make
        the profit system
        more profitable.

---

213. Also known as "Profit Seekers." Only minor word choices differentiated the essays.

3. In order to make
 the profit system
 more profitable
 business men
 replace men
 with machinery.
4. It is true
 that machines
 don't strike,
 but neither do they eat.
5. By replacing men
 with machinery
 business men
 increase
 the producing power
 and decrease
 the consuming power.

V. Sit-Downers {306} — 1 time

1. In putting more machines
 into factories
 business men
 have given up their job
 of providing jobs.
2. The job providers
 have to admit
 that they sit down
 on their job
 of providing jobs.
3. Because the job providers
 have sat down
 on their job
 of providing jobs,
 the Government.
 has taken up the job
 of providing jobs.

4. But the Government
         can only rob Peter
         to pay Paul
         and by doing so
         endanger its own credit.

VI. W.P.A. {281}

VII. If You Want to Know {307} — 1 time

   1. If you want to know
         why the things are
         what they are
         read:
         a) *Man, the Unknown,*
         by Dr. Alexis Carrel.
         b) *What Man Has Made of Man,*
         by Mortimer Adler.
         c) *The Bourgeois Mind,*
         by Nicholas Berdyaev.
   2. If you want to know
         how we got that way
         read:
         a) *A Guildsman's Interpretation of History,*
         by Arthur Penty.
         b) *Charles of Europe,*
         by Wyndham Lewis
         c) *Religion and the Rise of Capitalism,*
         by R. H. Tawney.
   3. If you want to know
         the way out
         read:
         a) *Personalist Manifesto,*
         by Emmanuel Mounier.
         b) *Freedom in the Modern World,*
         by Jacques Maritain.
         c) *A Philosophy of Work,*
         by Étienne Borne.

DECEMBER 1938
FROM RICHELIEU TO HITLER[214]

I. 100% Frenchman[215] {308} — 2 times

1. Cardinal Richelieu
    was a cardinal
    of the Catholic Church
    and Premier Minister
    to a Catholic King.
2. He ought to have been
    a 100% Catholic.
3. He chose to be
    a 100% Frenchman.
4. As a 100% Frenchman
    he wanted France stronger
    and Austria weaker.
5. He wanted France
    to be the dictator
    of continental Europe.

II. Thirty Years' War {309} — 1 time

1. It was during
    the Thirty Years' War.
2. Northern Germany
    and Sweden
    were fighting
    against Southern Germany
    and Austria.

---

214. Maurin's purpose in this arrangement of essays was to stress that political power was not only the primary motivator of war and global discord during his lifetime, but that it was also the primary reason during the so-called wars of religion since the Reformation.

215. Also known as "Richelieu." The second version contained minor word changes from the original and was longer, replacing stanza five with the following two lines: "To make Austria weaker he sided with Protestant Germany and Sweden against Catholic Germany and Austria. The Treaty of Westphalia kept Germany divided in more than 300 principalities." For more on the Treaty of Westphalia, see the footnote for essay {310}.

3. It was a civil war
    between Protestant Germany
    and Catholic Germany.
4. To make France stronger
    and Austria weaker
    Cardinal Richelieu
    took the side
    of Protestant Germany
    and Sweden
    against Catholic Germany
    and Austria.

III. Treaty of Westphalia[216] {310} — 1 time

1. Protestant Germany
    and Sweden
    won the war
    with the help of France.
2. The Treaty of Westphalia
    signed in 1648
    gave to France
    part of Alsace.
3. While France was united
    the Treaty of Westphalia
    kept Germany divided
    in 300 principalities.
4. The acquisition
    of part of Alsace
    by France
    did not keep Alsace
    from remaining
    a bone of contention

---

216. The Treaty of Westphalia, also known as the Peace of Westphalia, refers to numerous treaties signed during 1648 that ended the Thirty Years' War and the Eighty Years' War. These treaties gave precedence to national sovereignty, emphasized noninterference with other states, and were a precursor to international law.

between France
and Germany.

IV. Birth of Prussia[217] {311} — 1 time

1. While France was united
   and the King used to say
   "I am the State"
   Germany was divided
   in 300 principalities.
2. But Germany
   did not remain divided.
3. Around 1700
   the Principality of
   Hohenzollern,
   the Margraviate of Brandenburg
   and the Dukedom of Prussia
   formed a new nation
   which they called Prussia.
4. Eager to receive
   English recognition,
   the new nation
   took the side of England
   against Spain
   in the war
   of Spanish Succession.
5. It was in this war
   that England
   got Gibraltar.

---

217. By this essay, Maurin hoped to illustrate that the desire for political power was a greater driving force in politics than differences in Christian denomination. The Principality of Hohenzollern, or Province of Hohenzollern, was an area in the Holy Roman Empire that was south of Prussia, but not directly connected to it. Unlike the Margraviate of Brandenburg and the Dukedom of Prussia, which were solidly Lutheran and Calvinist, Hohenzollern was solidly Catholic. Though essentially a Protestant country, Prussia was known for its policy of religious toleration. Since the geography of Prussia made it very susceptible to incursions from neighboring nations, King Frederick I of Prussia would readily switch political alliances to preserve his kingdom and his power.

V. Seven Years' War[218] {312} — 1 time

1. During the Seven Years' War,
    known in America
    as the French and Indian War,
    Prussia again took
    the side of England.
2. While during
    the Thirty Years' War
    France was fighting
    against Austria,
    during the Seven Years' War
    France was fighting
    on the side of Austria.
3. In the war game
    friends of today
    become the enemies
    of tomorrow
    and enemies of today
    become the friends
    of tomorrow.
4. During this war
    Austria lost Silesia,
    and France
    lost Canada
    as well as
    colonies in India.

VI. Place in the Sun {313} — 1 time

1. In the meantime
    France as well as Austria
    was becoming weaker
    and England
    as well as Germany
    was becoming stronger.

---

218. Maurin was providing another example of a war in which political alliances changed to protect political power without regard to religious affiliation.

2. The war against Denmark
and the war against France
made Prussia stronger,
and in 1871
the King of Prussia
was made German Emperor
at Versailles.
3. The new German Empire
became envious
of French and English
Colonial Empires
and started to cry
for a place in the sun.
4. But the place in the sun
had been taken
by France and England
who were bragging
about the fact
that the sun never set
on their domains.

VII. United Germany {314} — 1 time

1. The Great War
was an attempt
on the part of Germany
to get a place in the sun.
2. But Germany
failed to get
its place in the sun,
while France and England
succeeded in getting
a bigger place in the sun.
3. The Germans still think
that they should have
a bigger and better
place in the sun.

4. They have annexed
> the Austrian Germans
> and the Sudeten Germans
> on the ground
> that it is for the good
> of the Austrian Germans
> and the Sudeten Germans.

VIII. Nations and Notions {315} — 1 time

1. The French are united,
> the English are united,
> the Italians are united,
> the Russians are united,
> the Germans are united
> but the world
> is still divided.
2. The League of Nations
> is a failure
> because nations
> have wrong notions.
3. Right notions
> must be spread
> among nations
> before we can have
> a genuine
> League of Nations.
4. Germany and Italy
> are now on the level
> of France and England.
5. Germany and Italy
> cannot be expected
> to be on the level
> when France and England
> are not on the level.

JANUARY 1939
NON-CATHOLIC CATHOLICS

I. Apologetic Catholics {316} — 1 time

1. Some Catholics
    like to apologize
    for being Catholics.
2. Since Catholicism
    is the truth,
    it is foolish
    to apologize
    for being Catholics.
3. Since Catholicism
    is the truth,
    then Catholics
    ought to let non-Catholics
    apologize
    for not being Catholics.
4. To let non-Catholics
    apologize
    for not being Catholics
    is good apologetics.
5. To apologize
    for being Catholics
    is bad apologetics.

II. Led by the Nose {317} — 1 time

1. Non-Catholics say
    that Catholics
    are led by the nose
    by the clergy.
2. Real Catholics
    are not led by the nose
    by the clergy.
3. Real Catholics
    follow their consciences.

4. I must admit
    that some Catholics
    are led by the nose.
5. These Catholics
    who are led by the nose
    are not led by the nose
    by the clergy.
6. They are led by the nose
    by non-Catholics.
7. These Catholics
    who allow themselves
    to be led by the nose
    by non-Catholics
    ought to be called
    non-Catholic Catholics.

III. A Wrong Way {318} — 1 time

1. Non-Catholic Catholics
    tell us
    that one cannot
    lead a Catholic life
    in a Protestant country.
2. The protestation
    of Protestants
    is not a protestation
    against the Catholicism
    of non-Catholic Catholics.
3. It is a protestation
    against the lack
    of Catholicism
    of non-Catholic Catholics.
4. Non-Catholic Catholics
    are giving to Protestants
    a wrong view
    of Catholicism.
5. To give to Protestants
    a wrong view
    of Catholicism

is not the right way
to make Catholics
out of Protestants.

IV. Catholic Principles {319} — 1 time

1. Protestants
   have principles
   but Catholics
   have more principles
   than Protestants.
2. But principles
   must be applied.
3. To have principles
   and not to apply them
   is worse
   than not having any.
4. Non-Catholic Catholics
   fail to bring
   Catholic principles
   to Protestants
   because
   they do not dare
   to exemplify
   those Catholic principles
   that Protestants
   do not have.

V. Imitators {320} — 1 time

1. Non-Catholic Catholics
   like to tell
   their Protestant friends,
   "we are just as good
   as you are."
2. They ought to tell
   their Protestant friends,
   "we are just as bad
   as you are."

3. Their Protestant friends
    ought to tell
    the non-Catholic Catholics,
    "you are not
    just as bad
    as we are;
    you are much worse
    than we are
    for you are
    our imitators,
    you are not,
    yourselves."

FEBRUARY 1939
NOT LIBERALS BUT RADICALS

I. The Word Liberal {321} — 1 time

1. The word liberal
    is used in Europe
    in a different way
    from the way
    it is used
    in America.[219]
2. In Europe
    a liberal is a man
    who believes in liberty
    without knowing
    what to do with it.
3. Harold Laski
    accuses liberals
    of having used

---

219. Maurin is likely referring to how the term "liberalism" in the United States became synonymous with Roosevelt's New Deal during the 1930s. This newer American version viewed the government as having a positive role to play in promoting the general welfare. Although the term did not remain static in the Europe, Maurin was probably referring to the classical political/economic notion of a liberal as someone who believed in individual liberty, laissez-faire capitalism, and small government. Maurin criticized the classical sense of the term for divorcing economics from Christian morality.

their intelligence
without knowing
what to do with it.

II. Too Broadminded {13}

III. Not Liberators {322} — 1 time

1. Liberals
    don't like to be
    religious fanatics,
    philosophical fanatics,
    or social fanatics.
2. Liberals
    prefer to be
    liberal fanatics.
3. The only kind
    of fanaticism
    that appeals to liberals
    is liberal fanaticism.
4. Liberal fanaticism
    is what keeps liberals
    from being liberators.
5. They are intellectuals
    who don't seem to know
    how to use
    their intelligence.

IV. Secularism {22}

V. Radicals {323} — 1 time

1. Liberals
    are too liberal
    to be radicals.
2. To be a radical
    is to go to the roots.
3. Liberals
    don't go to the roots;
    they only
    scratch the surface.

4. The only way
   to go to the roots
   is to bring religion
   into education,
   into politics,
   into business.
5. To bring religion
   into the profane
   is the best way
   to take profanity
   out of the profane.
6. To take profanity
   out of the profane
   is to bring sanity
   into the profane.
7. Because we aim
   to do just that
   we like to be called
   radicals.

TWO LETTERS FROM PETER

[These two letters are placed here because they appeared in this month's issue of the *New York Catholic Worker*. The letters addressed topics that were discussed among American Catholics in 1939, like Fr. Coughlin and Francisco Franco. These letters are presented to show how Maurin wrote to friends and gave updates. Of note, he wrote his personal letters using the format of Easy Essays.]

Portland, Oregon
January 19, 1939

Dear Dorothy:
I just received your letter
    and read the January issue
    of *The Catholic Worker*.
I had written a letter
    when I arrived in Seattle
    which I failed
    to send to you.

I am sending it to you
> with a fifty-dollar check.
I am now leaving
> for San Francisco
> and will write to you
> when I arrive there.

> > —Your fellow worker in Christ,
> > Peter Maurin

Seattle, Washington
December 28, 1938

Dear Dorothy:
I arrived in Seattle
> safe and sound
> except for a couple bruises
> on the chin.
We were driving
> back to Spokane
> from the Jesuit
> House of Studies.
Fr. Robinson,
> Dean of Gonzaga College
> was the driver.
I was sitting in the back
> with a Jesuit Scholastic.
Our conversation
> was so interesting
> for Fr. Robinson
> that he forgot to stop
> at a red light
> and ran into the middle
> of a city bus.
The head of his car
> was smashed.
His nose was cut
> while his glasses,
> which he was wearing,
> were not broken.

The Jesuit Scholastic
    had a cut
    above the left eye.
I was hurt
    by bumping my chin
    against the front seat.
The schools being closed
    I was only able
    to talk to the Scholastics
    in the House of Studies.
It was Bishop White
    who phoned Fr. Robinson
    about me being in town.
I am coming back to Spokane
    the 9, 10, 11 January.
I spent Christmas in Butte
    with Elias Seaman.
With a Catholic Hindu
    student in the School of Mines
    we went to midnight Mass
    at a Croatian Church.
This Croatian pastor
    is a great friend
    of *The Catholic Worker.*
I am sending you
    a fifty-dollar check.
    to help pay the debts.
While in St. Paul
    I paid fifty-two dollars
    and forty cents
    for a 5,569 mile trip.
That trip takes me
    from St. Paul to Seattle,
    then to Los Angeles,
    then to Denver,
    then to Omaha,
    then to St. Paul.

I can stop
    anywhere I want
    and it is good
    for 150 days.
They intend
    to start a Catholic Worker
    group in Minneapolis.
It is also a question
    of a farming commune.
Father Le Beau
    at St. Thomas College,
    Fr. Loosen
    at St. Mary's Hospital,
    Sister Helen Angelica
    at St. Joseph's Hospital,
    are great boosters
    of *The Catholic Worker*.
Dr. John Giesen
    is actively connected
    with a Mexican center.
Dr. Bauer,
    a German sociologist,
    is now at St. Thomas
    and is eager to cooperate
    with *The Catholic Worker*.
Before leaving St. Paul
    I made a short trip
    to Eau Claire and
    La Crosse.
The pastor of Eau Claire
    agrees with us:
    the youth need a cause.
A Y.M.C.A. secretary
    in La Crosse
    is very much in sympathy
    with the idea
    of an Unpopular Front
    on Personalist Democracy.

I found that the reaction
> to *The Catholic Worker*
> propaganda
> is very favorable.
There was very little talk
> either about Franco
> or Fr. Coughlin.
I wish you all
> a Happy New Year.

>> —Yours in Christ the Worker,
>> Peter Maurin

MARCH 1939
LOOKING BACKWARD

I. In New England {324} — 1 time

1. There are three kinds of people
   > in New England:
   > the foreigners,
   > the Irish,
   > and the Yankees.
2. The foreigners of New England
   > have given up
   > their own traditions
   > to keep up
   > with the Irish.
3. The Irish of New England
   > have given up
   > their own scholarship
   > to keep up
   > with the Yankees.
4. The Yankees of New England
   > have given up
   > their New England conscience
   > to keep up
   > with the utilitarian, futilitarian
   > political economists

　　　　of the Manchester School
　　　　of political economy.
　5. So what can you expect
　　　　from New England?

II. In Louisiana {325} — 1 time

　1. Waldo Frank says
　　　　that America
　　　　is a lost continent
　　　　and that to rediscover itself
　　　　America must go back
　　　　to Mediterranean thought.
　2. Mediterranean thought
　　　　was brought to Louisiana
　　　　by the founders of Louisiana.
　3. But the people of Louisiana
　　　　have turned over
　　　　the State of Louisiana
　　　　to greedy corporations.
　4. The Catholic people
　　　　of the State of Louisiana
　　　　had to have
　　　　a Baptist lawyer
　　　　by the name of Huey Long
　　　　to save them
　　　　from the grip
　　　　that greedy corporations
　　　　had on the Catholic people
　　　　of the State of Louisiana.

III. In Texas {326} — 1 time

　1. Spanish Franciscans
　　　　went to Texas
　　　　when Texas was part
　　　　of Old Mexico.

2. Spanish Franciscans
    taught the Indians
    to build churches,
    to build schools,
    to build mission-storehouses.
3. The ruins of those churches,
    the ruins of those schools,
    the ruins of those mission-storehouses
    can still be seen
    in the State of Texas.
4. But the Catholic people
    of Texas
    are not interested
    in the ideology
    of the Spanish Franciscans.
5. They are interested
    in keeping up
    with the Yankees.

IV. In California {327} — 1 time

1. The Yankees were not able
    to make wage-slaves
    out of the Indians.
2. The Yankees used to say:
    "A good Indian
    is a dead Indian."
3. By combining cult,
    that is to say Liturgy,
    with culture,
    that is to say Literature,
    with cultivation,
    that is to say Agriculture,
    the Spanish Franciscans
    who went to California
    succeeded in making willing workers
    out of the Indians.

4. The Catholics of California
         have not found the way
         to do for the Catholic unemployed
         what the Spanish Franciscans
         did for the Indians.
   5. In the meantime
         the people of California
         are looking for a panacea
         at the expense
         of the taxpayers.

V. Going to the Right {328} — 1 time

   1. Frey[220] of the A.F. of L.
         says that the Communist Party
         is pushing Roosevelt
         to the left.
   2. The A.F. of L.
         does not know enough
         to push Roosevelt
         to the right.
   3. Going to the left
         is going towards
         the Industrial Socialism
         of Stalin.
   4. Going to the right
         is going towards
         the Rural Communism
         of the Franciscan Founders
         who founded Rural Communes
         in what are now
         the State of Texas,
         the State of New Mexico,
         the State of California.

220. This is a reference to John P. Frey (1871–1957).

[The Easy Essays from May and June 1939 are not included in this volume. The essays for those two months of the paper were repeated collections from earlier issues of the paper that were not chosen by Maurin. An open letter from Dorothy Day to Peter Maurin on the front page of the June 1939 issue indicated she had not heard from Maurin in two months. As stated in the introduction, Maurin had taken a brief hiatus from the Catholic Worker, probably because Day had spent funds for the bread line that Maurin had sent to her for building a farming commune. Maurin reconciled with Day shortly afterward and submitted essays for the July-August issue of the paper.][221]

JULY–AUGUST 1939
LET'S KEEP THE JEWS FOR CHRIST'S SAKE

I. A Mystery {329} — 1 time

1. The Jews
    are a mystery
    to themselves.
2. They are not a nation
    although the Zionists
    try to build up one
    in Palestine.
3. They are not a race
    for they have intermarried
    with many other races.
4. They are not a religion
    since their belief
    calls for one Temple
    and the Jewish Temple
    has not been in existence
    for nearly 2,000 years.

---

221. Marc H. Ellis, *Peter Maurin: Prophet in the Twentieth Century* (New York: Paulist Press, 1981), 132–40; Day, "Open Letter to Peter Maurin From Editor," *New York Catholic Worker*, June 1939.

II. In Spain {330} — 1 time

1. St. Vincent Ferrer,
    a Spanish Dominican,
    succeeded in converting
    25,000 Jews.
2. When the Spaniards decided
    to drive the Moors out
    they also decided
    to drive the Jews out.
3. St. Vincent Ferrer
    tried to convert the Jews,
    he did not start a crusade
    to drive them out.
4. Driven out of Spain,
    the Jews found a refuge
    in Salonique
    which was then
    under the Turkish flag.
5. Spanish is still spoken
    by Jewish workmen
    in Salonique.

III. In the Papal States {331} — 1 time

1. The Popes never did
    start a crusade
    to drive the Jews
    out of the Papal States.
2. Jews have lived in Rome
    and the adjoining territory
    since the Roman Empire.
3. The Roman Empire
    protected the Jews
    living under its rule
    and so did the Popes
    in the Papal States.

4. The Jews themselves
    admit the fairness
    with which they were treated
    in the Papal States.

IV. In the Shadow of the Cross {332} — 1 time

1. While the Spaniards
    refused to keep the Jews
    the Popes consented
    to keep the Jews.
2. The Jews
    were the chosen people
    and they are still,
    for God does not change.
3. Because the Jews
    did not recognize Christ
    is not a good reason
    for acting towards them
    in a non-Christian manner.
4. The presence of the Jews
    all over the world
    is a reminder to the world
    of the coming of Christ.
5. The Jews who refused
    to accept the Cross
    find their best protection
    in the shadow
    of the Cross.

V. In Germany {333} — 1 time

1. Under the shadow of the Cross
    the Jews were protected;
    under the Swastika
    they are persecuted.
2. The Cross
    stands for one thing;

the Swastika
for another thing.
3. The Cross stands
for race equality;
the Swastika stands
for race superiority.
4. The Catholic Church
stands for human brotherhood,
the Nazi Regime
stands for the expansion
of one race
at the expense
of the other races.

VI. In America {334} — 1 time

1. The English Puritans
found a refuge
in America.
2. The French Huguenots
found a refuge
in America.
3. The Irish Catholics
found a refuge
in America.
4. The German Liberals
found a refuge
in America.
5. America
is big enough
to find a refuge
for persecuted Jews
as well as
persecuted Christians.[222]

---

222. Since early in 1938, Jewish applicants for visas to the United States far outstripped the number of visas the United States was willing to issue. Maurin likely wrote this essay in response to a highly publicized incident in May and June of 1939, where over 900 Jewish refugees sailing from Hamburg, Germany, were denied entry to the

VII. In Palestine {335} — 1 time

1. America can produce
    more than
    it can consume.
2. What America needs
    is more consumers.
3. More Jews in America
    means more consumers
    for America.
4. It is said that the Jews
    flock to the cities
    and become
    middlemen,
    and that there are
    too many middlemen
    in America.
5. But in Palestine
    the Jews are building
    both cities and country.
6. What the Jews are doing
    in Palestine
    they can do also
    in America.

SEPTEMBER 1939
EUROPEAN MESS

I. Safe for Dictators {336} — 1 time

1. America
    went into the last war
    to make the world
    safe for democracy.

United States. They had sailed to the United States after Cuba canceled most of their previously approved visas. Over 25 percent of the passengers who returned to Europe were known to have died in the Holocaust.

2. But England
    was not interested
    in helping America
    to make the world
    safe for democracy.
3. Because England
    as well as France
    was not interested
    in Wilson's 14 points
    the world
    is in the process
    of being made safe
    for dictators.
4. Because the Treaty of Versailles
    was not based
    on Wilson's 14 points
    it did not make for peace;
    it made for war.

II. League of Nations[223] {337} — 2 times

1. To please Wilson
    the Allies established
    the League of Nations.
2. But the League of Nations
    failed to impart notions
    to the nations
    of the League of Nations.
3. In spite of the League of Nations
    Japan went to Manchuria
    as well as China.
4. In spite of the League of Nations
    Italy went to Ethiopia
    as well as Albania.
5. In spite of the League of Nations
    Poland took Vilna
    from Lithuania.

---

223. Also known as "Pax Geneva." The other version of the essay is the same.

III. German Extension {338} — 1 time

1. The Treaty of Versailles
    disarmed Germany
    but Germany
    refused to stay disarmed.
2. And the League of Nations
    was powerless
    to keep Germany
    from rearming.
3. Once rearmed
    Germany
    started to revise
    the Treaty of Versailles,
    by going to Austria
    as well as Czechoslovakia.
4. And now Germany
    is in Poland.

IV. Nations and the Pope {339} — 1 time

1. The English believe
    in colonial expansion.
2. The French believe
    in colonial expansion.
3. The Germans believe
    in continental expansion.
4. The Pope does not believe
    in colonial expansion
    or continental expansion.
5. Nations thought
    that they could do
    without the Pope.
6. Nations need right notions
    and the Pope
    has the right notions
    that nations
    are in need of.

V. Prayer for Peace {340} — 1 time

1. Dismayed
    by the horrors of war
    which bring ruin
    to people and nations,
    we turn, O Jesus,
    to Thy most loving Heart,
    to our last hope.
2. O King of Peace,
    we humbly implore
    the peace for which we long.
3. From Thy Sacred Heart
    Thou didst send forth
    over the world
    divine charity,
    so that discord might end
    and love alone
    reign among men.
4. Do Thou inspire
    rulers and people
    with counsels of meekness,
    do Thou heal the discords
    that tear nations asunder.
5. Some trust in chariots,
    and some in horses,
    but we will call
    upon the name
    of the Lord our God.

—Benedict XV[224]

LAND AND CRAFTS {341} — 1 time

1. The Fascists
    do not believe in Marxism.

---

224. This is a version of Pope Benedict's peace prayer. Benedict directed all Catholics in the United States to recite it in their churches on 21 March 1915, which he designated as Peace Sunday.

2. The Marxists
    do not believe in Capitalism.
3. The Capitalists
    do not believe in a
    Land and Crafts society.
4. But if we had
    a Land and Crafts society
    we would not have Capitalism.
5. And if we did not have Capitalism
    we would not have Marxism.
6. And if we did not have Marxism
    we would not have Fascism.
7. So to foster
    a Land and Crafts Society
    is to oppose
    Capitalism, Marxism,
    Fascism.

OCTOBER 1939
PAX

I. Pax Geneva {337}

II. Pax Romana {342} — 1 time

1. Mussolini
    never did like
    the law and order
    that the League of Nations
    tried to enforce.
2. Mussolini
    went to the Roman Empire
    for a different concept
    of law and order.
3. Mussolini's policy
    has been to substitute
    the Pax Romana
    of the Roman Empire
    for the Pax Geneva
    of the League of Nations.

III. Pax Germania {343} — 1 time

1. Germany contends
     that the Holy Roman Empire
     was the heir
     to the Roman Empire,
     and that the Germans
     were the rulers
     of the non-German people
     of the Holy Roman Empire
2. Germany contends
     that the German race
     is more pure
     than the other races.
3. Germany contends
     that a pure race
     must increase
     and occupy territory
     now occupied
     by mongrel races.
4. Germany contends
     that enforced unanimity
     is the way to bring about
     national unity.

IV. Pax Muscova {344} — 1 time

1. Russia contends
     that the Russian Empire
     was the heir
     to the Byzantine Empire.
2. Russia contends
     that Russian Sovietism
     is the instrument
     for the realization
     of the Marxist dream.
3. While the Mahometans
     tried to force on the world
     their brand of Theism,
     Soviet Russia

tries to force on the world
its brand of Atheism.

V. Pax Britannica {345} — 1 time

1. England asks:
    "Is not Pax Britannica
    better than Pax Geneva,
    better than Pax Romana,
    better than Pax Germania,
    better than Pax Muscova?"
2. But Gandhi says:
    "England is not in India
    for the sake of India
    but for the sake of England."
3. De Valera says:
    "What England
    did to Ireland
    is not to the credit
    of Pax Britannica."
4. The United States
    is not convinced
    that the way to bring about
    the United States of the World
    is by joining
    the British Commonwealth.

VI. Pax Hibernia[225] {346} — 1 time

1. The world is cursed
    with imperialists.
2. What the world needs
    is missionaries
    not imperialists.

---

225. "Hibernia" is the Classical Latin name for Ireland.

3. When the Irish
    were scholars
    they were missionaries;
4. They were not
    imperialists.
5. When the Irish
    were missionaries
    they went all over Europe
    starting with England.
6. They had
    not swords or guns,
    but knowledge and zeal.
7. Through words and deeds
    they taught people
    to rule themselves.

VII. Pax Vaticana {347} — 1 time

1. What the Irish scholars taught
    is what the Christian Fathers taught.
2. What the Christian Fathers taught
    is what the Holy Father teaches.
3. The Holy Father teaches
    the supremacy
    of the spiritual
    over the material.
4. During the first world war
    a Protestant minister
    suggested that the warring nations
    accept the Pope
    as the arbiter.
5. The appeal for peace
    of Benedict XV
    was ignored
    in the last war.
6. Why not learn
    from the mistakes
    of the last war?

NOVEMBER 1939
PERSONALIST DEMOCRACY

I. Bourgeois Democracy {348} — 1 time

1. The economic royalists
   who believe in property
   without responsibility
   do not have
   the right concept
   of liberty.
2. They use liberty
   to become rugged individualists.
3. They don't use liberty
   to become gentlemen
   who try to be gentle.
4. In a letter addressed
   to French Catholics
   Cardinal Pacelli,
   now Pius XII,
   reminded them
   that "liberty
   does not grant
   license to act
   against the moral law
   nor should social liberties
   infringe upon the civil order
   and the common good."

II. Arithmocracy[226] {349} — 1 time

1. People used to say:
   "The king can do no wrong."
2. But kings can do wrong,
   and very often
   they did wrong.

---

226. "Arithmocracy" means rule by the majority of the population.

3. The kings that did wrong
   were the kings
   that had lost the sense
   of kingship.
4. Some seem to think
   that the majority
   can do no wrong.
5. But the majority
   can do wrong
   and it often does wrong
   because the majority
   has not yet acquired
   what makes people kind
   to mankind.

III. Poetry and Dictatorship {350} — 1 time

Padraic Colum says:
1. "In our time
    a political philosophy
    has arisen
    that tends to contradict
    what poets
    among all races,
    at all times,
    in all places
    have felt
    and shown.
2. "This philosophy insists
    that the individual
    has no dignity
    in himself,
    but only
    through his association
    with a race,
    a state,
    or a class.

3. "More and more
      it limits
      freedom of choice."

IV. Liberty or Discipline {351} — 1 time

1. Fascist countries
      discard liberty
      for the sake of discipline.
2. The greatness of a nation
      is the greatness
      of people's character.
3. Some people
      have good character.
4. Some people
      have bad character.
5. Some people
      have no character;
      they are yes men.
6. Through the power
      of thought and example
      people of good character
      transform the people
      of bad character.

V. Liberty or Security {352} — 1 time

1. Patrick Henry said:
      "Give me liberty
      or give me death."
2. Patrick Henry wanted
      the power to think,
      the power to choose,
      the power to act.
3. Many people today
      are willing
      to give up liberty
      for the sake
      of economic security.

4. When everybody
    looks for economic security
    nobody gets it.
5. But when nobody
    looks for economic security
    and uses liberty
    trying to be
    what he wants
    the other fellow to be
    then everybody gets
    economic security.

VI. They and We {166}

DECEMBER 1939
UNEMPLOYMENT

I. Profit Seekers {305}

II. Employers of Labor {280}

III. W.P.A. {281}

IV. On a Farming Commune {353} — 1 time

1. The remedy
    for unemployment
    is employment.
2. What the unemployed need
    is free rent,
    free fuel,
    free food;
    to acquire skill,
    to improve their minds,
    to receive
    spiritual guidance.
3. They can have all that,
    on a Farming Commune.

4. On a Farming Commune
    you eat
    what you raise,
    and raise
    what you want to eat.
5. On a Farming Commune
    a child is an asset,
    not a liability.
6. On a Farming Commune
    scholars
    become workers,
    and workers
    become scholars.

V. Firing the Boss[227] {354} — 2 times

1. The C.I.O.
    and the A.F. of L.
    help the worker
    fight the boss.
2. But the worker
    must have a boss
    before the C.I.O.
    and the A.F. of L.
    can be of any help
    to the worker
    in fighting a boss.
3. If it is a good thing
    to be a boss,
    it is a good thing
    to help the worker
    to be his own boss.

---

227. Also known as "Be Your Own Boss." The other version of the essay from February 1941 diverged after the first two stanzas with the following: "3. But if a worker cannot find a boss to fight, he can always go to a Farming Commune and be his own boss. 4. If it is a bad thing to exploit the worker, it is a good thing for the worker to exploit himself in a Farming Commune."

4. If it is a bad thing
   to exploit the worker,
   it is a good thing
   to help the worker
   exploit himself.
5. "Fire the boss
   and be your own boss"
   is a good slogan
   for the worker.

JANUARY 1940
WHY PICK ON THE JEWS?

I. Treaty of Versailles {355} — 1 time

1. Hitler likes
   to pick on the Jews.
2. The sufferings of Germany
   were the product
   of the Treaty of Versailles.
3. The Jews cannot be blamed
   for the Treaty of Versailles.
4. We must place the blame
   for the Treaty of Versailles
   on the English Machiavellian
   by the name of Lloyd George
   and on the French Machiavellian
   by the name of Clemenceau.

II. Bourgeois Capitalism[228] {356} — 2 times

1. In a book entitled
   Judaism and Capitalism,
   Werner Sombart
   blames the Jews
   for the development
   of Bourgeois Capitalism.

---

228. The other version of the essay is the same.

2. Adam Smith and Ricardo,
>   the theoreticians
>   of Bourgeois Capitalism
>   were not Jews.
3. The fostering
>   of Bourgeois Capitalism,
>   in modern Germany
>   is due to Bismarck.
4. To Kaiser William[229]
>   is also due
>   the fostering
>   of Bourgeois Capitalism
>   in modern Germany.

III. Turning Sharp Corners[230] {357} — 2 times

1. Business men say
>   that Bourgeois Capitalism
>   is all right
>   and that what is wrong
>   in Bourgeois Capitalism
>   are the abuses.
2. Rotarians have tried
>   without much success
>   to correct the abuses
>   of Bourgeois Capitalism.
3. The turning of sharp corners
>   by business men
>   must be laid to the door
>   of Christians
>   as well as Jews.
4. The assertion
>   that religion
>   has nothing to do
>   with business

---

229. It is unclear whether this is a reference to Wilhelm I (1797–1888) or Wilhelm II (1859–1941).

230. The other version of the essay is the same.

is the assertion
of Christians
as well as Jews.

IV. Modern Liberals[231] {358} — 2 times

1. The separation
    of the spiritual
    from the material
    was fostered
    by modern liberals.
2. Modern liberals
    were so broad-minded
    that they did not know enough
    to make up their minds.
3. Modern liberals
    were the defenders
    of Bourgeois Capitalism
    before becoming
    the fellow-travelers
    of Bolshevist Socialism.
4. Jews can be found
    among Bourgeois Capitalists,
    among Bolshevist Socialists,
    and among disillusioned
    fellow-travelers.

V. Racialism[232] {359} — 2 times

1. Having given up
    Jewish Orthodoxy
    some Jews tried to foster
    Jewish Racialism.
2. The Jews were
    a chosen people
    but they were never
    a superior race.

231. The other version of the essay is the same.
232. The other version of the essay is the same.

3. The Nordics were never
   a chosen people
   or a superior race.
4. And it is not
   because some Jews
   became racial-minded
   that other people
   should be racial-minded.
5. Racial-minded Jews
   are a nuisance
   and so are
   racial-minded Nordics.

VI. Promised Land[233] {360} — 2 times

1. When the Jews
   were themselves
   they taught the doctrine
   of a personal God
   as well as
   social ethics.
2. Bourgeois Capitalists
   as well as
   Bolshevist Socialists
   need the belief
   in a personal God
   as well as
   sound social ethics.
3. Hitler needs to read
   the Old Testament
   and the New Testament
   if he wants
   to lead men
   into the Promised Land
   where people
   do no longer try
   to cut each other's throats

---

233. Also known as "Personal God." The other version of the essay is only composed of the first two stanzas.

and where the lion
comes to lie down
with the lamb.

A NEW VENTURE

I. Turning to the Church {361} — 1 time

1. When I was in Saint Louis
    I met a Maryknoll Father
    who had recently returned
    to the United States
    after 8 years in China
    as a Maryknoll Missionary.
2. He is pleased to see
    that non-Catholics
    in the United States
    are much more curious
    about the Catholic Church
    than they were
    before he left for China
    ten years ago.
3. While modern nations
    give the sad spectacle
    of going back on their word,
    intelligent people
    are turning to the Church
    as the one moral security
    left in the world.

II. Beginning February First[234] {362} — 1 time

1. Father McSorley,
    great friend of
    The Catholic Worker,
    has always favored

---

234. This essay refers to the short-lived Discussion Center on Catholic Doctrine. The purpose of the Center was to promote Catholic thought among non-Catholics, particularly Jews, but very few non-Catholics chose to visit; Ellis, *Peter Maurin*, 149–53.

      the opening of small offices
      where non-Catholics
      curious about the Church
      could receive information.
2. Such an office
      has just been rented
      by Fr. Krimm,
      a Redemptorist Father.
3. It is located:
      196 East 3rd Street,
      near First Avenue.
4. It will be open
      from 2 to 5 p.m.
      and 7 to 10 p.m.,
      beginning February First.
5. Tell your non-Catholic friends
      curious about the Church
      that this office
      has just been opened
      for their benefit.

PROSTITUTION

I. Prostitution of Marriage[235] {363} — 2 times

  1. Birth control[236]
      is not self-control.

---

235. Also known as "Prostitution Plus." The essay from March 1940 concludes as follows after stanza 4: "Prostitution of marriage is prostitution legalized. Prostitution legalized is prostitution plus hypocrisy."

236. This essay in January 1940 and an arrangement of essays in March 1940 comprised the only essays in which Maurin addressed birth control. Maurin's argument against birth control was typical of Catholic teaching at the time. In December 1930, Pius XI issued his encyclical *Casti connubii*, which condemned the use of birth control. The encyclical was a reaction to two events: (1) the wide availability of latex condoms during the latter half of the 1920s, and (2) the approval of birth control within the confines of marriage by the Anglican Church in July 1930. Maurin's discussion of birth control can seem out of place after nearly seven years of essays that never mentioned the topic. Although his exact reason for writing these essays in 1940 is unclear, it probably

2. What is not self-control
   is self-indulgence.
3. What is self-indulgence
   is prostitution
   of functions.
4. Prostitution in marriage
   is prostitution
   of marriage.
5. Prostitution of marriage
   is prostitution
   plus hypocrisy.

II. Prostitution of Education {364} — 1 time

1. To educate
   is to elevate.
2. To elevate
   is to raise.
3. To raise wheat
   on a piece of land
   is to enable
   that piece of land
   to produce wheat
   instead of weeds.
4. To raise men
   from the animal state
   to the cultural state
   is to educate men.
5. The teaching of facts
   without understanding
   is a prostitution
   of education.

---

concerned his intention to open the Discussion Center on Catholic Doctrine to evangelize Jews and non-Catholics in February 1940. The Catholic ban on birth control may have been viewed as a hindrance to evangelization. This explanation is strengthened by Maurin's references to Herbert Ratner and Heywood Broun in March 1940, couched in essays discussing birth control. Both were recent converts to the Catholic faith.

III. Prostitution of the Press {365} — 1 time

1. Modern newspapermen
    try to give people
    what they want.
2. Newspapermen
    ought to give people
    what they need.
3. To give people
    what they want
    but should not have
    is to pander.
4. To give people
    what they need
    or in other terms
    to make them want
    what they ought to want,
    is to foster.
5. To pander
    to the bad in men
    is to make men
    inhuman to men.
6. To foster the good in men
    is to make men
    human to men.

IV. Prostitution of Politics {366} — 1 time

1. The Republicans say:
    "Let's turn the rascals out."
2. The Democrats say:
    "Let's turn the rascals out."
3. The Republicans
    call the Democrats rascals.
4. The Democrats
    call the Republicans rascals.
5. For the Republicans
    as well as
    for the Democrats

politics
is just profitable business.
6. By making a business
out of politics
politicians
have prostituted
the noble calling
of politics.

V. Prostitution of Property {367} — 1 time

1. All the land
belongs to God.
2. God wants us
to be our brother's keeper.
3. Our superfluous goods
must be used
to relieve the needs
of our brother.
4. What we do for our brother
for Christ's sake
is what we carry with us
when we die.
5. This is what the poor are for,
to give to the rich
the occasion to do good
for Christ's sake.
6. To use property
to acquire more property
is not the proper use
of property,
7. It is a prostitution
of property.

VI. Prostitution of the Theatre {368} — 1 time

1. What applies to the Press
applies also
to the Theatre.

2. In the Middle Ages
> the Theatre
> was considered
> as an efficient way
> of preaching.
3. They liked to produce
> Mystery Plays.
4. They aimed to preach
> and not to pander.
5. Pandering to the crowd
> has brought the degradation
> of the theatre.
6. The Theatre started
> in the Church.
7. The Theatre has ended
> in the gutter.

VII. Prostitution of Art {369} — 1 time

1. In the Middle Ages
> the artists
> were not called artists,
> they were called artisans.
2. When the artists
> were artisans
> they had the community spirit.
3. They had the community spirit
> because they believed
> in the doctrine
> of the common good.
4. Now that the artists
> do no longer believe
> in the doctrine
> of the common good
> they sell their work
> to art speculators.
5. As Eric Gill says:
> they have become

"the lap-dogs"
of the Bourgeoisie.²³⁷

FEBRUARY 1940
JUDAISM AND CATHOLICISM

I. Jacques Maritain {370} — 1 time

1. General Franco's
    brother-in-law
    accuses Maritain
    of being a converted Jew.
2. Maritain says
    that he is a convert,
    but not
    a converted Jew.
3. He adds
    that if he were
    he would not be
    ashamed of it.
4. He would, on the contrary,
    be proud,
    as his wife is proud
    of coming from a people
    who gave the Blessed Mother
    to the world.

II. Mrs. Maritain {371} — 1 time

1. Mrs. Maritain
    is a convert
    from Judaism.

---

237. This quote is from Eric Gill, *Autobiography* (London: J. Cape, 1940), 182. This essay shared Gill's general argument that most artists in the twentieth century were more concerned about pleasing their wealthy benefactors and did not ground their work in the Ultimate.

2. Mrs. Maritain
       thinks that Catholicism
       is Judaism plus.
  3. In becoming Catholic
       Mrs. Maritain thinks
       that she has kept
       her Judaism
       and added to it
       what Catholicism has
       that Judaism
       does not have.
  4. Mrs. Maritain thinks
       that she is now
       100% Jewish.

III. Dr. Herbert Ratner {372} — 1 time

  1. Dr. Herbert Ratner
       of the University of Chicago
       became a Catholic
       two years ago.
  2. His father, a Russian Jew,
       gave him the name Herbert
       in the hope
       that he would keep up
       with Herbert Spencer.
  3. He tried to get
       what modern liberals,
       including Herbert Spencer,
       had to offer.
  4. He was not satisfied
       with what modern liberals
       had to offer.
  5. He now says:
       "We were not
       attracted to the Church
       by Catholics;

we were pushed
into the Church
by non-Catholics who
did not have the stuff."

IV. Father Arthur Klyber {373} — 1 time

1. Father Arthur Klyber,
    a Redemptorist,
    was born on the East Side.
2. After a few years
    in the Navy
    he became a Catholic
    in Los Angeles.
3. The good example
    of Catholics
    from Los Angeles
    brought Fr. Klyber,
    an East Side Jew,
    into the Church.
4. The Catholic friends
    were always friendly
    to Klyber, the Jew,
    because they did not allow
    the poison of anti-Semitism
    to poison
    their human relations.
5. As a result
    Father Klyber is now
    a Catholic priest.

V. Six Other Priests {374} — 1 time

1. Six other converts
    from Judaism
    are now
    Catholic priests
    in the United States.

2. If they had remained Jews
  they might have
  become Rabbis.
3. As Rabbis,
  they would be
  commenting on the message
  of the Jewish Prophets.
4. As priests,
  they announce
  the good news
  that the Messiah,
  announced by the Prophets,
  died on Calvary.
5. As priests of Christ
  they again offer
  Christ's sacrifice
  on the altars
  of the Catholic Church.

MARCH 1940
BIRTH CONTROL

I. Gina Lombroso {375} — 1 time

1. In a book entitled
    The Soul of Woman,
    Gina Lombroso says
    that the basis of the home
    is the love of the woman
    for the man.
2. She adds that no woman
    can love a man
    whom she cannot admire.
3. The woman's scale of values
    is higher and lower
    than man's scale of values.
4. Because of that,
    no woman
    can admire a man

     who tries to induce her
     to practice birth control.
  5. She takes the man
     as a meal ticket.

II. Heywood Broun {376} — 1 time

  1. Margaret Sanger
     believes in birth control.
  2. The Catholic Church
     does not believe
     in birth control.
  3. If Margaret Sanger
     is right
     then the Catholic Church
     is wrong.
  4. Heywood Broun
     thought a long time
     about that question.
  5. He finally
     came to the conclusion
     that the Catholic Church
     is right
     and that Margaret Sanger
     is wrong.
  6. And he entered
     the Catholic Church.

III. Dr. Herbert Ratner {377} — 1 time

  1. Dr. Herbert Ratner
     is a convert
     from Judaism.
  2. The study of sex
     brought Dr. Herbert Ratner
     into the Catholic Church.
  3. As a scientist
     and as a philosopher,
     he maintains

that the Catholic Church
is foolproof
in the matter of sex.
4. He intends
to teach biology
and to lecture
on marriage.

IV. Prostitution Plus {363}

MAY 1940
KARL'S MARXISM VERSUS MY COMMUNISM

I. A Communist Society {303}

II. I Agree {72}

III. Means and Ends[238] {378} — 2 times
1. It is not true
that the end
justifies the means.
2. Good ends
require right means.
3. To use wrong means
to achieve good ends
is to forget the means
for the sake of the ends.
4. Class struggle
and proletarian dictatorship
are not the means
to bring about
a communist society.

---

238. The May 1941 essay contained several changes from the original, such as speaking of "pure means" instead of "right means." In addition, the May 1941 essay omitted the fourth stanza and switched stanzas two and three.

5. The means to bring about
a communist society
are Christian charity
and voluntary poverty.
6. We can create
a new society
within the shell of the old
with the philosophy of the new
which is not a new philosophy
but a very old philosophy;
a philosophy so old
that it looks like new.

IV. Curry Russian Favor[239] {379} — 1 time

1. "Our motives
were not based on principles.
2. "They were not concerned
with the interests
of the labor movement
as a whole.
3. "We did not want
to be found in opposition
to the Russian leaders
even if we believed

---

239. The next three essays feature quotes from prominent American leftists who had previously supported the Soviet Union, but were now outspoken critics of Stalin. The context for this change was twofold: (1) the Great Purge of the late 1930s in which Stalin exiled, imprisoned, and/or executed around one million Russians, including Communist Party members, government and army officials, and intellectuals; and (2) the Hitler-Stalin Nonaggression Pact of 1939, which was signed just days before the beginning of World War II. The Great Purge had already bewildered and disgusted many Soviet supporters in America, and the Hitler-Stalin Pact was viewed as an additional betrayal. The previous Soviet opposition to Hitler and fascism, which Communists viewed as a symptom of capitalism, had aided the growth and influence of American Communism. The pact hurt the credibility of Communism in America, with many leftists seeing it as a betrayal of Communist values.

that they were wrong,
because the Russians
never tolerated opposition."
4. "We had to curry favor
with the Russians
in order to maintain
our leadership
of the American Party."
5. "The Russian whip
could drive us out
just as quickly
as the Russian pat on the back
had put us in."

—Benjamin Gitlow,
in *I Confess*

V. Victims of a False Theory {380} — 1 time

1. "These men were victims
of a theory
according to which
no matter what they did
socialism
would ultimately come.
2. "The result
was a readiness
to use any means at hand,
an intellectual irresponsibility
in situations
where genuine alternatives
were present.
3. "It was a deadening
of moral sensibilities.
4. "The be-all
and end-all of life
was to stay
on the locomotive
of the revolution
as it speeds
towards Inferno.

5. "They were confident in the belief
    that a mystical,
    diabolical necessity
    was guiding it
    to a paradise on earth."

—Sidney Hook,
in a review of *I Confess*,
in *New York Tribune*

VI. They Were Wrong {381} — 1 time

1. "If we liberals were right
    on certain single aspects
    of the Russian Revolution,
    we were wrong,
    disgracefully wrong
    on the question as a whole.
2. "We were wrong
    because in our enthusiasm
    over Russia's liberation
    from the Tsar,
    our hope
    for the further liberation
    of the Russian people
    from economic
    as well as
    political serfdom
    and our vision of a new world
    springing from the womb
    of the Russian experiment,
    we permitted ourselves
    to condone wrongs
    that we knew to be wrongs.
3. "We consented
    to violations of principle
    that we knew to be fatal
    to the moral integrity
    of mankind."

—John Haynes Holmes

VII. Christian Charity {188}

VIII. On Selling Labor {16}

JUNE 1940
THE SIXTH COLUMN

I. Christianity Untried {135}

II. An Ethical Problem {2}

III. Roman Law {382} — 1 time

1. In a book entitled:
    *A Guildsman's
    Interpretation of History,*
    Arthur Penty
    has much to say
    about the revival
    of Roman Law.
2. To the revival
    of Roman Law
    must be attributed
    the historical disputes
    between Kings and Popes.
3. Jacques Maritain told us
    that Machiavellianism
    is the modern heresy.
4. By refusing
    to mind the Popes
    the Kings allowed Machiavellianism
    to become
    their guiding principle.
5. "Divide to rule"[240]
    is their slogan.

---

240. The exact origin of the quote is unknown, but its Latin variant, "*divide et impera,*" has been attributed to Alexander the Great's father, Philip II of Macedon (382–36 B.C.E.).

IV. Minding the Pope {383} — 1 time

1. Voltaire used to say:
    "If God did not exist
    He would have
    to be invented."
2. If the Pope
    did not exist
    he would have
    to be invented.
3. Because they refuse
    to mind the Pope
    modern nations
    are now busy
    cutting their own throats.
4. In time of peace
    modern nations
    prepare for war.
5. In time of war
    modern nations
    do not find time
    to prepare for peace.
6. If modern nations
    listened to the Pope
    when he talks about peace
    they would not
    have to worry
    about being ready
    for the next war.

V. We Catholics Believe[241] {384} — 2 times

1. We Catholics believe
    what Dualist Humanists believe,
    that there is
    good and bad

---

241. Also known as "We Catholics." The other version shortened the first stanza and inserted this additional stanza at the beginning: "We Catholics believe in beliefs."

in men
and that men
ought to express the good
to get rid of the bad.
2. We Catholics believe
what Orthodox Jews
and Quakers believe:
the Fatherhood of God
and the Brotherhood of Men.
3. We Catholics believe
what Fundamentalists believe:
Virgin Birth
and Redemption through Christ.
4. We Catholics believe
what the other believers believe
plus beliefs
that the other believers
don't believe:
Papal Supremacy
and the Universal Church.

VI. The Catholic Worker Isms {385} -1 time

1. *The Catholic Worker*
    stands for cooperativism
    against capitalism.
2. *The Catholic Worker*
    stands for personalism
    against socialism.
3. *The Catholic Worker*
    stands for leadership
    against dictatorship.
4. *The Catholic Worker*
    stands for agrarianism
    against industrialism.
5. *The Catholic Worker*
    stands for decentralism
    against totalitarianism.

JULY–AUGUST 1940
FOR PROTECTION'S SAKE

I. Protecting France {182}

II. Protecting England {183}

III. Protecting Japan {386} — 1 time

1. The French
    are doing their best
    to protect themselves
    and so do the English
    and so do the Japanese.
2. To protect themselves
    they went to Korea.
3. To protect themselves
    they went to Port Arthur.
4. To protect themselves
    they went to Manchuria.
5. To protect themselves
    they are in China.
6. They are in China
    for the same reason
    that European nations
    went to China.

IV. Protecting Russia {387} — 1 time

1. Russians used to think
    that they needed Constantinople
    for their protection.
2. The Crimean War was fought
    by France and England
    to keep Russia
    out of Constantinople.
3. The Russians think
    that in order to be able
    to protect themselves

they must be allowed
   by the Baltic States
   to have naval bases
   on the Baltic Sea.
4. The Russians say
   that they went to Poland,
   as well as Finland,
   not because they like war
   but because they like
   to protect themselves.
5. They have already
   the largest area
   of any nation
   and they still think
   that the world
   would be better off
   if they had more.

V. Protecting Italy {388} — 1 time

1. The Italians thought
   that in order to be protected
   they ought to have
   the Papal States.
2. They have the Papal States
   and now they think
   that they will never
   be protected
   until the Mediterranean Sea
   is under Italian control.
3. In the meantime
   they went to Libya
   as well as to Ethiopia,
   without forgetting
   Albania.
4. The Italians think
   that Italy
   will be better protected

when the Italian flag,
instead of the French flag,
flies over Djibouti
as well as Tunisia
as well as Corsica.

VI. Protecting Germany {389} — 1 time

1. The Germans also
    believe in protection.
2. For their own protection
    they went to Austria.
3. For their own protection
    they went to Czechoslovakia.
4. For their own protection
    they went to Denmark
    as well as Norway.
5. For their own protection
    they went to Holland
    as well as Belgium.
6. For their own protection
    they are in France.
7. For their own protection
    they intend
    to go to England.
8. Where will they not go
    for their own protection?

VII. Protecting Humanity {390} — 1 time

1. Each nation thinks
    that what it needs
    is to be protected
    against other nations.
2. But the fear
    of other nations
    does not take the place
    of the fear of God.

3. If we had
    the fear of God,
    we would have less fear
    of other nations.
4. Humanity
    is not protected
    when people
    cut each other's throats
    for fear of each other.
5. God may ask us,
    as He did of Cain:
    "Where is thy brother?"
6. Will God be satisfied
    if we answer Him:
    "I am not my brother's
    keeper"?
7. Is not the fear of God
    the best protection
    that humanity can have?

SEPTEMBER 1940
REVOLUTIONS

I. English Revolution {391} — 1 time

1. When Watt discovered
    the power of steam
    he brought into existence
    the factory system.
2. It is in England
    that the factory system
    had its beginning.
3. The factory system
    ran into competition
    with the crafts system.
4. The factory system
    brought about the system
    of stock ownership.

5. Stock ownership
    is absentee ownership.
6. Absentee ownership
    is property
    without responsibility.
7. Property without responsibility
    is now challenged
    by dictatorships.

II. French Revolution {392} — 1 time

1. French nobility
    had forgotten
    that "*noblesse oblige.*"
2. French peasants
    were oppressed
    by French nobility,
    which had ceased
    to be noble.
3. The French bourgeoisie
    sponsored the grievances
    of the peasants
    and made the Revolution
    not for the benefit
    of the peasants
    but for the benefit
    of the bourgeoisie.
4. Bourgeois revolutionaries
    sent each other
    to the guillotine
    while talking about
    Liberty, Equality, Fraternity.
5. Those who were not killed
    offered their services
    to Napoleon Bonaparte.
6. Adolph Hitler
    is now keeping up
    with Napoleon Bonaparte.

III. Russian Revolution {393} — 1 time

1. Lenin said
    that the world cannot be
    half industrial
    and half agricultural.
2. Because England
    had built up an Empire
    by giving up
    agrarianism
    and taking up
    industrialism
    Lenin thought
    that Russia
    should also
    be industrialistic.
3. Lenin thought
    that he could save time
    by building up
    State Socialism
    without passing
    through Private Capitalism
    and State Capitalism.
4. Lenin hoped
    that some day
    the State would wither away,
    but Stalin sees to it
    that the State
    does not wither away.

IV. American Revolution {394} — 1 time

1. The American Revolution
    stands for the right
    of the individual
    to be the master
    of his own destiny.
2. The American Revolution
    stands for personalism
    and not for Socialism.

3. The American Revolution
    stands for pluralism
    and not totalitarianism.
4. "*E Pluribus Unum*"
    is an American slogan.
5. America stands
    for freedom of speech,
    freedom of the press,
    freedom of worship.
6. The Declaration of Independence,
    the American Constitution,
    including the Bill of Rights,
    are important
    American documents.
7. The purpose of these documents
    is to protect the individual
    from majority rule.
8. The founders of America
    did not believe
    that the majority
    could do no wrong,
    any more than a dictator.
9. They believed
    in the right use of liberty;
    that is to say
    the power to think straight,
    the power to choose intelligently,
    the power to act wisely.

OCTOBER 1940
WRECKERS OF EUROPE

I. Philip the Fair {395} — 1 time

1. In the middle
    of the thirteenth century
    some Universities
    gave up the exclusive

teaching of Canon Law
and started to teach
Roman Law.
2. Roman-Law-minded
lawyers backed Philip the Fair
in his disputes
with Boniface VIII.
3. The aim of Roman Law
is to enable the rich men
to live among poor men
by teaching the rich men
how to keep the poor men poor.
4. The aim of Canon Law
is to enable the good men
to live among bad men
by teaching the good men
to carry their cross
and not to double-cross.

II. Machiavelli {396} — 1 time

1. According to R. H. Tawney,
high ethics
were taught to people
when the Canon Law
was the Law of the Land.
2. While Savonarola
was trying to bring back
the high ethics
of the Canon Law
Machiavelli
in his book *The Prince*
was trying to teach the rulers
how to rule people
by dividing them.
3. "Dividing to rule"
has been the slogan
of politicians
since Machiavelli
with few exceptions.

4. So today we say
         that politics
         is only politics.

III. Luther {397} — 1 time

   1. Christ established the Church
         to be the teacher
         of the human race.
   2. Luther told the people
         not to listen to the Church
         as the teacher
         established by Christ
         but to find from the Bible
         what Christ
         wants them to do.
   3. Since Luther
         people meet in churches
         to listen to somebody
         who gives them
         his personal interpretation
         of what is in the Bible
         while they profess to believe
         not in the preacher's interpretation
         but in their personal interpretation.
   4. In the meantime
         they are doing
         what the ruler wants.
   5. They refuse
         to listen to the teachings
         of the Church of Christ
         and yes the ruler.

IV. Richelieu {308}

V. Adam Smith {398} — 1 time

   1. Adam Smith
         expounded the theory
         that everything

would be lovely
if everybody took in
each other's washing
and got paid for it.
2. England first
and other nations afterward
acted on that theory.
3. The search for markets
and raw materials
is at the base
of modern imperialism.
4. And modern imperialism
is at the base
of modern wars.

VI. Napoleon {399} — 1 time

1. The French nobility
having become ignoble,
the French bourgeoisie
decided to get rid
of the French nobility.
2. Having got rid
of the French nobility,
the French bourgeoisie
split in two
and brought about
the French terror.
3. Napoleon Bonaparte
ended the French terror
and started a war
for the extermination
of foreign nobility.
4. Napoleonic rule
ended at Waterloo
and the Treaty of Vienna[242]

---

242. The Treaty of Vienna (1815) refers to a peace settlement between the major political powers of Europe following continual war and unrest for about twenty-five years,

established a compromise
between landed aristocracy
and plutocratic bourgeoisie.

VII. Hitler {400} — 1 time

1. In the nineteenth century
   secularist educators
   spread the idea
   that the Nordic race
   is a superior race.
2. What secularist educators
   used to believe
   Hitler now believes.
3. Hitler believes
   that inferior races
   ought to make room
   for superior races.
4. In 1914
   the Allies claimed
   that their job was
   to make the world
   safe for democracy.
5. Hitler claims
   that democracy
   is dangerous
   for the reason
   that under it
   the world is made safe
   for inferior races.

---

from the time of the French Revolution through the Napoleonic Wars. The new boundaries drawn by the settlement were meant to balance the major European powers and lead to a more peaceful Europe. As Maurin indicated, the peace and stability that the Treaty established benefited those already in power.

NOVEMBER 1940
EDUCATIONAL SECULARISM

I. To Worship God[243] {401} — 1 time

    1. Puritans came to America
        so they could worship God
        the way they wanted
        to worship God.
    2. Quakers came to America
        so they could worship God
        the way they wanted
        to worship God.
    3. Huguenots came to America
        so they could worship God
        the way they wanted
        to worship God.
    4. English Catholics
        came to America
        so they could worship God
        the way they wanted
        to worship God.

II. In the Public Schools {402} — 1 time

    1. The founders of America
        agreed in this
        that there is a God
        and that God wants
        to be worshipped.
    2. The founders of America
        did not agree
        about the way

---

243. All four of the groups that Maurin mentioned in this essay fled religious persecution. Only the fourth group mentioned was Catholic. It should be noted that in all four cases, political allegiances also played a role in the persecutions.

God wants
to be worshipped.
3. That there is a God
and that God wants
to be worshipped
is no longer taught
in the public schools
of America.
4. Religion
is no longer taught
in the public schools
of America,
but politics and business
are still taught
in the public schools
of America.

III. Secularism {22} (part 2)

IV. Hotbeds of Materialism {403} — 1 time

1. The Marxists
and the Chambers of Commerce
agree in this
that religion
ought to be kept
out of the public schools.
2. And American Protestants
keep silent
about the secularism
of the public schools.
3. In the nineteenth century
public schools
were the hotbeds
of Bourgeois Capitalism.
4. In the twentieth century
public schools
are the hotbeds
of Bolshevist Socialism.

DECEMBER 1940
NOT JEWISH WEALTH BUT IRISH CULTURE

I. Job or Mission {404} — 1 time

1. By grabbing
    Jewish wealth
    the Christian Mobilizers[244]
    hope to be able
    to give jobs
    to everybody.
2. By grabbing
    everybody's wealth
    the Bolshevist Socialists
    hope to be able
    to give jobs
    to everybody.
3. What everybody needs
    is not a job,
    but a mission.
4. When the Irish were Irish,
    they were missionaries.
5. By grabbing
    Irish Culture,
    as it was done,
    by Irish missionaries,
    we hope to be able
    to give a mission
    to everybody.

II. Land of Refuge[245] {405} — 2 times

1. After the fall
    of the Roman Empire,

---

244. The Christian Mobilizers were a 1939 offshoot of the Father Coughlin–inspired Christian Front. They proposed a very militant and even violent approach in confronting Jews and Communists. Their extreme views caused Father Coughlin to openly reject the group.

245. Also known as "Laying the Foundation." The other version of the essay only differed in grammar and punctuation usage.

the scholars,
scattered all over
the Roman Empire
looked for a refuge
and found a refuge
in Ireland,
where the Roman Empire
did not reach
and where the Teutonic
Barbarians did not go.
2. In Ireland,
the scholars formulated
an intellectual synthesis
and a technique of action.
3. Having formulated
that intellectual synthesis
and that technique of action,
the scholars decided
to lay the foundations
of Medieval Europe.

III. Salons de Culture[246] {406} — 2 times

1. In order to lay the foundations
of medieval Europe,
the Irish Scholars
established Salons de Culture
in all the cities of Europe,
as far as Constantinople,
where people
could look for thought
so they could have light.
2. And it was
in the so-called Dark Ages,
which were not so dark,
when the Irish
were the light.

---

246. Also known as "Literary Colonies." The other version of the essay referred to the "salons" as "literary colonies" and contained minor word changes.

3. But we are now living
    in a real Dark Age,
    and one of the reasons why
    the modern age
    is so dark,
    is because
    too few Irish
    have the light.

IV. Free Guest Houses[247] {407} — 2 times

1. The Irish Scholars established
    Free Guest Houses
    all over Europe
    to exemplify
    Christian charity.
2. This made
    pagan Teutonic rulers
    tell pagan Teutonic people:
    "The Irish are good people
    busy doing good."
3. And when the Irish
    were good people
    busy doing good,
    they did not bother
    about empires.
4. That is why we never heard
    about an Irish Empire.
5. We heard about
    all kinds of empires,
    including the British Empire,
    but never about
    an Irish Empire,
    because the Irish

---

247. The other version was only different from a structural standpoint.

did not bother about empires
when they were busy
doing good.

V. Agricultural Centers[248] {408} — 2 times

1. The Irish Scholars established
    Agricultural Centers
    all over Europe
    where they combined:
    cult,
    that is to say liturgy,
    with culture,
    that is to say literature,
    with cultivation,
    that is to say agriculture.
2. And the word America
    was for the first time
    printed on a map
    in a town in east France
    called Saint-Die,
    where an Irish scholar
    by the name Deodad[249]
    founded an Agricultural Center.
3. What was done
    by Irish Missionaries
    after the fall
    of the Roman Empire
    can be done today
    during and after the fall
    of modern empires.

---

248. Also known as "Rural Centers." The first two stanzas of the alternate essay were the same except that it substituted the term "rural center" for "agricultural center." The alternate version concluded with a completely different third stanza: "In the CATHOLIC WORKER we refuse to keep up with modern industrialists and choose to keep up with the radicalism of Irish Scholars."

249. This is a reference to St. Deodatus of Nevers (d. 679).

JANUARY 1941
CHRISTIANITY AND DEMOCRACY

I. Leo XIII {409} — 1 time

1. On several occasions
    Pope Leo XIII
    wrote on the legitimacy
    of several forms
    of government.
2. In the encyclical
    Diuturnum illud[250]
    we find this sentence:
    "Nothing prevents the Church
    from giving its approval
    to the government
    of one man
    or several men
    as long as the government
    is a just government
    and applies itself
    to foster the common good."

II. Pius X {410} — 1 time

1. In a letter
    condemning the *Sillon*[251]
    Pope Pius X
    takes up that doctrine.

---

250. In the English-speaking world, this encyclical is usually just called *Diuturnum*. Published in 1881, it stressed respect for rulers, the notion that justice was foundational for any society, and that God was the source of all political authority.

251. As noted in the introduction, Maurin was briefly associated with the *Le Sillon* movement. The movement was led by Marc Sangnier and promoted a social vision in which democracy could be reconciled to Catholicism as a viable alternative to Communism. In 1910, St. Pope Pius X condemned *Le Sillon* in his encyclical *Notre charge apostolique*, believing it to be tainted with the ideas of Communism and liberalism.

2. "The *Sillon*," says Abbe Leclercq
    editor of *La Cite Chretienne*
    "was a Christian
    democratic movement
    founded by Marc Sangnier.
3. "It was full of enthusiasm
    and generosity
    but lacked deep thought.
4. "It had allowed itself
    to present democracy
    as the only political regime
    in conformity
    with Christianity.
5. "Denounced in Rome,"
    continues Abbe Leclercq
    "it was condemned
    for the preceding reason
    as well as imprudences
    in thought and language."

III. Freda Kirchwey {411} — 1 time

1. Freda Kirchwey,
    editor of the *Nation*,
    has an article
    on Religion
    and Democracy.
2. "Democracy," she says,
    "may be Christian
    or it may be Jewish.
3. "It is related
    to whatever culture
    or whatever religious
    or nonreligious ideas
    flourish in the society
    that breeds it.

4. "Democracy," she continues,
>　"has nothing on earth to do
>　with any particular faith."[252]

IV. Agrees with Two Popes {412} — 1 time

1. The editor of *The Nation*
>　agrees with Leo XIII
>　as well as Pius X
>　in the contention
>　that Christianity
>　is not tied up
>　with any particular form
>　of government.
2. Don Sturzo
>　attacks Fascism
>　and several bishops
>　are defending it.
3. A government
>　can be autocratic
>　or aristocratic
>　or democratic.
4. The duty of a government,
>　whether it be
>　autocratic
>　or aristocratic
>　or democratic,
>　is to foster
>　the common good.

V. The Common Good {413} — 1 time

1. The common good
>　is not common,
>　　because common sense
>　　does not prevail.

---

252. Kirchwey, "Religion and Democracy," *Nation*, 30 November 1940, 521–22.

2. In a good autocracy
    the common good
    is incarnated
    in a good autocrat.
3. In a good aristocracy
    the common good
    is incarnated
    in the good aristocrats.
4. In a good democracy
    the common good
    is incarnated
    in the good democrats.
5. The good democrats
    are democrats
    with the democratic spirit.
6. They are the elite
    in a democracy.

VI. Democratic Elite {414} — 1 time

1. Henry Bérenger
    followed Jusserand
    as French Ambassador
    in Washington.
2. Bérenger was an agnostic
    who could not conceive
    of a democracy
    without a cultural elite.
3. The elite in a democracy
    is imbued
    with what we call
    the right spirit.
4. The democratic elite
    is the spearhead
    of a democratic society.
5. The democratic elite
    is recruited
    from all classes
    of a democratic society.

6. The democratic elite
    is not moved
    by greed for wealth
    or greed for power.
7. It is moved
    by clear thinking.

VII. Faith, Hope and Charity {415} — 1 time

1. Agnostic intellectuals
    lack faith
    in Christ the Redeemer
    as well as
    in God the Omnipotent.
2. And now
    they are losing faith
    in the power of man
    to pull himself up
    by his own bootstraps.
3. Faith in Christ the Redeemer,
    hope in the life to come,
    and charity toward all men
    are motivating forces
    in the fostering
    of a democratic elite—
    without which
    a democratic society
    becomes the laughing-stock
    of totalitarian societies.

FEBRUARY 1940
ROAD TO COMMUNISM

I. Paraguay Reductions {416} — 1 time

1. In a book entitled:
    The Magic Mountain
    Thomas Mann has a character

who has become
a Jesuit after having been
a Marxist.
2. As a Jesuit
he could understand
Communism much better
than he could understand
it as a Marxist.
3. In Paraguay
the Jesuits established
a Communist society.
4. Part of the land
was held individually.
5. The other part
known as God's land
was cultivated in common.
6. The produce was used
for the maintenance
of the aged,
the infirm
and the young.

II. Proudhon and Marx {417} — 1 time

1. "Communism is a society
where each one works
according to his ability
and gets
according to his needs."
2. Such a definition
does not come from Marx;
it comes from Proudhon.
3. Proudhon wrote two volumes
on *The Philosophy of Poverty*
which Karl Marx
read in two days.
4. Karl Marx wrote a volume
on *The Poverty of Philosophy*.

5. Karl Marx
>   was too much of a materialist
>   to understand
>   the philosophical
>   and therefore social value
>   of voluntary poverty.

III. A Blunderer {418} — 1 time

1. "If my wants
>   should be much increased
>   the labor required
>   to supply them
>   would become a drudgery.
2. "If I should sell
>   both my forenoons
>   and afternoons
>   to society
>   I am sure that for me
>   there would be nothing
>   left worth living for.
3. "I trust that I shall never
>   sell my birthright
>   for a mess of pottage.
4. "I wish to suggest
>   that a man
>   may be very industrious
>   and yet
>   not spend his time well.
5. "There is
>   no more fatal blunderer
>   than he who consumes
>   the greater part of his life
>   getting a living."

—Henry Thoreau

IV. Functional Poverty {419} — 1 time

1. "Now frankly
    most of us
    have our hands
    so full of baubles
    that we haven't
    even a finger free
    which to reach out
    and satisfy the claim
    of unlimited liability.
2. "Poverty,
    or some approximation of it,
    willingly assumed
    would set us free
    both for finding
    our responsibility
    and for fulfilling it
    when found.
3. "That is why
    I have called it
    functional poverty.
4. "It is to be taken up
    not as a shirking
    of the responsibility
    of wealth or privilege
    but as acceptance
    of wider responsibility."

—Mildred Binns Young

V. Holy Poverty {420} — 1 time

1. "This poverty consists
    in the voluntary renunciation
    of every possession
    for reasons of love
    and through divine inspiration.

2. "It is quite the opposite
    of that forced
    and unlovable poverty
    preached by
    some ancient philosophers.
3. "It was embraced by Francis
    with so much affection
    that he called her
    in loving accents
    Lady, Mother, Spouse.
4. "In this respect
    Saint Bonaventure writes:
    'No one was ever
    so eager for gold
    as he was for poverty;
    no more jealous
    in the custody
    of a treasure
    than he was
    for the pearl
    of the Gospel.'"[253]

—Pius XI

VI. Selling Their Labor {16}

VII. Farming Commune {94}

VIII. Be Your Own Boss {354}

---

[253]. This quote is from Pope Pius XI's 1926 previously mentioned encyclical on St. Francis of Assisi, *Rite expiatis* 15.

MARCH 1941
PIE IN THE SKY[254]

I. Bourgeois Capitalists {421} — 1 time

1. Bourgeois Capitalists
   don't want their pie
   in the sky
   when they die.
2. They want their pie
   here and now.
3. To get their pie
   here and now
   Bourgeois Capitalists
   give us
   better and bigger
   commercial wars
   for the sake of markets
   and raw materials.
4. But as Sherman says:
   "War is hell."
5. So we get hell
   here and now
   because Bourgeois Capitalists
   don't want their pie
   in the sky
   when they die,
   but want their pie
   here and now.

II. Bolshevist Socialists {422} — 1 time

1. Bolshevist Socialists
   like Bourgeois Capitalists

---

254. "Pie in the sky" was first employed in a 1911 song for the Industrial Workers of the World entitled, "The Preacher and the Slave." The song critiqued religion for promising a glorious afterlife if one accepted injustice and poverty in the present life.

   don't want their pie
   in the sky
   when they die.
2. They want their pie
   here and now.
3. To get their pie
   here and now.
   Bolshevist Socialists
   give us
   better and bigger
   class wars
   for the sake
   of capturing the control
   of the means of production
   and distribution.
4. But war is hell
   whether it is
   a commercial war
   or a class war.
5. So we get hell
   here and now
   because Bolshevist Socialists
   don't want their pie
   in the sky
   when they die
   but want their pie
   here and now.

III. Catholic Communionism {423} — 1 time

1. Bolshevist Socialists
   as well as
   Bourgeois Capitalists
   give us hell
   here and now
   without
   leaving us the hope
   of getting our pie
   in the sky
   when we die.

2. We just
   get hell.
3. Catholic Communionism
   leaves us the hope
   of getting our pie
   in the sky
   when we die
   without
   giving us hell
   here and now.

IV. Two of a Kind[255] {424} — 2 times

1. The Bourgeois Capitalist
   tells the Bolshevist Socialist:
   "We got what we got
   because we got it,
   and we are going to keep it
   no matter how we got it."
2. The Bolshevist Socialist
   tells the Bourgeois Capitalist:
   "We want what we want
   because we want it,
   and we want
   what you got;
   and we are going to get it,
   no matter how we get it."
3. The Bolshevist Socialist
   is the spiritual son
   of the Bourgeois Capitalist.
4. All the sins of the father,
   the Bourgeois Capitalist,
   are found in the son,
   the Bolshevist Socialist.

---

255. The other version omitted stanza four, substituted "rugged individualist" for "Bourgeois Capitalist" and "rugged collectivist" for "Bolshevist Socialist," and added the following line to conclude the first stanza: "And if your fellows try to get it we will organize vigilantes."

5. He is a chip from the old block;
> and the old block
> is a blockhead
> who has not learned
> to use his head.

V. Class Struggle {233}

VI. Were I a Marxist {425} — 1 time

1. Were I a Marxist
   > I would desert
   > the working class
   > and join the capitalist class
   > so as to be able
   > to bring class consciousness
   > to the working class.
2. A class conscious capitalist class
   > would put the screws
   > on the working class
   > and by doing so
   > bring class consciousness
   > to the working class.
3. A class conscious capitalist class
   > and a class conscious
   > working class
   > would fight for supremacy
   > and bring about
   > a bloody revolution.
4. In the clash
   > between two opposite classes
   > I as a member
   > of the capitalist class
   > would be killed
   > by the working class,
   > but by my death
   > would have contributed
   > to bring about
   > the emancipation
   > of the working class.

5. But I am not a Marxist;
   I am a Christian.

VII. Grave Diggers {426} — 1 time

1. Bolshevist Socialists
      want to be
      the grave-diggers
      of Bourgeois Capitalism.
2. They refuse
      to let the Bourgeois Capitalists
      dig their own graves.
3. Fascists refuse
      to let the Bolshevist Socialists
      dig the graves
      of Bourgeois Capitalism.
4. Fascists maintain
      that Bourgeois Capitalism
      is not dead yet
      and they will try
      to keep it alive.
5. By trying to be
      the grave-diggers
      of Bourgeois Capitalism,
      Bolshevist Socialists
      bring in Fascism.

VIII. A New Society {427} — 1 time

1. Why not let
      Bourgeois Capitalists
      dig their own graves?
2. And while the Bourgeois
      Capitalists
      dig their own graves
      why not create
      a new society
      within the shell of the old
      with the philosophy of the new
      which is not

a new philosophy
but a very old philosophy,
a philosophy so old
that it looks like new.

APRIL 1941
THE CANON LAW AND THE LAW OF THE CANNON

I. R. H. Tawney {68}

II. St. Thomas More {428} — 1 time

1. St. Thomas More believed
   in the Common Law.[256]
2. The Common Law
   that St. Thomas More
   believed in
   was rooted
   in Canon Law.
3. Henry VIII believed
   that since he was a king
   he was the Law.
4. St. Thomas More
   did not believe
   in Henry VIII's
   interpretation
   of Common Law.
5. The Common Law
   as it exists
   in today's England
   has little relation
   to Canon Law.

---

256. Common law came to prominence in England during the mid-twelfth century by the order of King Henry II. Incorporating local customs, he instituted a law that was common for the entire kingdom. In very general terms, common law courts are more inductive, beginning with the facts of the case and examining previous cases for the closest analogy. Civil law courts, largely based on Roman Law, are more deductive and begin a case by searching for statutes that can be universally applied.

III. Judge Cardozo {429} — 1 time

1. Judge Cardozo said
    that Common Law
    as it exists today
    in the United States
    does not make sense.
2. Judge Cardozo proposed
    to discard Common Law
    and go back
    to Roman Law.
3. If modern Common Law
    is bad,
    modern Roman Law
    is worse.
4. Hitler and Mussolini
    believe in Roman Law.
5. "To grab and to hold"[257]
    is the aim
    of Roman Law.
6. "Divide to rule"
    is the motto
    of the Roman Law-
    minded Lawyers.

IV. Arthur Penty {430} — 1 time

1. In a book entitled:
    *A Guildsman's
    Interpretation of History*
    Arthur Penty
    has a chapter
    on the revival of
    Roman Law.
2. The revival
    of Roman Law
    in the 13th century

---

257. This quote is not from Roman Law; it simply underscores Maurin's view that the purpose of Roman Law was to protect property owners and the wealthy.

>   brought about the disputes
>   between kings and popes.
> 3. The Kings
>   are on the go.
> 4. The Pope
>   is still on the job.
> 5. He writes encyclicals,
>   but business men
>   and politicians
>   pay little attention
>   to what he has to say.
> 6. In the meantime,
>   we are worrying
>   about what Stalin,
>   Hitler, and Mussolini
>   will do to us.

MAY 1941
BEYOND MARXISM

I. A Communist Society {303}

II. I Agree {72}

III. Means and Ends {378}

IV. He Left So Much[258] {431} — 2 times

> 1. When a man dies
>   and leaves a lot of money
>   the papers say:
>   "He left so much."
> 2. But they say:
>   "He left so much."
> 3. Why did he
>   leave so much?

---

258. The other version of the essay contained minor variations, omitted the second stanza, and added an additional stanza at the end that contains two words: "Too dumb."

4. Well, he did not know
    enough
    to carry it with him
    when he died
    by giving it
    to the poor
    for Christ's sake
    during his lifetime.

V. Better and Better Off {50}

VI. Logical and Practical[259] {432} — 2 times

1. What is not logical
    is not practical
    even if it is practiced.
2. What is logical
    is practical
    even if it is not practiced.
3. To practice
    what is not logical
    though it is practical
    is to be a bourgeois.
4. A bourgeois is a fellow
    who tries to be somebody
    by trying to be
    like everybody,
    which makes him
    nobody.
5. To practice
    what is logical
    even if it is not practiced
    is to be a leader.

---

259. The alternate version was shorter and contained a different final stanza: "A follower is a fellow who follows the leader because he sponsors the cause that the leader follows." The alternate version reworded stanza three as follows: "To practice what is not logical for the only reason that it is practiced is to be a bourgeois."

6. A leader is a fellow
   who follows a cause.
7. The Sermon on the Mount
   will be called practical
   when Christians make up
   their mind
   to practice it.

JUNE 1941
BEYOND NATIONALISM

I. Right and Wrong {181}

II. Barbarians and Civilized {275}

III. Germans and Poles {433} — 1 time

1. The Germans think
    that they are civilized
    and the Poles
    are barbarians.
2. The Germans
    invaded Poland
    to place Poland
    where they think it belongs
    under the German rule.
3. German rule
    is a military rule,
    not a personalist rule.
4. A military rule
    breaks the will of the people,
    but does not change
    the heart of the people.
5. A military rule
    is materially efficient,
    but it is not
    spiritually efficient.

IV. Polish Writers {434} — 1 time

1. After the first World War
    Poland established
    a personalist constitution.[260]
2. But military men in Poland
    discarded it
    so as to establish
    a more dictatorial
    military State.
3. But Polish writers
    are not like
    most German writers.
4. Polish writers believe
    in spiritual values
    while German writers
    believe in materialist values.
5. Polish writers believe
    in the power of the word;
    German writers believe
    in the power of the sword.

V. Catholic Extremism {435} — 1 time

1. Poland does not exist
    as a nation,
    but Poland exists
    as a culture.

---

260. This is a reference to Poland's March Constitution of 1921. The Constitution instituted three branches of government: an executive, legislative, and judicial branch. The most powerful branch of government was the legislative branch, which was broken into two groups, the Senate and the *Sejm*. The strong legislative branch was meant to ensure broad protections for ethnic and religious minorities. The Constitution was never fully implemented, and a military coup in 1926 resulted in its termination. It is likely that Maurin was attracted to the aspects of the Constitution that protected the rights of minorities and placed substantial power on the local level.

2. The expression of that culture
     by Polish writers
     in the Polish language
     will spread the Polish spirit
     among the Polish people.
3. The Germans are suffering
     from extreme nationalism;
     the Poles must face them
     with extreme Catholicism.
4. The extreme nationalism
     of Germany
     is the logical product
     of the deformation
     of Christian doctrine
     and practice by the Reformation.
5. Catholic people
     must quit looking up
     to Protestant people
     and return
     to the Catholic extremism
     of primitive Christians.

TRUE STORIES[261]

I. Only a Frenchman {436} — 1 time

1. When I was in Spokane
     a Catholic Sister
     told me:
     "I have a little story
     to tell you,
     and I think you will
     like it.
2. "I met an Indian woman
     who was carrying
     what looked like
     a white boy.

---

261. This section contains jokes by Peter Maurin. In this case, his humor focuses on ethnic assumptions.

3. "I said to her:
'You don't mean to tell me
that you married
a white man.'
4. "'Oh no,' she said,
'Just a Frenchman.'"

II. Nine Englishmen {437} — 1 time

1. An Englishman
and an American
were flying over
the Egyptian Soudan.[262]
2. Under them
was a stretch of houses
four miles long.
3. The American
asked the Englishman:
"What is the population
of this town?"
4. "Nine Englishmen,"
answered the Englishman.

III. Germans and English {438} — 1 time

1. A German
owned a fruit-farm
in British Columbia.
2. He and his wife
were considered
as second-class citizens
by the British element.
3. His wife succeeded
in inducing him
to sell the fruit-farm
and go back to Germany.

---

262. Egyptian Soudan is a reference to Anglo-Egyptian Sudan, which was under British and Egyptian control from 1899 to 1956. The name indicated how Sudan was subjugated during this period.

4. She could not stand
    to be considered inferior
    by the British element.
5. The English think
    that they are superior
    to the Germans.
6. And the Germans think
    they are superior
    to the English.
7. They cannot stand
    to be considered
    inferiors.
8. They can give it
    but cannot take it.

JULY–AUGUST 1941
LET'S BE CHARITABLE FOR CHRIST'S SAKE

I. Fallacy of Saving {38}

II. Wisdom of Giving {123}

III. He Left So Much {431}

IV. First Christians {188}

V. Rich and Poor {254}

SEPTEMBER 1941
LET'S BE FAIR TO THE NEGROES FOR CHRIST'S SAKE

I. Anthropologists Say {439} — 1 time

1. The anthropologists say
    that the western world
    is anthropologically
    divided into four kinds of
    people.

2. They are:
    a) the Nordics,
    b) the Alpines,
    c) the Mediterraneans,
    d) the Negroes.
3. Anthropologists add
    that there is nothing
    in science
    to prove
    that one race
    is superior
    to another race.
4. Science cannot prove
    that the Nordics
    are superior
    to the Negroes.

II. Theologians Say {440} — 1 time

1. Theologians say
    that Christ died
    for the redemption
    of the Negroes
    as well as
    the Nordics.
2. The Nordics
    were created
    by the same Creator
    and redeemed
    by the same Redeemer
    as the Negroes.
3. The redeemed Nordics
    will enjoy
    the beatific vision
    in the same Heaven
    as the Negroes.
4. The redeemed Nordics
    receive the same Christ

at the altar rail
as the Negroes.
5. The redeemed Nordics
belong to the same
Mystical Body
as the Negroes.

III. Nordic and Negro Bishops {441} — 1 time

1. The Holy Father
has recently selected
African Negro priests
and made them bishops.
2. The Negro bishops
of Africa
have the same powers
as the Nordic bishops
of Germany.
3. Nordic bishops
are all right
for Nordic people
and Negro bishops
are all right
for Negro people.
4. The Catholic Church
wants Nordic bishops
to lead Nordic people
and Negro bishops
to lead Negro people.
5. The Catholic Church
does not differentiate
between Nordic bishops
and Negro bishops.

IV. American Negroes {442} — 1 time

1. American Negroes
think they must keep up
with white people.

2. American Negroes
    don't need to keep up
    with white people.
3. American Negroes
    can keep up
    with St. Augustine.
4. St. Augustine,
    who lived
    in North Africa
    is one of the Fathers
    of the Catholic Church.
5. If American Negroes
    made up their minds
    to keep up
    with St. Augustine
    they would be able
    to make white Nordics
    look up to them
    instead of looking up
    to white Nordics.

THE MONEY SYSTEM

I. Humiliation and Doubt {443} — 1 time

1. "I believe
    there must be persons
    who like myself
    were deeply shaken
    by the events
    of September, 1938.
2. "It was a feeling of humiliation
    which seemed to
    demand an act of personal
    contrition, repentance,
    and amendment,
    as well as a doubt
    in the validity
    of a civilization.

3. "Was our society
      which had always been
      so assured of its
      superiority and
      rectitude,
      so confident
      of its unexamined premisses,
      assembled
      around anything
      more permanent
      than a congeries of banks,
      insurance companies
      and industries?"

                                    —T. S. Eliot

II. Because the State {5}

III. Thomas Wilson {444} — 1 time

1. John Calvin
      was the first man
      to legalize
      money lending at interest.
2. John Knox,
      a Scotchman,
      brought the idea
      to Scotland.
3. From Scotland,
      it went to England
      where they legalized it
      around 1575.
4. Thomas Wilson
      wrote a discourse
      on usury in 1572
      where he quotes
      the Prophets of Israel
      and the Fathers of the Church.

5. When Thomas Wilson
    was a student
    Thomas More
    was Chancellor of England
    and the Catholic doctrine
    on usury
    was still taught
    in the schools of England.

IV. Maynard Keynes {445} — 1 time

1. Maynard Keynes
    was the financial
    representative of the
    English government
    at Versailles.
2. After Versailles
    Maynard Keynes
    wrote a book entitled:
    *The Economic
    Consequences of the Peace*.
3. In this book
    Maynard Keynes pointed out
    the bad economic
    consequences
    that would result
    from the Treaty of
    Versailles.
4. France and England
    paid little attention
    to what he had to say.
5. Later on,
    Maynard Keynes declared
    that "modern economists
    ought to ask themselves
    if Medieval economists
    were not sound

> when they condemned
> money lending at interest."

V. A Better Way {446} — 1 time

1. Hitler has a way
    to solve the problem
    of money lending
    at interest.
2. But there is a better way
    than Hitler's way.
3. That better way
    is the way
    of the Prophets of Israel
    and the Fathers of the Church.
4. On this way
    the Jews and the
    Christians ought to
    agree.
5. Since the State
    has legalized
    money lending at interest
    in spite of the teachings
    of the Prophets of Israel
    and the Fathers of the Church,
    let the State
    make illegal
    money lending at interest
    and oblige money
    borrowers
    to pay one percent
    of the money lent
    every year
    during a period
    of hundred years.

VI. Christianity Untried {135}

OCTOBER 1941
FOR GOD'S SAKE

I. Honest to God {447} — 1 time

1. One of the slogans
    of the Middle Ages was
    "Honest to God."
2. We have ceased to be
    "Honest to God."
3. We think more
    about ourselves
    than we do
    about God.
4. We have ceased to be
    God-centered
    and have become
    self-centered.

II. Father Denifle {448} — 1 time

1. Father Denifle
    was an Austrian
    Dominican.
2. In 1872,
    he delivered four sermons
    in Graz, Austria,
    about "Humanity,
    its destiny
    and the means
    to achieve it."
3. Translated by a priest
    of Covington, Kentucky,
    these four sermons
    were published in America
    by Pustet,[263] the editor.

---

263. This is a reference to Fr. Pustet, which published the book Heinrich Denifle, *Humanity: Its Destiny and the Means to Attain it; A Series of Discourses* (Ratisbon, N.Y., 1909).

4. Father Denifle emphasizes
that having forgotten God,
humanity
cannot realize
its own destiny.
5. God has not
forgotten man,
but man has
forgotten God.

III. American Founders {449} — 1 time

1. The founders of America
came to America
to serve God
the way they thought
God wants to be served.
2. How God
wants to be served
is no longer taught
in American schools.
3. How to be successful
is still taught
in American schools.
4. Thinking of time
in terms of money
is at the base
of the thinking
of our business men.
5. We put on our coins:
"In God we trust,"
but persist in thinking
that everybody else
ought to pay cash.

IV. Cardinal Gasquet {450} — 1 time

1. Cardinal Gasquet
was an English
Benedictine.

2. He was a student
    of that period
    of English history
    that preceded
    the Reformation.
3. In a book entitled:
    *The Eve of the
    Reformation*
    he points out
    that externalism
    —another word
    for materialism—
    prevailed in that period
    of English history.
4. The externalism
    of English bishops
    made them
    follow the King
    instead of the Pope
    when the King ceased
    to mind the Pope.

V. St. Augustine {451} — 1 time

1. St. Augustine said,
    "Love God
    and do what you please."
2. We do what we please
    but we don't love God.
3. We don't love God
    because we don't know
    God.
4. We don't know God
    because we don't try
    to know God.
5. And man was created
    in the image of God
    and every creature
    speaks to us
    about God

and the Son of God
came to earth
to tell us
about God.

NOVEMBER 1941
PLURALIST PERSONALISM

I. We Catholics {384}

II. If {452} — 1 time
   1. What a fine place
         this world would be
         if Dualist Humanists
         tried to be human
         to men.
   2. What a fine place
         this world would be
         if Personalist Theists
         tried to be
         their brother's keeper
         as God
         wants them to be.
   3. What a fine place
         this world would be
         if Fundamentalist Protestants
         tried to exemplify
         the Sermon on the Mount.
   4. What a fine place
         this world would be
         if Roman Catholics
         tried to keep up
         with St. Francis of Assisi.

III. Logical and Practical {432}

IV. They and We {166}

V. Better and Better Off {50}

VI. Big Shots and Little Shots {56}

VII. Two of a Kind {424}

DECEMBER 1941
THE POPE AND THE WORLD

I. That Grey Eminence {453} — 1 time
1. In his book entitled
    Grey Eminence
    Aldous Huxley says
    that the business
    of theocentrists
    is to help the people
    to see the world
    the way God
    sees the world.
2. Father Joseph[264] said he
    made the big mistake
    to help Richelieu
    side with Protestant Germany
    and Sweden
    against Catholic Germany
    and Austria
    during the Thirty Years' War.
3. While France was united
    under one King
    the Treaty of Westphalia
    of 1648
    kept Germany divided
    in 300 principalities.

---

264. This is a reference to François Leclerc du Tremblay, who was also known as Fr. Joseph. In the biographical glossary, he can be found under "Leclerc du Tremblay, François."

II. Worldly Empires {454} — 1 time

1. Under the leadership
    of the Hohenzollern
    the 300 German principalities
    became united
    and formed
    the German Empire.
2. The German Empire
    was first
    a Continental Empire
    but later on
    it decided to become
    a Colonial Empire
    like the British Empire
    and the French Empire.
3. The aim
    of the British Empire
    of the French Empire
    of the German Empire
    is to exchange food
    and raw materials
    for gadgets.
5. The French Empire
    has gone to pieces
    and the British Empire
    is fighting
    the German Empire.

III. A Theocentric Pope[265] {455} — 1 time

1. The German Empire
    controls much of the land

---

265. "Theocentric" is a reference to Aldous Huxley's book *Grey Eminence* (1941; repr. New York: Harper & Row, 1966). For more info, see the biographical entry on Aldous Huxley. This essay referred to the British blockade of Vichy France, or unoccupied France, which was a pawn of the Nazi regime after the Nazis occupied northern France in 1940. Certain groups in the United States wished to deliver food and medicine to Vichy France, and even Pope Pius XII had contacted Britain for leniency. This issue was probably dear to Maurin, as his family lived in that region.

but the British Empire
   controls the sea.
2. The French Government
   wants to buy food
   in America
   to feed the people
   but the British Empire,
   who controls the sea,
   refuses to let the food
   pass the British blockade.
3. A theocentric Pope
   tells the world
   that God wants
   that the poor be fed
   but people in control
   of the British Empire
   tell the theocentric Pope
   to mind his own business.
4. But the business
   of a theocentric Pope
   is to tell the world
   what God wants him
   to tell the world.

JANUARY 1942
ON SPECIALIZATION

I. A College Professor {44}

II. A Negro Student {456} — 1 time

1. A Negro student
   had a father
   who was a Baptist minister.
2. The Baptist minister
   gave to his son
   Baptist theology,
   but no science.

3. And the son
    wanted to know science.
4. In the University of Pittsburgh
    the Negro student
    learned several sciences
    without correlation.
5. And the Negro student
    was complaining
    about the University of
    Pittsburgh
    for having failed
    to give him
    a correlated knowledge.

III. Henry Adams {46}

IV. Dr. Herbert E. Cory {457} — 1 time

1. Dr. Herbert E. Cory
    is now Dean
    of the Department
    of Liberal Arts
    of the State University
    of Washington.
2. The problem of specialization
    used to worry him
    when he was an atheist
    and a Marxist.
3. With the help of a Jesuit
    he found the solution.
4. And this led him
    into the Catholic Church.
5. You can find the presentation
    of the correlated knowledge
    of Dr. Herbert E. Cory
    in his book entitled:
    *The Emancipation
    of a Freethinker.*
6. Bruce of Milwaukee,
    is the publisher.

FEBRUARY 1942
ON PERSONALISM

I. Individual {458} — 1 time

1. A stone
    is not an individual.
2. You can make little ones
    out of big ones.
3. A tree
    is an individual.
4. It comes
    from a germ.
5. "Only God
    can make a tree,"[266]
    says the poet.
6. A horse
    is an individual.
7. The horse is not an individual
    the way the tree
    is an individual.
8. It has animal life.
9. Man is an individual
    and has animal life
    like the horse.
10. Man has also reason
    which the horse has not.

II. A Person {459} — 1 time

1. As an animal,
    man is an individual.
2. As a reasoning animal
    man is a person.
3. The difference
    between an individual
    and a person
    is the power of reasoning.

---

266. This is the last line of Joyce Kilmer's 1913 poem "Trees."

4. Through the use of reason
   man becomes aware
   of the existence of God.
5. Through the use of reason
   man becomes aware
   of his rights
   as well as
   his responsibilities.
6. Man's rights and responsibilities
   come from God
   who made him
   a reasoning animal.
7. Man's primary duty
   is to act
   according to reason.

III. Faith {460} — 1 time

1. To guide himself
   man has
   not only reason
   but also faith.
2. Faith
   is not opposed to reason,
   it is above reason.
3. The use of reason
   leads to faith
   but reason
   cannot understand
   all the faith.
4. The truths of faith
   that reason
   cannot understand
   we call them
   the mysteries of faith.
5. To use reason
   is to philosophize

and philosophy
is the hand maid of faith.
6. Some truths
we get through reason
and some truths
we get through faith.

IV. Emmanuel Mounier {461} — 1 time

1. Emmanuel Mounier
wrote a book entitled
A Personalist Manifesto.
2. Emmanuel Mounier
has been influenced
by Charles Péguy.
3. Charles Péguy once said:
"There are two things
in the world:
politics and mysticism."
4. For Charles Péguy,
as well as Mounier,
politics
is the struggle for power
while mysticism
is the realism
of the spirit.
5. For the man-of-the-street
politics
is just politics
and mysticism
is the right spirit.
6. In his *Personalist Manifesto*
Mounier
tries to explain
what the man-of-the-street
calls "the right spirit."

MARCH 1942
FIVE FORMS OF CAPITALISM

I. Mercantile Capitalism {462} — 1 time

    1. In the Middle Ages
        the consumer
        went to see the producer
        and asked the producer
        to produce something
        for him.
    2. There was no middle man
        between the producer
        and the consumer.
    3. When the producer
        started to sell his products
        to the middle man
        he no longer
        saw the consumer.
    4. The producer
        saw only the middle man
        and the consumer
        saw only the middle man
        and the middle man
        was only interested
        in buying cheap
        and selling dear.
    5. And the functional society
        ceased to exist
        and the acquisitive society
        came into existence.
    6. And everybody shouted:
        "Time is money!"

II. Factory Capitalism {127}

III. Monopoly Capitalism {463} — 1 time

    1. With the American Civil War,
        monopoly capitalism
        came into existence.

2. With monopoly capitalism
    came the trusts.
3. With monopoly capitalism
    came high tariffs
    for the protection
    of infant industries.
4. With monopoly capitalism
    came unionism
    for the protection
    of proletarianized workers.
5. With monopoly capitalism
    came trust-busting laws
    for the protection
    of the buying public.
6. With monopoly capitalism
    came Federal laws
    for the conservation
    of raw materials.

IV. Finance Capitalism {464} — 1 time

1. With the first World War
    finance capitalism
    came into existence.
2. With finance capitalism
    came installment buying.
3. In January, 1927,
    Yale Review
    published an article
    by a business man
    in which he said
    that installment buying
    has the result
    to boom boom years
    and to starve lean years.[267]

---

267. This is a reference to Charles Reinold Noyes, "Financing Prosperity on Next Year's Income," *Yale Review* 16 (January 1927): 227–42. Essentially, Noyes argued that the extreme extent of credit purchasing that began after the First World War would cause an economic depression.

4. Installment buying
>> gave us the New Era
>> and the promise
>> of a two-car garage,
>> a chicken in every pot
>> and a sign "To Let"
>> in front of every poorhouse.
5. But this promise
>> failed to materialize
>> and people found themselves
>> in the midst of the depression.

V. State Capitalism {465} — 1 time

1. Finance capitalism
>> has not been able
>> to employ
>> the unemployed.
2. The State
>> has now assumed the task
>> to employ the unemployed.
3. Economic activities
>> are now supervised
>> by State bureaucrats.
4. State bureaucrats
>> can give the people
>> State supervision.
5. State supervision
>> is not a substitute
>> for personal vision.
6. And without personal vision
>> people perish.
7. Personalist vision
>> leads to personalist action.
8. Personalist action
>> means personal
>> responsibility.
9. Personal responsibility
>> means dynamic democracy.

APRIL 1942
FOR A NEW ORDER

I. The Age of Reason {466} — 1 time

1. In the seventeenth century,
    a Frenchman
    by the name of Descartes
    discarded Thomistic philosophy
    and formulated
    a philosophy of his own.
2. St. Thomas' philosophy
    starts with Aristotle
    and helps the reason
    to accept revelation.
3. For Saint Thomas Aquinas
    reason is the handmaid of faith;
    not so for Descartes.
4. The eighteenth century
    became known
    as the age of enlightenment
    or the age of reason.
5. An American
    by the name of Thomas Paine
    wrote a book entitled:
    The Age of Reason.

II. The Age of Treason {14}

III. The Age of Chaos {467} — 1 time

1. And we are now
    in the age of chaos.
2. In an age of chaos
    people look
    for a new order.
3. What makes for chaos
    is lack of order.

4. Because people are becoming
>   aware
>   of this lack of order
>   they would like to be able
>   to create order
>   out of chaos.
5. The time
>   to create order
>   out of chaos
>   is now.
6. The germ of the present
>   was in the past
>   and the germ of the future
>   is in the present.
7. The thing to do
>   is to give up old tricks
>   and start to play new tricks.

IV. The Age of Order {468} — 1 time

1. If we make
>   the right decisions
>   in the age of chaos
>   the effect of those decisions
>   will be a better order.
2. The new order
>   brought about
>   by right decisions
>   will be functional
>   not acquisitive,
>   personalist
>   not socialist,
>   communitarian
>   not collectivist,
>   organismic
>   not mechanistic.
3. The thing to do right now
>   is to create a new society
>   within the shell of the old
>   with the philosophy of the new

which is not a new philosophy
but a very old philosophy,
a philosophy so old
that it looks like new.

MAY 1942
EASY ESSAYS

I. "My Experience Teaches Me" {469} — 1 time
1. "I have lived
    in all the major
    dictatorships—
    Russia, Italy, Germany.
2. "My experience teaches me
    that democracy
    with all its faults
    is better
    than any of these.
3. "My experience teaches me
    that the maintenance
    of personal freedom
    should be
    the primary consideration
    of every human being.
4. "It is never a choice
    between freedom
    and a full stomach.
5. "No dictatorship
    has given either.
6. "Only men and women.
    who have freedom
    and who have not
    seen it abolished
    in dictatorships
    can fail to understand
    what it means
    to be deprived of it."

—Louis Fisher

II. Three Characteristics {470} — 1 time

1. At the base
    of the American spirit
    is the functionalism
    of frontier life,
    not the acquisitivism
    of the chamber of commerce.
2. The American spirit
    is characterized
    by the love of freedom,
    the spirit of initiative
    and the will to cooperate.
3. The American
    does not like
    to be pushed about
    and being sent
    where he does not want
    to go.
4. Even the business man
    likes to talk about
    the spirit of initiative
    which he calls
    free enterprise.
5. When in America
    someone is busy
    doing something
    for the common good
    he finds people
    willing to cooperate.

III. Love of Freedom {471} — 1 time

1. Freedom is a duty
    more than a right.
2. Man has a duty
    to be intelligent.

3. Man has a duty
    to choose intelligently
    between two alternatives.
4. Man has a duty
    to act intelligently
    using pure means
    to reach pure aims.
5. To use impure means
    to reach pure aims
    is to take the wrong road.
6. You cannot go
    where you want to go
    by taking a road
    which does not lead
    you there.
7. Having pure aims
    and using pure means
    is making the right use
    of freedom.

IV. Spirit of Initiative {472} — 1 time

1. The spirit of initiative
    is what business men call
    free enterprise.
2. A private enterprise
    must be carried out
    for the common good.
3. If a private enterprise
    is not carried out
    for the common good
    it turns out to be
    a public nuisance.
4. A public nuisance
    produces grievances.
5. Personal grievances
    against public nuisances
    produce demagogues

       who promise to wipe out
       public nuisances.
6. The spirit of initiative
       of social-minded people
       brings into existence
       social institutions
       that make for the welfare
       of the common people.

V. Will to Cooperate {473} — 1 time

1. When someone
       has done something
       considered by the
       common man
       as to be beneficial
       to the common good
       he is admired
       by the common man.
2. The admiration
       of unselfish men
       who are not afraid
       to take the initiative
       creates a desire
       among the admirers
       to climb on the bandwagon
       of men of initiative.
3. They want to be part
       of an unselfish
       movement.
4. They are willing
       to make sacrifices
       for the common cause.
5. So the will to cooperate
       is the result
       of the daring
       of unselfish men

who are not afraid
to take the initiative.

JUNE 1942
A THREE POINTS PROGRAM

I. Clarification of Thought {8}

II. Houses of Hospitality {9}

III. Farming Communes {94}

JULY–AUGUST 1942
INDUSTRIALISM

I. It Started with England {474} — 1 time

1. Lenin said:
    "The world cannot be
    half industrial
    and half agricultural."
2. Lenin made the mistake
    to industrialize Russia.
3. Lenin industrialized Russia
    because the Japanese
    industrialized Japan.
4. The Japanese industrialized Japan
    because the Americans
    industrialized America.
5. The Americans industrialized America
    because the Germans
    industrialized Germany.
6. The Germans industrialized Germany
    because the English
    industrialized England.
7. It started with England.

II. A Few Englishman {475} — 1 time

1. R. H. Tawney said
    that "the Englishmen
    wear blinkers."[268]
2. Because they wear blinkers
    the Englishmen
    lack vision.
3. Because they lack vision
    the Englishmen
    are very strong
    for supervision.
4. And supervision
    is not a substitute
    for vision.
5. A few Englishmen
    got rid of their blinkers.
6. Among the Englishmen
    who got rid of their blinkers
    one can name:
    William Cobbett
    John Ruskin
    William Morris
    Arthur Penty
    Eric Gill.
7. The best of all
    is Eric Gill.

III. Legalized Usury {476} — 1 time

1. "The sex problem,
    the marriage problem,
    the crime problem,
    the problem of armaments
    and international trade—

---

268. Maurin was paraphrasing a line from the first page of R. H. Tawney's *The Acquisitive Society* (New York: Harcourt, Brace, 1920). In this phrase, Tawney was arguing that the English perform their daily tasks without concern for the principles that shape their society.

all these problems
could be solved
if we would recognize
the necessity
of abolishing
the trade in money,
and especially
the international trade in money,
that is to say
the usury,
the legalized usury
practised by the banks
under the protection
of their charters
with the support
of the so-called
'orthodox' economists."
2. "That is the first thing
to be recognised."[269]

—Eric Gill

IV. God and Mammon {17}

SEPTEMBER 1942
KEEPING UP WITH THE IRISH SCHOLARS

I. Laying the Foundation {405}

II. Literary Colonies {406}

III. Free Guest Houses {407}

IV. Rural Centers {408}

---

269. The quote is from Gill, *Money & Morals* (London: Faber and Faber, 1934), 36–37. As indicated earlier, Maurin liked this book so much that he copied it in its entirety into Easy Essay format.

NOVEMBER 1942
WHY BLAME THE JEWS

I. Bourgeois Capitalism {356}

II. Turning Sharp Corners {357}

III. Modern Liberals {358}

IV. Racialism {359}

V. Personal God {360}

DECEMBER 1942
CATHOLIC ACTION

I. Our Business {477} — 1 time
   1. Catholic bourgeois
         used to tell the Clergy
         "Mind your own business
         and don't butt into our business."
   2. Catholic bourgeois
         by keeping up
         with non-Catholic bourgeois
         have made a mess
         of their own business.
   3. And now the Holy Father
         tells Catholic bourgeois
         "The Bishop's business
         is your business."

II. The Bishop's Voice {478} — 1 time
   1. The Bishop's business
         is to teach
         the Christian Doctrine.
   2. The Holy Father
         appoints a Bishop
         to a seat (a cathedra)

so people may hear the truth
that will set them free.
3. Clergy, teachers, journalists
are the amplifiers
of the Bishop's voice.
4. Fathers and mothers
must also be
the Bishop's voice.
5. Bishop O'Hara
is fostering the teaching
of Christian Doctrine
by fathers and mothers.
6. Everything connected
with the teaching
of Christian Doctrine
can be called
Catholic Action No. 1.

III. Works of Mercy {479} — 1 time

1. But the Bishop
although he is a Bishop
cannot teach
an empty stomach.
2. Some people
are Bishop shy
because they are
hungry, shivering or sleepy.
3. So the Bishop
asks the faithful
to feed the hungry
clothe the naked
shelter the homeless
at a sacrifice.
4. Feeding the hungry
clothing the naked
sheltering the homeless
at a sacrifice
was the daily practice
of the first Christians.

5. The daily practice
of the Works of Mercy
is what we can call
Catholic Action No. 2.

IV. Social Reconstruction {480} — 1 time

1. We are asked
by the Holy Father
to reconstruct
the social order.
2. Reconstructing the social order
means the creation
of a Catholic society
within the shell
of a non-Catholic society
with the philosophy
of a Catholic society.
3. Catholic bourgeois
made the mistake
of trying to keep up
with non-Catholic bourgeois.
4. Catholic reconstructors
must create
a Catholic technique
in harmony
with Catholic thought.
5. Social reconstruction
by Catholic laymen and women
is what we can call
Catholic Action No. 3.

V. Three Kinds {481} — 1 time

1. Catholic Action No. 1
or the teaching
of Christian Doctrine
must be carried out
with the Bishop's supervision.

2. Catholic Action No. 2
    or the daily practice
    of the Works of Mercy
    can be carried out
    with or without
    the Bishop's supervision.
3. Catholic Action No. 3
    or the reconstruction
    of the Social Order
    through the foundation
    of new Catholic institutions
    must be left
    to the initiative
    of Catholic men and women.
4. The function of the Bishops
    is to be
    not directors
    but moderators.
5. Political action
    is not to be considered
    as Catholic Action.

DECEMBER 1945[270]

I. CLASSES AND CLASHES {11}

II. Share Your Wealth {122}

III. Social Workers and Workers {482} — 1 time

1. The training of social workers
    enables them to help people
    to adjust themselves
    to the existing environment.

---

270. Between December 1942 and December 1945, Maurin did not publish any original essays. During this period, the paper republished previous arrangements and works by other authors that Maurin arranged into the Easy Essay format. It is unclear if Maurin submitted this arrangement in December 1945 to be published or if this was an older arrangement that was simply not published previously.

2. The training of social workers
    does not enable them
    to help people
    to change the environment.
3. Social workers
    must become social-minded
    before they can be
    critics of the existing environment
    and free creative agents
    of the new environment.
4. In Houses of Hospitality
    social workers can acquire
    that art of human contacts
    and that social-mindedness
    or understanding of social forces
    which will make them
    critical of the existing environment
    and free creative agents
    of a new environment.

Unpublished Easy Essays

This section presents essays that were not published in the *New York Catholic Worker* newspaper during Peter Maurin's lifetime. A few of the essays were published in the newspaper after his death or in books about Maurin, but most have never been published in any format. Almost all of the essays are located at the Dorothy Day–Catholic Worker Archives at Marquette University's Raynor Library. They are kept in two folders at the collection, which are noted before each grouping of essays. The final three essays were preserved only in Arthur Sheehan's 1959 biography, *Peter Maurin*.

A few of the essays were never completed, but most were finished. It is impossible to state definitively why most of the essays were never published. Some may have been omitted from arrangements in the newspaper for lack of space. Others may have been omitted because they did not fit within a larger arrangement.

The essays are presented in the same order they were found in the archive's folders, though this order should not be seen as denoting any possible time frame or chronological order for the essays. Unless an essay is dated, which is rare, the date is unknown. Notations are made for the cases in which a number of unpublished essays were purposefully grouped together.

The following essays are from the Marquette University Archives, DD-CW Series W-10, Box 1, Folder: Manuscripts, "Easy Essays," 1934, 1942, n.d.

An Appeal for Funds {483}
1. Readers of the *Catholic Worker* must ask themselves
   what I am trying to do with my essays.

2. I am trying to tell the clergy
    how to talk to the Bolshevists
    so as to make the Bolshevists
    eat from the hands of the Holy Father.
3. If the Clergy have not succeeded
    in making the Encyclicals click
    the reason must be found
    in a lack of historical background.
4. When in 1899 Thorstein Veblen wrote:
    The Theory of the Leisure Class
    students of economics began to realize
    that there were no ethics in modern society.
5. R. H. Tawney, an Oxford student, asked himself:
    "Were there no ethics in society before?"
6. He learned that there were high ethics in society
    when the Canon Law was the Law of the Land.
7. Having found out the high ethics of society
    when the Canon Law was the Law of the Land
    R. H. Tawney started to study the Canon Law
    so as to find out what kind of ethics were taught
    when the Canon Law was the Law of the Land.
8. Having found that out,
    R. H. Tawney asked himself:
    "How has society gone down
    from the high ethics of Canon Law
    to the no ethics of today?"
9. What R. H. Tawney found out
    about the history of ethics of the last five hundred years
    is embodied in his book:
    Religion and the Rise of Capitalism.
10. Although R. H. Tawney is not a Catholic
    this book ought to be read by all Catholics
    Clergymen as well as laymen and women.
11. If Catholics knew their own stuff
    they would not look to Washington
    for the solution of their economic problems.
12. If Catholics knew their own stuff
    they would not pass the buck to the State.

13. If Catholics knew their own stuff
    they would go back to the sociology
    of Saint Thomas Aquinas, Saint Francis of Assisi
    and Blessed Thomas More.
14. And if Catholics went back to the sociology
    of Saint Thomas Aquinas, Saint Francis of Assisi
    and Blessed Thomas More
    people would not be interested
    in the sociology of Karl Marx, Lenin and Stalin.
15. If Catholics were busy with Dynamic Catholic Action,
    people would not be interested
    in Dynamic Bolshevik Action.
16. Dorothy Willmann, one of Fr. Lord's able assistants
    calls the Catholic Worker
    "a clarion's call for Catholic Action."
17. If you want the Catholic Worker
    to be "a clarion's call for Catholic Action"
    send us a few words of encouragement
    and a contribution, if you can afford it.

—For the Catholic Worker,
Peter Maurin

For His Children's Sake[1] {484}

1. This American artist
    is taking with him
    an earnest cooperation
    which happens to be his wife
    and ten devoted pupils
    which are his ten children.
2. With him go two young men
    coming from a Catholic College
    who have learned through experience
    that Catholic colleges

---

1. According to a note included with this essay, it was originally supposed to go after "Flying From America" in the October 1934 issue of the *Catholic Worker*, but was obviously omitted.

> may prepare students
> for a life of business
> but do not necessarily prepare
> for the business of life.
> 3. This American artist
>> has saved his own children
>> from a commercialized education
>> but didn't know how to save them
>> from a commercialized environment.

Essays {485} to {490} were grouped together.

Mortimer Adler {485}

> Mortimer Adler Says:
> 1. "The professors
>> by and large
>> are positivists.
> 2. "The most serious threat
>> to Democracy
>> is the positivism
>> of the professors.
> 3. "It dominates every aspect
>> of modern education.
> 4. "It is the central corruption
>> of modern culture.
> 5. "Democracy
>> has much more to fear
>> from the mentality
>> of its teachers
>> than from the nihilism
>> of Hitler."[2]

---

2. This quote was from a paper that Adler wrote entitled "God and Professors." He presented it at the Science, Philosophy, and Religion in Their Relation to the Democratic Way of Life Conference at New York's Jewish Theological Seminary in 1940. The paper was included in *Science, Philosophy and Religion: A Symposium* (New York, 1941), 120–38.

Robert M. Hutchins {486}

Robert M. Hutchins says:
1. "The trouble is
    that the University
    cannot even
    assure the graduate
    important work.
2. "He may be doomed
    to the performance
    of routine tasks.
3. "These routine tasks
    which however important
    in keeping
    the wheels of civilization turning
    do not always seem important
    to those
    whose daily burden
    they are.
4. "The mechanization of life
    may have enlarged leisure.
5. "It has certainly helped
    to make the hours of work
    dull, monotonous,
    and to the worker
    insignificant."[3]

Walter Lippmann {487}

Walter Lippmann says:
1. "The prevailing education
    is destined,
    if it continues,
    to destroy western civilization
    and is in fact
    destroying it.

---

3. The source of this quote is unknown. It could be Maurin's summary of Hutchins's *Higher Learning in America*, or it could be a quote from another source.

2. "Our civilization
     cannot effectively
     be maintained
     where it still flourishes,
     or be restored
     where it has been crushed,
     without the revival
     of the central, continuous
     and perennial culture
     of the western world.
3. "Therefore,
     what is now required
     in the modern educational system
     is not the expansion
     of its facilities,
     or the specific reform
     of its curriculum
     and administration,
     but a thorough reconsideration
     of its underlying assumptions
     and of its purposes."

Raïssa Maritain {488}

Raïssa Maritain says:
1. "When at last Jacques and I
     went to the College of France
     where Bergson was teaching
     we were at the gates of despair.
2. "We struck a balance
     of all that our teachers
     at the Sorbonne
     had given us
     as a provision
     for our journey.
3. "We found this balance
     to be merely
     dust and death.

4. "Positivism, scientism,
        mechanism, relativism,
        —all these
        did violence in us
        'to that idea of the truth
        which is invincible
        to all skepticism'
        as Pascal puts it.
5. "And we could only oppose
        our own suffering
        to this demoralization
        of the mind."[4]

In Denmark {489}

1. In the middle
        of the last century
        a Lutheran bishop realized
        that there was something rotten
        in Denmark.
2. The rotten thing
        about Denmark
        was property
        without responsibility
        which is
        prostituted property.
3. To bring back
        to the Danish people
        the right concept of property,
        that is to say
        functional property,

---

4. The quote paraphrased a line from Raïssa Maritain's memoir, *We Have Been Friends Together* (1942; repr. New York: Longmans, Green, 1945), 79–80. The memoir was first published in English in 1942.

the Lutheran bishop
established
Danish Folk Schools.⁵

Near Easton {490}

1. To bring back American people
    back to the spirit
    of the Founders of America
    the Catholic Worker
    intends to transform
    the Farming Commune
    near Easton, Pennsylvania
    into a Folk School.
2. In that Folk School,
    people will learn:
    Farming
    Canning
    Bio-Dynamics⁶
    Building
    Furniture making
    Knitting
    Weaving
    Dancing
    Singing
    Public speaking.

Essays {2} to {493} were grouped together with a notation that they were written in 1941.

---

5. Maurin was referring to Nikolaj Frederik Severin Grundtvig (1783–1872). For more on Grundtvig and the creation of folk schools, see the entry on Grundtvig in the biographical glossary.

6. Biodynamic agriculture was the method of farming on which Rudolf Steiner (1861–1925) lectured to a group of farmers in 1924. The method quickly spread internationally. He viewed the farm as a single organism that should be rich with a biodiversity of plants and animals to be self-sustaining. His vision was the forerunner to organic farming, since it eschewed the use of chemical fertilizers and pesticides.

No Ethics {2} [1941]

Rerum Novarum {491} [1941]

1. The high ethics
    of the Canon Law
    are embodied
    in *Rerum novarum*.
2. It was published
    50 years ago
    in 1891.
3. People ought to have listened
    to the advice
    of Leo XIII.
4. But business men
    as well as labor leaders
    told the Pope:
    "Mind your own business
    and don't butt in our business."
5. And business men
    as well as labor leaders
    have made a mess
    of their own business.
6. And people worry
    about tomorrow
    and forget to change
    their way of thinking.

A.C.T.U.[7] {492} [1941]

1. In 1937
    46 years
    after the publication

---

7. The Association of Catholic Trade Unionists (ACTU) grew out of the New York Catholic Worker. Its primary purpose was to imbue the labor movement with the teaching and practices of *Rerum novarum* and *Quadragesimo anno*. They stressed the possibility of class harmony in contrast to the class-warfare rhetoric of Communists in the labor movement. The ACTU continued until 1973. One of the cofounders of the ACTU was John Cort (1913–2006), who lived at the New York Catholic Worker during the 1930s and would later join the editorial staff of *Commonweal*.

of *Rerum novarum*
the Association
of Catholic Trade Unionists
was founded in New York.
2. The purpose
of the A.C.T.U.
is to bring the ideology
of *Rerum novarum*
into the Labor Movement.
3. The ideology
of *Rerum novarum*
will make the Labor Movement
think in terms
of a functional society.
4. Because employers
are acquisitive minded
is not a reason
why the workers
should be acquisitive minded.

For an A.C.E. {493} [1941]

1. The main idea
running through
Rerum novarum
is the idea
of a functional society.
2. The idea
of a functional society
must permeate
the Labor Movement
as well as
the National Association
of Manufacturers.
3. The A.C.T.U.
is trying
to bring the concept
of a functional society
to the Labor Movement.

4. We are badly in need
 of an Association
 of Catholic Employers
 for the purpose
 of bringing the ideology
 of *Rerum novarum*
 to the National Association
 of Manufacturers.

Essays {494} to {496} were grouped together. They made an unpublished arrangement that Maurin named "German Madness."

GERMAN MADNESS

I. Nationalism {494}

1. Nationalism
 did not originate
 in Germany.
2. When Louis XIV
 King of France
 was declaring:
 "I am the State"
 Germany was divided
 in more than 300
 principalities.
3. When France
 under the leadership
 of Richelieu
 decided to take part
 in the Thirty Years' War
 on the side
 of Protestant Germany
 and Sweden
 it laid the foundations
 of German nationalism.

II. Socialism {495}

1. The word Socialism
    was first used
    by an Irishman
    of the name
    of William Thompson.
2. When Karl Marx,
    a German Jew,
    declared to the world
    that Capitalism
    carries in itself
    the seed
    of its own destruction
    he made people
    look up to Socialism
    as the next system
    of human society.
3. When Lenin
    decided to use the State
    as a bludgeon
    he linked Socialism
    with Nationalism.

III. Racialism {496}

1. The first expounder
    of Racialism
    was a Frenchman
    by the name Gobineau.
2. The second expounder
    of Racialism
    was an Englishman
    by the name Chamberlain.
3. The other expounder
    of Racialism
    is a Baltic baron
    by the name Rosenberg.

4. Nationalism,
    Socialism,
    Racialism,
    did not originate
    in Germany.
5. The cause
    of German madness
    must be found
    outside of Germany.

———————

Essays {497} to {501} were grouped together. They made an unpublished arrangement that Maurin named "A Good Samaritan."

A GOOD SAMARITAN

I. A Good Movie {497}

1. Vice President Marshall
    used to say:
    "What America needs
    is a good five cent cigar."
2. According to Fr. Curran
    of Athol, Massachusetts
    what America needs
    is a good movie.
3. The good movie
    that America needs
    according to Fr. Curran
    is a movie
    on "The Good Samaritan."
4. Hollywood has produced
    plenty of bad movies
    and a few good movies.
5. Hollywood would
    in the eyes of many people
    redeem itself

if it could produce
more fostering movies
and less pandering movies.

II. Does What He Preaches {498}

1. Fr. Curran is not satisfied
    to wish that Hollywood
    would place on the screen
    "The Good Samaritan."
2. He is not satisfied
    to be a wishful thinker,
    he is not afraid to be
    a willful doer.
3. He is not satisfied
    to talk about
    the Good Samaritan;
    he dares to be
    a Good Samaritan.
4. He dares to be
    a Good Samaritan
    to migratory workers.

III. Rented a Store {499}

1. He has rented a store
    filled with new beds
    and new blankets.
2. Besides a clean bed
    the men can have
    an evening meal
    and a morning breakfast
    in a clean restaurant
    located next door.
3. In the evening
    Fr. Curran comes
    to talk with the men
    about current events.

4. Fr. Curran's comments
    on current events
    are food for thought
    to those migratory workers.
5. Fr. Curran believes
    that you cannot talk
    on an empty stomach.

IV. No Red Tape {500}

1. I visited the place
    with John McGee
    and Arthur Sheehan.
2. The men we saw
    were well pleased.
3. One of them said:
    "This place is clean
    and we keep it clean
    as we would
    if it were our own."
4. He added:
    "We are treated
    in a courteous manner
    and there is no red tape."

V. On the Road {501}

1. This man told us
    the reason why
    he is on the road.
2. He could no longer
    get a job
    in his home town
    on account of his age.
3. Waiting for a job
    that failed to show up
    he had to borrow money.

4. Having thus
    become indebted
    to his friends
    and not being able
    to pay it back
    for lack of work
    he felt
    that he could no longer
    stay in his home town.
5. And that's the reason why
    he is on the road.

Essays {502} and {503} were grouped together. They made an unpublished arrangement that Maurin named "Jews in New York."

JEWS IN NEW YORK

I. Liberal Jews[8] {502}

1. Liberal Jews
    look forward.
2. Liberal Jews
    don't look backward.
3. Liberal Jews
    don't look back
    to the Jewish Prophets.
4. And because Liberal Jews
    don't look back
    to the Jewish Prophets

---

8. This may be a reference to Reform Judaism (also called Liberal Judaism), which is a denomination that has its roots in nineteenth-century Germany. This strand of Judaism places more stress on the continuous nature of revelation from God and less stress on biblical revelation found in the Exodus event and the prophets. Maurin believed this type of Judaism had lost its strong spiritual foundation and capitulated to capitalism and consumerism. This critique is similar to the one he had made about secularism infesting modern Christianity.

     is the reason why
     Liberal Jews
     are not able
     to make Jews Jews.
5. And when a Jew
     is not a Jew
     he isn't much a Jew.

II. In New York {503}

1. And when a Jew
     goes among Gentiles
     not to bring
     Jewish culture
     to the Gentiles
     but tries
     to make money
     through business deals
     with Gentiles
     he does not succeed
     in making the Gentiles
     gentle to the Jews.
2. They say
     that there are
     too many Jews
     in New York.
3. There are not
     too many Jews
     in New York.
4. There are
     not enough Gentiles
     for the Jews that are
     in New York.

Essays {22} to {508} were grouped together. They made an unpublished arrangement that Maurin named "Modern Isms."

MODERN ISMS

I. French Secularism {22} [part 2]

II. English Industrialism {504}
>   1. The Manchester school
>   of political economy
>   spread the idea
>   that everything
>   would be lovely
>   if people took in
>   each other's washing.
>   2. England went in the business
>   of buying raw materials
>   transforming them
>   into manufactured products
>   and going all over the world
>   looking for markets.
>   3. Since trade follows the flag
>   England harbored the Union Jack[9]
>   all over the world
>   for the sake of markets
>   and raw materials.
>   4. And now Germany
>   is fighting England
>   to drive England
>   out of the world markets
>   and sources
>   of raw materials.

III. German Racialism {505}
>   1. The Germans believe
>   that they are
>   a superior race

---

9. This is a name for the flag of England.

and that the world
needs to be ruled
by a superior race.
2. The German youth
is dying today
so the German race
can rule the world.
3. The Hindus of India
maintain that English rule
is alright
for the English
when the English
try to rule themselves
but that the English rule
of other races
is neither good
for the other races
or the English.
4. What the Hindus say
about English rule
can also be said
about the German rule.

IV. Italian Nationalism {506}

1. The Germans believe
that they ought
to rule the world
because they are
a superior race.
2. The Italians don't believe
that they are
a superior race.
3. The Italians believe
that they know
how to rule
because there was once
a Roman Empire

and that they incarnate
the ruling qualities
of the former Roman Empire.
4. Mussolini believes
that the English Empire
is an Empire
of shopkeepers
who think in terms
of materialism.
5. Mussolini says:
"All in the State,
nothing against the State
nothing outside of the State."[10]

V. Russian Socialism {507}

1. Marx said
that Capitalism
carries in itself
the seed
of its own destruction.
2. If Capitalism
destroys itself
we don't need to worry
about Capitalism.
3. Lenin thought
that Russia
could have Socialism
without passing
through Capitalism.
4. Lenin thought
that Socialism
could be built
through the use of the State
and that the State
would then wither away.

---

10. This quote is attributed to Benito Mussolini and was seen as his definition of fascism.

5. But the Russian State
    has not withered away
    and Stalin sees to it
    that the State
    does not wither away.

VI. Irish Messianism[11] {508}

1. When the Irish were Scholars,
    they were Christian minded.
2. They were not
    secular minded
    business minded
    racial minded
    State minded
    or Socialist minded.
3. When the Irish were Scholars,
    they knew how to civilize
    the Teutonic barbarians
    including
    the Ango-Saxons.
4. The Irish Scholars
    believed in Christ
    and in the Pope.
5. Because they believed
    in Christ and the Pope
    the Irish Scholars
    were missionaries
    and not soldiers
    or politicians
    or business men.

The following essays are from the Marquette University Archives, DD-CW Series W-10, Box 1, Folder "Easy Essay," Fragments, 1933–35, n.d.

---

11. This essay was previously published in Luke Stocking, "When the Irish Were Irish: Peter Maurin and the Green Revolution" (M.A. thesis, St. Michael's College, 2007), 199.

My Business {509}

1. American law and order
    is a law and order
    friendly to business.
2. Russian law and order
    is a law and order
    opposed to business.
3. But business is only business
    whether it is private business
    as in America
    or State business
    as in Russia.
4. And I am trying
    to make it my business
    to put all business
    out of business
    which is a big business.
5. And they tell me:
    "Mind your own business."
6. And I say:
    "Agitation that's my business."

Re-Discovering America {510}

1. The American merry-go-round
    is rooted
    in merry England.
2. And merry England
    was rooted
    in Florentine Machiavellianism.
3. And Florentine Machiavellianism
    was a breaking away
    from the social ethics
    that prevailed
    when Mediaeval communes
    were founded by Mediaeval philosophers.
4. To understand the sociology
    of a Thomas Jefferson
    we must go back
    to Colonial America.

5. And to understand
    Colonial America
    we must go back
    to Shakespearean England.
6. And to understand
    Shakespearean England
    we must go back
    to Mediterranean culture.
7. As Waldo Frank says:
    "It is only
    in Mediterranean culture
    that America
    can re-discover itself."[12]

Essays {511} through {514} were an unpublished grouping.

Waiting for Orders[13] {511}

1. While the Holy Father
    presents Saint Francis of Assisi
    as the standard to go by
    and the four last Popes
    present the Franciscan movement
    as the movement best able
    to create order out of chaos
    nothing has been done
    either by the 3 Franciscan Orders
    or the Third Order of Saint Francis.
2. The contention is
    that the 3 Franciscan Orders
    and the Third Order of Saint Francis
    cannot do anything
    without being asked by the Bishops.
3. And the contention of the Bishops is
    that the 3 Franciscan Orders

---

12. This is not a quote, but Maurin's summary of Waldo Frank's book *Re-Discovery of America* (New York and London: Charles Scribner's Sons, 1929).
13. Maurin wrote this unpublished Easy Essay to follow essay {54}.

and the Third Order of Saint Francis
do not know how to go about it
any more than the politicians.

Body of Social Thought {512}

1. Archbishop McNicholas says:
    "We have been guilty
    of encouraging tyranny
    in the financial world
    until it has become
    a veritable octopus
    strangling the life
    of our people."
2. Cardinal Bourne contends
    that we need more Catholic social research
    so as to be able
    to present to people
    a Catholic social body of thought.
3. So the Bishops seem to think
    that the Franciscan movement
    is not dynamic enough
    to be relied upon
    and that a social body of thought,
    that is to say
    a sociology based on theology,
    is a prerequisite
    of a dynamic social movement.

Bishops' Message[14] {513}

1. In their message of 1933
    the Bishops say
    that in common
    with other nations
    we have brought about
    our present unhappy conditions

---

14. This essay is an almost verbatim quote from *The Present Crisis* (1933), the previously mentioned document of the National Catholic Welfare Conference.

>   by divorcing education,
>   industry, politics,
>   business and economics
>   from morality and religion
>   and by ignoring for long decades
>   the innate dignity of man.
> 2. The Bishops add
>   that the program of social reform
>   presented by the Communists
>   is unassailable
>   because it is distinctly Christian
>   in origin and purport
>   but in the hands of the Communists
>   it is merely a snare.

St. Francis of Assisi[15] {514}

> 1. Writing about Saint Francis of Assisi
>   the Holy Father says:
>   "He who called himself
>   the 'Herald of the Great King'
>   was also rightly spoken of
>   as 'another Jesus Christ,'
>   appearing to his contemporaries
>   and to future generations
>   almost as if he were
>   the Risen Christ."
> 2. The Holy Father adds
>   that "the rules of the Orders
>   founded by him
>   were made to agree
>   most scrupulously
>   with the Gospels
>   and the religious life
>   of his followers
>   the life of the Apostles."

---

15. The essay quoted two passages from *Rite expiatis* (1926), the previously mentioned encyclical of Pius XI on Saint Francis of Assisi.

A Crisis of Collapse {515}

1. Karl Marx says, "There are such things
    as crisis of collapse."
2. Henri Bruening[16] says, "A crisis of collapse
    is an economic crisis
    plus a psychological crisis."
3. We seem to have come
    to a crisis of collapse.
4. But we don't need to wait
    till capitalism has collapsed
    to lay the foundations
    of the new society.
5. We can create a new society
    within the shell of the old
    with a philosophy of the new
    which is not a new philosophy
    but a very old philosophy;
    a philosophy so old
    that it looks like new.

Charity and Poverty[17] {516}

1. The philosophy of the capitalists with capital
    that is to say the bourgeois class
    is the philosophy of the fat belly.
2. And so is the philosophy of the capitalists without capital
    that is to say the working class.
3. To the philosophy of the fat belly
    which is the philosophy
    of both the bourgeois class and the working class
    must be substituted with the philosophy
    of Christian charity and Christian poverty.
4. Christian charity and Christian poverty
    will be brought to the common man
    through Round-Table Discussions

---

16. This was either a reference to Heinrich Brüning or to Henri Bruning. There are biographical entries for both individuals.

17. Published after Maurin's death in the February 1951 issue of the *Catholic Worker*.

      Houses of Hospitality
      and Agronomic Universities.
5. We cannot do better in the twentieth century
      than to do what the Irish people did in the seventh century
      when they laid the foundations of Mediaeval Europe
      under the Leadership of the Irish Fathers.
6. This is what I try to point out
      in the Easy Essays running in the *Catholic Worker*.

Institutions and Corporations {517}

1. The editor of the *Guildsman*
      a magazine published
      in Germantown, Illinois says
      "The way to reconstruct the social order
      is to reconstruct social institutions.
2. "An institution," says Emerson,
      "is the extension of the soul of a man."
3. It is in institutions
      that ethics are taught
      and acted upon.
4. When institutions
      take leaves from the book of business
      they are no longer institutions
      they are corporations.
5. Corporations are organized
      to procure wealth for the few.
6. Institutions are founded
      to promote the welfare of the many.
7. Corporations are moved by greed
      institutions are moved by creed.
8. The technique of institutions
      is idealistic
9. The technique of corporations
      is materialistic.

Christian Institutions {518}

1. Our Holy Father asks us
      to reconstruct the social order.

2. Some propose
> a reconstruction of the social order
> through benevolent corporations.
3. Others propose
> a reconstruction of the social order
> though vocational[18] organizations.
4. And others propose
> a reconstruction of the social order
> through Christian institutions.
5. "Institutions," says Emerson,
> "are the extension of the souls of men."
6. It is in Christian institutions
> that people express their creed
> through the practice
> of personal charity and voluntary poverty.
7. It is in Christian institutions,
> operating within the framework
> of Catholic Action,
> that Catholics can build a new society
> within the shell of the old
> but with the philosophy of the new.
8.[19]

Dome and Home {519}

1. Saint Peter of Rome and many other churches
> have a central "dome."
2. Under the church's "dome"
> people gather to worship God.
3. A dome is a house
> for God and men.
4. The new Cathedral of Liverpool
> will have a "cathedra"
> that is to say a "seat"
> from which the Archbishop will teach his people.

---

18. The word "vocational" is written above the word "militant," which Maurin crossed out.

19. It appears that Maurin intended to add at least one more stanza, but this Easy Essay ended after he wrote the number eight.

5. It will also have a "dome"
    under which people will worship God.
6. But besides a "cathedra" and a "dome"
    the Cathedral of Liverpool will have a "home."
7. Next to the "dome" and the "cathedra"
    there will be a "home"
    where the Archbishop will be able
    to extend hospitality to the homeless
    as the Divine Master wants him to do.

The Bishop's Cathedra {520}

1. The word "cathedra"
    means "seat."
2. The Bishop is appointed to a "cathedra"
    that is to say to a "seat."
3. From the Bishop's "seat"
    comes the Church's teaching.
4. When the Bishop gives us the Church's teaching
    from his "seat"
    he presents the teachings
    of the infallible Vicar of Christ.
5. Since the Bishop presents us Christ's teachings
    under the supervision of the infallible Vicar of Christ
    clergy, laymen and women are obliged
    to mind the Bishop's teaching.
6. To bring the Bishop's teaching to the common people
    to be the amplifiers of his voice
    such is the task of Catholic journalism.

Under the Leadership of the Irish Fathers[20] {521}

1. When the Irish Fathers were leading the Irish people
    in the seventh century
    the Irish people were the most cultured people in Europe.

---

20. This essay was published after Maurin's death in the February 1951 issue of the *Catholic Worker*.

2. When the Irish Fathers were leading the Irish people
    in the seventh century
    the Irish people established Round-Table Discussions
    where people could look for thought, so they could have light.
3. When the Irish Fathers were leading the Irish people
    in the seventh century
    the Irish people established Free Guest Houses
    where people could receive Christian hospitality.
4. When the Irish Fathers were leading the Irish people
    in the seventh century
    the Irish people established Agronomic Universities
    where scholars become workers
    and workers could become scholars.
5. When the Irish Fathers were leading the Irish people
    in the seventh century
    the Irish people were the Pathfinders of Europe.

Ideals[21] {522}

1. A scholar is a realizer of ideals.
2. He teaches ideals
    by speech, by writing and by example.
3. He gives what he has
    and you get what he gives.
4. He is driving at your heart
    not your pocketbook.
5. The contact that he has with you
    is ideal and not commercial.
6. What he gives to you is a gift
    as well as what you give to him.

Six Economies[22] {523}

1. In a Capitalist economy
    everybody is a coupon-clipper.

---

21. This essay was published after Maurin's death in the February 1951 issue of the *Catholic Worker*.

22. This essay was published after Maurin's death in the February 1951 issue of the *Catholic Worker*.

2. In a Fascist economy
    everybody is a soldier.
3. In a Bolshevik economy
    everybody is a State employee.
4. In a Syndicalist economy
    everybody is a union man.
5. In a Technocratic economy
    everybody is an applied scientist.
6. In an Agronomic economy
    every scholar is a worker
    and every worker can be a scholar.

Reinterpreting Karl Marx {524}

1. Karl Marx condemns capitalism
    not because it makes people unhappy
    but because it makes them inhuman.[23]

    —Sidney Hook

2. Communist policy
    is in danger of opening the door
    to a real growth of Fascism.

    —G. D. H. Cole

3. The most necessary thing in Russia
    is the development of a sensitiveness
    to peasant needs
    and peasant complaints.

    —Maurice Hindus

4. For Rousseau's democratic myth
    of the sovereign people
    Marx substitutes the socialist myth
    of a messianic proletarian class.

    —Sherwood Eddy

---

23. The quote was from Sidney Hook, *Towards the Understanding of Karl Marx* (New York: John Day, 1933), 99.

We Oppose[24] {525}

1. Economy of Plenty — Economy of Scarcity
2. Rugged Individualism — Gentle Personalism
3. Proletarian Dictatorship — Personalist Communities
4. Finance Industrialism — Rural Homesteadism
5. Supply and Demand — Demand and Supply

[No Title][25] {526}

1. Fr. Coughlin says:
    "The country is in good hands
    because there is a man
    in the White House."
2. Al Smith says:
    "I know the man in the White House
    and while he is a man
    I know that he doesn't know
    any more than I know
    and I know that I don't know.
3. And because President Roosevelt
    does not know
    any more than I know
    he carries on expensive experiments
    and for the life of me
    I cannot see the great idea
    back of [sic][26] Roosevelt's experiments.
4.[27]

---

24. In this brief essay, Maurin began each line with what he opposed and finished each line with what he supported.

25. The origin of both quotes in {526} is unknown. They could be from contemporary newspaper accounts that have not been digitized. The Al Smith quote is similar to other published speeches that Smith gave during 1936 criticizing Roosevelt's New Deal.

26. If Maurin had had time to refine this essay, perhaps this line would have read, "behind Roosevelt's experiments."

27. This Easy Essay was unfinished and stopped after Maurin wrote the number four.

[No Title] {527}

1. A Bourgeois does
    what the other bourgeois
    are doing;
    he keeps up
    with the Joneses.
2. A Gentleman does
    what is to be done
    and does not
    wait for George
    to do it—
    Be a gentleman.

Farming Commune Slogans {528}

1. Don't fight the bosses
    fire the boss.
2. Don't rush the can
    fire the can.[28]
3. Find a place
    for everything
    and put everything
    in its place.
4. Find time
    for everything
    and do everything
    on time.
5. Eat what you raise
    and raise
    what you want to eat.
6. Find out
    what is to be done
    fit yourself to do it
    and do it.
7. Don't wait for George
    to do it
    Be George.

---

28. The first two stanzas were crossed out.

8. Go to Mass
    and bring the Mass
    to the masses.
9. Give
    what you can give
    and get
    what is given to you.

Women, Men, and Manners {529}

1. H. L. Mencken says
    that women are endowed
    with natural intelligence.
2. A good use by women
    of their natural intelligence
    is the teaching of manners
    to ill-mannered men.
3. Blaise Pascal says
    that men's good manners
    come from women.
4. But no nagging woman
    has ever taught good manners
    to any man.
5. A nagging woman
    is to be pitied
    not to be admired
    or censored.
6. But when men
    try to outnag women
    they are not doing
    the manly thing.

On the Farming Commune[29] {530}

1. A Catholic Worker
    Farming Commune
    is a farm

---

29. Published after Maurin's death in the February 1951 issue of the *Catholic Worker*. It has also been previously published in Ellis, *Peter Maurin: Prophet in the Twentieth Century* (New York: Paulist Press, 1981), 131–32.

where Catholic Workers
work in community.
2. To work on a Farming Commune
is to cooperate with God
in the production of food
for the feeding of men.
3. Children and invalids
cannot work
but they must be fed.
4. Catholic workers
must do more than their share
so as to be able
to feed the children
and invalids.
5. Gentlemen farmers
and lady farmerettes
are not workers
they are shirkers.
6. Time is a gift of God
and must be used
to serve God
by serving men.
7. Gentlemen farmers
don't live on the sweat
of their own brow.
8. Gentlemen farmers
are neither gentlemen or farmers
and lady farmerettes
are not very useful
on a Farming Commune.

The following section of unpublished essays brings together a holistic formula that was a common theme and reference in many of Peter Maurin's essays: cult, culture, cultivation. Cult denotes the spiritual, culture denotes learning, and cultivation denotes physical work—usually on the land. Another way to express these three areas is as spirit, mind, and body. The three areas have traditionally been seen as the three aspects of the human person in Christian anthropology. As March H. Ellis explains,

FIGURE 5. Peter Maurin speaking at retreat, Maryfarm, Easton, Pennsylvania, September 1940; photo probably taken by William Gauchat (Courtesy of Marquette University)

during the summer of 1938, Maurin began spending more time at the Catholic Worker farm in Easton, Pennsylvania. At this time, he wrote Easy Essays on cult, culture, and cultivation, which he placed on the bulletin board every day for inspiration and as a basis for discussion on the farm.[30] Each arrangement of three essays following the cult, culture,

30. Ellis, *Peter Maurin*, 123, 126.

cultivation formula was numbered. Unfortunately, numbers 11 through 14 are missing.

No. 1

CULT — A Child of God {531}

1. Would you like
    to know a child
    who has the sweet name
    of child of God?
2. Perhaps you have not thought about it
    but every man and woman
    who has been baptized
    is a child of God.
3. Every baby
    who has been baptized
    even though
    he may not be old enough
    to walk or to talk
    is a child of God.
4. We are all children of God
    our heavenly Father.

—Dominican Sisters of Grand Rapids[31]

CULTURE — The Need of Today {532}

1. All genuine thought
    is rooted in personal needs,
    and my own thought
    since the war,

---

31. The Dominican Sisters of Grand Rapids are still in existence. During the late 1920s and '30s, they were involved with Fr. Virgil Michel and the liturgical renewal movement, and they published a number of books that had the purpose of being companions to the *Baltimore Catechism* for children and adults. Maurin's quotes from the Sisters are likely from one of these catechetical books for children. For more information, see Mona Schwind, *Period Pieces: An Account of the Grand Rapids Dominicans 1853–1966* (Grand Rapids, Mich.: Sister of St. Dominic, 1991), 171–80.

and indeed for some years previously,
is due to the need
that so many of us feel today
for social readjustment
and for the recovery
of a vital contact
between the spiritual life
of the individual
and the social
and economic organization
of modern culture.[32]

—Christopher Dawson

2. The need of today
is to find the way
to express the spiritual
through the material.

—Peter Maurin

CULTIVATION — Based on an Ideal {533}

1. When the social
and economic system
is on the rocks,
those who try to build
a better world
should make a picture,
in human terms,
of what they want
that world to be.
2. This picture is more important
than any Reform Bill.
3. If a reformation
is to endure,
it must be based

---

32. This quote and the following quotes attributed to Christopher Dawson are from his introduction to his book *Enquiries into Religion and Culture* (New York: Sheed & Ward, 1933), which collected a number of his previously published essays.

> on sound political
> and economic theory.
> 4. But if a reformation
> is even to begin,
> it must be based on an ideal
> that can stir the human heart.
>
> —Herbert Agar[33]
>
> 5. People must be told
> why things are
> what they are
> as well as [how] things should be
> if they were
> as they should be.
>
> —Peter Maurin

No. 2

CULT — There Is One {534}

> 1. Now that you know
> that you are
> a child of God
> you will want to know
> many other things too.
> 2. You will want to know more
> about God
> and about what you should do
> in order to live
> as His loving child.
> 3. There is One
> who has known God
> and His heavenly Father
> from all eternity.

---

33. This quote and the following quotes from Herbert Agar were from the introduction of a book that Agar coedited with Allen Tate, *Who Owns America? A New Declaration of Independence* (Boston and New York: Houghton Mifflin, 1936).

4. This One is the Son of God,
    our Lord and Savior Jesus Christ.
5. He has always
    loved His Father.
6. He has taught us
    how we should love God
    and He has obtained for us
    the grace to do so.

—Dominican Sisters of Grand Rapids

CULTURE — Social Detachment {535}

1. Social detachment
    is a necessary condition
    for the scientific study of society,
    but a difficult
    and dangerous state.
2. For the man who is separated
    from the organic life
    of his culture
    is in little better case
    than the oyster
    that has been extracted
    from its shell.

—Christopher Dawson

3. When man is separated
    from his environment
    he becomes academic.
4. When man can think
    while he is in contact
    with his environment
    he becomes dynamic.

—Peter Maurin

CULTIVATION — Hate and Reform {536}

1. No country can be reformed
    by the people who hate it.

2. The haters can supply
    useful criticism;
    they can show
    the frauds and injustices
    which corrode society.
3. They can even persuade men
    to overthrow a world
    which has grown sick
    with injustice.
4. But only those
    who have affection
    for the national idea
    can persuade a people
    to reform.

            —Herbert Agar

5. The art of creating order
    out of chaos
    is the art of inducing people
    to give up old habits
    and start to contract
    new habits.

            —Peter Maurin

No. 3

CULT — In the Catholic Church {537}

1. The life of a child
    is a beautiful life of love.
2. God loves you
    and you love God.
3. We all love one another
    in God.
4. We live this beautiful life of love
    in the Catholic Church.
5. In the Catholic Church
    Jesus-Christ

the Son of God
not only teaches you
how a child of God should live.
6. Through the Sacraments
He also gives you
part in His own life,
so that you really live in Him.
7. Through Him
and in Him
you love and serve God.

—Dominican Sisters of Grand Rapids

CULTURE — Happy Is the People {538}

1. Happy is the people
that is without a history,
and thrice happy
is the people
without a sociology.
2. For as long as we possess
a living culture
we are unconscious of it.
3. And it is only
when we are in danger
of losing it
or when it is already dead
that we begin
to realize its existence
and to study it scientifically.

—Christopher Dawson

4. When people try
to become better
they are called
cultured.
5. When people try
to become better off
they are called
civilized.

—Peter Maurin

CULTIVATION — [No Title] {539}

1. It is our belief
    that the American ideal
    is still one of the best acts
    of man's imagination.
2. It is our belief
    that the plain man
    throughout America
    is still moved
    by this ideal
    as by no other promise.
3. If he can be taught
    that there is a chance
    to realize the ideal,
    he will insist
    that the chance be taken.

—Herbert Agar

4. It is not a question
    of a New Deal;
    it is a question
    of an old game.
5. It is not a question
    of rugged individualism;
    it is a question
    of gentle personalism.

—Peter Maurin

No. 4

CULT — God Loves Us {540}

1. In His goodness
    our Heavenly Father
    has given us commandments
    which help us
    to love and serve Him.
2. As a faithful child of God
    you will want
    to learn more and more

about the commandments of God
so that you may know
just what to do
to please Him.
3. God our heavenly Father,
He loves us
more than we can tell.
4. He has many ways
of telling of His love
and He is always
finding new ways
of showing His love.
5. He gives us
all that we are
and all that we have.

—Dominican Sisters of Grand Rapids

CULTURE — There Is No Vision {541}

1. But this process
is not a uniform one.
2. It is plainly perceptible
to those who are concerned
with the spiritual functions of culture
—the poets and artists,
philosophers and religious thinkers—
as well as to those
who are socially unsuccessful
and in a state of spiritual revolt,
while all those who live
on the surface of society
—the politicians
and the men of business—
are still unconscious of it.

—Christopher Dawson

3. Someone said:
"There is no vision
in Washington."

4. There is no vision
   in Washington
   but there is plenty of supervision
   in Washington.
5. But State supervision
   is a poor substitute
   for personal vision.

—Peter Maurin

CULTIVATION — Liberty Leaguers {542}

1. But when he sees
   all the good words
   associated with America
   applied to all the bad features
   of cosmopolitan plutocracy,
   he begins to feel
   that perhaps
   the whole effort
   was a mistake.
2. A few more Liberty League dinners
   and the plain man
   will turn against liberty.

—Herbert Agar

3. The trouble with the Liberty League
   is that the Liberty Leagues
   don't know what to do
   with liberty.
4. If the Liberty Leaguers
   want to find out
   what to do with liberty
   let them read
   Maritain's book
   Freedom in the Modern World.[34]

—Peter Maurin

34. In the original Easy Essay, Maurin recommended *Liberty and the Modern World* when he obviously meant Jacques Maritain's *Freedom in the Modern World* (London: Sheed & Ward, 1935), which he regularly recommended in his Easy Essays for those

No. 5

CULT — God's Gift to Men {543}

1. God made us
    to love Him
    and He knows
    that we want
    to love Him.
2. He knows
    that we would like
    to give Him something
    to show our love.
3. Of course
    God does not
    need anything from us
    but He is a kind Father
    and He wants
    to make us happy.
4. He knows
    that we have nothing to give
    that is worthy of Him
    and in His goodness
    God gives us a gift
    which we may offer to Him.
5. This gift is
    His divine Son.

—Dominican Sisters of Grand Rapids

CULTURE — Men Are Divided {544}

1. Men today are divided
    between those
    who have kept their spiritual roots
    and lost their contact
    with the existing order of society,
    and those who have preserved

---

interested in authentic freedom and liberty. This error on Maurin's part is understandable, since the original French title of the book was *Du Régime Temporal et de la Liberté*.

their social contacts
   and lost their spiritual roots.
2. Such a state of things
   has not been unknown in the past,
   but whenever it has occurred
   it has marked the dissolution
   or the weakening
   of a culture.
                                            —Christopher Dawson

3. To live in the world
   without being of the world
   such is the problem
   of professing Christians.
4. Professing Christians
   must live in such a way
   that modern Pagans
   will say about them
   what Roman Pagans
   used to say
   about Roman Christians
   "See how they love each other."
                                                —Peter Maurin

CULTIVATION — Men Should Be Able to Count {545}

1. According to the American dream,
   the large majority
   should be able to count
   on the freedom of men
   who do not have
   to be anybody's dependent,
   or anybody's toady.
2. They should be able to count
   on the reasonable permanence,
   both of residence
   and occupation,
   which makes possible
   a stable family life.

3. They should be able to count
     on having the chance
     to do creative work,
     and to enjoy responsibility.
4. They should be able to count
     on living in an atmosphere of equality,
     in a world
     which puts relatively few barriers
     between man and man.

—Herbert Agar

5. A human society
     is a society
     where man chooses
     to be human
     to men.
6. A human society
     is a society
     where man tries to be
     what he wants
     the other fellow to be.

—Peter Maurin

No. 6

CULT — Holy Mass[35] {546}

1. We love God best
     when we offer a gift
     to Him.
2. And God shows His love
     by giving us a gift, too.
3. This sweet giving of gifts
     takes place at Holy Mass.
4. Holy Mass
     is the greatest act of love

---

35. Previously published in Ellis, *Peter Maurin*, 126–27.

between God
and His children.
—Dominican Sisters of Grand Rapids

CULTURE — Rooted in Religion[36] {547}

1. The central conviction
    which has dominated my mind
    ever since I began to write,
    and which has increased
    in intensity
    during the last twenty years,
    is the conviction
    that the society or culture
    which has lost its spiritual roots
    is a dying culture,
    however prosperous
    it may appear externally.
2. Consequently,
    the problem of social survival
    is not only
    a political or economic one.
3. It is above all things religious,
    since it is in religion
    that the ultimate spiritual roots
    both of society and of the individual
    are to be found.
—Christopher Dawson

4. The political problem
    is not a political problem;
    it is an economic problem.
5. The economic problem
    is not an economic problem;
    it is an ethical problem.

---

36. Previously published in Ellis, *Peter Maurin*, 127–28.

6. The ethical problem
   is not an ethical problem;
   it is a religious problem.

—Peter Maurin

CULTIVATION — Derided by Two Groups {548}

1. Today that dream,
   is derided by two groups.
2. First, by the Communists,
   who say that any attempt
   to realize it
   must be vain,
   since the attempt
   would contradict
   the law of Marx.
3. Second, by the friends of Big Business,
   who dishonor the dream
   by saying
   that it has been realized,
   that it lies all about us today.

—Herbert Agar

4. Communists believe
   in making of America
   a land of opportunity
   by taking over the control
   of the means of production
   and distribution
   and placing everybody
   under State control.
5. Capitalists believe
   in making of America
   a land of opportunity
   by tightening their control
   over the means of production
   and distribution
   and placing everybody
   under their control.

—Peter Maurin

No. 7.

CULT — Planting the Seeds {549}

1. When seeds are planted in the ground
    something wonderful happens.
2. After a few days
    of sunshine and rain
    the seeds begin to sprout.
3. Finally they push their way
    out of the ground
    and soon grow
    into strong green plants.
4. Perhaps in time
    they may bear flowers
    or fruits.

—Dominican Sisters of Grand Rapids

CULTURE — Without Roots {550}

1. When a man
    has found his roots,
    he has found
    his religion.
2. The irreligious man
    is precisely
    the man without roots.
3. The irreligious man
    lives on the surface of existence
    and recognizes
    no ultimate allegiance.
4. This view is, of course,
    diametrically opposed
    to the dominant social philosophy
    of the modern world,
    whether individualist
    or socialist.

—Christopher Dawson

5. Bourgeois-mindedness
    is the result
    of modern secularism.
6. Modern secularism
    is the separation
    of the spiritual
    from the material.
7. To recapture
    spiritual awareness
    is to go to the roots
    of the modern unrest.

—Peter Maurin

CULTIVATION — We Must Remind {551}

1. We must not
    allow our people
    to be persuaded
    that freedom,
    self-government,
    equality
    mean nothing better
    than what we have attained.
2. We must remind them
    that the monopoly capitalism
    of modern America
    is almost the antithesis
    of our ideal.

—Herbert Agar

3. Rugged individualism
    has nothing to do
    with true Americanism.
4. True Americanism consists
    in knowing what to do
    with personal liberty.
5. To choose to be
    gentle personalist
    and refuse to be

rugged individualist
or rugged collectivist
is to make the right use
of personal liberty.

—Peter Maurin

No. 8

CULT — Growing of the Seed {552}

1. Of course,
    you do not know
    just how this takes place.
2. But you know
    that if the seeds
    did not have the sunshine
    and the rain
    they would not grow.
3. The growing of the seed
    is one of the wonderful things
    that we see around us
    every day.
4. It is God's way
    of making the world beautiful
    for us
    and of giving us
    what we need.

—Dominican Sisters of Grand Rapids

CULTURE — Liberal Thinking {553}

1. The liberal thinkers
    and statesmen
    who were the makers
    of nineteenth century civilization
    regarded religion and culture
    as entirely independent phenomena.

2. Religion was entirely
    a matter for the individual conscience
    and it had nothing to do
    with social and economic life.

—Christopher Dawson

3. Religion has nothing to do
    with politics
    which made politics
    just politics.
4. Religion had nothing to do
    with business
    which made business
    just business.
5. And business went in politics
    and politics
    went in business
    which brought the world
    where it is.

—Peter Maurin

CULTIVATION — Monopoly Capitalism {554}

1. So far from providing freedom,
    monopoly capitalism
    does not even desire it.
2. To be sure,
    a cardinal tenet
    of its economics theory
    is that
    both capital and labor
    should be "free."
3. But this only means
    that they must be allowed
    to flow backward and forward
    from area to area
    and from industry to industry

wherever
the highest interest rate of profit
is to be found.

        —Herbert Agar

4. Monopoly capitalism
believes in an acquisitive society
not a functional society.
5. Monopoly capitalism
is a society of go-getters,
not a society of go-givers.

        —Peter Maurin

No. 9

CULT — A Mystery {555}

1. And just as there are many things
which God does
that we cannot understand
so there are things
about God Himself
which we cannot
fully understand.
2. A truth about God,
which we cannot
fully understand
is called a mystery,
just as He lets us
know something
of the way in which
the seeds grow
but we cannot even
understand it fully.

      —Dominican Sisters of Grand Rapids

CULTURE — Secularism and Marxism {556}

1. But the resulting
    secularism of culture
    which took place
    throughout Western Europe
    in the nineteenth century
    brought its own nemesis.
2. It led to the discredit
    of a religion
    that had no power
    over social life
    and of a culture
    that had no spiritual sanctions.
3. It found at once
    its logical conclusion
    and its refutation
    in the yet more radical
    secularization of life
    which characterized
    the Marxian philosophy.

—Christopher Dawson

4. The Bourgeois say
    that religion
    has nothing to do
    with business.
5. The Bolshevists say
    that religion
    has nothing to do
    with life.
6. The Communitarians say
    that religion
    must find its expression
    in everyday life.

—Peter Maurin

CULTIVATION — Landless and Toolless[37] {557}

1. In terms of labor
    this means
    that a workman
    had better be "free"
    from a home,
    because if he had a home
    he would not be
    sufficiently mobile.
2. He had better be free
    from personal responsibilities.
3. Above all,
    he had better be free
    from children.
4. Landless and toolless,
    vagrant as the red Indian
    his successive livelihoods
    at the mercy
    of an "economic law"
    which we have
    basely allowed
    to take the throne from morals
    —this man has, of course,
    the vote.

—Herbert Agar

5. Two rooms and kitchenette
    is not the right place
    for the home.
6. The right place for the home
    is a homestead.

—Peter Maurin

---

37. Previously published in Ellis, *Peter Maurin*, 128–29.

No. 10

CULT — The Greatest Mystery {558}

1. The greatest mystery
    about God
    is the mystery
    of the Most Blessed Trinity.
2. The Blessed Trinity
    is three divine Persons
    in one God.
3. There is only one God
    but in God
    there are three divine Persons,
    the Father, the Son and the Holy Ghost.
4. The Father
    is the first Person
    of the Blessed Trinity
    the Son
    is the second Person
    and the Holy Ghost
    is the third Person.
5. The Father is God
    the Son is God
    and the Holy Spirit is God.

—Dominican Sisters of Grand Rapids

CULTURE — Liberalism and Bolshevism {559}

1. While Liberalism
    had pushed religion
    on the side,
    Bolshevism
    eliminated it altogether.
2. So Bolshevism
    prepared the way
    for the complete re-absorption
    of the individual
    in the social organism.

3. Bolshevism at the same time,
    transformed the social organism
    into an economic mechanism.[38]
                                    —Christopher Dawson

4. Liberals
    were not serious enough
    to take religion seriously.
5. And because liberals
    failed to take religion seriously
    they failed to be liberators.
6. Liberals
    failed to think deeply
    as well as to act vigorously.
                                    —Peter Maurin

CULTIVATION — Boredom Justified by Fear {560}

1. So far from offering the chance
    to do creative work,
    monopoly capitalism
    subjects more and more laborers
    to a humiliating,
    nerve-racking boredom.
2. The boredom to be sure,
    is qualified by fear
    —fear of losing their jobs,
    fear of annoying their straw-bosses,
    fear sometimes
    that their private habits
    may not meet the taste
    of an impudent
    and nosy employer.
                                    —Herbert Agar

---

38. In the original text, the term "Communism" was used instead of "Bolshevism."

3. Monopoly capitalism
    has given us
    mass-production
    mass-education
    mass-mindedness.
4. But thinking is individual
    not collective.
5. Mass-thinking
    is mob-thinking
    and mob-thinking
    is no thinking.
6. "Man is a man
    for all of that"
    and man
    who is a man
    stands as a man
    not part of a mob.

—Peter Maurin

Numbers 11 through 14 are missing.

No. 15

CULT — No One Like God {561}

1. There is no one
    like God.
2. God know all things
    and sees all things.
3. God is holy,
    just and merciful.
4. God sees us
    always.
5. God is everywhere,
    but we cannot see Him
    because He has no body.
6. God is a pure spirit.

—Dominican Sisters of Grand Rapids

CULTURE — Illegitimate Element {562}

1. This quasi-religious element
    of Bolshevist Communism
    seems to me
    to be inseparable
    from its revolutionary phase.
2. It seems to me
    to be destined to pass away
    in proportion as Bolshevist Communism
    becomes an established order.
3. In any case,
    it must be recognized
    by Bolshevist Communists themselves
    as an illegitimate element
    that is alien
    to the true spirit
    of scientific socialism.[39]

    —Christopher Dawson

4. Many Catholics
    want to know
    what is the cause
    of the Communists 'peal. [sic]
5. The cause must be found
    in the quasi-religious element
    of Bolshevist Communism.

    —Peter Maurin

CULTIVATION — The Question Arises {563}

1. An unprecedented collapse of business
    and a drastic shrinkage
    of the power to produce
    followed the growth
    of mass production
    and large-scale industry.

---

39. In this quote, Maurin added the word "Bolshevist" in each instance.

2. The question naturally arises
>   whether mass production
>   is practical,
>   or whether
>   it must inevitably lead
>   to poverty and distress.[40]

—David Cushman Coyle

3. The question naturally arises
>   if mass production
>   brings mass distribution
>   or mass starvation.
4. The question naturally arises
>   if it is a question
>   of supply and demand
>   or demand and supply.
5. The question naturally arises
>   if an economy of plenty
>   is any better
>   than an economy of scarcity.

—Peter Maurin

No. 16

CULT — God Is Watching {564}

1. God is always
>   watching over us.
2. There is nothing
>   that God does not know
>   and see.
3. God knows
>   all that we think
>   and say
>   and do.

---

40. This was a quote from the opening paragraph of David Cushman Coyle's article "The Fallacy of Mass Production," in Agar and Tate, *Who Owns America?*.

4. We cannot
    hide any thought
    word or action
    from God.
                    —Dominican Sisters of Grand Rapids

CULTURE — Arbitrary Simplifications {565}

1. This disharmony
    between socialist theory
    and social practice
    itself shows
    the inadequacy
    of the Marxian philosophy,
    when it is applied
    to the complex realities
    of social life,
    which refuse to be reduced
    to purely economic terms.
2. A genuinely scientific sociology
    must reject
    all such arbitrary simplifications
    of the problem
    by the elimination
    of an essential factor.
                    —Christopher Dawson

3. Bolshevist Socialists
    are not convincing
    when they try to reconcile
    economic determinism
    with social dynamism.
4. Bolshevist materialism
    and Bourgeois materialism
    are related.
5. Sponsoring grievances
    is not the same thing
    as sponsoring ideals.
                    —Peter Maurin

CULTIVATION — The Question Is {566}

1. An unprecedented collapse
    of business
    and a drastic shrinkage
    of the power to produce
    followed the growth
    of mass production
    and of large-scale industry.
2. The question naturally arises
    whether mass production
    is practical,
    or whether
    it must inevitably lead
    to poverty and distress.[41]

—David Cushman Coyle

3. Technicians
    are applied scientists,
    they are not
    applied philosophers.
4. Technicians
    have found the secret
    of mass-production
    but not the secret
    of mass-distribution.
5. Technicians
    are specialists,
    they know more and more
    about less and less.

—Peter Maurin

Easy Essays from Other Sources

These final three essays have only been preserved in Arthur Sheehan's 1959 biography, *Peter Maurin*. Maurin read the first essay to the Rotarian

---

[41]. This is the same exact quote from Coyle that Maurin used in essay {563}.

club in Kingston, New York, to which he had been invited to speak in 1927. Easy Essay {89} referred to this talk.

[No Title][42] {567}

1. The other fellow says
    that I am queer;
    and that is normal.
2. When he says that I am queer
    he means that I am queer
    to him.
3. I may be queer to him
    but he is queerer to me
    than I am queer to him,
    and he being queerer to me
    than I am queer to him,
    he hasn't a chance
    to make me normal.
4. So I am trying to make him queer
    so we both can be normal.

Peter Maurin wrote the following two essays in 1936, just after the first Catholic Worker farm began near Easton, Pennsylvania, to energize his fellow Catholic Workers about possibilities for the farm.

The Truck Gardeners of Paris[43] {568}

1. In market gardening
    the soil is always made
    whatever it originally might have been.
2. In the renting contracts
    of the truck gardeners of Paris,
    it is sometimes stipulated

---

42. This essay was preserved by Arthur Sheehan in Sheehan, *Peter Maurin: Gay Believer* (Garden City, N.Y.: Hanover House, 1959), 85–86.

43. This essay and the following one were preserved by Arthur Sheehan in Sheehan, *Peter Maurin*, 132.

>   that the gardener
>   may carry away its soil
>   down to a certain depth
>   when he quits his tenancy.
> 3. He himself makes it
>   and when he moves to another plot
>   he carts his soil away
>   together with his frames,
>   his water-pipes and other belongings.

The Case of Mr. Ponce {569}

> 1. In two and seven-tenth acres
>   Mr. Ponce cultivated every year
>   20,000 lbs. of carrots,
>   more than 20,000 lbs. of onions, radishes
>   and other vegetables sold by weight,
>   5000 heads of cabbage,
>   3000 of cauliflower,
>   5000 baskets of tomatoes,
>   5000 dozen of choice fruit,
>   154,000 heads of lettuce,
>   in short, a total of 250,000 lbs.
>   of vegetables.

Appendixes

Appendix I: Four Interviews with Peter Maurin

The *New York Catholic Worker* published Arthur Sheehan's interview of Peter Maurin during 1943. The interview was published in four parts in four consecutive issues. The headings denote the month in which the interview was published. The interview covered a wide range of topics and presented a comprehensive view of Maurin's vision in a relatively concise and brief manner.

FIGURE 6. Peter Maurin reading in his room, ca. 1936 (Courtesy of Marquette University)

April 1943

AS: Do you believe that people must have an agricultural college training before going on the land?

PM: These colleges don't always educate persons to stay on the land. I am in favor of people learning by doing.

AS: How can this return to the land be made a dynamic movement?

PM: It takes dynamic persons.

AS: What do you mean by dynamic persons?

PM: Persons with convictions, who foster actions based on convictions, not based on someone giving orders.

AS: Then the driving impulse must come from within people, you would say?

PM: A leader must be a personalist. If he is a personalist, he will not be a dictator. He will change the attitude of others through the power of example. It takes an awful lot of patience.

Community Spirit

AS: Would you have the members of your farming commune all eat at a common table?

PM: No, I am against the community kitchen idea. Each family should have their own house.

AS: How about the single persons on a farming commune?

PM: The ideal is to have them live in the homes of the married couples. However, this must not be forced but must come through the couples themselves accepting the single persons.

AS: Why do you prefer this way?

PM: To develop a community spirit. In my town, there were two brothers, one married with a wife and children and the other unmarried. The latter lived with his brother. One day, the married brother was killed by a tree as they were working together. The unmarried brother then became the guardian of the family. That was the true Christian spirit.

AS: How would you break down that feeling of isolation people have in the country?

PM: It must come from the development of a community spirit. We wish to be halfway between the collectivist idea of everything in common and the hermit way with people being rugged individualists.

AS: Could you mention a book where some ideas on the personalist and communitarian way could be found?
PM: There is something on it in Guardini's book, *The Church and the Catholic*.

The Three C's

AS: How about community prayer?
PM: There should be some prayer life in common but it should come from an inner desire, not be forced. There also must be intellectual discussion as well as the work to be done in the fields and crafts.
AS: You speak of the three C's often. What are they?
PM: They are cult, culture and cultivation.
AS: By cult, do you mean liturgical prayer?
PM: Yes, community prayer and the relationship of our work to it. For this study, I recommend Guardini's book.
AS: What do you mean by culture?
PM: There must be intellectual discussion, but it must come spontaneously, not be forced. It can be in the fields when you're working. It makes the labor lighter and breaks down that rugged individualist spirit which comes when people work alone.
AS: Have you any books along this line to recommend?
PM: Yes, there is one by a Polish priest, *Is Modern Culture Doomed?*[1]
AS: And what about cultivation?
PM: The private gardens needn't be so big. Then they will not take too much time for isolated work. More time can be spent in the fields together.
AS: Have you a book that might interest along this line?
PM: I would advise this book by Father McNabb, *Old Principles and the New Order*.[2]

---

1. The Polish priest was Rev. Andrzej Krzesiński (1884–1964).
2. *Old Principles and the New Order* (New York: Sheed & Ward, 1942) was a book by Vincent McNabb. Like his book *The Church and the Land* (1926; Norfolk, Va.: IHS, 2003), it argued that cities presented too much temptation and fostered isolation. McNabb contended that cities should be eschewed for a life on the land where authentic community could be cultivated.

Balance and Vocation

AS: On which of these three phases should the emphasis be placed?

PM: If too much attention is paid to one to the detriment of another, things go wrong. There must be a balance. Different persons have different inclinations. Those whose inclination is to work with their hands more than their heads will become disgruntled if too much time is given to discussion. If not enough time is given to discussion and there is too much physical work, the intellectually minded will fall away. People must sense when there is a lack of proportion.

AS: What makes for a good morale on a farming commune?

PM: It comes from harmony when the emphasis on prayer, discussion and work is rightly balanced.

AS: How many families do you think there should be on a farming commune?

PM: You must adjust yourself to your acreage. It does not make for the ideal to have limits. It ceases to be a personal idea. There must be crafts besides farming.

AS: Are you in favor of small groups?

PM: People must know each other. You must try to do away with factionalism. Even one family could begin on a farm and build for others. You build as you go along. It is a progressive thing.

AS: In other words, you want to get people on the land?

PM: First to get them thinking so that they see they should go on the land.

Learn by Doing

AS: Why don't you believe in a formal training previous to going on the land?

PM: Education is a life process. People learn by doing. Trouble is, people want blueprints. I don't want to give blueprints. Let them struggle with it. As they face problems, they get light. I must be available to discuss problems with them for clarification.

If the place is too small, there are not enough crafts, not enough variety. One thousand families wouldn't be too many, if they had the right idea. The craftsmen were the villagers. St. Dunstan's College on Prince Edward Island is doing the right thing, fostering a movement to bring craftsmen back to the villages. Then the farmers there wouldn't have to sell their wheat and fish and have to ship them out at a loss.

My grandfather was a craftsman and a farmer. He was a carpenter, a quarryman, a slate worker and he made baskets to carry dough to the bakers. Dick Aherne, of the Philadelphia group, was a city boy but he learned so that now he can teach others. He learned by working. The trouble with agricultural colleges is that they prepare people for business farming. Better go out to a farmer to learn.

My aim is to make people think. I am a personalist medievalist, which makes me a medievalist communist.

Private Ownership and Common Ownership

AS: But what about ownership, Peter? Families want their own land, their own house, although St. Gertrude said, "Property, the more common it becomes, the more holy it becomes."

PM: About ownership, the size of a piece of land depends on the size of the family. There can be the combination of the two kinds, private ownership and communal ownership. I always make a case for the communal ownership which is the ideal. Here in America people homesteaded but they became the victims of their isolation and their children left the farms and went to the cities. They forgot the village idea which was in Europe but went off by themselves. It was really the spirit of individualism which came from the Reformation, and Catholics unfortunately followed it, forgetting the community, the liturgical idea.

May 1943 — On Land and Children

AS: Peter, why do you say that being on the land is better for children?
PM: It's a matter of fresh food, fresh air and being away from city streets.
AS: Do you think that children get a better outlook on life in the country?
PM: Life on the land makes a child reflective. He watches the different life processes working out before his eyes, and it makes him think. He watches the growth of the animals and plants, and he gets an organic view of life.
AS: By organic, you mean he sees the function or purpose of each part?

PM: Yes; he sees the purpose through the medium of his own eyes. It doesn't come through books and through the memory, as a city child has to learn these things. The child absorbs more in a leisurely way through life on the land.

Asset or Liability?

AS: Why do you often say "a child is an asset on the farm, a liability in the city"?

PM: When the child sees his father doing useful work on a farm, the desire to be useful is born in the child. The child then wants to help his father, and it is good for the child to work with its father. I was plowing at eleven. The work on the farm gives the child the right form of exercise. It is exercise with a purpose, not just exercise for the sake of exercise, as is so often the case in sports. We say that we should read with a purpose, then why not exercise with a purpose?

AS: Then you would say that the boundless energy of the child is used up usefully on the farm, whereas in the city the child dissipates a lot of his energy in wasteful sports?

PM: Yes, the purpose of exercise is health, but why not get it while doing the more useful work? The farm work gives the child the right opportunity.

Teachers at Fault

AS: How explain then, Peter, the fact that children often wish to get away from the farm?

PM: The schools most often are to blame. They hold up city ideals. The children are educated even in country schools to look up to city living as a superior form of living. It doesn't help to make the child realize the fact that the country is more important than the city. The ideal that working with your head is superior to working with your head and your hands is taught or implied. This is how we get so many crazy ideas in society today.

AS: But the parents must see these things, too, Peter, else how can they point them out to the children?

PM: Yes, often the farmer doesn't see the superiority of this working with hands and head. The farmers often feel inferior to "so-called educated" city folks. The city people look down too much on the farmers.

AS: That is really a form of snobbery.
PM: Yes, it is.

Realization Too Late

AS: Isn't it strange, Peter, that men have to break down and be sent to mental hospitals before there is a realization of the importance of farm and craft work as a means to mental health?
PM: When the system has shattered their minds, they have to go to those places. The working in crafts and in gardens is known to bring a better balance to their minds.
Ade de Bethune once said that many persons can only see abstract principles through the medium of the material which they mould or shape with their hands.
I know a woman who has come to an understanding of Catholic dogma through studying Ade's drawings. She just couldn't grasp it otherwise. (Ade tries to explain the importance of little actions, such as cooking, carpentry work, all the different actions of housekeeping, as a means to developing the whole person.)

Stewardship Not Ownership

AS: Does the idea of a piece of land for himself have to be held up to the child as an ideal so that he will stay on the land?
PM: Something much more than that is necessary. You must realize the selfishness that is in the child and try to offset it. If the child is taught to consider material ownership as a sole badge of respect, he is not being taught enough. He must be taught the idea of using material things to help other people. This is the idea of stewardship, which is so opposed to the idea of absolute ownership of property. The child wishes to be recognized, but he should be taught to see that the right kind of recognition is to be recognized by your fellow man as one who helps people and not as one merely possessing things.
AS: You often speak of folk schools such as they have in Denmark. Do you think they are a better way of education?
PM: Yes, I do. Take the matter of folk dances. Through these dances the child comes to see the necessity of co-operation with other children to perform the dances. The children are attracted to the music through

the senses, and through the music they get the idea. The songs stick easily in the memory. Folk dances lead to folk songs.

AS: I remember, Peter, someone saying that in parts of Newfoundland they create songs at their parties.

PM: Yes, that is true of many folk cultures. The song brings ideas to the mind in an attractive way. Then you don't have to look to Tin Pan Alley[3] to create your music for you.

Sin of the Intellectuals

PM: The purpose of the music is to get ideas into the head. The idea then should start the will into action, and when it does, the soul is happy. Action must follow ideas. The sin of the intellectuals is to let the good ideas stay in their heads. They do not result in action, and, since they should be the leaders and are looked up to by the workers as leaders, this irresponsibility on their part is the reason why the workers turn against the intellectuals.

AS: It all goes back to what you say about the scholars having to become workers and the workers becoming scholars, if we are to bring right order into society.

PM: The knowledge-for-knowledge-sake business is no good. It must be used for the common good. The worker often doesn't think, and consequently doesn't have the answers. If the intellectuals just talk, they make no impression on him. When the worker sees the intellectual putting his ideas into action, he says, "What's the great idea?" and he watches him. He sees that he reads books for enlightenment, and he is attracted to reading them, too, and that is what he needs, namely, to cultivate his mind.

June 1943

AS: We were speaking about folk schools the last time. Have you any further ideas on them, Peter?

---

3. Tin Pan Alley is a reference to the powerful group of music publishers and writers who monopolized the popular music scene in New York City from the mid-1880s to the 1950s. These groups made money by selling sheet music to which they had purchased the copyright.

PM: We need these folk schools so that people can understand the significance of folk cultures and can learn from these cultures. The folk dances and folk songs help us to understand. Consider the Negro spirituals. The rhythms came from Africa and the Negroes of the South applied them to what they had learned of Christian teaching, and out of the two came a new cultural development.

AS: You mentioned one time something Kenkel, the editor of *Social Justice and Central Blatt*, once said about folk proverbs.

PM: He said that the proverbs of the German peasants would fill several volumes the size of Webster's if they were published. They weren't translated into English and so we find the English speaking people falling for the proverbs of the Manchester school: "Time is money," "Business is business," "Your dollar is your best friend."

I have been trying to find Irish proverbs. I have found some by a policeman from Dublin in a book called *Twenty Years A-Growing*.[4]

And speaking of the effect of folk songs, there is something which Professor Donald Davidson of Vanderbilt University told me. He said that many of the anti-Catholic prejudices among the Kentucky hill people came from old Elizabethan ballads handed down from the last part of the 16th century.

AS: You can see the effect of good liturgical music in a parish where there is a participation of the people in the singing.

PM: That is a good way to convey the liturgical spirit. After all, it is through military music that the military spirit is conveyed to the people. Good Gregorian chant, participated in by the people, will increase the spirit of prayer and wonder, the true liturgical spirit.

AS: Victor Smith was saying that in making the crib sets, with their figures of the Nativity scene, you couldn't help but come to a deepened respect for the religious spirit represented by the scenes.

PM: That comes from work which has a significance. The trouble today is that recreation tends to take people away from Christian thoughts. Hence you hear people listening to crooners and such like.

AS: But the people crave music, Peter.

PM: But it must be worthwhile, like the music of the monks at Solesmes. You can trace this work back to Dom Abbe Guéranger, who sponsored

---

4. *Twenty Years A-Growing* (New York: Viking, 1933) was a book by Irish police officer Maurice O'Sullivan (1904–50).

the revival of this work among the Benedictines and through them around the world.

AS: Somewhere I read, Peter, that much of the religious spirit of the Middle Ages came from the common practice of learning the psalms by heart. Then when the people were working the phrases constantly made them try to create a synthesis between the matter they were working with and the spiritual significance of their work.

PM: That is how they related all things to God. There is an interesting thing that happened in Guatemala. When the Spaniards were there, they frightened away the Indians because they used to take them and make beasts of burden of them. When the Jesuits tried to Christianize them, they fled. The Jesuits began to sing their hymns and the natives were attracted, and when they saw they weren't harmed they cooperated. That was how some of the Jesuit Reductions began.

(These Reductions were farming communes started in various South American countries. They were self-sufficient agricultural communities.)

AS: Couldn't school teachers do much to bring a return to the crafts by introducing them in the schools, Peter? Weaving has been encouraged in some parts of Canada in the schools.

PM: Yes, it would be a good thing. The trouble is that the country schools imitate the city schools and so fail to prepare the children for a constructive life on the farm. I think that the Ladies of the Grail,[5] with their summer school near Chicago, are on the right track. The folk schools will help people to get the vision of a good rural economy. Professor Davidson was telling me that the Catholic Worker should start schools of this type. I think it would be good. Then people wouldn't be looking for entertainers to entertain them, but would find their own entertainment in creating beautiful things, and incidentally things they could find a market for.

July–August 1943

AS: Will you tell us something about the farming methods in your home in France? That was folk farming, the real peasant kind, and should be

---

5. The Grail is an international laywomen's movement that began in 1921 in Holland with the belief that women outside the context of a religious order could play a vital role in transforming the world. In 1940, at the invitation of Archbishop Stritch of Chicago, they opened a summer camp for inner city youth in Libertyville, Illinois.

enlightening to those who wish to know more about folk cultures and cultivation.

PM: There were about 3,500 sheep in our village and a thousand of these belonged to the people of the village. The others belonged to others from some distance away who brought them to our sheep herders to care for at certain times of the year.

AS: Did the sheep graze on the communal lands?

PM: Yes, in the daytime. Of course, sometimes when fields were lying fallow they would graze on private lands.

AS: Why do you say daytime?

PM: The sheep were brought into the private lands at night by the sheep herders for purpose of manuring.

AS: How was this arranged?

PM: It depended upon the number of fields a farmer had. The sheep were brought into the fields of the particular farmer whose night it was to have the sheep. The farmer's family prepared the meals for the sheep herders for that day. At two in the morning the sheep herders would move the sheep from field to field, and in this way twice as much land was manured. The sheep were as close packed as possible. All the families had their sheep in this communal grazing. Our family had eighty sheep.

AS: You had other fertilizing methods, didn't you?

PM: Yes, we used the fertilizer of oxen and cows, but we weren't perhaps as scientific about using it as we should have been.

AS: You used no commercial fertilizer?

PM: No; we never even had heard of it.

AS: In that book by Lord Howard[6] you gave me, entitled *An Agricultural Testament*, the author makes an awful strong case against the use of commercial fertilizer. He says that it ruins the fungi and humus of the top soil and so makes for a weakened soil. Such a soil makes the plants weak and easily hurt by the bugs and insects.

PM: Yes, I know. At home we used to have big burrowing rats in the fields—taupes, we called them. They helped to work the soil. The commercial fertilizer would certainly have killed them.

AS: Perhaps they were like our gophers. But, anyway, Peter, if what Lord Howard says is true, and he gives a whole lifetime of study to back his ideas, then our methods of farming have been nothing short of criminal.

---

6. This is a reference to Albert Howard (1873–1947).

PM: Yes, our farmers too often aren't farmers at all. They are land miners. They just take stuff out of the soil and don't replace it right. The miner just takes things out of the earth and never returns anything. Look how different a psychology that creates from that of the farmer who tries to preserve the fertility of the land for coming generations. It's really soil robbing, and practices of this kind don't make for good character. If we had folk schools, these ideas could be brought out. You can see the amount of miseducation that has gotten around.

AS: The other night I gave a talk on Catholic books, and the connection between reading poor books and soil conservation struck me vividly. The trees are torn down to make the cheap books. The land becomes eroded because the trees aren't replaced. The patriot would be then the person who read only the fewer good books, not the person who reads the trash.

PM: We begin to see all the connections when we think in this organic way. A good farmer plants trees along the edges of his fields. That keeps the wind from eroding the soil.

AS: Yes, and it also lessens the impact of the rain, which is apt to wash out plants and make the good top soil run off, especially on hills. When I think how banks lend money on mortgages to farmers who only "mine" their land, I wonder how stupid they are. The land may look the same, but the loss is in the soil. I don't think that many mortgages demand that the land be returned in the same good condition it was received.

PM: Speaking about mortgages, my father had to borrow money from time to time. But he borrowed it on his honor as a farmer, and a good farmer. There was no mortgage. When the man who loaned the money wanted it back, my father paid it if he had it, or if he didn't he tried to find another person to lend him the money until he could pay it. He would then repay the first lender. It was all done on honor; no mortgages.

AS: Getting back to the sheep, Peter. How often were these sheared?

PM: Once a year—in June.

AS: Did you do your own carding and spinning?

PM: We did formerly, but got away from it.

AS: How about chickens? Did you have to buy grain?

PM: No, because we processed our own grain. We grew it ourselves. The chickens ate the gleanings, and there was a lot of undigested grain from the animals around, too. The wheat straw was mixed with the silage, and there was often some grain on it. The chickens scratched for the undigested grain. The chickens got the leftovers from the meals, too. We had no ice, and food wasn't kept from one meal to another.

AS: Did you make your own bread in the villages?

PM: Yes, the bread was made in the village oven, which was an outdoor oven. It had a covering in front to protect the bakers from the rain. The people from the village used to gather around the oven when baking was going on. It was a great place for round-table discussions.

AS: The meat you ate, then, would be mostly chicken and mutton and lamb?

PM: No, we sold our chickens and sheep, and ate pork and sausages and the different pork meats.

AS: How about replanting of trees? When you cut trees for firewood, did you have a system of replacing them by replanting?

PM: Our trees weren't so many, and so we only cut the branches. This was in three-year periods. We tried to pick trees whose leaves the sheep would eat.

Appendix II: Peter Maurin's Radio Interview

Below is a transcript of a radio interview with Peter Maurin, printed in the November 1937 issue of the *Catholic Worker*. It is unknown either who performed the interview or on which radio station it was broadcast. Similar to the preceding interview with Sheehan, it briefly and concisely communicates Maurin's understanding of contemporary economic problems and his solution for a functional society.

FIGURE 7. Peter Maurin, undated (Courtesy of Marquette University)

Q: What would you suggest as the first step toward the solution of economic ills?

A: Feed the hungry for Christ's sake, clothe the naked for Christ's sake, shelter the homeless for Christ's sake, instruct the ignorant for Christ's sake, as the first Christians used to do, which made the pagans say about the Christians: "See how they love one another."

Q: Your first step then would be to spiritualize service to others by expressing the spiritual in the material. How would you do this?

A: My idea is to have people who choose to be voluntary poor live under the same roof and sit at the same table with the involuntary poor, setting an example in spiritualization of human relations, thus influencing others to follow this standard.

Q: How can we carry this influence into our everyday work life?

A: By having the voluntary poor and their associates remind the owners of capital of the responsibilities of ownership and teach the wage workers that labor is a gift, not a commodity to be sold for "what the traffic can bear."

Q: What do you mean by the responsibility of ownership?

A: Ownership does not exist to acquire more wealth, since all wealth belongs to God and therefore must be used for the service of God's children. The owner is God's trustee. God wants us to be our brother's keeper; what the rich do for the poor for Christ's sake is what they carry with them when they die, for Jean-Jacques Rousseau says that when a man dies, he carries in his clutched hands only that which he has given away during his lifetime.

Q: To what extent does this apply to industrial owners?

A: Industrial owners must use the profits of industry as Léon Harmel, an industrial owner, was using them, looking after the needy of his community and acting as an aristocrat rather than a plutocrat towards his workers, having a sense of *"noblesse oblige."*

Q: What are the working man's responsibilities toward the common good?

A: He must see to it that the things he makes are fit to use rather than to sell. He must take pride in work well done, and think less about fighting the boss, and he must realize that labor is related to thought and thought is a spiritual faculty, not a commodity.

Q: What would be the ultimate outcome of the realization on the part of the worker and the industrial owner of their responsibilities?

A: Through awareness of the employer's responsibility as well as the worker's, we will bring about a functional society based on Christian charity which will replace our acquisitive society. Capital as well as labor must aim to create a new society within the shell of the old, with the philosophy of the new, which is not a new philosophy but a very old one, so old that it looks like new.

Q: Will you tell us what you mean by a functional society?

A: A functional society is a society in which each member strives to foster the common good, a society of go-givers instead of go-getters, a society of idealists instead of materialists.

Q: Could you suggest some practical way of developing this functional society?

A: The practical ways of getting it are left to the initiative of individuals who have learned what to do with liberty, and who keep always in mind the importance of pure means; means that harmonize with the ultimate aims to be pursued.

Q: Where will we find the guiding principles of social reconstruction which will bring about this order based on justice and love?

A: We will find them in the social teachings of the Catholic Church through the centuries. In recent years these teachings have been reiterated in the encyclicals, especially in those of Pius XI and Leo XIII, and in the writings of churchmen, sociologists and economists such as Cardinal Manning, Bishop Von Ketteler, Prof. Toniolo[1] and the Marquis de La Tour du Pin.

Q: Your ideas for the common good have struck a responsive chord in my mind, and this leads me to believe that many of our listeners are wondering, at this point, how they could help to bring about this social order?

A: First, by the daily practice of the Works of Mercy at a personal sacrifice.

Second, by round-table discussion and study groups, to clarify thought; to learn to teach and to carry into action.

Third, the working man should belong to workingmen's associations, the employer should belong to employers' associations, and through joint collective action these associations are morally obligated to foster collective bargaining.

Fourth, the Catholic working man and the Catholic employer should impregnate the working men's associations and the employers' associations with Christian principles.

---

1. This is a reference to Blessed Giuseppe Toniolo (1845–1918).

Fifth, foster farming communes for the employment of the unemployed.

And finally, each individual should assume the responsibility of understanding and participating in this program wherever and however he finds the opportunity. Just one word of warning: this participation should always be that of a thinking, reasoning person.

Q: Some people say that Christianity has failed in allowing our present conditions to exist. What do you think about this?

A: "The Christian ideal has not failed," said Chesterton, "it has been found difficult and left untried." It has not been tried because people thought that it was not practical and men have tried everything except Christianity. Everything that men have tried has failed, and to fail in everything that man tries is not considered practical by the so-called practical people. So, the so-called practical people will begin to be practical when they start to practice the Christianity they profess to believe in.

Appendix III: Peter Maurin's Book Recommendations

Peter Maurin was a voracious reader and liked to recommend books. Maurin rarely agreed wholeheartedly with a book's entire argument, but he recommended books that he believed had important ideas. He made these recommendations in the pages of the *Catholic Worker* in Easy Essays, standalone recommendation lists that he published in the *Catholic Worker* (which were not included in the Easy Essays), and in the context of the interviews included in Appendixes I and II.

Previous collections of Easy Essays have included Maurin's book lists, but the one included here is the most complete. Other lists omit books recommended in interviews and those that Maurin recommended in essays and lists from September 1941 onward. In instances where a book's name or author was incorrectly written in the newspaper, the error has been corrected. Traditionally, the lists have been compiled in alphabetical order according to the name of the book, but this list is according to the author.

Mortimer Adler, *What Man Has Made of Man*
Herbert Agar, *Land of the Free*
Robert Hugh Benson, *Lord of the World*
Nicholas Berdyaev, *The Bourgeois Mind*
———, *Christianity and Class War*
Étienne Borne and François Henry, *A Philosophy of Work*
Ralph Borsodi, *Flight from the City*
George Boyle, *Democracy's Second Chance*
Alexis Carrel, *Man, the Unknown*
Jean-Baptiste Chautard, *The Soul of the Apostolate*
G. K. Chesterton, *The Outline of Sanity*
———, *Saint Francis of Assisi*
Amleto Cicognani, *The Great Commandment of the Gospel*
Herbert E. Cory, *The Emancipation of a Free Thinker*

Christopher Dawson, *Enquiries into Religion and Culture*
———, *The Making of Europe*
———, *Progress and Religion*
———, *Religion and the Modern State*
Charles Du Bos, *What Is Literature?*
Gerald Ellard, *Christian Life and Worship*
Amintore Fanfani, *Catholicism, Protestantism, and Capitalism*
Benedict Fitzpatrick, *Ireland and the Foundation of Europe*
Paul Hanly Furfey, *Fire on the Earth*
Francis A. Gasquet, *The Eve of the Reformation*
Agostino Gemelli, *The Franciscan Message to the World*
Eric Gill, *Art and a Changing Civilization*
———, *Christianity and the Machine Age*
———, *Work and Leisure*
T. S. Gregory, *The Unfinished Universe*
Romano Guardini, *The Church and the Catholic*
Waldemar Gurian, *The Future of Bolshevism*
Patrick J. Healy, *The Valerian Persecution*
Christopher Hollis, *The Two Nations*
Hélène Iswolsky, *Soviet Man—Now*
Toyohiko Kagawa, *Brotherhood Economics*
Peter Kropotkin, *Fields, Factories, and Workshops*
Andrzej Krzesiński, *Is Modern Culture Doomed?*
Gustave Le Bon, *The Crowd*
D. B. Wyndham Lewis, *Charles of Europe*
Joseph Lortz, *History of the Church*
Alphonse Lugan, *Social Principles of the Gospel*
Jacques Maritain, *Freedom in the Modern World*
———, *Integral Humanism*
———, *The Things That Are Not Caesar's*
Vincent McNabb, *The Church and the Land*
———, *Nazareth or Social Chaos*
———, *Old Principles and the New Order*
Suzanne Michel, *La Notion Thomiste du Bien Commun*[1]
Emmanuel Mounier, *A Personalist Manifesto*

---

1. Maurin recommended this work as *The Thomistic Doctrine of the Common Good*, by Séraphine Michel. Perhaps Michel also went by the name Séraphine. Nevertheless, this was obviously a reference to the French work, which was published in 1932 by Librairie Philosophique J. Vrin. It has never been translated into English.

———, *Révolution Personnaliste et Communautaire*[2]
National Catholic Rural Life Conference, *Manifesto on Rural Life*
Albert Jay Nock, *Our Enemy the State*
Arthur Penty, *Guilds, Trade, and Agriculture*
———, *A Guildsman's Interpretation of History*
———, *Means and Ends*
———, *Post-Industrialism*
———, *Towards a Christian Sociology*
Ehrenfried Pfeiffer, *Bio-Dynamic Farming and Gardening*
Paul Pigors, *Leadership or Domination*
Weston Price, *Nutrition and Physical Degeneration*
Fulton Sheen, *The Mystical Body of Christ*
George N. Shuster, *The Catholic Spirit in Modern English Literature*
R. H. Tawney, *Religion and the Rise of Capitalism*
Twelve Southerners, *I'll Take My Stand*
Thorstein Veblen, *The Theory of the Leisure Class*
Theodore Wesseling, *Liturgy and Life*
Oswin William Wilcox, *Nations Can Live at Home*[3]
Thomas Wilson, *A Discourse on Usury*
Maurice Zundel, *Our Lady of Wisdom*

2. This work has never been translated into English.
3. When Maurin originally recommended this book, the newspaper mistakenly printed *Nations Can Stay at Home*, by B. O. Wilcox.

Biographical Glossary to Peter Maurin's Easy Essays

ADAMS, HENRY (1838–1918) was an American historian and the grandson and great-grandson of John Quincy Adams and John Adams, respectively. The autobiography that Maurin alluded to was *The Education of Henry Adams*. Adams saw his autobiography as a sequel to *Mont-Saint-Michel and Chartres*, which was a personal meditation on the unity of thought that existed in France from 1150 to 1250. Adams believed the great cathedrals built in France during that period to honor the Virgin Mary illustrated that she was the most powerful force in the history of Western civilization. His autobiography argued his belief that civilization had fragmented since 1250 and has continued to do so at an accelerated rate. As he was not religious, Adams was not arguing for people to join the Catholic Church, but simply relating his pessimistic view of the modern world.

ADAMS, JAMES TRUSLOW (1878–1949) was a Pulitzer Prize–winning American historian famous for coining the term "American Dream" in his popular book *The Epic of America* (1931). Before becoming a writer, he was a successful businessman for a New York brokerage house. Maurin's quotation of Adams paraphrased an 1873 speech from Wisconsin Chief Justice Edward G. Ryan in Adams, *The Epic of America* (Boston: Little, Brown, 1931), 297.

ADLER, MORTIMER J. (1902–2001) was an American philosopher and lifelong advocate of the thought of Aristotle and Aquinas. He played a critical role in creating the Great Books of the Western World curriculum to foster a conversation between students and the great ideas of Western thought. He only officially became Catholic near the end of his life. He also aided Jacques Maritain in finding publishers to publish some of his early works in English.

AGAR, HERBERT (1897–1980) was a Pulitzer Prize–winning American journalist, author, and Southern Agrarian who promoted distributism. The quotes from Agar were from the introduction of a book that Agar coedited with Allen Tate, *Who Owns America? A New Declaration of Independence* (1936). Agar believed that the freedom at the heart of the American ideal had been trampled by monopoly capitalism, which removed creativity, responsibility, and job security from laborers. His works about the Civil War indicated a belief that Southern views on race should be tolerated by the federal government.

AHERNE, DICK (d. 2005) was one of the founders of the Philadelphia Catholic Worker house in the 1930s. Aherne was passionate about farming and played a key role in the farm that the Philadelphia group opened in the late 1930s. When he was drafted in the early 1940s, he entered military service for World War II. After the war, he had a farm in Hamburg, Pennsylvania, and later worked for the United States Department of Agriculture.

AMBROSE, ST. (340–397), a theologian and the Archbishop of Milan, was influential in the conversion of St. Augustine. As a bishop, Ambrose was known for living very simply and for his generosity toward the poor. He also interpreted the Genesis creation story to imply that private property was contrary to nature and that God created all things to be held in common.

AMIEL, HENRI FRÉDÉRIC (1821–81) was a Swiss philosopher and poet whose cited book, *Journal Intime* (or *Private Journal*), was published posthumously. His journal, which possessed Calvinist tendencies, stressed the importance of love and duty. Maurin appreciated how the journal recast Amiel's life within the framework of a metaphysical argument that promoted intellectual and moral ideals.

ARISTOTLE (384–22 B.C.E.) was a Greek philosopher whose understanding of knowledge, nature, and ethics played a pivotal role in the theology of Thomas Aquinas. Aristotle's moderate realism, which asserted that the human intellect could discern truth outside of itself, was perhaps the core idea that Aquinas appropriated from Aristotle. For Maurin, Maritain, and other Thomists, this ability to know truth laid the foundation for and was consistent with a Catholic theology that could reconcile faith and reason. In essay {193}, Maurin highlighted Aristotle's contempt for Sophists. Although Sophists began with a good reputation, by the time of Aristotle they were known as expensive teachers of rhetoric who simply taught manipulation, as opposed to truth, so that their students might obtain successful and lucrative careers.

AUGUSTINE, ST. (354–430), arguably the most important theologian of Western Christianity, was Bishop of Hippo from 395 until his death in 430. A prolific writer, it is impossible in a footnote to discuss the numerous ways his life and writings have affected Western Christianity. For our purposes, it is important to note Augustine's stress on the relationship between loving God and loving others. In {451}, Maurin provided his only quote of Augustine: "Love God and do what you please." This same essay made clear that since every person was made in the image of God, St. Augustine was calling us to love everyone.

BARRÈS, MAURICE (1862–1923), a writer and politician, became involved in politics when he was elected to France's Chamber of Deputies in 1889 as a Boulangist, a populist group with a strong nationalist orientation. He was a leading writer in the proto-Fascist movement, *Action française*; Barrès's writing contributed to the rise of French nationalism during the early twentieth century with his emphasis on reverencing "*la terre et les morts*" ("the land and the dead"). Maurin would have agreed with Barrès's respect for one's land and cultural heritage, but not his nationalism and belief in French superiority. Barrès's 1914 book *The Great Pity of the Churches of France* collected speeches where he derided the French government for allowing churches to fall into disrepair since the government had officially taken ownership of church buildings in 1905. Barrès's arguments were not grounded in a strong Catholic faith, but a belief in the pivotal role that the Catholic Church played in French cultural identity.

BELLOC, HILAIRE (1870–1953) was a Catholic writer who was born in France and later obtained dual citizenship with Britain. He collaborated with G. K. Chesterton and was an ardent supporter of distributism. Maurin was very fond of Belloc's 1912 book *The Servile State*, which related the story of European economic history and foretold of a society dependent on the state because of the state's addressing the ills of capitalism through regulation. As an alternative solution for capitalism, Belloc proposed widespread ownership of land and the means of production.

BENDA, JULIEN (1867–1956) was a French philosopher and prolific novelist of Jewish heritage. His most famous work, *The Treason of the Intellectuals*, accused German and French intellectuals of the nineteenth and twentieth centuries of becoming propagandists of nationalism instead of voices for justice and liberty. Many of the nationalists he attacked—including Maurice Barrès, whom Maurin later mentions—were connected to the proto-Fascist movement *Action française*.

BENEDICT XV, POPE (1854–1922), pope from 1914 to 1922, tried unsuccessfully to broker peace during World War I. Both sides saw him as biased toward the other. In several essays, Maurin brought up Benedict's promotion of a peaceful resolution to World War I. In one essay, Maurin employed Benedict to promote the possibility of the Third Order of Saint Francis as a leaven of Christ's message for the modern world.

BENEDICT OF NURSIA, ST. (480–527) founded several monastic communities, but his largest influence was as the author of the "Rule of Saint Benedict," which laid down a practical foundation and guidelines for monastic life. *Ora et Labora* (pray and work) is often seen as the summation of his rule.

BERDYAEV, NICHOLAS (1874–1948) was a Russian Christian political philosopher who, after being exiled from the Soviet Union in 1922, settled in France for the remainder of his life. His book *The Bourgeois Mind* (1934) emphasized that the spirit, or worldview, of the bourgeois person had infected society, and especially the middle class, with a rugged materialism that was spiritually bankrupt. Rejecting violent revolutions, he proposed that a change in the bourgeois spirit of society could only occur through spiritual transformation.

BÉRENGER, HENRY (1867–1952) was a French writer and politician who served as the French ambassador to the United States in 1925 and 1926. He promoted the notion that an elite was necessary to push forward the ideals of democracy. I have corrected a mistake that Maurin made regarding Bérenger's name. Essay {414} used "Jules Beranger" instead of "Henry Bérenger." Maurin accidentally conflated the names of Henry Bérenger and Jean Jules Jusserand. A misleading statement by Maurin remains in the essay when he states that Bérenger followed Jean Jules Jusserand. Bérenger was not Jusserand's immediate successor, but the second person to serve in the position after Jusserand's service as ambassador concluded.

BERGSON, HENRI (1859–1941) was a French philosopher who stressed the importance of experience and intuition to discover knowledge and truth. The Maritains appreciated the thought of Bergson as students because he persuaded them that absolute truth existed and could be known. Nevertheless, Jacques Maritain's first book, *Bergsonian Philosophy and Thomism*, argued for the superiority of Aquinas, who believed that the rational intellect played the prominent role in uncovering knowledge. Bergson's belief that intuition could uncover truths without an explicitly religious framework was very influential for Emmanuel Mounier and the interreligious spirit that imbued *Esprit*.

BONAPARTE, NAPOLEON (1769–1821) was a military leader and the French emperor from 1804 to 1815. He rose to power in the wake of the French Revolution and controlled most of continental Europe before his defeat in 1815. Maurin was drawing purposeful parallels between the ambitions for controlling all of Europe by both Napoleon and Hitler.

BONAVENTURE, ST. (1221–74), an Italian Franciscan priest, was a prominent theologian during the thirteenth century. As minister general of the Franciscan Order, he played a crucial role in forming the Franciscan Order after the death of St. Francis of Assisi and is often referred to as the second founder of the Franciscans. The quote in essay {420} is from Bonaventure's 1263 biography of St. Francis of Assisi, *Legenda maior S. Francisci*, chapter 7.

BORNE, ÉTIENNE (1907–93), a French journalist and philosopher, was part of Mounier's personalist school of thought during the 1930s. In 1944, he cofounded the Popular Republican Movement, a Christian democratic political party. *A Philosophy of Work*, cowritten with François Henry, was published in English in

1938. The book proposed a philosophy of work grounded in Catholic theology where work was an extension of friendship and charity.

BOSSUET, JACQUES-BÉNIGNE (1627–1704) was the French Bishop of Meaux and a theologian known for his oratory skills who served as court preacher to King Louis XIV. He was strongly influenced by St. Vincent de Paul's (1581–1660) example of service to the poor. Bossuet cited scripture to ground his belief that the poor were first-class citizens in the kingdom of God. Consequently, he argued that the rich must become poor to enter the kingdom of God. Maurin's only quotation from Bossuet is from a sermon that he delivered.

BOURNE, FRANCIS CARDINAL (1861–1935), Archbishop of Westminster from 1903 until his death in 1935, was an influential figure in the English Catholic Church. He was known for promoting the rights of Arabs in Palestine and for being critical of ecumenical dialogue with Anglicans. He had a profound belief in the ability of the Catholic faith to transform society, but did not support Catholics founding their own universities or political parties.

BRANHAM, GRACE (1887–1978) was involved with the Catholic Worker during the late 1930s and 1940s. She was a school teacher from Baltimore who in 1936 donated $1,000 toward the purchase of the Easton Farm.

BRIAND, ARISTIDE (1862–1932) was a French politician who was prime minister of France multiple times between 1909 and 1929. He also coauthored the Kellogg-Briand Pact of 1928, in which sixty-two countries, including the United States, France, and Germany, promised to refrain from war to solve international disputes. The treaty did not have any mechanism for enforcement and was subsequently ignored.

BRIFFAULT, ROBERT (1876–1948) was a European surgeon who later became an author, novelist, and anthropologist. He achieved international fame for his novel *Europa: A Novel of the Days of Ignorance*, which was the tenth-bestselling novel in the United States in 1935. In 1932, he had released another book: *Breakdown: The Collapse of Traditional Civilisation*. Both books portrayed contemporary Western society as immersed in trivialities that were leading to its own deterioration.

BROOKS, VAN WYCK (1886–1963) was an American writer and literary critic. In essay {134}, Maurin was probably referencing Brooks's 1934 book *Three Essays on America*, which was published by E. P. Dutton. In the essay "Our Awakeners," Brooks asserted that pragmatists value intelligence over imagination and believe the present reality to be the norm and ideal. For Brooks, this led to complacency and a lack of poetic vision for the future.

BROUN, HEYWOOD (1888–1939), an American journalist, founded the American Newspaper Guild. He wrote for several New York newspapers and believed that journalists could play a role in improving society. Although Broun converted to the Catholic faith seven months before his death, he had previously been an avid supporter of birth control with Margaret Sanger.

BRUEHL, REV. CHARLES P. (1876–1963), a professor of fundamental dogmatic theology at the Theological Seminary of Saint Charles Borromeo in Overbrook, Pennsylvania, authored several articles on social justice and eugenics during the 1920s and 1930s for Catholic magazines such as the *Christian Front* and *Homiletic and Pastoral Review*.

BRÜNING, HEINRICH (1885–1970), chancellor of Germany from 1930 to 1932. Before the First World War, he had earned a doctorate in economics; after fleeing to the United States in 1935, he taught political science at Harvard University.

BRUNING, HENRI (1900–1983) was a prominent Dutch Catholic poet and writer in the years before World War II. During the Nazi occupation of the Netherlands, he served as a literary censor for the Nazis.

BURNS, ROBERT (1759–96) was a Scottish pre-Romantic poet and lyricist famous worldwide for songs such as "A Man's a Man for A' That," and "Auld Lang Syne." His work, including the former song mentioned by Maurin, evinced strong egalitarian ideals.

BUSCH, JOSEPH FRANCIS (1866–1953) was Bishop of St. Cloud, Minnesota, from 1915 until his death in 1953. As a priest, he had been a secretary to Archbishop of St. Paul John Ireland, who was known for his support of labor unions and social justice. Busch shared these attributes.

CALVIN, JOHN (1509–64) was a French theologian and one of the principal Protestant reformers. His theology of predestination identified material well-being as evidence of eternal salvation. Of the Protestant reformers, he was the most supportive of lending money at interest, but his support was qualified. Maurin unfairly laid the entire blame for the legalization of interest on the shoulders of Calvin. It should be remembered that the Fifth Lateran Council for the Roman Catholic Church (1512–17) also provided qualified support for certain lending institutions to collect fees on loans. In other words, qualified support for usury began to enter both Catholic and Protestant thought during the early sixteenth century and cannot be blamed solely on the Reformers.

CARDOZO, BENJAMIN N. (1870–1938), an American jurist, served on the United States Supreme Court from 1932 until his death in 1938. Before serving on the Supreme Court, he served on the New York Court of Appeals. He was a strong proponent and reformer of common law, or laws created by judges by case precedent. He participated in and supported attempts to restate common law, which consisted of analyzing previous cases to find guiding principles for future cases. In all instances, he saw common law as dependent on the state and preceding case law precedent. In essay {429}, it is uncertain where Maurin found the reference for Cardozo favoring Roman law and in what context the source should be understood. Cardozo did favor a relationship between modern law and morality, which he saw as necessary for popular respect for law. Cardozo also viewed the Roman Stoic vision of law as expressed in natural law as an example par excellence of morality being wed to law. Maurin would not have been opposed to this conception of the Roman Law, but his own understanding of Roman Law saw it favoring the private property of the rich over the common good of society as protected in canon law. Cardozo never mentioned Maurin's sense of the Roman Law in his writings.

CARLYLE, THOMAS (1795–1881) was a Scottish philosopher, historian, and satirical writer. The quote in essay {156} about the blessedness of work is a famous quote from his 1843 book *Past and Present*. In the book, Carlyle argued that genuine work was noble, sacred, and eternal. He viewed love of money and concern only for oneself as the critical problems of nineteenth-century England. The only solution was a return to God and communal responsibility.

CARR, REV. HENRY (1880–1963) was a Canadian Basilian priest dedicated to providing quality Catholic education in North America. He cofounded the Institute of Medieval Studies at St. Michael's College of the University of Toronto in 1929, which in 1939 would be named a pontifical institute. He also served as superior general of the Basilians from 1930 until 1942.

CARREL, ALEXIS (1873–1944) was a Nobel Prize–winning surgeon and biologist from France. The book mentioned by Maurin was *Man, the Unknown* (1935). Carrel's book proposed that industrialization and urbanization were leading to cultural deterioration. His solution involved forced eugenics and a society led by elite intellectuals. Maurin obviously suggested this book because of its critique of society, not for its solution.

CHAMBERLAIN, HOUSTON STEWART (1855–1927) was an English-born political philosopher and scientist who later became a German citizen. His most famous work, *The Foundations of the Nineteenth Century* (1899), proposed the racial superiority of Aryans in general and Germans above all. Chamberlain was an early member of the Nazi party, and Adolf Hitler visited his home multiple times in the 1920s.

CHANSON, PAUL was president of the *Fédération Maritime Patronale du Port de Calais* in France, also known as the Maritime Employers' Syndicate. Eschewing class warfare, he believed that the problems of capitalism could be solved by guilds that brought together workers and employers. His social thought was greatly influenced by Leo XIII's *Rerum novarum* and Pius XI's *Quadragesimo anno*. Chanson's cited book in essay {251} was probably a reference to *Les Droits du Travailleur et le Corporatisme* (1935), which has not been translated into English.

CHARDONNEL, ABBÉ simply means Fr. Chardonnel. It is probably a reference to Fr. Louis Le Cardonnel (1862–1936), who was a poet before his religious conversion during his early thirties. Very little of his work has been translated into English.

CHESTERTON, G. K. (1874–1936) was a prolific English writer, philosopher, and convert to the Catholic faith. Although he was an apologist for the Catholic faith and held economic ideas on distributism that Maurin admired, Maurin's essays only quoted his phrase that Christianity has never been tried (from Chesterton's *What's Wrong with the World* [1910]). Maurin employed this quote because he did not believe that Christianity was idealistic to the point of unrealistic, but that an authentically lived Christianity could be the bedrock for a flourishing society. Maurin recommended two of Chesterton's books: *The Outline of Sanity* (1927) and *Saint Francis of Assisi* (1923). The former book argued for the reasonableness and possible first steps for achieving a distributist agrarian economy while revealing the insanity of capitalism. The latter book was a biography of St. Francis that stressed his imitation of Christ, love for God, asceticism, and joy.

CICOGNANI, AMLETO GIOVANNI (1883–1973) was an archbishop who served as the apostolic delegate to the United States from 1933 to 1959. His 1915 book (1931 in English), *The Great Commandment of the Gospel in the Early Church*, proposed a societal foundation of "brotherly love" and "Christian charity" as illuminated by the scriptures and the early Church.

CLEMENCEAU, GEORGES (1841–1929) was the French prime minister from 1906 to 1909 and 1917 to 1920. He was one of the chief architects of the Treaty of Versailles, in which he was successful in achieving ruthless reparations from Germany after the War.

COBBETT, WILLIAM (1763–1835), a British writer and farmer, was an ardent supporter of political and agricultural reform. Two of his better-known books were *Cottage Economy* (1822), which was a guide to family self-sufficiency that provided such information as bread recipes and advice on raising livestock, and

Rural Rides (1830), a detailed travel journal of his wanderings throughout the English countryside.

COLE, GEORGE DOUGLAS HOWARD (1889–1959) was an English economist, historian, and proponent of the cooperative movement. The quote in essay {524} was a paraphrase from Cole, *What Marx Really Meant* (New York: A. A. Knopf, 1934), 163–64. In the passage, Cole argued that the work of Communists to gain influence in capitalist countries may cause conservative elements in those countries to embrace fascist regimes. Cole continued that this did not bother Communists because the war-mongering nature of fascist regimes destabilized their countries to the point of making them more susceptible for Communist revolutions. During the 1930s, Cole advocated the Popular Front—an alliance of moderate, liberal, and Communist political parties against the threat of fascism. He believed cooperation with Communists, rather than hostility, could prevent the growth of fascism.

COLUM, PADRAIC (1881–1972) was an Irish poet, novelist, and children's book writer. A major theme in his work was the inherent dignity of peasants, despite the poverty, discrimination, and suffering they endured. In the United States, he was also known for his essays in *Commonweal, New Republic, the Nation, Saturday Review*, and *Catholic World*.

CONSIDERANT, VICTOR PROSPER (1808–93) was a French utopian Socialist who advocated a peaceful transformation of society through the reconciliation of capital and labor. His critique of bourgeois society to which Maurin referred was Considerant's *Principles of Socialism: Manifesto of Nineteenth Century Democracy*. In this work, Considerant presented a historical narrative of oppression in which bourgeois society, or capitalism, came into existence after the bourgeoisie, often equated with businessmen, overpowered the feudal aristocracy that ruled during the Middle Ages. The bourgeoisie proclaimed political liberation while continuing to economically exploit the proletariat, or poor working classes. Marx incorporated this historical narrative into the *Communist Manifesto*, but greatly diverged with Considerant regarding the antidote for bourgeois society.

COOLIDGE, CALVIN (1872–1933) was vice president until 1923, when Harding unexpectedly died and Coolidge became president of the United States until 1929. He promoted laissez-faire polices and was president during the Roaring Twenties. His fiscal policies promoted speculative investments that contributed to the Great Depression.

CORBETT, REV. JOHN was a Jesuit priest who had been stationed at Fordham University during the early 1930s. He was a friend of the New York Catholic

Worker, and an interview with him was published in the same issue of the paper as the essay that mentioned him (Easy Essay {28}). The interview concerned the importance of Catholic learning for Catholic children in both Catholic and public schools.

CORY, HERBERT E. (d. 1947) was a well-known convert to the Catholic faith. His autobiography, *The Emancipation of a Freethinker* (1941), was very popular when it was first published. The autobiography documented his two-decade journey from Congregationalist, to agnostic humanist, to Marxist, to scholastic, to Catholic. Cory stressed the rational nature of his conclusion regarding the revolutionary truth of Catholicism.

COUGHLIN, REV. CHARLES (1891–1979) was a famous radio priest during the 1930s who helped legitimize the social justice encyclicals of Leo XIII and Pius XI among his 30 million listeners. Although Maurin approved of Coughlin's condemnation of capitalism and banking practices, he would have disparaged his intellectual imprecision, anti-Semitism, and fascist leanings, which became more pronounced at the end of the 1930s. Coughlin was emblematic of figures that Maurin would employ to strengthen his argument, even if the person possessed other problematic characteristics. As Dorothy Day wrote in in 1951, "[Peter] used to embarrass us sometimes by dragging in Marshall Petain and Fr. Coughlin and citing something good they had said, even when we were combating the point of view they were representing. Just as we shock people by quoting Marx, Lenin, Mao-Tse-Tung, or Ramakrishna to restate the case for our common humanity, the brotherhood of man and the fatherhood of God."

COYLE, DAVID CUSHMAN (1887–1969) was an engineer, economist, and popular writer. In addition to designing the Washington State capitol, he also served as a technical advisor to Roosevelt's Public Works Administration, which built hospitals, dams, bridges, and other large-scale projects. Although Coyle believed that technology served the common good, he condemned capitalism's propensity for mass production. The quote in essays {563} and {566} began a 1936 article, "The Fallacy of Mass Production," in *Who Owns America? A New Declaration of Independence*, edited by Herbert Agar and Allen Tate.

CRAM, RALPH ADAMS (1863–1942) was an American Episcopalian architect known for designing church and college buildings. He was an Anglo-Catholic who had profound respect for Catholicism and an interest in the back-to-the-land movement. Essay {160} was inspired by an article, "Cities of Refuge," that Cram wrote for the 16 August 1935 issue of *Commonweal*.

CURRAN, REV. MICHAEL J. (1875–1954) was a priest who started his own hostel, which he self-funded for about $35 per week. In addition to providing shelter, he paid for meals at a local restaurant; Sheehan, *Peter Maurin*, 176. Curran was born in Massachusetts; his parents were from Ireland. He was the pastor of Immaculate Conception Catholic Church during the 1920s and 1930s and pastor of St. Bernard Parish during the 1940s.

DAVIDSON, DONALD (1893–1968) was an American poet, social critic, and Southern Agrarian. In addition to promoting a regional-focused identity, his poems glorified the Confederate South and promoted a racially segregated society based on white racial superiority. During the 1950s, he chaired the pro-segregation Tennessee Federation for Constitutional Government.

DAWSON, CHRISTOPHER (1889–1970), a British scholar and Catholic historian, asserted the importance of Catholic monks in laying the groundwork for medieval Europe. He believed that this common cultural foundation was more essential to European identity than national origin. Dawson was one of Maurin's favorite historians regarding the Middle Ages.

DE BECKER, RAYMOND (1912–69), a Belgian journalist and friend of Emmanuel Mounier, was a proponent of personalism and in 1933 founded the journal *L'Esprit Nouveau*, which was the Belgium counterpart to Mounier's *L'Esprit*. He proposed that lay Catholics, properly formed in the monastic lifestyle, would transform an ungodly world much in the same way that Maurin believed the Irish had saved European civilization during the early Middle Ages. De Becker, who had always harbored strong anti-Semitic tendencies, later renounced the Catholic faith, and in 1940 he became the general editor for a Nazi newspaper in Belgium.

DE BETHUNE, MARIE ADÉLAÏDE (1914–2002), commonly known as Ade Bethune, was a Catholic liturgical artist. She was born in Belgium and immigrated with her parents to the United States following World War I. She began volunteering her artistic talents to the Catholic Worker movement as a young student in 1934 and later professionally produced liturgical art.

DE GOBINEAU, ARTHUR (1816–82), a French aristocrat, was an early proponent of scientific racism. His 1850s book, *An Essay on the Inequality of the Races*, proposed that authentic history only occurred in or through the white Aryan race and that childbearing between whites with other races would destroy civilization.

DE VALERA, ÉAMON (1882–1975) was a leading Irish political figure during the first three-quarters of the twentieth century and a leader in the struggle for Irish independence. During most of the 1930s, he was president of the Executive Council of the Irish Free State, and he would serve as president of Ireland from 1959 to 1973.

DENIFLE, REV. HEINRICH SEUSE (1844–1905) was a Dominican priest, historian, and famous preacher in Austria. The book to which Maurin referred in essay {448}, *Humanity: Its Destiny and the Means to Attain it; A Series of Discourses* (1909), promoted the belief that Christ, as found in the Catholic Church, needed to become the center of human living.

DENNIS, LAWRENCE (1893–1977) was a controversial American author during the 1930s, who believed that capitalism would be replaced by a fascist government, which would have to exert strict control over the economy. He would later disassociate himself from these views.

DEODATUS OF NEVERS, ST. (d. 679) was probably born in western France, though it is possible he originally came from Ireland. At the very least, he was greatly influenced by Irish missionaries. He served as Bishop of Nevers in France from 655 until he resigned in 664. In retirement, he served as abbot of Jointures, a monastery that he founded, around which grew the town of Saint-Dié. It was in this town that the name "America" was first used on a map in 1507. Maurin employed him to argue for the lasting cultural effects of Irish agricultural centers.

DESCARTES, RENÉ (1596–1650) was French philosopher, mathematician, and scientist. With his famous phrase "Cogito, ergo sum" (I think, there for I am), Descartes attempted to use epistemological doubt as the starting point for knowledge. This was foreign to the moderate realism of Aquinas and Aristotle. Thomists like Maritain and Maurin believed that Descartes's pessimistic epistemology denied any certainty about the natural, the supernatural, and morality.

DEVAS, CHARLES STANTON (1848–1906) was an English political economist. He was a convert to Catholicism and was interested in presenting an authentically Christian economic theory, which he believed to be the only viable economic theory. The quotation in essay {156} about the dull and uncreative nature of industrial work is from his 1883 work *The Groundwork of Economics*, paragraph 81.

DEWEY, JOHN (1859–1952) was an American pragmatist philosopher and educational reformer. He promoted the need for widespread progressive education because he believed that democracy was only effective with an informed public who could intelligently interact in public discourse. In his book *Individualism: Old and New* (1930), Dewey argued that rugged individualism in American capitalist society placed profit before all else while, ironically, also suppressing individual creativity among factory workers.

BIOGRAPHICAL GLOSSARY 525

DONAHUE, JOHN B. (1901–70) was the editor of *Columbia*, the monthly magazine published by the Knights of Columbus since 1921.

DU PIN, FRANÇOIS RENÉ DE LA TOUR (1834–1924), Marquis de La Charce, was a French politician who was a proponent of a Christian social order and economy. Although he promoted subsidiarity, or decentralization, within society, he also believed that a monarch was necessary to promote the good of all.

EDDY, SHERWOOD (1871–1963) was an American Protestant missionary and author who spent time in Russia, the Middle East, and Southeast Asia. The quote in essay {524} was from Eddy's 1934 book *Russia Today: What Can We Learn From It?*, 38. Eddy saw a dualism in Marxism, which grouped together the proletariat, atheism, and virtue in contrast to the bourgeois mentality of greed, religion, and hypocrisy.

ELIOT, THOMAS STEARNS (1888–1965) was an American-born Nobel Prize–winning poet and writer who later moved to England and renounced his U.S. citizenship. Although raised Unitarian, he converted to Anglicanism as an adult and held a deep appreciation for the Catholic faith. Maurin's quote of Eliot in essay {443} was from his book *The Idea of a Christian Society* (1939), which collected three lectures that Eliot gave in March 1939. The quote was about the Munich Agreement, which was made with Germany by France, the United Kingdom, and Italy. France, the United Kingdom, and Italy hoped to appease Hitler by permitting him to annex the German-speaking border areas of Czechoslovakia. Czechoslovakia was not invited to the conference, and the border areas given to Germany contained not only Czechoslovakia's main military defenses, but also many of its prominent economic centers.

EMERSON, RALPH WALDO (1803–82) was an American philosopher and poet. He was a major figure in the Transcendental movement, in which he proposed the harmony between humans and nature with strong pantheistic overtones. Maurin regularly quoted Emerson as stating, "An institution is the extension of the soul of a man." This was likely paraphrasing a sentence from Emerson's essay "Self-Reliance" (1841): "An institution is the lengthened shadow of one man." In essay {198}, Maurin quoted Emerson as stating, "People have only the power we give them." This was probably paraphrasing a paragraph from Emerson's essay "Power" (1876): "Imbecility . . . victims of gravity, custom, and fear. This gives force to the strong,—that the multitude have no habit of self-reliance or original action." In essay {227}, Maurin quoted Emerson as stating, "The way to acquire the vernacular of the man of the street is to go to the street and listen to the man of the street." This is likely a summary of Emerson's essay "Art and Criticism" (1859), which included the line, "Speak with the vulgar, think with the wise." Like Emerson, Maurin was arguing that great truths need to be communicated using language that can be understood by non-academics.

FERRER, ST. VINCENT (1350–1419) was a Spanish Dominican priest who became famous as a successful missionary in Jewish communities. Although Ferrer prohibited overt violence against Jews to encourage conversion, he discouraged personal and economic interactions with Jews, which often led to increased anti-Semitism after his departure from an area. Maurin was probably not aware of the negative impact that Ferrer left on many Jewish communities.

FISHER, LOUIS (1896–1970) was an American Jewish journalist and author, whose 1950 biography of Gandhi was the basis for the 1982 film on Gandhi. The quote in essay {469} was from his autobiography, *Men and Politics* (1941), which documented his time as a journalist in Soviet Russia, Fascist Italy, Republican Spain, and Germany during the rise of Nazism. Stanza six has been changed to reflect the actual quote. The version in the paper, which was probably a typo, stated that only those who have never had their freedom abolished can understand what it means to be deprived of freedom.

FOERSTER, NORMAN (1887–1972), an American educator, promoted the new humanism of the early twentieth century, which argued for the freedom of the human will against scientific deterministic notions. He disavowed that science was the final arbiter of human nature and particularly disliked the social sciences. As Maurin noted, Foerster critiqued state universities in the United States for their fractured collection of specialized courses. He argued that Americans would be better educated from universities offering a general education, which featured a Great Books curriculum like that of Hutchins and Adler. He expressed these thoughts in his book *The American State University* (1937).

FRANCIS DE SALES, ST. (1567–1622) was the Bishop of Geneva and known for his deep personal faith. His book *Introduction to the Devout Life* (1609) presented his spiritual direction for Christians from various states of life. He believed that a life dedicated to Christian perfection should be the goal of every Christian, not only those who had undertaken religious life.

FRANCIS OF ASSISI, ST. (1181–1226) founded the Franciscan Order and was known for championing voluntary poverty. Arguably Maurin's favorite saint, Francis was born the son of a wealthy silk merchant and as a young man fought as a soldier for his town. As a Franciscan, he renounced possessions and violence. Maurin devoted the latter half of his life to emulating his interpretation of Francis's voluntary poverty and manual labor and offering his labor as a gift.

FRANK, GLENN (1887–1940) was president of the University of Wisconsin-Madison from 1925 to 1937 and was known for expanding the agricultural

BIOGRAPHICAL GLOSSARY 527

program. From 1927 to 1932, he was responsible for the existence of the University of Wisconsin Experimental College, which was a student-empowered great books program.

FRANK, WALDO (1889–1967) was an American novelist and social critic who served as chairman of the First American Writers' Congress in 1935 and was the first president of the League of American Writers in that same year. His 1929 book *The Re-Discovery of America* began from the premise that the cultures of the Mediterranean made up the soul of European and American culture. He argued that the marriage of these various cultures reached their peak in the Middle Ages. Therefore, America should strive to reintroduce that cultural ideal while also adding insights from certain Eastern cultures. Maurin would have agreed with Frank's argument that America needed to recover cultural insights from the Middle Ages.

FREY, JOHN P. (1871–1957), an American labor activist, was the influential president of the American Federation of Labor's (AFL) Metal Trades Department from 1934 to 1950. Maurin's discussion of Frey in essay {328} is probably about his testimony in 1938 before the House Un-American Activities Committee. Frey's testimony provided detailed examples of Communist Party members who held leadership positions in the Congress of Industrial Organizations (CIO) Union. The CIO had been a strong and influential supporter of Roosevelt and his New Deal legislation.

FURFEY, PAUL HANLY (1896–1992) was an American Catholic priest and sociologist who taught at the Catholic University of America from the 1930s to the early 1970s. His book *Fire on the Earth* (1936) proposed two sources for Catholic social action: (1) divine revelation and (2) the saints. The book also prioritized the role of faith and the importance of the supernatural. His system of Catholic social action, which included noncooperation with evil and the duty of bearing witness, was largely inspired by the Catholic Worker movement. His own preface stated that *Fire on the* Earth was not presenting an original idea, but trying to systematize the thought and actions of the Catholic Worker movement and like-minded groups.

GAGE, MARGUERITE, was involved with the Catholic Worker during the 1930s and 1940s. At one point, when the New York house was in debt from feeding striking workers, she paid the grocery bill. In 1940, she provided a dramatic reading of the Psalms at the New York house that left a very positive impression.

GANDHI, MOHANDAS (1869–1948) was an Indian activist who played a leading role in Indian independence from Britain through nonviolent methods. His nonviolent methods were greatly admired by both Dorothy Day and Peter Maurin. Gandhi also promoted economic self-sufficient villages that utilized agriculture and crafts. The quote in essay {155} about industrialism being evil does not appear to be an exact quote, but Maurin's summary of Gandhi's thought regarding industrialization. Gandhi thought that industry would only be acceptable on a small scale for local use and under local control.

GASQUET, FRANCIS AIDAN CARDINAL, O.S.B., (1846–1929) was an English historian whose scholarly work has, in retrospect, been called into question, particularly by the German-born English historian Sir Geoffrey Elton. The book Maurin cited, *The Eve of the Reformation* (1900), proposed that the people of England were happy and holy members of the Catholic Church before the events that led to the English Reformation.

GEORGE, DAVID LLOYD (1863–1945) was the prime minister of the United Kingdom from 1916 to 1922. He also played an integral role in negotiating the Treaty of Versailles. He struggled between satisfying the desire of British public opinion to harshly punish Germany and his own interests in long-term peace, preventing further Communist expansion into Europe, and maintaining Germany as a viable trading partner.

GERTRUDE, ST. (1256–1302) was a German Benedictine nun, mystic, theologian, and prolific writer. Unfortunately, very few of her writings have survived. The quote "Property, the more common it becomes, the more holy it becomes" is commonly attributed to St. Gertrude, but its origin is uncertain.

GILL, ERIC (1882–1940), an English sculptor, type-face designer, and stonecutter, was a leader in the Arts and Crafts movement. He believed that creativity should play a key role for workers in the production process. His Catholic faith imbued his writings, and he was arguably Peter Maurin's favorite contemporary writer. Maurin copied several of Gill's articles and books into Easy Essay form, including *Money and Morals* (1934), "Politics of Industrialism," in *New Blackfriars* (1934), *Work and Culture* (1939), several articles in *Christianity and the Machine Age* (1940), and "Leisure State," in *Last Essays* (1942). It came to light in 1989 that Gill sexually abused his children, had an incestuous relationship with his sister, was very promiscuous with other women even while married, and practiced bestiality.

GILLIS, REV. JAMES MARTIN (1876–1957), an American Paulist priest, was editor of the *Catholic World* from 1922 to 1948. Gillis regularly wrote in favor of smaller government, personal responsibility, and personal spiritual renewal. In essay {30}, Maurin was referencing Gillis's editorial from the *Catholic World* (August 1933). In that editorial, Gillis argued that materialism and human exploitation had destroyed modern civilization, just as it had the Roman Empire. He proposed building a new society based on Christian principles. In St. Augustine, Gillis saw a person who proposed the same and did so fearlessly.

GITLOW, BENJAMIN (1891–1965) was an American politician and founding member of the Communist Party USA in 1919. By the end of the 1930s, he had become a staunch opponent of Communism. The quote in essay {379} adapted some lines from his autobiography, *I Confess: The Truth about American Communism* (New York: E. P. Dutton, 1940), 390–91. In this passage, Gitlow confessed how he knowingly performed actions injurious to the American union movement to retain his position in the Communist Party and further Russia's desire to control American unions.

GORKY, MAXIM (1868–1936) was the pseudonym for Alexei Maximovich Peshkov, a Russian novelist and playwright who founded the socialist realism literary method. Socialist realism had the goal of bringing the reader to support Marxist beliefs. A significant example is Gorky's 1906 novel *The Mother*, which followed the life of a mother who was engrossed in her own problems of capitalistic-inspired poverty and transformed to become supportive of her son and other young people who become Communist revolutionaries.

GRUNDTVIG, NIKOLAJ FREDERIK SEVERIN (1783–1872) was a Danish Lutheran bishop, pastor, author, and education reformer. He is credited with creating the idea of the folk high school as a place that formed students for life in society. Common characteristics for these schools included discussions of literature from one's own language as well as learning crafts and folk songs to instill a sense of pride in rural life and one's own culture. This was in contrast to Danish schools at the time, which focused on training future scholars for the university, with an emphasis on reading classic Latin and Greek texts. Grundtvig did not found any schools, but about fifty folk schools were founded in Denmark during this lifetime. A couple prominent folk schools had recently opened in the United States: the John C. Campbell Folk School in North Carolina in 1925 and the Highlander Folk School in Tennessee in 1932.

GUARDINI, ROMANO (1885–1968) was a German priest and theologian whose family moved to Germany from Italy when he was one year old. His book, *The Church and the Catholic* (1923), discussed the need to move from a society of suspicion and individualism to one of communal love, sacrifice, and mutuality grounded in the Catholic Church and its liturgy.

GUÉRANGER, PROSPER LOUIS PASCAL (1805–75), a French Benedictine priest who founded Solesmes Abbey in 1833, effectively reintroduced the Benedictine Order in France in the wake of the French Revolution. Guéranger also restored Gregorian chant to the life of the community. In 1930, the Choir of Solesmes issued an LP with their Gregorian chant to support a textbook they had also published at the time, and in 1994 they had a Gregorian chant album reach number three on the American billboard charts.

GUNN, MICHAEL, led the Catholic Labor Guild in Brooklyn during the 1930s and was active in supporting protests against abusive employers. He was a brush maker by trade and, though his views did not conform entirely to those of the Catholic Worker, he regularly visited the New York Catholic Worker and gave talks there well into the 1950s.

HALL, BOLTON (1854–1938) was an American lawyer, author, and activist who became an ardent supporter of the back-to-the-land movement in the early twentieth century and was active in promoting gardening on vacant lots in New York City. Since the quotation in essay {172} mentioned the New Deal, it is clearly from the 1930s and cannot be from Bolton's 1907 book *Three Acres and Liberty*, which illustrated how a city dweller could provide for a family after purchasing a small piece of land. In essay {174}, Maurin explained that the previous essay was from a letter to the *New York Times*. The letter was probably entitled, "Putting the Land to Use." As Maurin explained, *Three Acres and Liberty* was mentioned to let the reader of the essay know Bolton's credentials.

HANNA, MARK (1837–1904) was a wealthy American businessman and U.S. senator best known for skillfully running the successful presidential bids of William McKinley in 1896 and 1900.

HARDING, WARREN G. (1865–1923) was president of the United States from 1921 until his death in 1923. He ran a successful presidential campaign by stating that he would bring the United States back to the normalcy that existed before World War I.

HARMEL, LÉON (1829–1915) was a French industrialist known implementing good working conditions in his factory, which he based on Catholic social thought. In addition to striving for a positive relationship with his workers, he provided a living wage, free medical care, retirement benefits, and time for leisure. He believed that it was natural for factory owners to be authority figures for their workers, but this authority implied a responsibility to provide for the basic spiritual and physical needs of one's employees. Like Maurin, Harmel idealized the Middle Ages as a time when God was viewed as the proper authority and the Medieval guilds protected the dignity of workers. Harmel also believed that the Renaissance had resulted in European society turning away from God, which caused the elimination of the guilds. He posited that both owners and workers needed faith and religion to guide their lives and direct their proper responsibility toward one another. To promote this idea, he organized numerous worker pilgrimages to Rome in the late nineteenth century, in which workers had audiences with Pope Leo XIII. These pilgrimages were influential for Leo XIII in authoring *Rerum novarum*. Though Maurin applauded Harmel's care and concern for his workers, he never promoted an industrial economy. In fact, Maurin's writings indicate a belief that industrialization cannot exist outside of a capitalist or Communist context.

HAYES, CARLTON J. H. (1882–1964) was an American historian who converted to Catholicism and was one of the founders of the American Catholic laity-managed journal *Commonweal* in 1924. His academic areas included European history and the rise of nationalism.

HAYES, REV. CORNELIUS. Maurin could be referring to one of two people. First, he could be referring to Rev. Cornelius Hayes (b. 1883), an Irish-born priest of the Missionaries of Our Lady of La Salette, who ministered in Hartford, Connecticut, as the director of a preparatory college, or a high school that prepares students for the academic rigor of college. Second, it could be a reference to Rev. Cornelius V. Hayes (b. 1891), a priest of the Archdiocese of New York, who was the pastor of St. Margaret Catholic Church in Pearl River, New York, during the 1930s.

HEALY, REV. PATRICK JOSEPH (1871–1937), an American Catholic theologian, was most famous for authoring *The Valerian Persecution*, which examined the Emperor Valerian's third-century persecution of Christians. Healy argued that this resulted from the incompatibility of Christian monotheism with Rome's polytheism. The book also detailed how Valerian's second wave of persecution included the confiscation of property from wealthy Christians, many of whom had shared their wealth with poor Christians during previous persecutions. Healy taught at the Catholic University of America in Washington, D.C., from 1903 until his death in 1937.

HENRY VIII (1491–1547) reigned as king of England from 1509 until his death in 1547. In essay {428}, Maurin stated that St. Thomas More and Henry VIII disagreed in their interpretation of common law, which Maurin believed was based on canon law. As More served at the behest of Henry in the position of lord chancellor, a position which oversaw the courts of England, from 1529 until he resigned from the position in 1532, this is unlikely. More would be executed for refusing to swear to Henry's Oath of Supremacy, which acknowledged the king as the head of the Church of England. More intrepated this oath as compromising the authority of the pope, but this was not a matter of common law.

HENRY, PATRICK (1736–99), an American politician, was involved in the movement for American independence and served as governor of Virginia. As a noted orator, he is perhaps most famous for the line Maurin quoted: "Give me liberty, or give me death!"

HERGENHAN, HERMAN (1883–1942) was friends with Maurin and very involved with the Catholic Worker during the 1930s. A German immigrant to the United States in 1906, Hergenhan lived with Maurin during his Harlem experiment in 1934 and 1935, worked as a carpenter on the first Catholic Worker farm at Easton, and wrote numerous articles for the *Catholic Worker*. For example, he wrote a two-part exposé on the City of New York's municipal lodging house for the May and June 1934 issues of the paper. He was only listed as the author in the second part of the story. Before 1941, *Catholic Worker* newspaper articles called him Herman Hergenhan, but articles from 1941 onward referred to him as Steve Hergenhan. According to U.S. census records, his name was Herman Hergenhan. The reason for this discrepancy is unknown.

HIGH, STANLEY (1895–1961) was an American journalist who spent part of his life as an aide, advisor, and speechwriter for Franklin Roosevelt. During the 1930s, he was a strong proponent of Roosevelt's New Deal.

HINDUS, MAURICE G. (1891–1969) was a Russian-born journalist whose parents immigrated to the United States when he was a teenager. During the 1920s and 1930s, he regularly visited Russia and wrote numerous books and articles on the conditions of peasants and regular folk there. These works were often critical of the Soviet government. The quote in essay {524} paraphrased a couple sentences from Hindus, *The Great Offensive* (New York: Harrison Smith and Robert Haas, 1933), 158. The quoted passage related not only broken promises, but also excessive collection of crops and animals from farming peasants by state officials. These practices had resulted in ill will, famine, and the desertion of farms by many peasant families.

HINSLEY, ARTHUR CARDINAL (1865–1943) was an English prelate and Archbishop of Westminster from 1935 until his death in 1943. He was an outspoken critic of both fascism and Nazism. In 1935, during the Ethiopian War, which is now called the Second Italo-Ethiopian War, Hinsley responded to criticism that Pope Pius XI had not condemned the actions of Mussolini. In referring to the Vatican's vulnerable situation as a state surrounded by Italy, Hinsley called the pope "a helpless old man." This widely publicized quote likely resulted in his delay in being elevated to the cardinalate until December 1937.

HITLER, ADOLF (1889–1945) was a German politician and leader of the Nazi Party. He became chancellor of Germany in 1933 and began ruling as Führer in

BIOGRAPHICAL GLOSSARY 533

1934. He would rule until 1945, when he committed suicide as World War II was coming to an end. Under Hitler's leadership and anti-Semitic policies, around six million Jews were murdered. In 1936, Maurin began critiquing the dictatorial manner and racism of Hitler and the people who flocked to his message. By the end of the 1930s, Maurin's essays were explicit in their condemnation of anti-Semitism, and many of his essays countered the arguments of anti-Semites who wanted to place blame for all the failings of Western society at the feet of the Jewish people.

HOBBES, THOMAS (1588–1679) was a British philosopher who purported that the natural state of human beings consisted of isolation from others, extreme individualism, and a perpetual state of war to obtain perceived needs. He believed that only the submission of individuals to a sovereign government could preserve humanity from a brutal and short existence. Hobbes's natural state differed from the Thomistic notion that human beings are naturally social and prone to form communities.

HOLMES, JOHN HAYNES (1879–1964) was a Unitarian minister and pacifist who played a founding role for both the National Association for the Advancement of Colored People and the American Civil Liberties Union. Holmes was initially supportive of the Russian Revolution. He was never a Communist, but viewed the Red Revolution as preferable to czarist Russia. He began critiquing the Soviet Union after the Great Purge. And after the Hitler-Stalin Pact, he helped engineer the expulsion of the Communists from the ACLU board in 1940. The quote in essay {381} was from a Sunday sermon and can be found in Eugene Lyons, *The Red Decade: The Stalinist Penetration of America* (Indianapolis: Bobbs-Merrill, 1941), 356.

HOOK, SIDNEY (1902–89) was an American philosopher. Like Benjamin Gitlow, he became a staunch critic of Communism after initially being an avid supporter. Stalin's political repression during the 1930s, which resulted in up to millions of deaths in Russia, particularly disgusted Hook.

HOWARD, ALBERT (1873–1947) was an English botanist and an early figure in the organic farming movement. After serving as an agricultural advisor for various government provinces in India during the 1920s, he became convinced that traditional organic Indian farming practices were superior to Western farming methods. His book *An Agricultural Testament* (1940) stressed the need to maintain soil fertility via organic farming practices and composting.

HUME, DAVID (1711–76) was a Scottish philosopher who placed greater importance on the passions and human sympathy as an indicator of morality than the intellect. Unlike Locke and Hobbes, he explicitly rejected organized religion and believed that religious systems must first be expunged before one can begin the search for knowledge and morality. He rejected any God-given moral sense and desired to use the scientific method to explain morality and human nature.

HUTCHINS, ROBERT MAYNARD (1899–1977), an educational philosopher, was president at the University of Chicago from 1929 to 1945 and chancellor from 1945 to 1951. He instituted a system of learning that revolved around the Great Books of the Western World (which he collaborated on with Mortimer Adler), Socratic dialogue, and comprehensive examinations. Instead of focusing on vocational training, he envisioned the university as a place where minds were formed in dialogue with the great ideas and minds of the Western world. Hutchins also invited Maritain to speak at the University of Chicago during the 1930s and '40s. Hutchins attempted to offer Maritain an appointment to the philosophy department multiple times, but the philosophy department always frustrated his plans.

HUXLEY, ALDOUS (1894–1963), an English writer and novelist, is most famous for his novel *Brave New World*. He was also a pacifist and a perennialist, believing that all religions have a common origin and rejecting modern materialism. *Grey Eminence: A Study in Religion and Politics* (1941) was a biography about Fr. Joseph, or François Leclerc du Tremblay. The book's primary purpose was to contrast a theocentric worldview from an anthropocentric worldview. He utilized Fr. Joseph to illustrate that even a prayerful priest compromised his theocentric worldview when he entered politics. From a historical perspective, Huxley argued that the actions of Fr. Joseph and Richelieu extended the Thirty Years' War, which finally ended with the Treaty of Westphalia and created a docile German population that had now fallen under the sway of Nazism.

IBSEN, HENRIK (1828–1906), a Norwegian playwright and poet, wrote plays that revealed the pitiable reality experienced by families and society that were ignored by contemporary playwrights. The quote from essay {227} inaccurately paraphrases the physician and protagonist in his 1882 play *An Enemy of the People*. According to the actual quote, a "normally constituted truth" has a life of no more than twenty years before it becomes a lie, at which point most people will accept it.

JARRETT, REV. BEDE (1881–1934) was an English Dominican priest famous for bringing the Dominican Order back to Oxford in 1921, establishing the Dominican journal *Blackfriars*, and as the author of numerous spiritual books and works on medieval social ethics. The quote that Maurin attributed to Jarrett in essay {227} paraphrased words from his original preface to *Meditations for Layfolk* (1915). The actual quote stated, "The Meditations of Challoner and of Wiseman had such an astonishing success, precisely because they adapted to the changing times unchanging principles. Now, because what is the novelty of one age is the platitude of the next, they have lost their effect." Jarrett hoped that the contemporary style of his book would bring timeless truths to another generation.

JEFFERSON, THOMAS (1743–1826) was the third president of the United States (1801–9) and the primary author of the Declaration of Independence. Jefferson strove during his presidency to reverse the increase in federal power that was implemented during the previous presidency of John Adams. A strong proponent of agrarianism, he believed that an economic foundation of small landowning farmers would create a strong democracy. He thought that manufacturing should be limited, as it removed ownership from the workers. And he was also wary of banks because of their propensity to foster long-term debt and their creation of monopolies through large borrowing. Maurin's quotation of Jefferson about less government, while commonly attributed to Jefferson, originated in 1837 in the pages of the now defunct *United States Magazine and Democratic Review*.

JOHNSON, HUGH SAMUEL "IRON PANTS" (1881–1942) was a former Army general whom Roosevelt placed in charge of the N.R.A. (National Recovery Administration). He was known to be difficult to work with and left the administration in 1934, shortly before the N.R.A. was ruled unconstitutional in 1935. Johnson left because of increasing difficulties in his relationship with Roosevelt and the administration. He became very critical of the direction that the N.R.A. took after he left.

JØRGENSEN, JOHANNES (1866–1956), a Danish poet, biographer, and convert to Catholicism, was known for his biographies of Catholic saints. Essay {53} was inspired by Johannes Jørgensen, *Saint Francis of Assisi: A Biography*, trans. T. O'Conor Sloane (New York: Longmans, Green, 1912), 79.

JUSSERAND, JEAN JULES (1855–1932), a French author and diplomat, served as the French ambassador to the United States from 1903 to 1924.

KAGAWA, TOYOHIKO (1888–1960), a Japanese convert to Christianity, was a pacifist, labor activist, Christian minister, and a leader in Japan's cooperative movement. During the 1950s, he was twice nominated for the Nobel Peace Prize. Maurin recommended Kagawa's book *Brotherhood Economics* (1936) to *Catholic Worker* readers. The book argued that the foundation for world peace was a Christian economy realized in cooperatives.

KALLENBACH, MARIE SCHULTE, contributed stories and poems for Catholic periodicals like *Commonweal* and the Paulist Fathers' *Catholic World* during the 1920s and 1930s.

KEATING, FREDERICK WILLIAM (1859–1928) was the Catholic Bishop of Northampton from 1908 until 1921. He then became the Archbishop of Liverpool, where he served from 1921 until his death in 1928. The college that Maurin referred to in the essay {69} was the Catholic Workers' College at Oxford, which was founded in 1922. The original purpose of the college was to form Catholic men and women in the social sciences. In 1965, it was renamed Plator College, which is its current name. It is technically unfair to say that Keating founded the college. Fr. Leo O'Hea, S.J., founded the college with the blessing of Keating.

KELLER, HELEN (1880–1968), deaf and blind since childhood, was an American social activist and author. She famously learned language from her teacher, who spelled the word "water" on one of her hands as water poured on the other. The quote in essay {95} was almost an exact quote from an article entitled, "The Common Good," which Keller published in the November 1934 issue of *Home Magazine*. The article focused on the need for Americans to live more simply and not be "dazzled" into a materialistic lifestyle.

KENKEL, FREDERICK (1863–1952) was an American Catholic sociologist and journalist. From 1909 to 1952, he was the director of the Central Bureau of the Catholic Central Verein of America, which was a German-American social justice organization. In addition to editing the group's journal, *Social Justice and Central Blatt*, he was involved with Catholic Charities of St. Louis and the Catholic Rural Life Conference.

KEYNES, JOHN MAYNARD (1883–1946), a British economist, was one of the most influential economists of the twentieth century and is considered one of the founders of modern macroeconomics. He believed government intervention was necessary to combat the unemployment that would naturally occur when a free market economy produced too many unwanted goods. He was supportive of the medieval condemnation of interest to the extent that saving prevented the investment of money in fruitful ventures. Keynes's argument for this can be found in his monumental book *The General Theory of Employment, Interest, and Money* (1936). Maurin explicitly mentioned his book *The Economic Consequences of Peace* (1919), which asserted that the economic reparations demanded at Versailles by England and France at the end of World War I would impoverish Germany, destabilize Europe, and lead to a more devastating war. Keynes resigned from his role at the Versailles Conference in May 1919 out of frustration with its determined course of action.

KIRCHWEY, FREDA (1893–1976) was an American journalist and editor of the *Nation* from 1933 to 1955. She supported the New Deal and was a staunch opponent of fascism and Nazism. *The Nation* is an American weekly magazine that covers politics and culture from the political left. It was founded in 1865 and continues to this day.

KLYBER, REV. ARTHUR (1900–1999) was an American Jewish convert to the Catholic faith. As a Catholic priest, he fought against anti-Semitism among Catholics and preached the Christian message to Jews.

KNOX, JOHN (1514–72) is regarded as the founder of Presbyterianism in Scotland. Presbyterianism was greatly influenced by the ideals that Knox appropriated after working with John Calvin in Geneva in the 1550s. Maurin's theory that Calvin's influence on Knox eventually led to the legalization of usury in England is difficult to prove. And although Maurin is correct that England legalized usury with the Usury Act of 1571, usury was previously legalized for a brief time under Henry VIII in 1545.

KOCH, EDWARD A., was a Catholic publisher of the journal the *Guildsman*, out of Germantown, Illinois, from 1932 until 1967. The journal attacked capitalism and advocated that workers hold control of their respective industries. Like Fr. Charles Coughlin, he took on stronger fascist and anti-Semitic views during the late 1930s and early 1940s.

KRIMM, REV. JOHN A. (1907–92) was a Redemptorist priest who gave talks at Maurin's short-lived Discussion Center on Catholic Doctrine and offered his services as a spiritual advisor to any possible converts.

KROPOTKIN, PRINCE PETER (1842–1921), a Russian scientist and socialist anarchist, was a major influence on the thought of Peter Maurin. Kropotkin believed that feudalism and capitalism created poverty and scarcity while promoting economic privilege for others. He proposed (like Maurin) a more decentralized economic system based on mutual aid and voluntary cooperation. He asserted that the tendencies for this kind of organization already existed both in evolution and in human society.

KRZESIŃSKI, REV. ANDRZEJ (1884–1964) was a Polish priest and philosopher who fled to the United States in 1939 as the Nazi threat increased. He would later become an American citizen. His book *Is Modern Culture Doomed?* (1942) explored the notion that materialism, particularly as found in Nazism and Communism, threatened to deprive the world of true freedom. He proposed a return to traditional Christian culture, which included the spiritual, creative, and dynamic aspects of the human person.

LASKI, HAROLD (1893–1950), a British economist and Marxist of Jewish heritage, was a professor at the London School of Economics from 1936 until his death in 1950. Although Maurin would have obviously disagreed with Laski's

538   BIOGRAPHICAL GLOSSARY

notion that a violent class war was the solution to capitalism, Maurin welcomed Laski's reading of the Middle Ages with Christianity playing a positive moral role in economics.

LE BON, GUSTAVE (1841–1931) was a French physician, anthropologist, and sociologist. Maurin referenced his best-known work, *The Crowd: A Study of the Popular Mind* (1895), which analyzed notions of mob mentality and groupthink. Maurin was particularly interested in Le Bon's argument that groups do not think logically and can be emotionally exploited to act in focused ways by savvy leaders.

LECLERC DU TREMBLAY, FRANÇOIS (1577–1638) was a French Capuchin friar, the war minister for France, and an advisor to Cardinal Richelieu during the Thirty Years' War. He was also known as Fr. Joseph or Grey Eminence. The term *éminence grise*, or grey eminence, was first coined in deference to Leclerc. "Grey" referred to his robes, while "eminence" was common nomenclature for cardinals, though Leclerc was never made a cardinal. For more on Fr. Joseph, see the entry on Aldous Huxley.

LECLERCQ, ABBÉ JACQUES (1891–1971), a Belgian Catholic theologian and priest, founded the journal *La Cité Chrétienne* and wrote several books during the 1930s on Catholic morality, natural law, and politics.

LENIN, VLADIMIR (1870–1924) was a Russian Marxist revolutionary who led the Soviet Republic from 1917 until his death in 1922. He wrote prolifically about his interpretation of Marxism and provided a practical blueprint for carrying out a revolution. Although Maurin disagreed with Lenin's theories, he appreciated the importance that Lenin placed on a theory of revolution.

LEO XIII, POPE (1810–1903) was pope from 1878 until his death in 1903. He is known for beginning the Catholic social encyclical tradition with *Rerum novarum* (1891), his encyclical on capital and labor. Maurin regularly referenced this encyclical, but also quoted from two additional encyclicals of Leo XIII: *Diuturnum* (1881) and *Auspicato concessum* (1882).

LEWIS, D. B. WYNDHAM (1891–1969), a British journalist and biographer, was a convert to the Catholic faith. In essay {307}, Maurin recommended a book of Lewis's that he called *Charles V*, though it was published as *Charles-Quint, Empereur d'Occident* in French, *Charles of Europe* in 1931 in the United States, and *Emperor of the West: A Study of Charles the Fifth* in 1932 in England. In that essay and on the recommended book appendix, I changed the name of the book to *Charles of Europe*. In the book, Lewis examined the history of Europe during the Reformation, paying particular attention to Charles V, who was the Holy Roman Emperor, as well as ruler of Spain and the Netherlands. Charles was the tragic hero of the book who failed to preserve Europe's identity and cultural unity within a Catholic framework.

LEWISOHN, LUDWIG (1882–1955), a Jewish novelist, was born in Germany, but brought by his parents to the United States. He was extremely critical of Jewish attempts at appropriating American values. He would become an avid supporter of the Zionist movement during World War II.

LIÉNART, ACHILLE CARDINAL (1884–1973) was a French prelate who served as Bishop of Lille from 1928 to 1968. He was an ardent supporter of social reform, trade unionism, and the worker priest movement. Maurin exaggerated when he stated that Liénart formed Catholic unions, though the prelate strongly advocated for the legitimacy of the Catholic workers unions that were striking against Catholic textile owners in northern France in 1929. The owners falsely complained to Rome that the unions were Communist-controlled, but Vatican officials supported Liénart's interpretation of events, and he was made a cardinal in 1930.

LIPPMANN, WALTER (1889–1974) was an American Pulitzer Prize–winning journalist and political commentator. The quote in essay {487} was from a 1940 address by Lippmann entitled, "Education v. Western Civilization" and can be found in *The Essential Lippmann: A Political Philosophy for Liberal Democracy* (Cambridge, Mass.: Harvard University Press, 1982), 418–22. This address emphasized the need for education to ground itself in the great cultural and religious ideas of Western culture. For achieving this purpose, he suggested the Great Books curriculum of Alder and Hutchins, which Maurin also admired.

LOCKE, JOHN (1632–1704) was a British philosopher who proposed ideas promoting the separation of church and state, the natural rights of man, and the social contract, in which people form governments to protect their persons and possessions. He was one of the first British empiricists and believed that all knowledge was derived from experience.

LOMBROSO, GINA (1872–1944) was an Italian anthropologist and writer of Jewish descent. In addition to being staunchly against birth control, she advanced the notion that women were more altruistic by their maternal nature while men were more self-centered. Therefore, she argued that women may be particularly suited for professions in areas such as medicine and education. Her 1920 book *L'amina Della Donna* (in English, *The Soul of Woman: Reflections on Life* [1923]), compared the egoism, indifference, passivity, and reason of men to the altero-centrism, passion, activity, and intuition of women. She viewed neither of these essentialist gender qualities as bad; they simply implied different courses of action to lead moral and fulfilling lives.

LONG, HUEY (1893–1935) was an American politician and governor of Louisiana from 1928 to 1932. He also served as a member of the U.S. Senate from 1932 until his assassination in 1935. He supported wealth redistribution and social programs for the poor. As governor, he wrested political control of Louisiana away from business, plantation, and oil interests while shifting the tax burden from the poor to large businesses, wealthy citizens, and oil operators. In 1929, Standard Oil tried unsuccessfully to have him removed from office.

LORD, REV. DANIEL A. (1888–1955) was an American Jesuit priest known for his writings on politics and decency in movies. He authored the 1930 Motion Picture Production Code, which set guidelines for censorship in movies. From 1925 to 1948, he was also the director of the Sodality of the Blessed Virgin Mary, which organized students for charitable and devotional activities at Jesuit schools. During the 1930s, the Sodalists would pass out the *Catholic Worker* newspaper during May Day parades in large cities.

LUGAN, REV. ALPHONSE-MARIE (1869–1931) was a French Jesuit and religious writer. The English edition of his book *Social Principles of the Gospel* (1928) was an abridged edition of his two-volume French work from the early 1920s entitled, *Les Grandes Directives Sociales*, which was part of a greater project that Lugan wrote on the social teachings of Jesus. The book utilized the historical Jesus to inspire a social framework for human equality and social responsibility.

LUTHER, MARTIN (1483–1546) was a German Catholic priest who became the leading figure in the Protestant Reformation during the sixteenth century. He eventually rejected the teaching authority of the Catholic Church, first in the practical realm of indulgences and then in the theological realm in prioritizing the Bible's teaching authority over and above that of the Catholic Church. During the German Peasants' War (1524–25), he supported the nobility as upholders of the peace, even while recognizing the injustices faced by the peasants. Maurin's primary critiques of Luther were his rejection of the Catholic Church and his uncritical acceptance of the state.

LYONS, EUGENE (1898–1985), an American journalist, was an early supporter of Marxism and lived in the Soviet Union from 1928 to 1934. By the late 1930s, when Maurin wrote essay {278}, Lyons had started to become critical of the violence and repression he had witnessed in the Soviet Union. By the early 1940s, his critique would turn to a complete rejection of Communism.

LYTLE, ANDREW NELSON (1902–95), an American novelist and professor of literature, was a prominent spokesman for the Southern Agrarians. The Southern Agrarians were a group of twelve writers associated with Vanderbilt University during the 1920s and 1930s who promoted a strong connection between the land, social conservatism, and religiosity in response to the urbanization and industrialization of the South. Lytle wrote a 1931 biography on Bedford Forrest, praising Forrest's ingenuity as a Confederate lieutenant general and as first Grand Wizard of the Klu Klux Klan. The paraphrased quote in essay {159} is from his essay "The Hind Tit," 203–4, in *I'll Take My Stand: The South and the Agrarian Tradition*, by Twelve Southerners. The article argued that the Civil War and northern industrialism ruined the Southern agrarian economy and created substantial white poverty. He displayed no concern for enslaved blacks, whom he saw as a "menace" after the Civil War (215).

MACDONALD, RAMSAY (1866–1937) was one of the founders of the Labour Party, and he became the first Labour prime minister of the United Kingdom during 1924. He reprised this role from 1929 to 1935, though he was expelled from the Labour Party in 1931 when he formed a new government coalition with the Conservative and Liberal parties.

MACHIAVELLI, NICCOLÒ DI BERNARDO DEI (1469–1527) was an Italian historian and political philosopher. His philosophy, famously proclaimed in his political treatise *The Prince*, promoted the idea that violence and deceit were at times necessary for political stability. His thought led to the term "Machiavellianism," which implies the use of violence and deceit by rulers and others in their quest for power.

MANN, THOMAS (1875–1955), a German novelist and winner of the Nobel Prize in Literature, was known for updating biblical accounts in many of his stories. *The Magic Mountain* (*Der Zauberberg*) was a 1924 novel in which the protagonist met individuals representing the major philosophical strands of thought in Europe before World War I. A character named Leo Naphta, an irrational Jesuit with Communist ideals about historical destiny and the proletariat, ranted against industrialism and idealized the Middle Ages. Naphta was written as a caricature of the Marxist philosopher György Lukács (1885–1971).

MANNING, HENRY EDWARD CARDINAL (1808–92) was the English Catholic Archbishop of Westminster from 1865 until his death in 1892. Like John Henry Newman, he was an Anglican priest who converted to the Catholic faith. He was an ardent supporter of the working poor and successfully mediated the London Dock Strike of 1889. Guild supporters, like Maurin, appreciated how he peacefully brought together owners and workers. This notion of owners and workers cooperating would be a major tenet of Leo XIII's *Rerum novarum*.

MARITAIN, JACQUES (1882–1973) was a French Catholic philosopher whose thought was grounded in Thomas Aquinas. He was a friend of the Catholic

Worker movement, and Maurin was very impressed with his ideas on pure means and a pluralistic state, which were based on the Catholic notion of the human person as one with inherent dignity who was oriented to the divine. He played a drafting role in the Universal Declaration of Human Rights (1948), and his thought deeply influenced the social thought of Pope Paul VI. The lectures that Maurin mentioned in essay {171} would be published as *Integral Humanism*. In his Easy Essays, Maurin regularly recommended Maritain's *Freedom in the Modern World*, in which Maritain argued that freedom was not an end in itself, but an instrument that permitted human fulfillment by conforming ourselves to the Truth of the Created Order, God. It was also from this book that Maurin borrowed the term "pure means." Maritain believed that the authentic construction of a social order oriented toward the common good could only occur through nonviolent means like those promoted by Gandhi. Unlike Dorothy Day, Maritain was not a pacifist, and he believed that violence was at times necessary. Nevertheless, Maritain believed that violence and coercion were often viewed as the only option even when nonviolence was a viable alternative.

MARITAIN, RAÏSSA (1883–1960) was born in Russia and raised as a Hasidic Jew. At age ten, her family immigrated to France. Though largely known because of her marriage to Jacques Maritain, she was an accomplished poet and philosopher in her own right. Both Jacques and Raïssa, while searching for Truth, became enthralled with Thomistic theology and philosophy and converted to the Catholic faith.

MARSHALL, DONALD, wrote articles and pamphlets during the 1930s for publications such as *Catholic World* on the relationship of Catholicism to capitalism and industrialism.

MARSHALL, THOMAS R. (1854–1925) was vice president of the United States under Woodrow Wilson from 1913 to 1921. Marshall was known for his sense of humor, which was the only way Maurin utilized him.

MARX, KARL (1818–83) was a German philosopher and economist who theorized that capitalism would result in a class struggle between the owners of factories and laborers. This struggle would inevitably lead to the dictatorship of the proletariat, or Communism. His two most notable works were *Das Kapital* and *The Communist Manifesto*. The prominence of Communist thought during the 1930s made Marx a regular opponent in Maurin's Easy Essays. Maurin disagreed with Marx that class struggle was inevitable.

MCCALL, CHESTER H., served as assistant secretary of Commerce under Daniel C. Roper during the Franklin D. Roosevelt Administration, from 1933 to 1937. He ran the administrative, public relations, and publications efforts for the

BIOGRAPHICAL GLOSSARY 543

department's Bureau of Foreign and Domestic Commerce, National Bureau of Standards, and Bureau of Air Commerce. He was also a member of the Executive Board of the National Youth Administration.

MCGEE, JOHN, with Arthur Sheehan, was a founder of the Catholic Worker house in Boston during the 1930s.

MCGOWAN, REV. RAYMOND A., was the assistant director of the social action department of the National Catholic Welfare Conference, which would go on to become the United States Conference of Catholic Bishops. A strong proponent of social justice and labor unions, he worked for the conference from 1919 until his retirement in 1954.

MCNABB, REV. VINCENT (1868–1943) was an Irish priest who joined an English Dominican order. His book *The Church and the Land* (1926) was very critical of urban life, which he believed was harmful for families and Christian morality. He strongly promoted a vision of distributism that emphasized homesteading families on the land to replace industrialized cities.

MCNICHOLAS, ARCHBISHOP JOHN T. (1877–1950) was the Archbishop of Cincinnati from 1925 until his death in 1950. He criticized excessive wealth and greedy corporations during the Great Depression, for which he was quoted by both Day and other writers in the New York *Catholic Worker* newspaper. In 1937, Day even visited him in Cincinnati at his invitation. In 1938, he issued a pastoral supporting conscientious objection, portions of which were reprinted in the April 1938 *Catholic Worker* newspaper. Nevertheless, he was most famous for founding the Catholic Legion of Decency in 1933 with the purpose of combating objectionable content in cinema.

MCSORLEY, REV. JOSEPH (1874–1963), a Paulist priest and early friend of the Catholic Worker movement, was Dorothy Day's first spiritual advisor. He also served as an official advisor, approved by the Archdiocese of New York, for the New York *Catholic Worker* during its first years in the wake of numerous complaints about the publication. From 1924 to 1929, he served as superior general of the Paulists.

MEIKLEJOHN, ALEXANDER (1872–1964) was an English philosopher and university administrator. During the 1920s and 1930s, he taught at the University of Wisconsin–Madison at the invitation of Glenn Frank and organized an experimental college that stressed an interdisciplinary liberal education and read much of the classic literature of Western civilization.

MENCKEN, HENRY LOUIS (1880–1956) was an American journalist and acerbic polemicist. Though he promoted the notion that women were intelligent and intuitive, he did not believe that women should have a greater participatory role in society. His most well-known work on the subject was his book *In Defense of Women* (1919).

MICHEL, SUZANNE, was a French lawyer who authored a book on Thomas Aquinas's notion of the common good. Dorothy Day wrote in 1963, "One of the first books Peter used to discourse on, was *The Thomistic Doctrine of the Common Good*." This is a reference to Michel's French book *La Notion Thomiste du Bien Commun*, which was published in 1932 by Librairie Philosophique J. Vrin. It has never been translated into English. In the *Catholic Worker* newspaper, Séraphine Michel was erroneously given as the author. Perhaps Michel also went by the name Séraphine, but her actual name was Suzanne.

MIRABEAU was Honoré Gabriel Riqueti, Count of Mirabeau (1749–91), a French revolutionary, writer, and politician. As a moderate during the French Revolution, he argued for a constitutional monarchy. Because of his close connection with King Louis XVI, there are still arguments regarding whether his loyalties resided with the revolutionaries, the king, or simply his own interests.

MOLEY, RAYMOND (1886–1975) was an early supporter and architect of President Franklin Roosevelt's New Deal, but his political allegiance began to change during 1933. By the end of the 1930s and for the remainder of his life, he was a conservative Republican and avid supporter of free-market policies.

MORE, ST. THOMAS (1478–1535), an English lawyer and social philosopher, was councilor to King Henry VIII until he was executed for refusing to acknowledge the king as head of the church. He was elevated to sainthood in the Catholic Church in May 1935. This explains why some essays referred to him as St. Thomas More while others referred to him as Blessed Thomas More. More's most famous work, *Utopia*, began with his critique of the Bourgeois society, because the wealthy were moving to enclose formerly public lands. This resulted in many peasant owners and renters being removed from the land. *Utopia* told of a society with clear laws, good education, and communal ownership. This equated to a society without money or private property, where people lived simply, and all participated in the practical work of providing for the basic needs of society. There was no rich or leisure class, and those in leadership would be removed if they became infatuated with material goods. Maurin believed that More's utopian sociology was grounded in a theological sociology, which stressed the common good. More was trained in the common law tradition, of which he saw equity as a key component. When he oversaw England's courts as Lord Chancellor, he tried to persuade the judges of the common law courts to prioritize equity over the letter of the law. Maurin and some of his contemporaries argued that the common law had its origin in canon law, which was an oversimplification. For more on common law and canon law, see notes on Judge Benjamin Cardozo and Arthur Penty.

MORRIS, WILLIAM (1834–96) was a British writer, artist, and textile manufacturer. Regarding the last, he created many patterns, resurrected preindustrial methods for producing many of his patterns, and believed that the designer and manufacturer of goods should be the same person.

MOUNIER, EMMANUEL (1905–50) was a French philosopher who founded the French magazine *Esprit* in 1932 and was the main proponent of the personalist movement. Personalism envisioned a spiritual revolution grounded in a transcendent Christian faith, which would lead to a communal sense of responsibility for fellow humans and prioritize the dignity of human beings above other societal concerns (e.g., profit, material possessions, etc.). Nevertheless, as Maurin noted, Mounier and *Esprit* did not believe that the transcendental spirit that animated this revolution had to be explicitly Christian. In this sense, the journal contained an ecumenical and interreligious element. Maurin is often credited with introducing Mounier's personalism to the United States through his sharing of the idea with fellow Catholic Workers and writing about it in his Easy Essays.

MUSSOLINI, BENITO (1883–1945) was an Italian politician of the National Fascist Party. He ruled Italy as a dictator from 1925 until 1943. During World War II he allied Italy with Nazi Germany, and he was executed while trying to flee Italy in 1945. Maurin's essays that mentioned Mussolini emphasized his ruthless military power, order, and discipline.

NEWMAN, JOHN HENRY CARDINAL (1801–90) was a nineteenth-century convert to Catholicism. He had been a prominent Anglican priest in the Oxford movement. The Oxford Movement was an endeavor to renew the Church of England through the incorporation of early Catholic theology and spirituality by a group of clergy at Oxford University from 1833 to 1845. Newman's study of Catholic theology eventually led to his conversion. As a Catholic, he wrote works on theology and education. The Catholic Newman was fiercely against liberalism, which he saw as promoting the notion that no religion or philosophy was superior to another and was, moreover, simply a matter of opinion. Perhaps Newman's most famous reference to liberalism as a grave error is from his Biglietto Speech (1879). Newman was canonized in 2010 by Pope Benedict XVI and is now referred to as Saint John Henry Newman.

NOCK, ALBERT J. (1870–1945) was an American journalist and author. He was a rugged individualist and acclaimed anarchist with libertarian and antistate views who strongly opposed Roosevelt's New Deal. In essay {206}, Maurin recommends Nock's 1935 book *Our Enemy the State*, which denounced Roosevelt's New Deal as a "coup d'état" that consolidated power from the people of society into the hands of the state. Nock viewed this as part of the continuing progression of state control in Western civilization that, for the moment, has no end in sight. He was also a vehement critic of anti-Semitism and the Nazi Party.

NOYES, CHARLES REINOLD (1884–1954) was an American economist from St. Paul, Minnesota. Maurin noted Noyes's January 1927 article in the *Yale Review*, "Financing Prosperity on Next Year's Income," in which Noyes argued that the extreme extent of credit purchasing that began after the First World War would cause an economic depression. Noyes was president of his family's wholesale drug company during the 1920s, and during the 1940s he held various executive posts for the National Bureau Economics Research in New York City.

O'HARA, EDWIN VINCENT (1881–1956), promoted adult study clubs as the Bishop of Great Falls, Montana, in 1931. When he left Great Falls to become the Bishop of Kansas City, Missouri (he was later named Archbishop of Kansas City), there were over seven hundred active study clubs in the Diocese of Great Falls. O'Hara was also an active supporter of the Catholic Worker movement. Maurin likely interacted with O'Hara through their mutual involvement in the National Catholic Rural Life Conference and O'Hara's visits to the New York Catholic Worker.

O'SULLIVAN, MAURICE (1904–50) was an Irish author and police officer. His book *Twenty Years A-Growing* (1933) recounted his growing up on a small island named Great Blasket off the coast of Ireland. The book paints a very romantic picture of traditional Irish culture.

PAINE, THOMAS (1737–1809) was born in England, but became an American revolutionary. He was a political theorist most famous for his work *Common Sense*, which he published anonymously in 1776. The work provided simple reasoning for immediate independence from England. Maurin noted another famous Paine work, *The Age of Reason* (printed in three parts between 1794 and 1807), which argued for the reasonableness of Deism and the unreasonableness of revealed religions, such as Christianity.

PARSONS, REV. WILFRID (1887–1958) was an American Jesuit theologian, journalist, and political scientist. He was editor-in-chief of *America* magazine from 1925 to 1936 and later taught political science at the Catholic University of America.

PASCAL, BLAISE (1623–62) was a French Catholic philosopher who also played a significant role in the development of mathematics. He viewed Christian faith and truth as gifts from God that could not be fully comprehended by human rationality, in contrast to some of his contemporaries who believed that authentic religious truth could be rationally comprehended. The quote in essay {488} was from Pascal's posthumously published *Pensées*.

PÉGUY, CHARLES (1873–1914) was a French Catholic essayist, journalist, and poet. After renouncing his faith early in life, he became a socialist. When he returned to Catholicism later in life, he remained a socialist, which challenged both his Catholic and socialist friends. Péguy wrote on politics and mysticism in his journal *Cahiers de la Quinzaine*. Maurin's use of Péguy could mislead someone to think that Péguy supported mysticism and opposed politics, which would be incorrect. As a socialist, Péguy was supportive of politics, but believed that politics needed to be informed by mysticism. His preference for combining mysticism and politics was best illustrated by his numerous works on St. Joan of Arc.

PENTY, ARTHUR (1875–1937) was a British architect who wrote extensively on guilds and distributism. His book *Post-Industrialism* (1922) posited the dangers of machinery and the subdivision of labor. His solution included the rejuvenation of the arts and crafts movement as well as the guilds movement, of which he believed medieval society offered an example par excellence. In three essays, Maurin cited Penty's *A Guildsman's Interpretation of History* (1920), which blamed the economic problems of the modern age on the creation of currency and the influence of Roman Law. Maurin was particularly interested in Penty's contrast between Canon Law of the Church and Roman Law. Penty viewed Canon Law as grounded in God's authority, communal, and concerned with moral and just solutions. He viewed Roman Law as grounded in an earthly leader's authority, individualistic, and overly concerned with protecting private property and maintaining order. Although there is some truth to Penty's demarcations of the Roman and Canon laws, his analysis is too simplistic The laws' histories are intertwined, and they influenced each other in their respective developments.

PHILIP THE FAIR (1268–1314), also known as Philip IV, was King of France from 1285 until his death. His dispute with Pope Boniface VIII and the French Church regarded taxing clergy and other church revenue without the pope's consent as well as limiting the jurisdiction for ecclesiastical courts. Maurin viewed Philip's victories in these disputes as the beginning of Christianity's relegation from the public to the private sphere alone.

PIGORS, PAUL (1900–1994) was a professor of Industrial Relations at the Massachusetts Institute of Technology and a consultant to the U.S. Army Management Training Agency. His book *Leadership or Domination* (1935) defined leadership as cooperative and domination as coercive. Pigors believed leadership was the preferred method of governance, but saw a role for domination in times of crisis with a heterogeneous group or when interacting with immature individuals. He also believed that domination needed to play a limited role in modern politics to attain a just and peaceful society.

PIUS IX, POPE (1792–1878) reigned as pope from 1846 until his death in 1878. Though initially considered friendly to liberal ideas, he became a staunch opponent of liberalism. In 1864, he published his *Syllabus of Errors*, which condemned propositions such as the separation of church and state and freedom of religion. He believed these propositions pushed religion into the realm of personal opinion and placed religion outside the realm of public discourse and influence. He also called the First Vatican Council (1869–70), which declared the present teaching on papal infallibility.

PIUS X, POPE SAINT (1835–1914) was pope from 1903 until his death in 1914. He was a formidable opponent of modernist theology, which he saw as inappropriately conflating Catholic theology with Enlightenment ideals. In 1910 Pius condemned *Le Sillon*, the French group with which Maurin had been involved until shortly before the condemnation.

PIUS XI, POPE (1857–1939) reigned from 1922 to 1939. Maurin particularly liked his social encyclical *Quadragesimo anno* (1931), on the reconstruction of the social order. The encyclical promoted subsidiarity, the idea that matters should be governed as locally as possible. Maurin also appreciated Pius's encyclical *Rite expiatis* (1926) on St. Francis of Assisi and referenced Pius's statement from his encyclical *Mens nostra 7* (1929) that the separation of the spiritual from the material was a "deadly plague."

PIUS XII, POPE (1876–1958) was pope from 1939 until his death in 1958. He is most notable for infallibly declaring the Assumption of Mary into heaven, body and soul, and for being the pope during World War II. Regarding the latter, he is credited for saving Jews behind the scenes, but he is also criticized for not openly denouncing the Nazis during the war. Pius's quote in essay {348} represents the standard Catholic view of freedom, in which humans are given freedom to choose what is good and should not abuse this freedom for immorality or harm to others.

PROUDHON, PIERRE-JOSEPH (1809–65) was an early French anarchist who promoted workers' associations and cooperatives. He also promoted the possession of personal property when the property was utilized by the same person, but opposed private property, referring to an absolute right to property when it was not being used by the so-called owner. Maurin often utilized Proudhon to state that Marx stole his definition of communism: "A society where each one works according to his ability and gets according to his needs." Maurin erred in attributing the quote to Marx's *Communist Manifesto*. Rather, it was from Marx's *Critique of the Gotha Program*, which he wrote in 1875, though it was not published until after his death. Additionally, this definition of communism did not originate with Proudhon. Maurin was correct that the quote was French in origin, but it probably originated with Louis Blanc or Étienne-Gabriel Morelly. Proudhon analyzed the definition in *General Idea of the Revolution in the Nineteenth Century* (1851), but argued that it was idealistic and impractical.

RATNER, HERBERT (1907–97) was an American physician who would become a vocal proponent of informed consent regarding medical procedures. He was appointed as a senior member of the Committee of Liberal Arts at the University of Chicago in 1937 by Robert M. Hutchins. In this capacity, he worked closely with Mortimer Adler. Largely through his interaction with Thomistic theology and philosophy, he converted to the Catholic faith in 1938. He was the descendent of Russian Jews, though he was not raised in any faith. Essay {377} refers to Ratner's opposition to artificial contraception and his belief that human sexuality needs to follow the laws of nature.

RICARDO, DAVID (1772–1823) was an English political economist most known for his theory of comparative advantage. This theory assumed international free trade and advocated that each nation only grows and produces those items in which it had the greatest competitive advantage. Other items could be obtained by international trade. Maurin would have opposed such a theory especially because it opposed local self-sufficient economies.

RICHELIEU, CARDINAL (1585–1642) was a French bishop and the secretary of state for King Louis XIII. He successfully consolidated the royal authority in France and played a key role during the Thirty Years' War in weakening the Catholic Habsburg dynasty, which was particularly prominent in Spain and Austria. Richelieu was utilized as the primary antagonist in Alexandre Dumas's *Three Musketeers*.

RIVERA, DIEGO (1886–1957) was a prominent Mexican mural painter and the husband of artist Frida Kahlo. Many of his murals, as public pieces of art, served as propaganda to glorify the Mexican revolution and indigenous cultures. Rivera was not the originator of the quote that Maurin attributed to him; it may have been Upton Sinclair in his 1925 book *Mammonart: An Essay in Economic Interpretation*.

ROBERTSON, JOHN M. (1856–1933) was a British writer and politician who, in addition to his ideas about money, argued against the historicity of Jesus. In his book *The Fallacy of Saving*, Robertson argued that saved money was not being utilized for current and future industry, which in turn endangered the future economic life of the community. Since he believed that substantial saving by the middle class was for retirement, he proposed government-run old-age pensions to help dissuade people from saving. Maurin, in essay {94}, offered farming communes as an alternative solution to old-age pensions. Therefore, any type of saving would become unnecessary.

ROOSEVELT, FRANKLIN D. (1882–1945) was the president of the United States from 1933 until his death in 1945. Roosevelt came into office at the height of the Great Depression. In response to the Great Depression, his administration instituted the "New Deal," which included work projects, financial reforms, and the N.R.A. (National Recovery Administration). The N.R.A., which was empowered to legislate prices, wages, and business practices for various industries, was ruled unconstitutional in 1935. Maurin was extremely critical of the New Deal, which he viewed as costly experiment that consolidated too much power with the federal government.

ROOSEVELT, THEODORE (1858–1919) was the president of the United States from 1901 to 1909. In essay {59}, Maurin alluded to Roosevelt's critique of President Woodrow Wilson for playing too passive a role in World War I. Additionally, Roosevelt had berated Wilson for not strengthening American military forces on the eve of World War I. This probably led Maurin to attribute the following quote to Rossevelt: "If you want peace, prepare for war." The origin of the quote is a Latin adage from Publius Flavius Vegetius Renatus's tract *De re militari* (fourth or fifth century C.E., though the notion itself can be found in Greek and Chinese literature from centuries earlier.

ROPER, DANIEL C. (1867–1943) was the secretary of commerce for President Franklin D. Roosevelt from 1933 to 1938. He was particularly interested in promoting an irenic relationship between business and the federal government during the Great Depression.

ROSENBERG, ALFRED (1893–1946) was an influential Nazi party member who held several governmental posts and authored numerous Nazi racial tracts. He was born in modern Estonia, which was then part of the Russian Empire, and was executed at the end of World War II.

ROUSSEAU, JEAN-JACQUES (1712–78) was a Genevan philosopher, novelist, and music composer. He stressed the goodness of humanity in its natural state and advocated the formation of citizenship through individuals banding together in a social contract to ensure that weaker members of society were not bullied. In essays {1} and {304}, Maurin employed the following quote: "Man is naturally good, but institutions make him bad, so let us overthrow institutions."

Rousseau believed that most modern institutions, such as private property, further removed humans from their natural state and corrupted them.

RUSKIN, JOHN (1819–1900) was a British art and social critic. He decried the separation of art from labor, which he saw as a hallmark of modern industrialism.

RYAN, REV. ARTHUR, was an Irish priest and philosophy professor at Queen's University Belfast in Ireland. He was an outspoken critic of fascism and Communism during the 1930s and 1940s.

SANGER, MARGARET (1879–1966) was an American nurse and birth control activist. She believed that the empowerment of women required the ability of women to regulate pregnancy. In addition to founding Planned Parenthood and opening the first birth control clinic in the United States, she also supported the sterilization of people whom she considered genetically unfit.

SANGNIER, MARC (1873–1950) was a French Catholic activist who founded the *Le Sillon* movement in 1894. The movement was condemned in 1910 for conflating Catholicism with democracy. After the condemnation, Sangnier was active in French politics and founded a number of newspapers that promoted democratic ideals. It is not known if Maurin and Sangnier ever met. Although Maurin had ideological differences with Sangnier as indicated in essay {410}, Maurin seemingly adopted many of *Le Sillon*'s practices. For example, for both *Le Sillon* and the Catholic Worker, there was no enrollment, dues, salary, or structured leadership. People could freely join or leave both movements. Where the Catholic Worker hosted clarifications of thought, *Le Sillon* organized small study clubs to discuss social questions of the day in light of the Catholic faith.

SAVONAROLA, GIROLAMO (1452–98), an Italian Dominican priest, who by way of his preaching and prophecies turned out the corrupt ruling family in Florence and established a democratic republic. Under his influence and promise of wealth, Florence enacted several laws against vice. During this time, Christ was considered the King of Florence and Christ's laws were seen as the foundation of their society. Because of political pressure, Pope Alexander VI excommunicated Savonarola, and he was later executed.

SCHMITT, CARL (1889–1989), an American Catholic painter, spoke of justice beginning with the individual Catholic who lived an authentically Catholic life and inspired others by his or her example. He was an early visitor to the Catholic Worker in New York. He is sometimes confused with the German philosopher by the same name who lived during roughly the same time period. Adding to this confusion, the German Schmitt was a prominent Catholic in the 1920s who contributed writings to the English distributist movement. By the 1930s,

552   BIOGRAPHICAL GLOSSARY

the German Schmitt had rejected his Catholic faith and later became active in the Nazi party.

SHAKESPEARE, WILLIAM (1564–1616) was an English playwright, considered by many to be England's greatest writer. The quote "be yourself" is a reference to the line "To thine own self be true," which was spoken by Polonius in the first act of *Hamlet*.

SHEEHAN, ARTHUR (d. 1975), along with John McGee, was a founder of the Catholic Worker house in Boston during the 1930s. Afterward, Sheehan was very involved at the New York house until the time of Peter Maurin's death in 1949. He published the first biography on Maurin, *Peter Maurin: Gay Believer* (1959).

SHEELY, REV. PATRICK, S.J.—Unfortunately, to whom Maurin was referring is unknown.

SHEEN, FULTON J. (1895–1979) was an American priest who eventually became Bishop of Rochester, New York. As a priest theologian, he hosted a popular radio program, *The Catholic Hour*, from 1930 to 1950. After being elevated to bishop in 1951, he hosted a television show during the 1950s and 1960s. His legacy is the result of his ingenious use of radio and television to communicate the complexities of Catholic theology largely through relatable stories and examples.

SHERMAN, WILLIAM TECUMSEH (1820–91) was a Union Army general during the American Civil War. He is most famous for marching his troops through Georgia in 1864, destroying both military targets and infrastructure. He popularized the quote in essay {421}, which is attributed to him, when speaking to a group of cadets years later.

SHUSTER, GEORGE N. (1884–1977) was the editor of *Commonweal* from 1925 to 1937. As its editor, he was responsible for publishing several articles by Dorothy Day. Peter Maurin also knew Shuster from stopping by the *Commonweal* offices, and it was partly on Shuster's recommendation that Maurin sought out Day in 1932. Shuster would later be president of Hunter College (1940–60) and assistant to the president of Notre Dame University (1960–76).

SIEGFRIED, ANDRÉ (1875–1959) was a French geographer who launched the field of electoral geography, the interaction between geography, culture, economics, and politics. Within his prolific writings, he wrote on America, Canada, Europe, South America, India, and New Zealand. In his 1927 book *America Comes of Age: A French Analysis*, he wrote about the necessity of knowing the "Puritan spirit" if one wished to understand America.

BIOGRAPHICAL GLOSSARY 553

SINCLAIR, UPTON (1878–1968) was an American socialist and author most famous for his book *The Jungle* (1906), which exposed the horrors of the meatpacking industry in Chicago. This book played a pivotal role in making Dorothy Day aware of the need for social justice. Sinclair is mentioned in one Easy Essay, but only as the promoter of a socialist utopia that Maurin did not support.

SMITH, ADAM (1723–90), a Scottish philosopher, is considered the founder of modern economic theory. Although there is controversy surrounding the proper interpretation of his views, he is generally seen as promoting self-interest, competition, and laissez-faire economics. Maurin was very critical of Smith's most well-known book, which encapsulated Smith's basic economic views: *An Inquiry into the Nature and Causes of the Wealth of Nations* (1776), often simply called *The Wealth of Nations*.

SMITH, AL (1873–1944) was an American Catholic politician who was the governor of New York for four terms, but was defeated in his presidential bid in 1928. He was the first Catholic presidential candidate, but anti-Catholic prejudice that he would be answerable to the pope played a significant role in his defeat. Essays {83} and {526} are likely in reference to Smith's opposition to Roosevelt's New Deal, for which Smith joined the American Liberty League, an organization founded largely by pro-business Democrats to oppose the New Deal. The quote attributed to Smith in essay {526}, where Smith stated that neither he nor Roosevelt knew the solution to Great Depression, may explain why Maurin believed Smith was "wondering," and that both Roosevelt and Smith were "out to sea" in essay {83}.

SMITH, VICTOR (1907–64) was a journalist before he decided to join the New York Catholic Worker in the 1930s. After marrying a fellow Catholic Worker, they moved to Maryfarm, the first Catholic Worker farm in Easton, Pennsylvania. They raised ten children there, and he lived there until his death in 1964. The Smiths were one of the families that stayed on the farm after Dorothy Day decided to disassociate the Catholic Worker movement from the farm in the late 1940s. For more about Day's dissociation from the farm, see Hennessy, *Dorothy Day*, 165–70.

SOMBART, WERNER (1863–1941) was a German economist and sociologist. For much of his life he was a committed Marxist. During the 1930s, he held an ambivalent relationship to Nazism. His 1911 book *The Jews and Modern Capitalism* proposed that Jewish merchants brought about the rise of capitalism after being excluded from the European guild system.

SOMERVILLE, HENRY (1889–1953) was an English Catholic journalist who immigrated to Canada at the request of Archbishop Neil McNeil of Toronto around 1933 to be the editor of the *Catholic Register*, Canada's oldest English-speaking Catholic newspaper. He became a leading proponent of Catholic Social Teaching in Canada during the 1930s.

SOREL, GEORGES (1847–1922) was a French philosopher known for promoting the power of myth, or metanarratives, and supporting violence to achieve just ends. His thought was embraced by many Communists and fascists. Sorel held to anarcho-syndicalist principles, in which workers owned the means of production in a relatively anarchistic society.

SPENCER, HERBERT (1820–1903), a famous English philosopher and sociologist in the nineteenth century, was a very early proponent of evolution and coined the term "survival of the fittest." Dispensing with the Christian faith, Spencer believed that everything could be explained by the natural laws of the universe, which science had the power to discover.

STALIN, JOSEPH (1878–1953) was a ruthless dictator for the Soviet Union from 1922 until his death in 1953. During his tenure, he implemented a program of state centralization and industrialization. In order to consolidate power and retain it, he coordinated the Great Purge during the 1930s, in which 600,000 to 1.2 million Russians were executed.

STEFFENS, LINCOLN (1866–1936) was an American reporter whose most famous book, *The Shame of the Cities* (1904), connected political corruption at all levels of American government to bribes, kickbacks, and other manifestations of greed. This led Steffens to conclude that the political problem was an economic problem. He was initially encouraged by the Russian Revolution during the 1920s, but lost his enthusiasm for Communism by 1930.

STEVENSON, ROBERT LOUIS (1850–94) was a Scottish novelist and poet most famous for his books *Treasure Island* and the *Strange Case of Dr. Jekyll and Mr. Hyde*. Maurin's quotations of Stevenson were from a posthumously published fragment of Stevenson's writing from 1879 entitled, "Lay Morals." Stevenson is usually considered an atheist or an agnostic.

STRACHEY, JOHN (1901–63) was one of the most widely read British Marxist-Leninist theorists of the 1930s. He later broke with Communism and, beginning in 1945, held several government posts as a member of Britain's Labour Party.

STURZO, DON LUIGI (1871–1959), an Italian Catholic priest and politician, was a fierce critic of fascism and Mussolini. In 1919, he cofounded the Italian People's Party, a Christian democratic political party that played a significant role in Italian politics until Mussolini came to power in 1922. His opposition to Mussolini resulted in his forced exile from Italy from 1924 to 1946.

TAWNEY, RICHARD HENRY (1880–1962), an English Christian socialist and economic historian, was a professor at the London School of Economics during the 1930s and 1940s. His book *The Acquisitive Society* (1920) critiqued the onset of capitalism and the resultant elimination of ethics from the realm of economics. Maurin was particularly fond of Tawney's book *Religion and the Rise of Capitalism* (1926), which critiqued and augmented Max Weber's (1864–1920) thesis that Calvin and English Puritanism played a significant role in the onset of capitalism. Tawney took a more nuanced view, but essentially agreed. He posited that capitalism became a dominating force because Catholic ethics viewed economics as an interpersonal affair instead of a social and cultural reality. The inability of Catholic ethics to properly understand and adapt to changing economic conditions meant that it could not adequately address capitalism.

THOMAS, NORMAN (1884–1968), an American socialist and author, was critical of Marxist Communism. He was a minister in the Presbyterian Church until 1931. He rose to prominence in 1928 when he ran for president of the United States on the Socialist Party ticket. He would also run in the next five presidential elections.

THOMAS AQUINAS, ST. (1225–74) was an Italian Dominican priest and theologian. He was undoubtedly the most important theologian of the Middle Ages, and his work is still important in Catholic theology. Maurin was most interested in promoting Thomas's idea of the common good and the responsibility of the individual to the community. Maurin contrasted this to rugged individualism, which placed the needs of the individual over that of the community. During the first half of the twentieth century, Aquinas's emphasis on the ability of the intellect to ascertain knowledge was appreciated by Robert Hutchins and Mortimer Adler at the University of Chicago. Thomas's metaphysics, which envisioned a unified hierarchy of truths, was influential for their Great Books of the Western World curriculum. At the invitation of Hutchins, Jacques Maritain spoke at the University of Chicago on numerous occasions during the 1930s and 1940s. Hutchins and Adler greatly admired Jacques Maritain for his neo-Thomist writings, and all three shared similar thoughts on education, which they thought should be more interdisciplinary and emphasize essential cultural values. Aquinas's influence on Hutchins, Adler, and Maritain are noted here because their Thomism made them all prominent figures for Maurin. Last, it should also be noted that Catholic interest in Thomas Aquinas in the early twentieth century was largely because of Leo XIII's encyclical *Aeterni patris*

(1879), which promoted the use of Aquinas in theology, philosophy, and education as a sure antidote to combat the errors of modern times.

THOMPSON, WILLIAM (1775–1833), an Irish utilitarian philosopher, was critical of capitalism and a proponent of the cooperative movement. His writings, which influenced Karl Marx, argued that created wealth should remain with its true creators, the workers. His most prominent work on economics was *An Inquiry into the Principles of the Distribution of Wealth Most Conducive to Human Happiness: Applied to the Newly Proposed System of Voluntary Equality of Wealth* (1824). In essay {495}, Maurin claimed that Thompson was the first to use the term "socialism." The term "socialism" came into use in the 1830s, but it is uncertain who originally coined the term.

THOREAU, HENRY DAVID (1817–62) was an American poet, naturalist, and social critic. His writings on civil disobedience, as well as his example of spending a day in jail for his refusal to pay a tax because of his stand against the Mexican-American War and slavery, influenced Tolstoy, Gandhi, and Martin Luther King Jr. The quote in essay {418} was from his 1854 essay "Life without Principle," in which Thoreau briefly shared some thoughts on living a good and meaningful life.

TONIOLO, BLESSED GIUSEPPE (1845–1918) was an Italian Catholic economist layman who saw the economy within a religious framework that included care and concern for one's neighbor. He was a supporter of unions and the principle of subsidiarity, meaning that the decision and performance of a task should be controlled by the smallest and most local group possible.

TOWNSEND, FRANCIS (1867–1960) campaigned for an old-age security program in 1933 that eventually became the Roosevelt administration's Social Security old-age pension program in 1935.

TROTSKY, LEON (1879–1940) was a Russian Marxist revolutionary and theorist. He played a key coordinating role with the Red Army during the Russian Civil War (1918–22). After failing to prevent the rise of Stalin to power in the 1920s, he was deported in 1929. In 1940, he was assassinated in Mexico by order of Stalin. The primary reasons for Trotsky's opposition to Stalin were Trotsky's aversion to Stalin's bureaucratization of the Communist Russia and stifling of divergent opinions within the party.

VAN ZEELAND, PAUL (1893–1973) was a Belgian economist and Catholic politician. He was prime minister of Belgium from 1935 to 1937, leading a coalition government that implemented reforms to support the working class. It is uncertain why Maurin referred to van Zeeland as a communitarian. Van Zeeland's popular reputation in 1936 may have led supporters, such as de Becker, to paint an inaccurate picture.

VEBLEN, THORSTEIN (1857–1929) was an American economist and critic of capitalism most famous for his book *The Theory of the Leisure Class* (1899). He believed that human ethics had its source in one's environment and in evolutionary biology. He argued that the ideal put forth by the leisure class of a labor-free life with wasteful consumption had demeaned meaningful labor and efficient consumption. Though in later Easy Essays Maurin attributed the quote in essay {2} ("There is no ethics in modern society.") to *The Theory of the Leisure Class*, it was not a direct quote, but rather represented a sentiment that Maurin gleaned from the book. In the context provided by the Easy Essays, the quote could imply that ethics were taught in medieval society, but Veblen believed that the problem of the leisure class was a hallmark in barbaric, medieval, and modern societies.

VERDIER, JEAN CARDINAL (1864–1940), a fierce opponent of fascism, was a French prelate and the Archbishop of Paris from 1929 until his death in 1940. He was made both the Archbishop of Paris and a cardinal by Pope Pius XI in 1929.

VOLTAIRE (1694–1778), whose real name was François-Marie Arouet, was a French Enlightenment writer known for his critique of the Catholic Church and his support for freedom of religion and the separation of church and state.

VON BISMARCK, OTTO (1815–98) was a Protestant Prussian statesman who was largely responsible for the unification of most German states in 1871. He was chancellor of Germany from 1871 to 1890. Between 1871 and 1878, he orchestrated the *Kulturkampf*, a campaign against Catholic political power in Germany and Prussia that he abandoned when he needed Catholic support against Communism. He was not a proponent of colonization, but relented under popular opinion and political pressure. He believed that colonies were a greater burden to the colonizer than the actual benefits received. He had no problem with French colonial expansion, since he believed that it ultimately weakened French power and influence.

VON KETTELER, WILHELM EMMANUEL (1811–77) was the Bishop of Mainz in Germany from 1850 until his death. He viewed the labor question as the most critical issue of the day and vehemently advocated state protections for workers and the formation of unions to protect workers from exploitation in factories. His 1864 book *The Labor Question and Christianity* was influential on Pope Leo XIII's *Rerum novarum*. Von Ketteler was passionate about serving the poor, even taking his own "vow of poverty" to dedicate his superfluous goods for charitable purposes. He believed that there was no exclusive right to private property, since all property truly belonged to God. He asserted that it was God's intention that all people would be sustained by the earth's goods. Additionally, as Maurin noted in essay {211}, von Ketteler argued that anyone refusing "to help a poor man who is in *extreme necessity*" was in mortal sin. Von Ketteler, quoted in George Metlake, *Christian Social Reform* (Philadelphia: Dolphin, 1912), 66.

WATT, JAMES (1736–1819) was a Scottish inventor and mechanical engineer most well known for making the steam engine more efficient and practical. His updates to the steam engine played a pivotal role in furthering the Industrial Revolution.

WILHELM I (1797–1888) was the German emperor and king of Prussia during most of the latter nineteenth century. He oversaw changes in Germany that made it more amenable to centralization, industrialization, and the growth of banks.

WILHELM II (1859–1941), the grandson of Wilhelm I, was the last German emperor and king of Prussia from 1888 to 1918. After World War I, he fled to the Netherlands. Wilhelm II oversaw the perpetuation of many of his grandfather's policies. From 1888 to 1907, there was a shift from equal parts of the population involved in either industrial occupations or farming to twice the population working in industrial occupations as in farming.

WILLMANN, DOROTHY J. (1900–1987) was a laywoman who worked on the staff of the *Queen's Work*, an American Jesuit publication. During that time, the publication was edited by Fr. Daniel Lord and essentially acted as an arm of the Sodality movement. She also served as an executive for the Sodality of the Blessed Virgin Mary.

WILSON, THOMAS (1524–81) was an English rhetorician and government official under Queen Elizabeth I. The work to which Maurin referred was *A Discourse upon Usury by Way of Dialogue and Orations*. Though he was Anglican and a humanist, Wilson's book cited not only scripture and early church theologians, but also canon law. The 1925 edition of the book contained a 172–page introduction by one of Maurin's favorite writers, R. H. Tawney.

WILSON, WOODROW (1856–1924) was president of the United States from 1913 to 1921. Wilson won the presidential election with an anti-war message, but entered World War I shortly after his election. He played a key role in forming the League of Nations after the War. In essays {287}, {336}, and {337}, Maurin painted a sympathetic picture of Wilson as a person whose Fourteen Points or aims for concluding the First World War, if they had been enacted, could have prevented the rise of fascism and Nazism in Spain and Germany, respectively.

YOUNG, MILDRED BINNS (1901–95) was an American Quaker who played a founding role in the interracial Delta Cooperative Farm in Rochdale, Mississippi, in 1936. Later in life she became active in the peace movement, authored pamphlets on nonviolence, and sat on the board of *Friends Journal*. The quote in essay {419} is from her 1939 pamphlet *Functional Poverty*.

YOUNG, OWEN (1874–1962), an American businessman, was chairman of General Electric during the 1920s and 1930s. He also made an unsuccessful bid for the Democratic presidential nomination in 1932. Although involved with manufacturing while at General Electric, he was born on his family's farm and returned to farming after retiring from General Electric in the late 1930s. He was also chairman of General Electric for a brief period during the 1940s. During his entire adult life, he diligently pursued avenues for farmers to earn a living wage.

Acknowledgments

Since I began working on this project back in 2012, archivist Phil Runkel of the Dorothy Day–Catholic Worker Collection at Marquette University's Raynor Memorial Libraries has played an indispensable role not only in retrieving old *Catholic Worker* newspapers and unpublished essays, but also in referring me to resources I did not even know about. I cannot express enough gratitude for Phil. I am also deeply grateful to Fredric Nachbaur and Fordham University Press for their invaluable feedback on and belief in this project. Fordham University Press has published some wonderful books related to the Catholic Worker that have deepened my understanding and appreciation of the movement.

I need to thank Peter Maurin and Dorothy Day. Their writings led me to the Casa Maria Catholic Worker community in Milwaukee, Wisconsin. Since joining this community in 1998, I have met so many wonderful people also inspired by the vision of the Catholic Worker, including Laura Pope, Michael Komba, Amada Morales, Reda Moore, Anna Hunter, Roberta Thurston, and Don Timmerman.

Easy Essay Index

{1} Institutions—Corporations, May 1933 (p. 19); Institutions and Corporations, December 1935 (p. 117)
{2} Ethics and Economics, May 1933 (p. 20); Listening to the Pope, November 1934 (p. 115); Ethics and Economics, June 1935 (p. 147); An Ethical Problem, June 1940 (p. 346); No Ethics, Unpublished, (p. 431)
{3} Blowing the Dynamite, May 1933 (p. 21); Blowing the Dynamite, 1 February 1934 (p. 64); Blowing the Dynamite, October 1936 (p. 218); Blowing the Dynamite, May 1937 (p. 249)
{4} The Money-Lenders' Dole, May 1933 (p. 22)
{5} Mortgaged, May 1933 (p. 23); Legalized Usury, 15 December 1933 (p. 54); [No Title], 15 December 1933 (p. 59); Legalized Usury, October 1934, (p 114); Mortgaged, May 1935 (p. 147); Mortgaged, June 1936 (p. 201); Because the State, September 1941 (p. 392)
{6} Out of the Temple, May 1933 (p. 24)
{7} Wealth-Producing Maniacs, May 1933 (p. 25); Wealth-Producing Maniac, 15 December 1933 (p. 54); Wealth-Producing Maniacs, May 1935 (p. 147); Wealth-Producing Maniacs, June 1936 (p. 201)
{8} Round-Table Discussions, June–July 1933 (p. 26); Round-Table Discussions, 1 March 1934 (p. 72); Round-Table Discussions, March 1935 (p. 138); Round-Table Discussions, September 1935 (p. 158); Clarification of Thought, June 1942 (p. 415)
{9} Houses of Hospitality, June–July 1933 (p. 27); Houses of Hospitality, October 1933 (p. 43); Houses of Hospitality, 1 March 1934 (p. 72); Houses of Hospitality, March 1935 (p. 138); Houses of Hospitality, September 1935 (p. 158); Houses of Hospitality, May 1936 (p. 200); Houses of Hospitality, June 1942 (p. 415)
{10} Agronomic Universities, June–July 1933 (p. 28); Farming Communes, November 1934 (p. 120); Farming Communes, January 1935 (p. 134); Farming Communes, March 1935 (p. 138); Farming Communes, September 1935 (p. 158); Framing Communes, November 1935 (p. 176); What the Unemployed Need, January 1937 (p. 229)
{11} Creating Problems, July–August 1933 (p. 29); Business Is Selfishness, July–August 1935 (p. 154); Business Is Business, December 1936 (p. 226); Business Is Business, August 1937 (p. 260); Business Is Selfishness, January 1938 (p. 269); Business Is Selfishness, October 1938 (p. 288); Classes and Clashes, December 1945 (p. 421)
{12} No Way to Turn, July–August 1933 (p. 29); Teaching Subjects, July–August 1935 (p. 154); Teachers of Subjects, December 1936 (p. 226)
{13} Liberal Fanatics, July–August 1933 (p. 30); Not a Liberal, October 1934, (p 105); Liberalism, January 1936 (p. 182); Liberals Not Liberators, November 1936 (p. 221); Liberals and Liberators, June 1937 (p. 254); Let's Be Liberators, July 1938 (p. 285); Too Broadminded, February 1939 (p. 301)

{14} The Age of Treason, July–August 1933 (p. 31); The Age of Treason, November 1936 (p. 221); The Age of Treason, June 1937 (p. 254); The Age of Treason, April 1942 (p. 409)

{15} Commercializers of Labor, July–August 1933 (p. 32); Capital and Labor, 1 April 1934 (p. 81); Capital and Labor, November 1934 (p. 120); Accumulators of Labor (part 1), April 1935 (p. 141); Sellers of Labor (part 2), April 1935 (p. 141); Capital and Labor, September 1935 (p. 158); Capital and Labor, May 1936 (p. 198)

{16} Selling Their Labor, July–August 1933 (p. 33); Selling Their Labor, 1 April 1934 (p. 81); Selling Their Labor, November 1934 (p. 120); Getting Left, April 1935 (p. 141); Selling Their Labor, September 1935 (p. 158); Selling Their Labor, May 1936 (p. 198); Selling Their Labor, September 1938 (p. 287); On Selling Labor, May 1940 (p. 346); Selling Their Labor, February 1941 (p. 374)

{17} God and Mammon, September 1933 (p. 34); God or Mammon, June 1936 (p. 200); God and Mammon, July–August 1942 (p. 417)

{18} When Civilization Decays, September 1933 (p. 35)

{19} Self-Organization, September 1933 (p. 36); Self-Organization, 1 April 1934 (p. 81); Self-Organization, November 1934 (p. 120); Self-Government, September 1938 (p. 287)

{20} Politics Is Politics, September 1933 (p. 37); Politics Is Politics, July–August 1935 (p. 153); Politics vs. Politics, December 1936 (p. 226)

{21} Church and State, September 1933 (p. 37)

{22} A Modern Plague, September 1933 (p. 38); A Modern Plague (part 1), 1 June 1934 (p. 86); Secularism (part 2), 1 June 1934 (p. 86); Secularism, January 1936 (p. 182); Secularism Is a Pest, November 1936 (p. 221); Secularism, May 1937 (p. 250); Secularism, July 1938 (p. 286); Secularism, February 1939 (p. 301); Secularism (part 2), November 1940 (p. 361); French Secularism (part 2), Unpublished (p. 440)

{23} The Duty of Hospitality, October 1933 (p. 40); Why Not Be a Beggar, May 1935 (p. 146); Hospitality, May 1936 (p. 23)

{24} The Municipal Lodgings, October 1933 (p. 41)

{25} Back to Hospitality, October 1933 (p. 42)

{26} Hospices, October 1933 (p. 43); Houses of Hospitality, January 1935 (p. 133)

{27} Parish Houses of Hospitality, October 1933 (p. 44)

{28} Houses of "Catholic Action," October 1933 (p. 45)

{29} The Spirit of the Mass / The Spirit of the Masses, October 1933 (p. 45)

{30} An Open Letter to Father Lord, M. Ag. (Master Agitator), October 1933 (p. 46)

{31} To Be a Marxian, November 1933 (p. 48)

{32} Karl Marx Soon Realized, November 1933 (p. 49)

{33} The Communist Manifesto, November 1933 (p. 50); The Communist Party, June 1935 (p. 147)

{34} For Catholic Action, November 1933 (p. 50); The Catholic Worker, June 1935 (p. 147)

{35} The Bishops' Program, November 1933 (p. 51)

{36} Reconstructing the Social Order, November 1933 (p. 52); Reconstruction, September 1934 (p. 101); Reconstructing the Social Order, October 1934, (p 110); Reconstructing the Social Order, December 1934 (p. 130); Reconstructing the Social Order, March 1935 (p. 137)

{37} Usurers Not Gentleman, 15 December 1933 (p. 53); [No Title], 15 December 1933 (p. 60); Peter Maurin

EASY ESSAY INDEX 565

Says Usurers are not Gentlemen! October 1934, (p 114)
{38} The Fallacy of Saving, 15 December 1933 (p. 54); [No Title], 15 December 1933 (p. 61); The Fallacy of Saving, May 1935 (p. 147); The Fallacy of Saving, May 1936 (p. 198); The Fallacy of Saving, June 1936 (p. 201); Fallacy of Saving, March 1938 (p. 274); Fallacy of Saving, July–August 1941 (p. 388)
{39} Avoiding Inflation, 15 December 1933 (p. 55); Avoiding Inflation, May 1935 (p. 147); Avoiding Inflation, June 1936 (p. 201)
{40} Another Open Letter to Father Lord M. Ag. (Master Agitator), 15 December 1933 (p. 56)
{41} Legalized Usury, 15 December 1933 (p. 57); Things Have Changed, July–August 1934 (p. 94); Things Have Changed, September 1934 (p. 97); Business Is the Bunk, October 1935 (p. 165); On the Campus, October 1937 (p. 266)
{42} [No Title], 15 December 1933 (p. 61); Going Back, April 1935 (p. 142)
{43} Hayes of Columbia Gives Opening Night Lecture of Catholic Workers' School, 1 February 1934 (p. 63)
{44} Coming to Union Square, 1 February 1934 (p. 63); Specialization, July–August 1935 (p. 44); Not My Subject, October 1935 (p. 44); Not My Subject, December 1936 (p. 226); Not My Subject, October 1937 (p. 266); A College Professor, January 1942 (p. 401)
{45} Scholars and Bourgeois, 1 February 1934 (p. 64); Scholar and Bourgeois (part 1), January 1937, (p. 228); Scholar and Worker (part 2), January 1937 (p. 228)
{46} Building Churches, 1 February 1934 (p. 65); Looking for an Education, October 1934, (p. 110); No Unity of Thought, January 1936 (p. 182); No Unity of Thought, July 1936 (p. 203); Unity of Thought, December 1936 (p. 226); Henry Adams, January 1942 (p. 402)
{47} Purpose of Catholic Workers' School in Detail, 1 March 1934 (p. 71)
{48} Communes, 1 March 1934 (p. 72)
{49} Catholic Social Philosophy, 1 March 1934 (p. 72)
{50} The Way Out, 1 April 1934 (p. 76); A Philosophy of Labor, November 1934 (p. 120); Better and Better Off, September 1935 (p. 158); Better and Better Off, May 1937 (p. 252); Better and Better Off, March 1938 (p. 274); Better and Better Off, May 1941 (p. 383); Better and Better Off, November 1941 (p. 399)
{51} Christianity, Capitalism, and Communism, 1 April 1934 (p. 77); Christianity, Capitalism, Communism, April 1935 (p. 141); Christianity, Capitalism, Communism, September 1935 (p. 156)
{52} Christ's Message, 1 April 1934 (p. 78); Christ's Message, April 1936 (p. 192); Christ's Message, May 1937 (p. 250)
{53} What Saint Francis Desired, 1 April 1934 (p. 79); What Saint Francis Desired, April 1935 (p. 141); What Saint Francis Desired, May 1935 (p. 146); What Saint Francis Desired, September 1935 (p. 158); Franciscan Radicalism, April 1936 (p. 192); What St. Francis Desired, May 1937 (p. 251); What Saint Francis Desired, March 1938 (p. 274); What St. Francis Desired, September 1938 (p. 287)
{54} The Third Order, 1 April 1934 (p. 79)
{55} Three Ways to Make a Living, 1 April 1934 (p. 81)
{56} Big Shots and Little Shots, 1 May 1934 (p. 85); Big Shots and Little Shots, May 1936 (p. 198); Big Shots and Little Shots, November 1941 (p. 399)
{57} Spiritualizing, 1 June 1934 (p. 86)

{58} Business-Like, 1 June 1934 (p. 87)
{59} Roosevelt's Experiment, 1 June 1934 (p. 87)
{60} The Forgotten Man, 1 June 1934 (p. 88); The Forgotten Man, September 1936 (p. 215)
{61} Rome or Moscow, 1 June 1934 (p. 89)
{62} [No Title], July–August 1934 (p. 91); I Was Told, September 1934 (p. 97)
{63} Looking for Light, July–August 1934 (p. 92); Looking for the Lights, September 1934 (p. 97)
{64} Shouting with Rotarians, July–August 1934 (p. 93); Shouting with Rotarians, September 1934 (p. 97); Shouting with Anglo-Saxons, December 1934 (p. 129); Shouting with Rotarians, October 1935 (p. 165); Bourgeois Slogans, September 1936 (p. 215); Bourgeois Slogans, December 1936 (p. 226); A Commencement, October 1937 (p. 266); Materialist Slogans, July 1938 (p. 286)
{65} Only Twenty-Five Cents, July–August 1934 (p. 95)
{66} A Protestant Agitator, July–August 1934 (p. 95)
{67} The Common Good, July–August 1934 (p. 96)
{68} Tawney's Books, July–August 1934 (p. 96); R. H. Tawney, April 1941 (p. 380)
{69} Catholic Social Research, September 1934 (p. 98); School of Social Studies, January 1935 (p. 131)
{70} School of Social Studies, September 1934 (p. 98)
{71} Putting Patches, September 1934 (p. 99)
{72} I Agree, September 1934 (p. 100); I Agree, June 1935 (p. 147); I Agree, May 1940 (p. 342); I Agree, May 1941 (p. 382)
{73} Personal Sacrifice, September 1934 (p. 101); At a Sacrifice, September 1935 (p. 158)

{74} A Third Open Letter to Father Lord, M. Ag. (Master Agitator), September 1934 (p. 102)
{75} On Being Crazy, October 1934 (p. 104); On Being Crazy, December 1934 (p. 123)
{76} Not a Conservative, October 1934 (p. 105)
{77} A Radical Change, October 1934, (p. 106); A Radical Change, March 1935 (p. 137)
{78} When Bankers Rule, October 1934, (p. 107); When Bankers Rule, March 1935 (p. 137); When Bankers Rule, June 1936 (p. 201)
{79} When Christ Is King, October 1934 (p. 108); When Christ Is King, March 1935 (p. 137)
{80} Rebellion Is Rebellion, October 1934 (p. 109)
{81} Constructing the Social Order, October 1934 (p. 109); Constructing the Social Order, March 1935 (p. 137)
{82} Flying from America, October 1934 (p. 110)
{83} Carl Schmitt the Artist, October 1934 (p. 111)
{84} What America Needs, October 1934 (p 111)
{85} Carl Schmitt Believes, October 1934 (p. 112)
{86} What Makes Man Human, October 1934 (p. 113); What Makes Man Human, April 1935 (p. 141); What Makes Man Human, March 1937 (p. 242); What Makes Man Human, September 1937 (p. 264); Human to Man, March 1938 (p. 274)
{87} Fighting Communism, October 1934 (p 114)
{88} Robertson's Book, November 1934 (p. 115)
{89} Before the Crash, November 1934 (p. 116)
{90} The Great Folly, November 1934 (p. 117)
{91} We Were Told, November 1934 (p. 118); 1933—New Deal, May 1935 (p. 151)

EASY ESSAY INDEX   567

{92} What Is Needed, November 1934 (p. 119)
{93} Professors of a Farming Commune, November 1934 (p. 120); Professors of a Farming Commune, March 1935 (p. 138); Professors of a Farming Commune, September 1935 (p. 158); Professors of a Farming Commune, November 1935 (p. 176); Professors of an Outdoor University, January 1937 (p. 229)
{94} Laborers of a Farming Commune, November 1934 (p. 121); Laborers of a Farming Commune, March 1935 (p. 138); Laborers of a Farming Commune, September 1935 (p. 158); Laborers of a Farming Commune, November 1935 (p. 176); Farming Communes, May 1936 (p. 198); Laborers of an Outdoor University, January 1937 (p. 229); Farming Commune, February 1941 (p. 374); Farming Communes, June 1942 (p. 414)
{95} The Common Good, November 1934 (p. 122)
{96} Not Communists, December 1934 (p. 123); Not Communists, May 1936 (p. 198); Bolshevik Socialists, January 1937 (p. 231)
{97} Two Reds, December 1934 (p. 124)
{98} Looking for a Boss, December 1934 (p. 125)
{99} America and Russia, December 1934 (p. 126)
{100} Red and Green, December 1934 (p. 127)
{101} Then and Now, December 1934 (p. 127)
{102} A Thousand Years Ago, December 1934 (p. 128)
{103} Palestine, Ireland, America, December 1934 (p. 129)
{104} Irish Scholars at Work, December 1934 (p. 130)
{105} Social Missionaries, January 1935 (p. 131)
{106} Study Clubs, January 1935 (p. 132)
{107} Works of Mercy, January 1935 (p. 132)
{108} Self-Employing Centers, January 1935 (p. 133)
{109} What Communists Say They Believe, February 1935 (p. 134)
{110} What Fascists Say They Believe, February 1935 (p. 135)
{111} What Socialists Say They Believe, February 1935 (p. 136)
{112} What Democrats Say They Believe, February 1935 (p. 136)
{113} What the Catholic Worker Believes, February 1935 (p. 137)
{114} [No Title], April 1935 (p. 138)
{115} Taking Over, April 1935 (p. 139)
{116} What is Communism? April 1935 (p. 140)
{117} What Labor Needs, April 1935 (p. 140)
{118} An Old Philosophy, April 1935 (p. 141)
{119} *Esprit*, April 1935 (p. 143)
{120} Communist Ideal, April 1935 (p. 144)
{121} The Hope of the People, April 1935, (p. 144)
{122} Share Your Wealth, May 1935 (p. 145); Share Your Wealth, December 1945 (p. 421)
{123} The Wisdom of Giving, May 1935 (p. 146); The Wisdom of Giving, September 1935 (p. 158); The Wisdom of Giving, May 1936 (p. 198); The Wisdom of Giving, October 1936 (p. 216); Wisdom of Giving, March 1938 (p. 274); Wisdom of Giving, July–August 1941 (p. 388)
{124} 1200—Guild System, May 1935 (p. 147)
{125} 1400—Middle Men, May 1935 (p. 148)
{126} 1600—Banker, May 1935 (p. 148)
{127} 1700—Manufacturer, May 1935 (p. 149); Factory Capitalism, March 1942 (p. 406)
{128} 1800—Economist, May 1935 (p. 150)
{129} 1914—World War, May 1935 (p. 150)
{130} 1929—World Depression, May 1935 (p. 151)

{131} 1933—Catholic Worker, May 1935 (p. 151)
{132} No Recourse, June 1935 (p. 152); No Recourse, December 1936 (p. 226); Makers of Depressions, April 1937 (p. 246); No Recourse, August 1937 (p. 260); No Recourse, January 1938 (p. 269); No Recourse, October 1938 (p. 288)
{133} Maker of Deals, July–August 1935 (p. 153); Business Is the Bunk, October 1935 (p. 165); Business Is Business, October 1937 (p. 266)
{134} Another Experiment, July–August 1935 (p. 154)
{135} Christianity Untried, July–August 1935 (p. 155); Christianity Untried, January 1936 (p. 183); Not Practical, May 1937 (p. 249); Christianity Untried, June 1940 (p. 346); Christianity Untried, September 1941 (p. 394)
{136} The Wisdom of Giving, July–August 1935 (p. 155)
{137} Looking at Property, September 1935 (p. 156)
{138} For Christ's Sake, September 1935 (p. 157)
{139} Invaders and Invaded, September 1935 (p. 158); Germans and French, December 1937 (p. 267)
{140} The Communist Party vs. The Catholic Worker, October 1935 (p. 159); The C.P. and C.M., May 1936 (p. 198); The Catholic Worker, January 1937 (p. 234)
{141} Taking Back Our Thunder, October 1935 (p. 160)
{142} Taking Back Our Name, October 1935 (p. 161)
{143} Confused Marxists; October 1935 (p. 162)
{144} Confused Catholics, October 1935 (p. 162)
{145} From a Non-Catholic, October 1935 (p. 163)
{146} From a Catholic, October 1935 (p. 164)
{147} Catholic Bourgeois, October 1935 (p. 164); Catholic Bourgeois, October 1937 (p. 266)
{148} College Graduates, October 1935 (p. 165); In a Changing World, October 1937 (p. 266)
{149} An Unhappy Lot, October 1935 (p. 166); Looking for Jobs, October 1937 (p. 266)
{150} Houses of Hospitality, October 1935 (p. 167)
{151} Indoctrination, October 1935 (p. 168); Indoctrination, October 1937 (p. 266)
{152} On Farming Communes, October 1935 (p. 169); On Farming Communes, October 1937 (p. 266)
{153} On the Level, November 1935 (p. 170)
{154} Industrialization, November 1935 (p. 170)
{155} Mechanized Labor, November 1935 (p. 171)
{156} No Pleasure in Work, November 1935 (p. 172)
{157} Industrialism and Art, November 1935 (p. 173)
{158} From a Chinese, November 1935 (p. 173)
{159} Regard for the Soil, November 1935 (p. 174)
{160} Up to Catholics, November 1935 (p. 175)
{161} Some Institutions, December 1935 (p. 176)
{162} American Institutions, December 1935 (p. 177)
{163} The N.R.A., December 1935 (p. 177); The N.R.A., December 1936 (p. 226)
{164} Bureaucracy, December 1935 (p. 178)
{165} Five Definitions, December 1935 (p. 179); Five Definitions, May 1936 (p. 198); Three Definitions, March 1937 (p. 240)
{166} They and We, December 1935 (p. 180); They and We, May 1936 (p. 198); They and We, September 1936 (p. 212); They and We, March 1937 (p. 240); They and We, September 1937 (p. 264); They and We, September 1938 (p. 287); They and We, November 1939 (p. 325);

EASY ESSAY INDEX   569

They and We, November 1941 (p. 398)
{167} A New Movement, December 1935 (p. 181); Communitarian Movement, May 1936 (p. 198)
{168} A Blackfriars Editorial, January 1936 (p. 182)
{169} The Hope of the People, January 1936 (p. 183)
{170} The Christian Front, January 1936 (p. 184)
{171} The New Apologetics, January 1936 (p. 185)
{172} Putting the Land to Use, January 1936 (p. 185)
{173} Rendering a Great Service, February 1936 (p. 186)
{174} Bolton Hall's Panacea, February 1936 (p. 187)
{175} Brainless Trustees, February 1936 (p. 188)
{176} Down to the Roots, April 1936 (p. 189)
{177} Poor Conservatives, April 1936 (p. 190)
{178} Radically Wrong, April 1936 (p. 190)
{179} A New Society, April 1936 (p. 191)
{180} Creating Order, April 1936 (p. 191)
{181} Right or Wrong, April 1936 (p. 192); Right and Wrong; December 1937 (p. 266); Right and Wrong, June 1941 (p. 384)
{182} Protecting France, April 1936 (p. 193); Protecting France, July–August 1940 (p. 349)
{183} Protecting England, April 1936 (p. 194); Protecting England, July–August 1940 (p. 349)
{184} Civilizing Ethiopia, April 1936 (p. 195)
{185} League of Nations, April 1936 (p. 196)
{186} Moral Disarmament, April 1936 (p. 196)
{187} Room Could be Found, April 1936 (p. 197)
{188} At a Sacrifice, May 1936 (p. 199); Then and Now, March 1938 (p. 274); Primitive Christianity, September 1938 (p. 287); Christian Charity, May 1940 (p. 346); First Christians, July–August 1941 (p. 388)
{189} Four Million Catholics, May 1936 (p. 200)
{190} Usurers Not Gentlemen, June 1936 (p. 200)
{191} Shouting a Word, July 1936 (p. 201)
{192} The Right Word, July 1936 (p. 202)
{193} Philosophy and Sophistry, July 1936 (p. 203)
{194} The City of God, July 1936 (p. 203)
{195} Integral Humanism, July 1936 (p. 204)
{196} Action and Thought, July 1936 (p. 205)
{197} Two Bourgeois, August 1936 (p. 206)
{198} Bourgeois Capitalist, August 1936 (p. 207)
{199} Bolshevist Socialist, August 1936 (p. 208)
{200} Personalist Communitarian, August 1936 (p. 208)
{201} Community Spirit, August 1936 (p. 209)
{202} Franciscans and Jesuits, August 1936 (p. 210)
{203} Counsels of the Gospel, August 1936 (p. 211)
{204} Basic Power, September 1936 (p. 212)
{205} Thinking Individual, September 1936 (p. 212)
{206} Social Power, September 1936 (p. 213)
{207} Give Me Liberty, September 1936 (p. 213)
{208} Leadership, September 1936 (p. 213)
{209} Communitarian Personalism, September 1936 (p. 214)
{210} The Problem of Today, October 1936 (p. 215)
{211} With Our Superfluous Goods, October 1936 (p. 215)
{212} Ambassadors of God, October 1936 (p. 216)

{213} We Seem to Think, October 1936 (p. 217)
{214} If, October 1936 (p. 217)
{215} The Stuff and the Push, October 1936 (p. 218)
{216} Houses of Hospitality, October 1936 (p. 218)
{217} Open Letter to Father Lord, S.J., October 1936 (p. 219)
{218} Utilitarian Thought, November 1936 (p. 221)
{219} Futilitarian Economics, November 1936 (p. 222)
{220} Futilitarian States, November 1936 (p. 222)
{221} Totalitarian States, November 1936 (p. 223)
{222} Pluralist Thought, November 1936 (p. 224)
{223} Pluralist State, November 1936 (p. 224)
{224} Allied Techniques, November 1936 (p. 225)
{225} About Textbooks, December 1936 (p. 226)
{226} It Must Be Used, December 1936 (p. 227)
{227} On to the Street, January 1937 (p. 228)
{228} Hands and Heads, January 1937 (p. 229)
{229} Silver Springs, January 1937 (p. 230)
{230} Three Books, January 1937 (p. 230)
{231} In Bolshevik Russia, January 1937 (p. 231)
{232} Economic Determinism, January 1937 (p. 232)
{233} Class Struggle, January 1937 (p. 232); March 1941 (p. 378)
{234} Proletarian Dictatorship, January 1937 (p. 233)
{235} Personalist Leadership, January 1937 (p. 234)
{236} The Thinking Man's Journalist, February 1937 (p. 235); Journalism: Good and Bad, February 1938 (p. 274)
{237} Caesar or God, March 1937 (p. 237)
{238} Fascist Caesar, March 1937 (p. 238)
{239} The Nazi Caesar, March 1937 (p. 239)
{240} The Bolshevik Caesar, March 1937 (p. 240)
{241} The Use of Liberty, March 1937 (p. 240)
{242} Modern Education, March 1937 (p. 241)
{243} On Gandhi Lines, April 1937 (p. 242)
{244} In the Middle Ages, April 1937 (p. 243)
{245} Economic Economy, April 1937 (p. 243)
{246} Proper Property, April 1937 (p. 244)
{247} Speed-Up System, April 1937 (p. 245)
{248} Collective Bargaining, April 1937 (p. 246)
{249} In the Rumble Seat, April 1937 (p. 246)
{250} The Modern Mind, April 1937 (p. 247)
{251} Paul Chanson, April 1937 (p. 248)
{252} Just as Bad, May 1937 (p. 249)
{253} The Law of Holiness, May 1937 (p. 250)
{254} Rich and Poor, May 1937 (p. 251); Rich and Poor, July–August 1941 (p. 388)
{255} Utilitarian Philosophers, June 1937 (p. 252)
{256} Futlitarian Economists, June 1937 (p. 252)
{257} Harold Laski Says, June 1937 (p. 253)
{258} Fascism and Marxism, June 1937 (p. 254)
{259} Capitalism, Fascism, Communism, June 1937 (p. 254)
{260} Without Comments, July 1937 (p. 255)
{261} Twenty and Forty, July 1937 (p. 256)
{262} Works of Mercy, July 1937 (p. 257)

{263} Irish Scholars, July 1937 (p. 257)
{264} Chinese Catholics, July 1937 (p. 258); Chinese Catholics, September 1937 (p. 265)
{265} Five Books, July 1937 (p. 259)
{266} Faith and Reason, July 1937 (p. 259)
{267} The Trouble Has Been, August 1937 (p. 260)
{268} Twin Cities, August 1937 (p. 261)
{269} Class-Consciousness, August 1937 (p. 261)
{270} Paul Chanson Says, August 1937 (p. 262)
{271} Four in One, September 1937 (p. 263)
{272} Jewish Jubilee, September 1937 (p. 264)
{273} Let the Jews Be Jews, September 1937 (p. 264)
{274} For Christ's Sake, September 1937 (p. 265)
{275} Barbarians and Civilized, December 1937 (p. 266); Barbarians and Civilized, June 1941 (p. 384)
{276} Italians and Ethiopians, December 1937 (p. 267)
{277} Spaniards and Moors, December 1937 (p. 268)
{278} Stalinites and Trotskyites, December 1937 (p. 269)
{279} Making Money, January 1938 (p. 269)
{280} Providing Jobs, January 1938 (p. 270); Employers of Labor, December 1939 (p. 325)
{281} W.P.A., January 1938 (p. 271); W.P.A., October 1938 (p. 290); W.P.A., December 1939 (p. 325)
{282} Government Control, January 1938 (p. 272)
{283} State Supervision, January 1938 (p. 273)
{284} Jeffersonian Democracy, January 1938 (p. 273)
{285} 1638–1938, April 1938 (p. 274)
{286} Ethiopia and Austria, April 1938 (p. 275)
{287} France and England, April 1938 (p. 275)
{288} Disarmament of the Heart, April 1938 (p. 276)
{289} A Practical Question, April 1938 (p. 276)
{290} Not Better, May 1938 (p. 277)
{291} Germans and Irish, May 1938 (p. 278)
{292} Soldiers and Scholars, May 1938 (p. 278)
{293} The Negro Problem, May 1938 (p. 279)
{294} The Power of Example, May 1938 (p. 280)
{295} The Outstretched Hand, June 1938 (p. 281)
{296} Cardinal Verdier, June 1938 (p. 282)
{297} Cardinal Liénart, June 1938 (p. 282)
{298} Cardinal Hinsley, June 1938 (p. 283)
{299} No Party Line, June 1938 (p. 283)
{300} Three Jews, July 1938 (p. 284)
{301} Modern Education, July 1938 (p. 285)
{302} Looking for Dictators, July 1938 (p. 286)
{303} U.S.S.R., September 1938 (p. 286); A Communist Society, May 1940 (p. 342); A Communist Society, May 1941 (p. 382)
{304} Priests and Policemen, October 1938 (p. 288)
{305} More Profitable, October 1938 (p. 288); Profit Seekers, December 1939 (p. 325)
{306} Sit-Downers, October 1938 (p. 289)
{307} If You Want to Know, October 1938 (p. 290)
{308} 100% Frenchman, December 1938 (p. 291); Richelieu, October 1940 (p. 357)
{309} Thirty Years' War, December 1938 (p. 291)
{310} Treaty of Westphalia, December 1938 (p. 292)
{311} Birth of Prussia, December 1938 (p. 293)

{312} Seven Years' War, December 1938 (p. 294)
{313} Place in the Sun, December 1938 (p. 294)
{314} United Germany, December 1938 (p. 295)
{315} Nations and Notions, December 1938 (p. 296)
{316} Apologetic Catholics, January 1939 (p. 297)
{317} Led by the Nose, January 1939 (p. 297)
{318} A Wrong Way, January 1939 (p. 298)
{319} Catholic Principles, January 1939 (p. 299)
{320} Imitators, January 1939 (p. 299)
{321} The Word Liberal, February 1939 (p. 300)
{322} Not Liberators, February 1939 (p. 301)
{323} Radicals, February 1939 (p. 301)
{324} In New England, March 1939 (p. 306)
{325} In Louisiana, March 1939 (p. 307)
{326} In Texas, March 1939 (p. 307)
{327} In California, March 1939 (p. 308)
{328} Going to the Right, March 1939 (p. 309)
{329} A Mystery, July–August 1939 (p. 310)
{330} In Spain, July–August 1939 (p. 311)
{331} In the Papal States, July–August 1939 (p. 311)
{332} In the Shadow of the Cross, July–August 1939 (p. 312)
{333} In Germany, July–August 1939 (p. 312)
{334} In America, July–August 1939 (p. 313)
{335} In Palestine, July–August 1939 (p. 314)
{336} Safe for Dictators, September 1939 (p. 314)
{337} League of Nations, September 1939 (p. 315); Pax Geneva, October 1939 (p. 318)
{338} German Extension, September 1939 (p. 316)
{339} Nations and the Pope, September 1939 (p. 316)
{340} Prayer for Peace, September 1939 (p. 317)
{341} Land and Crafts, September 1939 (p. 317)
{342} Pax Romana, October 1939 (p. 318)
{343} Pax Germania, October 1939 (p. 319)
{344} Pax Muscova, October 1939 (p. 319)
{345} Pax Britannica, October 1939 (p. 320)
{346} Pax Hibernia, October 1939 (p. 320)
{347} Pax Vaticana, October 1939 (p. 321)
{348} Bourgeois Democracy, November 1939 (p. 322)
{349} Arithmocracy, November 1939 (p. 322)
{350} Poetry and Dictatorship, November 1939 (p. 323)
{351} Liberty or Discipline, November 1939 (p. 324)
{352} Liberty or Security, November 1939 (p. 324)
{353} On Farming Communes, December 1939 (p. 325)
{354} Firing the Boss, December 1939 (p. 326); Be Your Own Boss, February 1941 (p. 374)
{355} Treaty of Versailles, January 1940 (p. 327)
{356} Bourgeois Capitalism, January 1940 (p. 327); Bourgeois Capitalism, November 1942 (p. 418)
{357} Turning Sharp Corners, January 1940 (p. 328); Turning Sharp Corners, November 1942 (p. 418)
{358} Modern Liberals, January 1940 (p. 329); Modern Liberals, November 1942 (p. 418)
{359} Racialism, January 1940 (p. 329); Racialism, November 1942 (p. 418)
{360} Promised Land, January 1940 (p. 330); Personal God, November 1942 (p. 418)

{361} Turning to the Church, January 1940 (p. 331)
{362} Beginning February First, January 1940 (p. 331)
{363} Prostitution of Marriage, January 1940 (p. 332); Prostitution Plus, March 1940 (p. 342)
{364} Prostitution of Education, January 1940 (p. 333)
{365} Prostitution of the Press, January 1940 (p. 334)
{366} Prostitution in Politics, January 1940 (p. 334)
{367} Prostitution of Property, January 1940 (p. 335)
{368} Prostitution of the Theatre, January 1940 (p. 335)
{369} Prostitution of Art, January 1940 (p. 336)
{370} Jacques Maritain, February 1940 (p. 337)
{371} Mrs. Maritain, February 1940 (p. 337)
{372} Dr. Herbert Ratner, February 1940 (p. 338)
{373} Father Arthur Klyber, February 1940 (p. 339)
{374} Six Other Priests, February 1940 (p. 339)
{375} Gina Lombroso, March 1940 (p. 340)
{376} Heywood Broun, March 1940 (p. 341)
{377} Dr. Herbert Ratner, March 1940 (p. 341)
{378} Means and Ends, May 1940 (p. 342); Means and Ends, May 1941 (p. 382)
{379} Curry Russian Favor, May 1940 (p. 343)
{380} Victims of a False Theory, May 1940 (p. 344)
{381} They Were Wrong, May 1940 (p. 345)
{382} Roman Law, June 1940 (p. 346)
{383} Minding the Pope, June 1940 (p. 347)
{384} We Catholics Believe, June 1940 (p. 347); We Catholics, November 1941 (p. 398)
{385} The Catholic Worker Isms, June 1940 (p. 348)
{386} Protecting Japan, July–August 1940 (p. 349)
{387} Protecting Russia, July–August 1940 (p. 349)
{388} Protecting Italy, July–August 1940 (p. 350)
{389} Protecting Germany, July–August 1940 (p. 351)
{390} Protecting Humanity, July–August 1940 (p. 351)
{391} English Revolution, September 1940 (p. 352)
{392} French Revolution, September 1940 (p. 353)
{393} Russian Revolution, September 1940 (p. 354)
{394} American Revolution, September 1940 (p. 354)
{395} Philip the Fair, October 1940 (p. 355)
{396} Machiavelli, October 1940 (p. 356)
{397} Luther, October 1940 (p. 357)
{398} Adam Smith, October 1940 (p. 357)
{399} Napoleon, October 1940 (p. 358)
{400} Hitler, October 1940 (p. 359)
{401} To Worship God, November 1940 (p. 360)
{402} In Public Schools, November 1940 (p. 360)
{403} Hotbeds of Materialism, November 1940 (p. 361)
{404} Job or Mission, December 1940 (p. 362)
{405} Land of Refuge, December 1940 (p. 362); Laying the Foundation, September 1942 (p. 417)
{406} Salons de Culture, December 1940 (p. 363); Literary Colonies, September 1942 (p. 417)
{407} Free Guest Houses, December 1940 (p. 364); Free Guest Houses, September 1942 (p. 417)
{408} Agricultural Centers, December 1940 (p. 365); Rural Centers, September 1942 (p. 417)
{409} Leo XIII, January 1941 (p. 366)

574 EASY ESSAY INDEX

{410} Pius X, January 1941 (p. 366)
{411} Freda Kirchwey, January 1941
    (p. 367)
{412} Agrees with Two Popes, January
    1941 (p. 368)
{413} The Common Good, January 1941
    (p. 368)
{414} Democratic Elite, January 1941
    (p. 369)
{415} Faith, Hope and Charity, January
    1941 (p. 370)
{416} Paraguay Reductions, February
    1941 (p. 370)
{417} Proudhon and Marx, February
    1941 (p. 371)
{418} Blunderer, February 1941 (p. 372)
{419} Functional Poverty, February 1941
    (p. 373)
{420} Holy Poverty, February 1941
    (p. 373)
{421} Bourgeois Capitalists, March 1941
    (p. 375)
{422} Bolshevist Socialist, March 1941
    (p. 375)
{423} Catholic Communionism, March
    1941 (p. 376)
{424} Two of a Kind, March 1941
    (p. 377); Two of a Kind, November
    1941 (p. 399)
{425} Were I a Marxist, March 1941
    (p. 378)
{426} Grave Diggers, March 1941
    (p. 379)
{427} A New Society, March 1941
    (p. 379)
{428} St. Thomas More, April 1941
    (p. 380)
{429} Judge Cardozo, April 1941 (p. 381)
{430} Arthur Penty, April 1941 (p. 381)
{431} He Left So Much, May 1941
    (p. 382); He Left So Much, July–
    August 1941 (p. 388)
{432} Logical and Practical; May 1941
    (p. 383); Logical and Practical,
    November 1941 (p. 398)
{433} Germans and Poles, June 1941
    (p. 384)
{434} Polish Writers, June 1941 (p. 385)
{435} Catholic Extremism, June 1941
    (p. 385)

{436} Only a Frenchman, June 1941
    (p. 386)
{437} Nine Englishmen, June 1941
    (p. 387)
{438} Germans and English, June 1941
    (p. 387)
{439} Anthropologists Say, September
    1941 (p. 388)
{440} Theologians Say, September 1941
    (p. 389)
{441} Nordic and Negro Bishops,
    September 1941 (p. 390)
{442} American Negroes, September
    1941 (p. 390)
{443} Humiliation and Doubt,
    September 1941 (p. 391)
{444} Thomas Wilson, September 1941
    (p. 392)
{445} Maynard Keynes, September 1941
    (p. 393)
{446} A Better Way, September 1941
    (p. 394)
{447} Honest to God, October 1941
    (p. 395)
{448} Fr. Denifle, October 1941 (p. 395)
{449} American Founders, October
    1941 (p. 396)
{450} Cardinal Gasquet, October 1941
    (p. 396)
{451} St. Augustine, October 1941
    (p. 397)
{452} If, November 1941 (p. 398)
{453} That Grey Eminence, December
    1941 (p. 399)
{454} Worldly Empires, December 1941
    (p. 400)
{455} A Theocentric Pope, December
    1941 (p. 400)
{456} A Negro Student, January 1942
    (p. 401)
{457} Dr. Herbert E. Cory, January 1942
    (p. 402)
{458} Individual, February 1942
    (p. 403)
{459} A Person, February 1942 (p. 403)
{460} Faith, February 1942 (p. 404)
{461} Emmanuel Mounier, February
    1942 (p. 413)
{462} Mercantile Capitalism, March
    1942 (p. 406)

{463} Monopoly Capitalism, March 1942 (p. 406)
{464} Finance Capitalism, March 1942 (p. 407)
{465} State Capitalism, March 1942 (p. 408)
{466} The Age of Reason, April 1942 (p. 409)
{467} Age of Chaos, April 1942 (p. 409)
{468} The Age of Order, April 1942 (p. 410)
{469} "My Experience Teaches Me," May 1942 (p. 411)
{470} Three Characteristics, May 1942 (p. 412)
{471} Love of Freedom, May 1942 (p. 412)
{472} Spirit of Initiative, May 1942 (p. 413)
{473} Will to Cooperate, May 1942 (p. 414)
{474} It Started with England, July–August 1942 (p. 415)
{475} A Few Englishmen, July–August 1942 (p. 416)
{476} Legalized Usury, July–August 1942 (p. 416)
{477} Our Business, December 1942 (p. 418)
{478} The Bishop's Voice, December 1942 (p. 418)
{479} Works of Mercy, December 1942 (p. 419)
{480} Social Reconstruction, December 1942 (p. 420)
{481} Three Kinds, December 1942 (p. 420)
{482} Social Workers and Workers, December 1945 (p. 421)
{483} An Appeal for Funds, Unpublished (p. 423)
{484} For His Children's Sake, Unpublished (p. 425)
{485} Mortimer Adler, Unpublished (p. 426)
{486} Robert M. Hutchins, Unpublished (p. 427)
{487} Walter Lippmann, Unpublished (p. 427)
{488} Raïssa Maritain, Unpublished (p. 428)
{489} In Denmark, Unpublished (p. 429)
{490} Near Easton, Unpublished (p. 430)
{491} *Rerum Novarum*, Unpublished (p. 431)
{492} A.C.T.U., Unpublished (p. 431)
{493} For an A.C.E., Unpublished (p. 432)
{494} Nationalism, Unpublished (p. 433)
{495} Socialism, Unpublished (p. 434)
{496} Racialism, Unpublished (p. 434)
{497} A Good Movie, Unpublished (p. 435)
{498} Does What He Preaches, Unpublished (p. 436)
{499} Rented a Store, Unpublished (p. 436)
{500} No Red Tape, Unpublished (p. 437)
{501} On the Road, Unpublished (p. 437)
{502} Liberal Jews, Unpublished (p. 438)
{503} In New York, Unpublished (p. 439)
{504} English Industrialism, Unpublished (p. 440)
{505} German Racialism, Unpublished (p. 440)
{506} Italian Nationalism, Unpublished (p. 441)
{507} Russian Socialism, Unpublished (p. 442)
{508} Irish Messianism, Unpublished (p. 443)
{509} My Business, Unpublished (p. 444)
{510} Re-Discovering America, Unpublished (p. 444)
{511} Waiting for Orders, Unpublished (p. 445)
{512} Body of Social Thought, Unpublished (p. 446)
{513} Bishops' Message, Unpublished (p. 446)
{514} St. Francis of Assisi, Unpublished (p. 447)
{515} Crisis of Collapse, Unpublished (p. 448)

{516} Charity and Poverty, Unpublished (p. 448)
{517} Institutions and Corporations, Unpublished (p. 449)
{518} Christian Institutions, Unpublished (p. 449)
{519} Dome and Home, Unpublished (p. 450)
{520} The Bishop's Cathedra, Unpublished (p. 451)
{521} Under the Leadership of the Irish Fathers, Unpublished (p. 451)
{522} Ideals, Unpublished (p. 452)
{523} Six Economies, Unpublished (p. 452)
{524} Reinterpreting Karl Marx, Unpublished (p. 453)
{525} We Oppose, Unpublished (p. 454)
{526} [No Title], Unpublished (p. 454)
{527} [No Title], Unpublished (p. 455)
{528} Farming Commune Slogans, Unpublished (p. 455)
{529} Women, Men, and Manners, Unpublished (p. 456)
{530} On the Farming Commune, Unpublished (p. 456)
{531} CULT — A Child of God, Unpublished (p. 459)
{532} CULTURE — The Need of Today, Unpublished (p. 459)
{533} CULTIVATION — Based on an Ideal, Unpublished (p. 460)
{534} CULT — There Is One, Unpublished (p. 461)
{535} CULTURE — Social Detachment, Unpublished (p. 462)
{536} CULTIVATION — Hate and Reform, Unpublished (p. 462)
{537} CULT — In the Catholic Church, Unpublished (p. 463)
{538} CULTURE — Happy Is the People, Unpublished (p. 464)
{539} CULTIVATION — [No Title], Unpublished (p. 465)
{540} CULT — God Loves Us, Unpublished (p. 465)
{541} CULTURE — There Is No Vision, Unpublished (p. 466)
{542} CULTIVATION — Liberty Leaguers, Unpublished (p. 467)
{543} CULT — God's Gift to Men, Unpublished (p. 468)
{544} CULTURE — Men Are Divided, Unpublished (p. 468)
{545} CULTIVATION — Men Should Be Able to Count, Unpublished (p. 469)
{546} CULT — Holy Mass, Unpublished (p. 470)
{547} CULTURE — Rooted in Religion, Unpublished (p. 471)
{548} CULTIVATION — Derided by Two Groups, Unpublished (p. 472)
{549} CULT — Planting the Seeds, Unpublished (p. 473)
{550} CULTURE — Without Roots, Unpublished (p. 473)
{551} CULTIVATION — We Must Remind, Unpublished (p. 474)
{552} CULT — Growing of the Seed, Unpublished (p. 475)
{553} CULTURE — Liberal Thinking, Unpublished (p. 475)
{554} CULTIVATION — Monopoly Capitalism, Unpublished (p. 476)
{555} CULT — A Mystery, Unpublished (p. 477)
{556} CULTURE — Secularism and Marxism, Unpublished (p. 478)
{557} CULTIVATION — Landless and Toolless, Unpublished (p. 479)
{558} CULT — The Greatest Mystery, Unpublished (p. 480)
{559} CULTURE — Liberalism and Bolshevism, Unpublished (p. 480)
{560} CULTIVATION — Boredom Justified by Fear, Unpublished (p. 481)
{561} CULT — No One Like God, Unpublished (p. 482)
{562} CULTURE — Illegitimate Element, Unpublished (p. 483)
{563} CULTIVATION — The Question Arises, Unpublished (p. 483)
{564} CULT — God Is Watching, Unpublished (p. 484)
{565} CULTURE — Arbitrary Simplifications, Unpublished (p. 485)
{566} CULTIVATION — The Question Is, Unpublished (p. 486)
{567} [No Title], Unpublished (p. 487)
{568} The Truck Gardeners of Paris, Unpublished (p. 487)
{569} The Case of Mr. Ponce, Unpublished (p. 488)

Name and Topic Index

Adams, Henry, 65, 285, 402, 513
Adams, James Truslow, 38, 513
Adler, Mortimer J., 203, 260, 285, 290, 426, 509, 513, 526, 534, 549, 555
Africa, 43–44, 193, 195–96, 280, 390
African Americans, 12, 84, 277–81, 388–91, 401–2, 499, 541
Agar, Herbert, 461, 463, 465, 467, 470, 472, 474, 477, 479, 481, 484, 509, 513, 522
agronomic universities, 28, 52, 70–70, 228–29, 449, 452. *See also* farms and farming: farming communes
Aherne, Dick, 495, 514
Alexander the Great, 346
Algeria, 193, 195
Ambrose, St., 156, 514
American Federation of Labor (A.F. of L.), 247, 249, 309, 326, 527
Amiel, Henri Frédéric, 236, 514
Anglada, Eric Cussen, 2, 15
Argentina, 14, 197–98
Aristotle, 189, 203, 260, 409, 513–14, 524
Association of Catholic Trade Unionists (A.C.T.U.), 431–32
Augustine, St., 47, 260, 278, 280–81, 391, 397, 514, 529
Australia, 14, 197–98
Austria and Austrians, 274–75, 291–92, 294, 296, 316, 351, 395, 399, 523, 549

Baldwin, Roger N., 12
bank, bank account, bankers, 25, 34–35, 70, 83, 107–8, 121, 137, 145, 148, 187, 200–1, 392, 417, 502, 522, 535, 558
barbarians, 14, 52, 83, 158–59, 266–67, 363, 384, 443, 557
Barrès, Maurice, 66, 514–15

Bede, Rev. Jarrett, 228, 534–35
Belloc, Hilaire, 82, 260, 515
Benda, Julien, 32, 284–85, 515
Benedict XV, Pope, 80, 276, 317, 321, 515
Benedict of Nursia, St., 67, 515
Benedictines, 67, 396, 500, 528–29
Benson, Robert Hugh, 509
Bentham, Jeremy, 221
Berdyaev, Nicholas, 259, 290, 509, 515–16
Bérenger, Henry, 369, 516
Bergson, Henri, 428, 516
Bethune, Ade. *See* De Bethune, Marie Adélaïde
Bonaparte, Napoleon, 353, 358, 516
Bonaventure, St., 374, 516
Boniface VIII, Pope, 356, 547
Borne, Étienne, 290, 509, 516–17
Borsodi, Ralph, 509
Bossuet, Jacques-Bénigne, 35, 44, 251, 517
Bourne, Francis Cardinal, 98, 446, 517
Boyle, George, 509
Branham, Grace, 256, 517
Briand, Aristide, 197, 276, 517
Briffault, Robert, 142, 517
Brooks, Van Wyck, 155, 517
Broun, Heywood, 333, 341, 518
Bruehl, Rev. Charles P., 254–55, 518
Brüning, Heinrich, 448, 518
Bruning, Henri, 448, 518
Burns, Robert, 214, 224, 518
Burrow, Elizabeth, 17
Busch, Bishop Joseph Francis, 189, 518

Calvin, John and Calvinist, 23, 25, 53, 148–49, 252, 293, 392, 514, 518, 537, 555
Canada, 2, 8, 14, 90, 194, 294, 500, 552, 553–54

canon law, 20, 44, 97, 200–1, 356, 380, 424, 431, 519, 531, 544–45, 547, 558
capital and capitalism, 14–15, 20, 31, 32–34, 48–50, 56, 59, 67, 69–70, 73, 77, 81, 84, 90, 96–97, 106, 111, 116, 120, 134–35, 138–41, 147, 149, 156, 158–60, 164, 171, 175, 198, 206–8, 212, 232–34, 243, 245, 247–48, 254–55, 262, 284–85, 290, 300, 318, 327–30, 343, 348, 354, 361, 375–79, 406–8, 418, 424, 434, 438, 442, 448, 452–53, 472, 474, 476–77, 481–82, 506–7, 510–11, 513, 515, 520–22, 524, 529, 531, 537–38, 542, 553, 555–57
Cardozo, Benjamin N., 381, 518–19, 545
Carlyle, Thomas, 172, 519
Carr, Rev. Henry, 156, 519
Carrel, Alexis, 259, 286, 290, 509, 519
Carthage, Council of, 43–44
Catholic Action, 21, 27, 45, 48, 50–52, 57, 62, 71, 76, 86–87, 89, 97, 99, 103–4, 418–21, 425, 450
Chamberlain, Houston Stewart, 434, 519
Chanson, Paul, 248–49, 262–63, 520
Charles V, 290, 510, 538–39
Chardonnel, Abbé, 48, 520
Chautard, Jean-Baptiste, 509
Chesterton, G. K., 85, 88, 90, 155, 211, 508–9, 515, 520
China and Chinese, 103, 173, 258, 315, 331, 349
Christian Front, 184, 254–55
Christian Mobilizers, 362
Cicognani, Amleto Giovanni, 100, 509, 520
clarification of thought. *See* round-table discussions
Clemenceau, Georges, 256, 276, 327, 520
Cobbett, William, 416, 520
Cole, George Douglas Howard, 453, 521
colleges and college students, 9, 30, 47, 56, 63–64, 88, 92–94, 98–99, 102–3, 116, 119, 164–69, 189, 216, 220, 227, 229, 235, 266, 303, 305, 401, 425, 428, 492, 494–95, 519, 522, 527, 531, 536, 543, 552
Colum, Padraic, 323, 521
common good, 51, 70, 72, 84, 95–96, 115, 122–23, 147–48, 209, 243, 263, 322, 336, 366, 368–69, 412–14, 498, 506–7, 510, 519, 522, 536, 541, 544, 555
communism (Catholic) or communitarianism, 9, 50–51, 62, 77, 114–15, 123–24, 140, 143–44, 156, 159, 161–62, 176, 179–81, 198–99, 208–10, 212, 214, 220, 225, 263, 287, 309, 342–43, 370–71, 376–77, 382, 410, 478, 493, 495, 511, 548–49, 556
Communism (Marxist or Bolshevist), 2, 10, 12, 15, 49, 50, 56–57, 62, 69, 77, 83–85, 89–92, 94–96, 100, 106, 114–15, 123–24, 134–35, 138–42, 144, 147, 151, 156, 159–62, 167, 171, 176, 180–81, 198, 206, 208, 210, 212–13, 231–33, 237, 240, 254–58, 262, 269, 284, 286–87, 309, 329–30, 342–43, 361–62, 366, 370–71, 375–77, 379, 382, 424–25, 431, 447, 453, 472, 478, 480–81, 483, 485, 510, 521, 527–29, 531, 533, 537, 539–40, 542, 548–49, 551, 554–57
Congress of Industrial Organizations (C.I.O.), 247, 326, 527
Considerant, Victor Prosper, 50, 521
conservatism and conservatives, 105–6, 190–91, 207, 521, 541–42, 544
Constantine, 40, 42
Coolidge, Calvin, 51, 117, 521
Corbett, Rev. John, 45, 521–22
corporations, 19–20, 125, 136, 176, 307, 449–50, 543, 545
Cort, John, 431
Cory, Herbert E., 402, 509, 522
Coughlin, Rev. Charles, 184–88, 302, 306, 362, 454, 522, 537
Coyle, David Cushman, 484, 486, 522
Cram, Ralph Adams, 175, 522
Cuba, 103, 314
Cummings, John J., 89–90
Curran, Rev. Michael J., 435–37, 522–23

Davidson, Donald, 499, 500, 523
Dawson, Christopher, 73, 259, 268, 460, 462, 464, 466, 469, 471, 473, 476, 478, 481, 483, 485, 510, 523
Day, Dorothy, 1–2, 4, 10–17, 53, 167, 211, 256, 302–3, 310, 423, 522, 528, 541, 543–44, 552–53, 561
De Becker, Raymond, 181, 183, 523, 557
De Bethune, Marie Adélaïde, 497, 523

De Gobineau, Arthur, 434, 523
De La Salle, Jean-Baptiste, 3
De Valera, Éamon, 320, 523
Denifle, Rev. Heinrich Seuse, 395–96, 524
Denmark, 295, 351, 429, 497, 529
Dennis, Lawrence, 134, 524
Deodad. *See* Deodatus of Nevers, St.
Deodatus of Nevers, St., 365, 524
Descartes, René, 409, 524
Devas, Charles Stanton, 172, 524
Deverall, Richard L. G., 184
Dewey, John, 154, 190, 524
distributism, 220, 287, 513, 515, 520, 543, 547, 551
Dominican Sisters of Grand Rapids, 459, 462, 464, 466, 468, 471, 473, 475, 477, 480, 482, 485
Donahue, John B., 160, 525
Du Bos, Charles, 510
Du Pin, François René de La Tour, 507, 525

Easton Farm, 4, 11–12, 14, 430, 458, 487, 517, 532, 553
Eddy, Sherwood, 453, 525
Eliot, Thomas Stearns, 392, 525
Ellard, Gerard, 510
Ellis, Marc, 7, 15–17, 310, 331, 456–58, 470–71, 479
Emerson, Ralph Waldo, 19, 207, 228–29, 449–50, 525–26
Engels, Friedrich, 124
England and English, 2, 14, 59, 66, 88, 116, 138, 150, 164, 171 194–95, 221, 223, 252, 256, 271, 275–76, 284, 287, 293–96, 306–7, 313, 315–16, 320–21, 327, 349, 351–52, 354, 358, 360, 380, 387–88, 392–93, 396–97, 415–16, 429, 434, 440–42, 444–45, 517, 519–21, 524–25, 528, 531–34, 536–38, 541, 543–46, 549, 551–55, 558
Enlightenment, 32, 409, 498, 548, 557
Ethiopia, 195–96, 267, 275, 283, 315, 350, 532

Fanfani, Amintore, 510
farms and farming, 7, 23, 59, 119, 170–71, 175, 387, 430, 456–57, 495–97, 500–2, 511, 514, 520, 532–33, 535, 558–59; farming

communes, 2, 4, 11–14, 28, 50, 52, 72, 76, 114, 120–22, 134, 137–38, 144, 158, 169, 176–77, 198, 266, 305, 310, 325–26, 374, 415, 430, 455–58, 487, 492, 494, 500, 508, 517, 532, 550, 553. *See also* outdoor universities
fascism, 56, 90, 96, 134–35, 151, 176, 181, 212–13, 237–38, 254–54, 260, 275, 282, 284, 317–18, 324, 343, 368, 379, 442, 453, 515, 521–22, 524, 526, 532, 536–37, 545, 551, 554, 557, 559
Ferrer, St. Vincent, 311, 526
Fisher, Louis, 411, 526
Fitzpatrick, Benedict, 510
Foerster, Norman, 285, 526
folks schools, 13, 430, 497–500; 502, 529
France and French, 3, 7–9, 11, 15, 17, 38, 66, 73, 143, 158, 161, 163, 178–79, 181, 193–96, 212, 223, 244, 249, 256, 263, 267, 274–76, 281, 284, 291–96, 313, 315, 322, 327, 349, 351, 353, 358–59, 365, 369, 386–87, 393, 399–401, 409, 428, 433–34, 440, 500, 513, 515–21, 523–25, 529–30, 535–36, 538–42, 544–49, 551–52, 554, 557
Francis, Pope, 1, 545
Francis de Sales, St., 250, 526
Francis of Assisi, St., 2, 62, 78, 79–80, 89, 141, 145–46, 158, 217, 251, 274, 287, 374, 398, 425, 445, 447, 509, 516, 520, 526, 535, 548
Franciscans, 11, 79–80, 189, 192, 210–11, 307–9, 445–46, 510, 515–16, 526
Frank, Glenn, 39, 93, 273, 526–27, 543
Frank, Waldo, 110–11, 204, 307, 445, 527
Frey, John P., 309, 527
Furfey, Paul Hanly, 11, 88, 510, 527

Gage, Marguerite, 256, 527
Gandhi, Mohandas, 171, 242, 247, 320, 526–28, 541, 556
Gasquet, Francis Cardinal Aidan, O.S.B., 396, 510, 528
Gemelli, Agostino, 510
George V of England (king), 88, 455
George, David Lloyd, 276, 327, 528
Germany and Germans, 14, 17, 67, 88, 90, 103–4, 143, 150–51, 158–59, 171,

Germany and Germans *(continued)*
178–79, 181, 194–95, 197–98, 223,
237, 239, 264, 267, 274–78, 291–96,
305, 312–13, 316, 319–20, 327–28,
351, 384–88, 390, 399–400, 411, 415,
433–35, 438, 440–41, 499, 515,
517–20, 523, 525–26, 528–29, 532,
534, 536–37, 539–40, 542, 545–46,
548, 550–53, 557–59
Gertrude, St., 495, 528
Gill, Eric, 173, 205, 336–37, 416–17, 510, 528
Gillis, Rev. James Martin, 47, 528–29
Gitlow, Benjamin, 344, 529, 533
Gobineau, Arthur. *See* De Gobineau, Arthur
Gold, Mike, 167
Gorky, Maxim, 204, 529
Grail, Ladies of the, 500
Great Depression, 1–2, 14, 25, 41, 54,
58, 61, 67–68, 70, 81, 94, 105, 117–18,
120, 151–52, 155, 163, 183, 218, 246,
407, 408, 521, 543, 546, 550, 553
Greek and Greeks, 37, 40, 93, 111,
128–29, 216, 218, 514, 529, 550
Green Revolution, 2, 15, 93, 127, 220, 443
Gregory, T. S., 510
Grundtvig, Nikolaj Frederik Severin, 430, 529
Guardini, Romano, 493, 510, 529
Guéranger, Prosper Louis Pascal, 499, 529
guilds, 67–68, 71, 73–76, 147–49, 176,
220, 225, 249, 259, 263, 290, 346,
381, 449, 511, 518, 520, 530, 537, 541,
547, 553
Gunn, Michael, 67, 73, 530
Gurian, Waldemar, 510

Hall, Bolton, 186–88, 530
Hanna, Mark, 235, 530
Harding, Warren G., 51, 104, 521, 530
Harlem, 12–13, 95, 124, 532
Harmel, Léon, 15, 62, 244, 506, 530–31
Hayes, Carlton J. H., 63, 220, 531
Hayes, Rev. Cornelius, 45, 531
Healy, Rev. Patrick Joseph, 110, 510, 531
Heaney, Ruth, 14
Hennessy, Kate, 17, 553

Henry II (king), 380
Henry VIII (king), 380, 531, 537, 544
Henry, François, 509, 516
Henry, Patrick, 213, 240, 286, 324, 532
Hergenhan, Herman, 41, 96, 532
High, Stanley, 134, 532
Hindus and Hinduism, 304, 441
Hindus, Maurice G., 453, 532
Hinsley, Arthur Cardinal, 283, 532
Hitler, Adolf, 202, 212, 214, 276, 278,
291, 327, 330, 343, 353, 359, 381–82,
394, 426, 516, 519, 525, 532–33
Hobbes, Thomas, 31, 221, 252, 533
Hollis, Christopher, 510
Holmes, John Haynes, 345, 533
Holy Roman Empire, 293, 319, 538
Hook, Sidney, 345, 453, 533
houses of hospitality and hospices, 2,
11–12, 14, 27, 40, 42–45, 52, 67–68,
72, 101, 114, 133–34, 137–38, 144, 158,
167–68, 176, 200, 218, 220, 257, 415,
422, 449
Howard, Albert, 501, 533
Huguenots, 313, 360
humanism, 96, 143, 204–5, 224–25,
263, 347, 398, 510, 522, 526, 541, 558
Hume, David, 221, 252, 533
Hutchins, Robert Maynard, 226–28,
285, 427, 526, 534, 539, 549, 555
Huxley, Aldous, 399–400, 534, 538

Ibsen, Henrik, 228, 534
India, 194–95, 294, 527, 533
Indo-China, 193
interest (usury), 22–23, 25, 53–55, 57,
59–61, 74–75, 114, 129, 148–49, 201,
392–94, 416–17, 477, 511, 518,
536–37, 558
institutions, 19–20, 27, 43, 51, 59, 99,
176–77, 414, 421, 449–50, 525,
550–51
Ireland and the Irish, 2, 10, 15–17, 22, 52,
74, 93, 114–15, 124, 127–30, 144, 257,
278–79, 306, 313, 320–21, 362–65,
417, 434, 443, 449, 451–52, 499, 510,
521, 523–24, 531, 543, 546, 551, 556
Islam, 40–41, 268
Iswolsky, Hélène, 510
Italy and Italians, 90, 103, 151, 195–98,
223, 267, 275–76, 296, 315, 350–51,

411, 441, 516, 525–26, 529, 532, 539, 541, 545, 551, 554–56

James, William, 154
Japan and Japanese, 171, 181, 195–98, 258, 315, 349, 415, 535
Jarrett, Rev. Bede, 228, 534–35
Jefferson, Thomas, 36, 241, 273–74, 444, 535
Jesuits, 11, 210–11, 220, 303–4, 371, 402, 500, 521, 540, 542, 546, 558
Jesus Christ, 3, 15, 24, 34, 45–46, 62, 71, 78, 80, 91, 100, 104, 108, 137, 145–46, 157, 164, 170, 192, 216, 219, 224, 235, 237, 250, 265, 303, 306, 310, 312, 317, 335, 340, 348, 357, 370, 383, 388–89, 443, 447, 451, 462–63, 506, 511, 515, 520, 523, 540, 549, 551
Jewish religion and people, 13, 24, 37, 53, 59, 93, 96, 127–29, 143, 225, 264–65, 268, 277–78, 284–85, 310–14, 327–31, 333, 337–40, 348, 362, 367, 394, 418, 426, 434, 438–39, 515, 526, 533, 537, 539, 542, 548–49, 553
Johnson, Hugh Samuel "Iron Pants," 118, 154–55, 178, 188, 215, 535
Jørgensen, Johannes, 79, 535
Jusserand, Jean Jules, 369, 516, 535

Kagawa, Toyohiko, 181, 510, 535
Kallenback, Marie Schulte, 130, 535
Keating, Frederick William, 98, 146, 536
Keller, Helen, 122–23, 536
Kenkel, Frederick, 499, 536
Keynes, John Maynard, 59, 393, 536
Kilmer, Joyce, 403
King, Martin Luther, Jr., 556
Kingston, New York, 8, 487
Kirchwey, Freda, 367–68, 536–37
Kiwanis, 181, 209–10
Klyber, Rev. Arthur, 339, 537
Knights of Columbus, 1, 160, 189, 525
Knox, John, 53, 392, 537
Koch, Edward A., 71, 537
Kohn, Eugene, 12
Krimm, Rev. John A., 332, 537
Kropotkin, Peter, 20, 510, 537
Krupa, Stephen T., 17
Krzesiński, Rev. Andrzej, 493, 510, 537

labor and labor unions, 2, 7–8, 10–11, 32–34, 53, 67–70, 73–76, 81, 97–98, 102, 115, 118, 120–22, 136, 138, 140–43, 158, 162, 171–72, 176, 198, 207, 229, 230, 244, 247–48, 255, 263, 270, 287, 325, 343, 346, 372, 374, 431–32, 476, 479, 481, 493, 506–7, 513, 518, 521, 526–27, 530, 535, 538, 542–43, 547, 551, 557. *See also* American Federation of Labor; Congress of Industrial Organizations
LaFarge, Rev. John, S.J., 11
laissez faire, 31, 51, 221, 300, 521, 553
Laski, Harold, 243, 253–54, 284, 300, 537–38
League of Nations, 196, 296, 315–16, 318, 558
Le Bon, Gustave, 212, 510, 538
Lebbe, Rev. Vincent, 258
Leclerc du Tremblay, François, 399, 534, 538
Leclercq, Abbé Jacques, 367, 538
Lenin, Vladimir, 49–50, 62, 84, 89, 170, 232, 269, 354, 415, 425, 434, 442, 522, 538, 554
Leo XIII, Pope, 20, 75, 80, 96, 115, 366, 368, 431, 507, 520, 522, 531, 538, 541, 555, 557
Lewis, D. B. Wyndham, 290, 510, 538–39
Lewisohn, Ludwig, 264, 539
liberals and liberalism, 30–32, 105–6, 182, 184, 221, 243, 248, 254, 259, 284–86, 300–1, 313, 329, 338, 345, 366, 418, 438, 439, 475, 480–81, 521, 539, 542, 545, 548
Liberty League, 213, 467, 553
Liénart, Achille Cardinal, 282–83, 539
Lippmann, Walter, 527, 539
Locke, John, 31, 221, 252, 533, 539
Lombroso, Gina, 340, 539
Long, Huey, 307, 540
Lord, Rev. Daniel A., S.J., 46, 56, 97, 102, 219, 425, 540, 558
Lortz, Joseph, 510
Louis XIII (king), 549
Louis XIV (king), 443, 517
Louis XVI (king), 544
Lugan, Rev. Alphonse-Marie, 73, 510, 540

582   NAME AND TOPIC INDEX

Luther, Martin, 252, 259, 357, 540
Lutheranism, 293, 430, 529
Libya, 350
Lyons, Eugene, 269, 533, 540
Lytle, Andrew Nelson, 174, 540–41

MacDonald, Ramsay, 141, 541
Machiavelli, Niccolò di Bernardo dei, 356, 541
Machiavellianism, 327, 346, 444, 541
Manchuria, 195–96, 315, 349
Mann, Thomas, 370, 541
Manning, Henry Edward Cardinal, 507, 541
Maritain, Jacques, 11, 185, 203, 205, 213, 231, 242–43, 259, 290, 337, 346, 467, 510, 513–14, 516, 524, 534, 541–42, 555
Maritain, Raïssa, 337–38, 428–29, 516, 542
Marshall, Donald, 172, 542
Marshall, Thomas R., 112, 435, 542
Marx, Karl, 32, 48–51, 62, 69, 89, 161–62, 170, 232, 287, 371–72, 425, 434, 442, 448, 453, 472, 521–22, 542, 548–49, 556
Marxism and Marxists, 48–49, 162, 183–84, 200, 204–5, 220, 254, 258, 260, 281, 286, 317–19, 342, 361, 371, 378–79, 382, 402, 478, 485, 522, 525, 529, 537–38, 540, 542, 553–56
Mason, David, 15
McCall, Chester H., 102, 542–43
McGee John, 437, 543, 552
McGowan, Rev. Raymond A., 190, 543
McKenna, Norman C., 184
McNabb, Rev. Vincent, O.P., 231, 287, 493, 510, 543
McNicholas, Archbishop John T., 24, 276–77, 446, 543
McSorley, Rev. Joseph, 45, 331, 543
medieval and medievalists, 38, 45, 52, 59, 65, 147, 221, 243–44, 253, 257, 279, 336, 355, 363, 393, 395, 406, 444, 449, 495, 500, 519, 521, 523, 527, 530, 534, 536, 538, 542, 547, 555, 557
Meiklejohn, Alexander, 93, 543
Mencken, Henry Louis, 456, 543–44
Mexico and Mexican, 2, 14, 103, 305, 307, 549, 556
Michel, Suzanne, 72, 510, 544

Michel, Virgil, 11, 459
Mirabeau, 81, 544
Moley, Raymond, 57–58, 544
More, St. Thomas, 50, 62, 89, 115, 380, 393, 425, 531, 544
Morris, William, 416, 545
Mounier, Emmanuel, 1, 143, 181, 290, 405, 510, 516, 523, 545
Mussolini, Benito, 89, 202, 212, 214, 270, 276, 283, 318, 381–82, 442, 532, 545, 554–55
Muste, A. J., 12

National Association of Manufacturers, 432–33
National Catholic Rural Life Conference, 13, 511, 536, 546
National Recovery Act (N.R.A.), 53, 105, 118–19, 154, 163, 177–78, 188, 226, 247, 535, 550
Native Americans, 294, 308–9, 386, 479, 500
Nazis and Nazism, 17, 151, 179, 181, 237, 239, 275, 313, 400, 518–19, 523, 526, 532, 534, 536–37, 545–56, 548, 550, 552–53, 559
Newman, John Henry Cardinal, 30–31, 226–28, 541, 545
noblesse oblige, 35, 75, 353, 506
Nock, Albert J., 21, 161, 213, 511, 545–46
Noyes, Charles Reinold, 117, 407, 546

O'Grady, Brendan Anthony, 3, 15
O'Hara, Edwin Vincent, 132, 419, 546
O'Hea, Rev. Leo, S.J., 536
O'Sullivan, Maurice, 499, 546
outdoor universities, 28, 120–21, 228–29

pagans and paganism, 62, 89–90, 101, 107, 114, 130, 133, 159, 199, 216, 218, 257, 265, 277, 364, 469, 506
Palestine, 22, 129, 310, 314, 517
Paine, Thomas, 32, 259, 409, 546
Parguay, 370–71
Parsons, Rev. Wilfrid, 11, 201, 247, 546
Pascal, Blaise, 429, 456, 546–47
Péguy, Charles, 35, 66, 113, 405, 547
Peirce, Charles Sanders, 154
Penty, Arthur, 231, 259, 290, 346, 381, 416, 511, 545, 547

Pfeiffer, Ehrenfried, 511
Philip II of Macedon, 346
Philip the Fair (king), 355–56, 547
Piehl, Mel, 16
Pigors, Paul, 214, 511, 547–48
Pius IX, Pope, 30–31, 548
Pius X, Pope St., 80, 366, 368, 548
Pius XI, Pope, 20, 39, 56, 80, 250, 332, 374, 447, 507, 520, 522, 532, 548, 557
Pius XII, Pope, 322, 400, 548
Poland and Poles, 315–16, 350, 384–86, 493, 537
politics and politicians, 20, 37–39, 51, 56, 82, 86–91, 98, 102–5, 107–9, 113, 119, 125, 129, 131–32, 152–53, 179, 200, 213, 217, 221–23, 226, 248, 253–54, 272, 275, 291, 293–94, 300, 302, 306–7, 323, 334–35, 345, 356–58, 360–61, 366–67, 382, 405, 421, 440, 443, 446–47, 461, 466, 471, 476, 514–21, 524–26, 528–29, 532–34, 537–41, 544–49, 551–57
poor and poverty, 7, 10–11, 27, 35, 40–41, 43–44, 69, 77–78, 82, 98, 101, 117, 122, 136, 145–47, 151, 156, 163, 165, 176, 196, 198–99, 216–17, 235, 251–52, 335, 356, 371, 374–75, 383, 388, 401, 408, 484, 486, 506, 514, 517, 521, 529, 531, 537, 540–41, 557–58. *See also* voluntary poverty
Price, Weston, 511
Proudhon, Pierre-Joseph, 50, 140, 161, 371, 548–49
Prussia, 293–95, 557–58
Puritans and Puritanism, 38, 163–64, 313, 360, 552, 555

Quadragesimo anno, 431, 530, 548
Quakers, 348, 360, 559

Ratner, Herbert, 333, 338, 341, 549
Rerum Novarum, 75, 431–33, 520, 531, 538, 541, 557
Ricardo, David, 253, 328, 549
Richelieu, Cardinal, 291–92, 357, 399, 433, 534, 538, 549
Rivera, Diego, 48, 549
Robertson, John M., 115–17, 549–50
Roman Empire, 38, 52, 114, 158, 237, 279, 311, 318–20, 362–63, 365, 441–42, 469, 529. *See also* Holy Roman Empire
Roman law, 111, 200, 346, 356, 380–81, 519, 547
Roosevelt, Franklin D., 51, 53, 57, 87, 88, 105, 111, 118–19, 300, 309, 454, 522, 527, 532, 535, 542, 544–46, 550, 553, 556
Roosevelt, Theodore, 88, 196, 550
Roper, Daniel C., 102, 542, 550
Rosenberg, Alfred, 434, 550
Rotary Clubs, 8, 16, 93, 97, 116, 165, 181, 209–10, 328, 486–87
round-table discussions, 2, 10, 13, 26, 45, 52, 57, 61, 72, 114, 138, 144, 158, 176, 415, 448, 494, 452, 503, 507, 551
Rousseau, Jean-Jacques, 19, 27, 32, 146, 156, 288, 453, 506, 550–51
Runkel, Phil, 16, 561
Ruskin, John, 416, 551
Russia and Russians, 2, 103, 106, 123–24, 126–27, 143–44, 151, 159, 162, 171, 223, 231–32, 287, 296, 319, 338, 343–45, 349–50, 354, 411, 415, 442–44, 453, 515, 525–26, 529, 532–33, 537–38, 542, 549–50, 554, 556
Ryan, Rev. Arthur, 199, 551
Ryan, Edward G., 38, 513
Ryan, Rev. John A., 11

Sanger, Margaret, 341, 518, 551
Sangnier, Marc, 366–67, 551
Savonarola, Girolamo, 356, 551
Schmitt, Carl, 111–13, 551–52
Scotland and Scottish, 252, 392, 518–19, 533, 537, 553–54, 558
Scully, Fr. Joseph, 8
Second Sino-Japanese War, 258
selfishness, 29, 62, 73, 153–54, 190–91, 269, 288, 414, 497
Seven Years' War, 294
Shakespeare, William, 180, 227, 445, 552
Sheehan, Arthur, 4–5, 15–17, 423, 437, 486–87, 491–503, 505, 523, 543, 552
Sheely, Rev. Patrick, S.J, 98, 552
Sheen, Rev. Fulton, 90, 190, 511, 552
Sherman, William Tecumseh, 375, 552
Shuster, George N., 10, 20, 511, 552
Sicius, Francis, 15–17

Siegfried, André, 163, 552
Sillon, Le, 7–8, 366–67, 548, 551
Sinclair, Upton, 185, 549, 553
Smith, Adam, 31, 150, 221, 253, 328, 357, 553
Smith, Al, 111, 131, 454, 553
Smith, Victor, 499, 553
sociology, 11, 62, 67, 88–89, 165–66, 190, 192, 255, 305, 425, 444, 446, 464, 485, 507, 511, 527, 536, 538, 544, 553–54
Sombart, Werner, 327, 553
Somerville, Henry, 164, 553–54
Sorel, Georges, 261, 554
Spain and Spanish, 194, 217, 268, 274, 284, 293, 307–9, 311–12, 428, 500, 526, 538, 549, 559
Spanish Civil War, 284
Spencer, Herbert, 338, 554
Stalin, Joseph, 62, 84, 89, 212, 214, 269, 309, 343, 354, 382, 425, 443, 533, 554, 556
Steffens, Lincoln, 20, 554
Steiner, Rudolf, 430
Stevenson, Robert Louis, 34, 78, 554
Stocking, Luke, 15–17, 443
Strachey, John, 134, 138, 287, 554
Sturzo, Don Luigi, 368, 554–55
Sudan, 194, 296, 387
Sullivan, Thomas, 17
Sweden, 274, 291–92, 399, 433

Tate, Allen, 461, 484, 513, 522
Tawney, R. H., 20, 59, 96–97, 164, 290, 356, 380, 416, 424, 511, 555, 558
Tertullian, 101
Thirty Years' War, 291–92, 294, 399, 433, 534, 538, 549
Thomas, Norman, 134, 141, 555
Thomas Aquinas, Saint, 51, 72–73, 84, 89, 95, 115, 189, 259–60, 263, 409, 425, 510, 514, 516, 524, 533, 541–42, 544, 549, 555–56
Thompson, William, 434, 556
Thoreau, Henry David, 372, 556
Toniolo, Blessed Giuseppe, 507, 556
Townsend, Francis, 186, 556
Treaty of Versailles, 275–76, 315–16, 327, 393, 520, 528
Treaty of Vienna, 358–59
Treaty of Westphalia, 291–92, 399, 534

Troester, Rosalie Riegle, 14
Trotsky, Leon, 269, 556
Twelve Southerners, 511, 540–41

Uganda, 14
unemployed and unemployment, 2, 10–11, 16, 22, 27–28, 40, 42, 45, 54, 61–62, 68–69, 72, 107, 118–19, 121, 133, 141, 146, 152–53, 167–69, 186, 188, 200, 216, 220, 229, 245, 309, 325, 408, 508, 536
usury. *See* interest

Van Zeeland, Paul, 181, 556–57
Veblen, Thorstein, 20, 97, 424, 511, 557
Verdier, Jean Cardinal, 282, 557
Vishnewski, Stanley, 14
Voltaire, 32, 347, 557
voluntary poverty, 2, 11, 27, 52, 69, 77, 79, 101, 211, 217, 274, 343, 372–74, 448, 450, 526, 558–59
Von Bismarck, Otto, 275, 328, 557
Von Ketteler, Wilhelm Emmanuel, 215, 507, 557–58

Watt, James, 352, 558
Wesseling, Theodore, 511
Wilcox, Oswin William, 511
Wilhelm I (emperor), 328, 558
Wilhelm II (emperor), 328, 558
Willmann, Dorothy J., 425, 558
Wilson, Thomas, 392–93, 511, 558
Wilson, Woodrow, 88, 104, 150, 275–76, 315, 542, 550, 558–59
Works of Mercy, 27, 50, 100–1, 104, 110, 112, 114, 132, 133, 137, 257, 282, 419–21, 507
World War I, 8, 51, 74, 88, 102, 104, 150–51, 165, 195–97, 223, 275–76, 295, 314–15, 321, 385, 407, 515, 518, 520, 523, 530, 536, 542, 546, 550, 558–59
World War II, 17, 194, 196, 246, 315, 343, 514, 518, 533, 536, 539, 545, 548, 550

Young, Mildred Binns, 373, 559
Young, Owen, 170, 559

Zundel, Maurice, 511

LINCOLN RICE received his Ph.D. in Moral Theology from Marquette and is the author of *Healing the Divide: A Catholic Racial Justice Framework Inspired by Dr. Arthur Falls.* He currently teaches theology at Marquette University and is a member of the Casa Maria Catholic Worker in Milwaukee.

CATHOLIC PRACTICE IN NORTH AMERICA

James T. Fisher and Margaret M. McGuinness (eds.), *The Catholic Studies Reader*
Jeremy Bonner, Christopher D. Denny, and Mary Beth Fraser Connolly (eds.), *Empowering the People of God: Catholic Action before and after Vatican II*
Christine Firer Hinze and J. Patrick Hornbeck II (eds.), *More than a Monologue: Sexual Diversity and the Catholic Church. Volume I: Voices of Our Times*
J. Patrick Hornbeck II and Michael A. Norko (eds.), *More than a Monologue: Sexual Diversity and the Catholic Church. Volume II: Inquiry, Thought, and Expression*
Jack Lee Downey, *The Bread of the Strong: Lacouturisme and the Folly of the Cross, 1910–1985*
Michael McGregor, *Pure Act: The Uncommon Life of Robert Lax*
Mary Dunn, *The Cruelest of All Mothers: Marie de l'Incarnation, Motherhood, and Christian Tradition*
Dorothy Day and the Catholic Worker: The Miracle of Our Continuance. Photographs by Vivian Cherry, Text by Dorothy Day, Edited, with an Introduction and Additional Text by Kate Hennessy
Nicholas K. Rademacher, *Paul Hanly Furfey: Priest, Scientist, Social Reformer*
Margaret M. McGuinness and James T. Fisher (eds.), *Roman Catholicism in the United States: A Thematic History*
Gary J. Adler Jr., Tricia C. Bruce, and Brian Starks (eds.), *American Parishes: Remaking Local Catholicism*
Stephanie N. Brehm, *America's Most Famous Catholic (According to Himself): Stephen Colbert and American Religion in the Twenty-First Century*
Matthew T. Eggemeier and Peter Joseph Fritz, *Send Lazarus: Catholicism and the Crises of Liberalism*
John C. Seitz and Christine Firer Hinze (eds.), *Working Alternatives: American and Catholic Experiments in Work and Economy*
Lincoln Rice (ed.), *The Forgotten Radical Peter Maurin: Easy Essays from the Catholic Worker*
Jill Peterfeso, *Womanpriest: Tradition and Transgression in the Contemporary Roman Catholic Church*

www.ingramcontent.com/pod-product-compliance
Lightning Source LLC
Chambersburg PA
CBHW022102290426
44112CB00008B/514